GREEK
and ROMAN
MYTHOLOGY

Second Custom Edition for
Grant MacEwan College

Custom Publishing

New York Boston San Francisco
London Toronto Sydney Tokyo Singapore Madrid
Mexico City Munich Paris Cape Town Hong Kong Montreal

Pearson
Custom Publishing
is a division of

www.pearsonhighered.com

ISBN 10: 0-558-36940-5
ISBN 13: 978-0-558-36940-8

Copyright Acknowledgments

Contents

Homer, *The Iliad*
Books 1, 3, and 6

BOOK ONE

The Rage of Achilles

Rage—Goddess, sing the rage of Peleus' son Achilles,
murderous, doomed, that cost the Achaeans countless losses,
hurling down to the House of Death so many sturdy souls,
great fighters' souls, but made their bodies carrion,
feasts for the dogs and birds,
and the will of Zeus was moving toward its end.
Begin, Muse, when the two first broke and clashed,
Agamemnon lord of men and brilliant Achilles.

What god drove them to fight with such a fury?
Apollo the son of Zeus and Leto. Incensed at the king   10
he swept a fatal plague through the army—men were dying
and all because Agamemnon spurned Apollo's priest.
Yes, Chryses approached the Achaeans' fast ships
to win his daughter back, bringing a priceless ransom

and bearing high in hand, wound on a golden staff,
the wreaths of the god, the distant deadly Archer.
He begged the whole Achaean army but most of all
the two supreme commanders, Atreus' two sons,
"Agamemnon, Menelaus—all Argives geared for war!
May the gods who hold the halls of Olympus give you   20
Priam's city to plunder, then safe passage home.
Just set my daughter free, my dear one . . . here,
accept these gifts, this ransom. Honor the god
who strikes from worlds away—the son of Zeus, Apollo!"

    And all ranks of Achaeans cried out their assent:
"Respect the priest, accept the shining ransom!"
But it brought no joy to the heart of Agamemnon.
The king dismissed the priest with a brutal order
ringing in his ears: "Never again, old man,
let me catch sight of you by the hollow ships!   30
Not loitering now, not slinking back tomorrow.
The staff and the wreaths of god will never save you then.
The girl—I won't give up the girl. Long before that,
old age will overtake her in *my* house, in Argos,
far from her fatherland, slaving back and forth
at the loom, forced to share my bed!
                              Now go,
don't tempt my wrath—and you may depart alive."

    The old man was terrified. He obeyed the order,
turning, trailing away in silence down the shore
where the battle lines of breakers crash and drag.   40
And moving off to a safe distance, over and over
the old priest prayed to the son of sleek-haired Leto,
lord Apollo, "Hear me, Apollo! God of the silver bow
who strides the walls of Chryse and Cilla sacrosanct—
lord in power of Tenedos—Smintheus, god of the plague!
If I ever roofed a shrine to please your heart,
ever burned the long rich bones of bulls and goats
on your holy altar, now, now bring my prayer to pass.
Pay the Danaans back—your arrows for my tears!"

His prayer went up and Phoebus Apollo heard him.   50
Down he strode from Olympus' peaks, storming at heart
with his bow and hooded quiver slung across his shoulders.
The arrows clanged at his back as the god quaked with rage,
the god himself on the march and down he came like night.
Over against the ships he dropped to a knee, let fly a shaft
and a terrifying clash rang out from the great silver bow.
First he went for the mules and circling dogs but then,
launching a piercing shaft at the men themselves,
he cut them down in droves—
and the corpse-fires burned on, night and day, no end in sight.   60

Nine days the arrows of god swept through the army.
On the tenth Achilles called all ranks to muster—
the impulse seized him, sent by white-armed Hera
grieving to see Achaean fighters drop and die.
Once they'd gathered, crowding the meeting grounds,
the swift runner Achilles rose and spoke among them:
"Son of Atreus, now we are beaten back, I fear,
the long campaign is lost. So home we sail . . .
if we can escape our death—if war and plague
are joining forces now to crush the Argives.   70
But wait: let us question a holy man,
a prophet, even a man skilled with dreams—
dreams as well can come our way from Zeus—
come, someone to tell us why Apollo rages so,
whether he blames us for a vow we failed, or sacrifice.
If only the god would share the smoky savor of lambs
and full-grown goats, Apollo might be willing, still,
somehow, to save us from this plague."
                                        So he proposed
and down he sat again as Calchas rose among them,
Thestor's son, the clearest by far of all the seers   80
who scan the flight of birds. He knew all things that are,
all things that are past and all that are to come,
the seer who had led the Argive ships to Troy
with the second sight that god Apollo gave him.
For the armies' good the seer began to speak:

"Achilles, dear to Zeus . . .
you order me to explain Apollo's anger,
the distant deadly Archer? I will tell it all.
But strike a pact with me, swear you will defend me
with all your heart, with words and strength of hand.   90
For there is a man I will enrage—I see it now—
a powerful man who lords it over all the Argives,
one the Achaeans must obey . . . A mighty king,
raging against an inferior, is too strong.
Even if he can swallow down his wrath today,
still he will nurse the burning in his chest
until, sooner or later, he sends it bursting forth.
Consider it closely, Achilles. Will you save me?"

    And the matchless runner reassured him: "Courage!
Out with it now, Calchas. Reveal the will of god,   100
whatever you may know. And I swear by Apollo
dear to Zeus, the power you pray to, Calchas,
when you reveal god's will to the Argives—no one,
not while I am alive and see the light on earth, no one
will lay his heavy hands on you by the hollow ships.
None among all the armies. Not even if you mean
Agamemnon here who now claims to be, by far,
the best of the Achaeans."
                                    The seer took heart
and this time he spoke out, bravely: "Beware—
he casts no blame for a vow we failed, a sacrifice.   110
The god's enraged because Agamemnon spurned his priest,
he refused to free his daughter, he refused the ransom.
That's why the Archer sends us pains and he will send us more
and never drive this shameful destruction from the Argives,
not till we give back the girl with sparkling eyes
to her loving father—no price, no ransom paid—
and carry a sacred hundred bulls to Chryse town.
Then we can calm the god, and only then appease him."

    So he declared and sat down. But among them rose
the fighting son of Atreus, lord of the far-flung kingdoms,   120

Agamemnon—furious, his dark heart filled to the brim,
blazing with anger now, his eyes like searing fire.
With a sudden, killing look he wheeled on Calchas first:
"Seer of misery! Never a word that works to my advantage!
Always misery warms your heart, your prophecies—
never a word of profit said or brought to pass.
Now, again, you divine god's will for the armies,
bruit it about, as fact, why the deadly Archer
multiplies our pains: because I, I refused
that glittering price for the young girl Chryseis.   130
Indeed, I prefer *her* by far, the girl herself,
I want her mine in my own house! I rank her higher
than Clytemnestra, my wedded wife—she's nothing less
in build or breeding, in mind or works of hand.
But I am willing to give her back, even so,
if that is best for all. What I really want
is to keep my people safe, not see them dying.
But fetch me another prize, and straight off too,
else I alone of the Argives go without my honor.
That would be a disgrace. You are all witness,   140
look—*my* prize is snatched away!"
                                        But the swift runner
Achilles answered him at once, "Just how, Agamemnon,
great field marshal . . . most grasping man alive,
how can the generous Argives give you prizes now?
I know of no troves of treasure, piled, lying idle,
anywhere. Whatever we dragged from towns we plundered,
all's been portioned out. But collect it, call it back
from the rank and file? *That* would be the disgrace.
So return the girl to the god, at least for now.
We Achaeans will pay you back, three, four times over,   150
if Zeus will grant us the gift, somehow, someday,
to raze Troy's massive ramparts to the ground."

   But King Agamemnon countered, "Not so quickly,
brave as you are, godlike Achilles—trying to cheat *me*.
Oh no, you won't get past me, take me in that way!
What do you want? To cling to your own prize

while I sit calmly by—empty-handed here?
Is that why you order me to give her back?
No—if our generous Argives *will* give me a prize,
a match for my desires, equal to what I've lost,   160
well and good. But if they give me nothing
I will take a prize myself—your own, or Ajax'
or Odysseus' prize—I'll commandeer her myself
and let that man I go to visit choke with rage!
Enough. We'll deal with all this later, in due time.
Now come, we haul a black ship down to the bright sea,
gather a decent number of oarsmen along her locks
and put aboard a sacrifice, and Chryseis herself,
in all her beauty . . . we embark her too.
Let one of the leading captains take command.   170
Ajax, Idomeneus, trusty Odysseus or you, Achilles,
you—the most violent man alive—so you can perform
the rites for us and calm the god yourself."
                                        A dark glance
and the headstrong runner answered him in kind: "Shameless—
armored in shamelessness—always shrewd with greed!
How could any Argive soldier obey your orders,
freely and gladly do your sailing for you
or fight your enemies, full force? Not I, no.
It wasn't Trojan spearmen who brought me here to fight.
The Trojans never did *me* damage, not in the least,   180
they never stole my cattle or my horses, never
in Phthia where the rich soil breeds strong men
did they lay waste my crops. How could they?
Look at the endless miles that lie between us . . .
shadowy mountain ranges, seas that surge and thunder.
No, you colossal, shameless—we all followed you,
to please you, to fight for you, to win your honor
back from the Trojans—Menelaus and you, you dog-face!
What do *you* care? Nothing. You don't look right or left.
And now you threaten to strip me of my prize in person—   190
the one I fought for long and hard, and sons of Achaea
handed her to me.

My honors never equal yours,
whenever we sack some wealthy Trojan stronghold—
my arms bear the brunt of the raw, savage fighting,
true, but when it comes to dividing up the plunder
the lion's share is yours, and back I go to my ships,
clutching some scrap, some pittance that I love,
when I have fought to exhaustion.

No more now—
back I go to Phthia. Better that way by far,
to journey home in the beaked ships of war.   200
I have no mind to linger here disgraced,
brimming your cup and piling up your plunder."

But the lord of men Agamemnon shot back,
"*Desert*, by all means—if the spirit drives you home!
I will never beg you to stay, not on *my* account.
Never—others will take my side and do me honor,
Zeus above all, whose wisdom rules the world.
You—I hate you most of all the warlords
loved by the gods. Always dear to your heart,
strife, yes, and battles, the bloody grind of war.   210
What if you are a great soldier? That's just a gift of god.
Go home with your ships and comrades, lord it over
        your Myrmidons!
You *are* nothing to me—you and your overweening anger!
But let this be my warning on your way:
since Apollo insists on taking my Chryseis,
I'll send her back in my own ships with *my* crew.
But I, I will be there in person at your tents
to take Briseis in all her beauty, your own prize—
so you can learn just how much greater I am than you
and the next man up may shrink from matching words with me, 220
from hoping to rival Agamemnon strength for strength!"

He broke off and anguish gripped Achilles.
The heart in his rugged chest was pounding, torn . . .
Should he draw the long sharp sword slung at his hip,

thrust through the ranks and kill Agamemnon now?—
or check his rage and beat his fury down?
As his racing spirit veered back and forth,
just as he drew his huge blade from its sheath,
down from the vaulting heavens swept Athena,
the white-armed goddess Hera sped her down: 230
Hera loved both men and cared for both alike.
Rearing behind him Pallas seized his fiery hair—
only Achilles saw her, none of the other fighters—
struck with wonder he spun around, he knew her at once,
Pallas Athena! the terrible blazing of those eyes,
and his winged words went flying: "Why, why now?
Child of Zeus with the shield of thunder, why come now?
To witness the outrage Agamemnon just committed?
I tell you this, and so help me it's the truth—
he'll soon pay for his arrogance with his life!"   240

Her gray eyes clear, the goddess Athena answered,
"Down from the skies I come to check your rage
if only you will yield.
The white-armed goddess Hera sped me down:
she loves you both, she cares for you both alike.
Stop this fighting, now. Don't lay hand to sword.
Lash him with threats of the price that he will face.
And I tell you this—and I *know* it is the truth—
one day glittering gifts will lie before you,
three times over to pay for all his outrage.   250
Hold back now. Obey us both."
                              So she urged
and the swift runner complied at once: "I must—
when the two of you hand down commands, Goddess,
a man submits though his heart breaks with fury.
Better for him by far. If a man obeys the gods
they're quick to hear his prayers."
                              And with that
Achilles stayed his burly hand on the silver hilt
and slid the huge blade back in its sheath.
He would not fight the orders of Athena.

Soaring home to Olympus, she rejoined the gods   260
aloft in the halls of Zeus whose shield is thunder.

　　But Achilles rounded on Agamemnon once again,
lashing out at him, not relaxing his anger for a moment:
"Staggering drunk, with your dog's eyes, your fawn's heart!
Never once did you arm with the troops and go to battle
or risk an ambush packed with Achaea's picked men—
you lack the courage, you can see death coming.
Safer by far, you find, to foray all through camp,
commandeering the prize of any man who speaks against you.
King who devours his people! Worthless husks, the men you rule—   270
if not, Atrides, this outrage would have been your last.
I tell you this, and I swear a mighty oath upon it . . .
by this, this scepter, look,
that never again will put forth crown and branches,
now it's left its stump on the mountain ridge forever,
nor will it sprout new green again, now the brazen ax
has stripped its bark and leaves, and now the sons of Achaea
pass it back and forth as they hand their judgments down,
upholding the honored customs whenever Zeus commands—
This scepter will be the mighty force behind my oath: 280
someday, I swear, a yearning for Achilles will strike
Achaea's sons and all your armies! But then, Atrides,
harrowed as you will be, *nothing* you do can save you—
not when your hordes of fighters drop and die,
cut down by the hands of man-killing Hector! Then—
then you will tear your heart out, desperate, raging
that you disgraced the best of the Achaeans!"
　　　　　　　　　　　　　　　　　Down on the ground
he dashed the scepter studded bright with golden nails,
then took his seat again. The son of Atreus smoldered,
glaring across at him, but Nestor rose between them,   290
the man of winning words, the clear speaker of Pylos . . .
Sweeter than honey from his tongue the voice flowed on and on.
Two generations of mortal men he had seen go down by now,
those who were born and bred with him in the old days,
in Pylos' holy realm, and now he ruled the third.

He pleaded with both kings, with clear good will,
"No more—or enormous sorrow comes to all Achaea!
How they would exult, Priam and Priam's sons
and all the Trojans. Oh they'd leap for joy
to hear the two of you battling on this way,   300
you who excel us all, first in Achaean councils,
first in the ways of war.
                              Stop. Please.
Listen to Nestor. You are both younger than I,
and in my time I struck up with better men than you,
even you, but never once did they make light of me.
I've never seen such men, I never will again . . .
men like Pirithous, Dryas, that fine captain,
Caeneus and Exadius, and Polyphemus, royal prince,
and Theseus, Aegeus' boy, a match for the immortals.
They were the strongest mortals ever bred on earth,   310
the strongest, and they fought against the strongest too,
shaggy Centaurs, wild brutes of the mountains—
they hacked them down, terrible, deadly work.
And I was in their ranks, fresh out of Pylos,
far away from home—they enlisted me themselves
and I fought on my own, a free lance, single-handed.
And none of the men who walk the earth these days
could battle with those fighters, none, but they,
they took to heart my counsels, marked my words.
So now you listen too. Yielding is far better . . .   320
Don't seize the girl, Agamemnon, powerful as you are—
leave her, just as the sons of Achaea gave her,
his prize from the very first.
And you, Achilles, never hope to fight it out
with your king, pitting force against his force:
no one can match the honors dealt a king, you know,
a sceptered king to whom great Zeus gives glory.
Strong as you are—a goddess was your mother—
he has more power because he rules more men.
Atrides, end your anger—look, it's Nestor!   330
I beg you, cool your fury against Achilles.

Here the man stands over all Achaea's armies,
our rugged bulwark braced for shocks of war."

   But King Agamemnon answered him in haste,
"True, old man—all you say is fit and proper—
but this soldier wants to tower over the armies,
he wants to rule over all, to lord it over all,
give out orders to every man in sight. Well,
there's one, I trust, who will never yield to *him*!
What if the everlasting gods have made a spearman of him?   340
Have they entitled him to hurl abuse at *me*?"

   "Yes!"—blazing Achilles broke in quickly—
"What a worthless, burnt-out coward I'd be called
if I would submit to you and all your orders,
whatever you blurt out. Fling them at others,
don't give me commands!
Never again, *I* trust, will Achilles yield to *you*.
And I tell you this—take it to heart, I warn you—
my hands will never do battle for that girl,
neither with you, King, nor any man alive.   350
You Achaeans gave her, now you've snatched her back.
But all the rest I possess beside my fast black ship—
not one bit of it can you seize against my will, Atrides.
Come, try it! So the men can see, that instant,
your black blood gush and spurt around my spear!"

   Once the two had fought it out with words,
battling face-to-face, both sprang to their feet
and broke up the muster beside the Argive squadrons.
Achilles strode off to his trim ships and shelters,
back to his friend Patroclus and their comrades.   360
Agamemnon had a vessel hauled down to the sea,
he picked out twenty oarsmen to man her locks,
put aboard the cattle for sacrifice to the god
and led Chryseis in all her beauty amidships.

Versatile Odysseus took the helm as captain.

                               All embarked,
the party launched out on the sea's foaming lanes
while the son of Atreus told his troops to wash,
to purify themselves from the filth of plague.
They scoured it off, threw scourings in the surf
and sacrificed to Apollo full-grown bulls and goats   370
along the beaten shore of the fallow barren sea
and savory smoke went swirling up the skies.

   So the men were engaged throughout the camp.
But King Agamemnon would not stop the quarrel,
the first threat he hurled against Achilles.
He called Talthybius and Eurybates briskly,
his two heralds, ready, willing aides:
"Go to Achilles' lodge. Take Briseis at once,
his beauty Briseis by the hand and bring her here.
But if he will not surrender her, I'll go myself,   380
I'll seize her myself, with an army at my back—
and all the worse for him!"

                          He sent them off
with the strict order ringing in their ears.
Against their will the two men made their way
along the breaking surf of the barren salt sea
and reached the Myrmidon shelters and their ships.
They found him beside his lodge and black hull,
seated grimly—and Achilles took no joy
when he saw the two approaching.
They were afraid, they held the king in awe   390
and stood there, silent. Not a word to Achilles,
not a question. But he sensed it all in his heart,
their fear, their charge, and broke the silence for them:
"Welcome, couriers! Good heralds of Zeus and men,
here, come closer. You have done nothing to me.
You are not to blame. No one but Agamemnon—
he is the one who sent you for Briseis.
Go, Patroclus, Prince, bring out the girl
and hand her to them so they can take her back.

But let them both bear witness to my loss . . .   400
in the face of blissful gods and mortal men,
in the face of that unbending, ruthless king—
if the day should come when the armies need *me*
to save their ranks from ignominious, stark defeat.
The man is raving—with all the murderous fury in his heart.
He lacks the sense to see a day behind, a day ahead,
and safeguard the Achaeans battling by the ships."

    Patroclus obeyed his great friend's command.
He led Briseis in all her beauty from the lodge
and handed her over to the men to take away.   410
And the two walked back along the Argive ships
while she trailed on behind, reluctant, every step.
But Achilles wept, and slipping away from his companions,
far apart, sat down on the beach of the heaving gray sea
and scanned the endless ocean. Reaching out his arms,
again and again he prayed to his dear mother: "Mother!
You gave me life, short as that life will be,
so at least Olympian Zeus, thundering up on high,
should give me honor—but now he gives me nothing.
Atreus' son Agamemnon, for all his far-flung kingdoms—   420
the man disgraces me, seizes and keeps my prize,
he tears her away himself!"
                   So he wept and prayed
and his noble mother heard him, seated near her father,
the Old Man of the Sea in the salt green depths.
Suddenly up she rose from the churning surf
like mist and settling down beside him as he wept,
stroked Achilles gently, whispering his name, "My child—
why in tears? What sorrow has touched your heart?
Tell me, please. Don't harbor it deep inside you.
We must share it all."
            And now from his depths·   430
the proud runner groaned: "You know, you know,
why labor through it all? You know it all so well . . .
We raided Thebe once, Eetion's sacred citadel,
we ravaged the place, hauled all the plunder here

and the armies passed it round, share and share alike,
and they chose the beauty Chryseis for Agamemnon.
But soon her father, the holy priest of Apollo
the distant deadly Archer, Chryses approached
the fast trim ships of the Argives armed in bronze
to win his daughter back, bringing a priceless ransom   440
and bearing high in hand, wound on a golden staff,
the wreaths of the god who strikes from worlds away.
He begged the whole Achaean army but most of all
the two supreme commanders, Atreus' two sons,
and all ranks of Achaeans cried out their assent,
'Respect the priest, accept the shining ransom!'
But it brought no joy to the heart of Agamemnon,
our high and mighty king dismissed the priest
with a brutal order ringing in his ears.
And shattered with anger, the old man withdrew   450
but Apollo heard his prayer—he loved him, deeply—
he loosed his shaft at the Argives, withering plague,
and now the troops began to drop and die in droves,
the arrows of god went showering left and right,
whipping through the Achaeans' vast encampment.
But the old seer who knew the cause full well
revealed the will of the archer god Apollo.
And I was the first, mother, I urged them all,
'Appease the god at once!' That's when the fury
gripped the son of Atreus. Agamemnon leapt to his feet   460
and hurled his threat—his threat's been driven home.
One girl, Chryseis, the fiery-eyed Achaeans
ferry out in a fast trim ship to Chryse Island,
laden with presents for the god. The other girl,
just now the heralds came and led her away from camp,
Briseus' daughter, the prize the armies gave me.
But you, mother, if you have any power at all,
protect your son! Go to Olympus, plead with Zeus,
if you ever warmed his heart with a word or any action . . .

Time and again I heard your claims in father's halls,   470
boasting how you and you alone of all the immortals

rescued Zeus, the lord of the dark storm cloud,
from ignominious, stark defeat . . .
That day the Olympians tried to chain him down,
Hera, Poseidon lord of the sea, and Pallas Athena—
you rushed to Zeus, dear Goddess, broke those chains,
quickly ordered the hundred-hander to steep Olympus,
that monster whom the immortals call Briareus
but every mortal calls the Sea-god's son, Aegaeon,
though he's stronger than his father. Down he sat,   480
flanking Cronus' son, gargantuan in the glory of it all,
and the blessed gods were struck with terror then,
they stopped shackling Zeus.
                                        Remind him of that,
now, go and sit beside him, grasp his knees . . .
persuade him, somehow, to help the Trojan cause,
to pin the Achaeans back against their ships,
trap them round the bay and mow them down.
So all can reap the benefits of their king—
so even mighty Atrides can see how mad he was
to disgrace Achilles, the best of the Achaeans!"   490

    And Thetis answered, bursting into tears,
"O my son, my sorrow, why did I ever bear you?
All I bore was doom . . .
Would to god you could linger by your ships
without a grief in the world, without a torment!
Doomed to a short life, you have so little time.
And not only short, now, but filled with heartbreak too,
more than all other men alive—doomed twice over.
Ah to a cruel fate I bore you in our halls!
Still, I shall go to Olympus crowned with snow   500
and repeat your prayer to Zeus who loves the lightning.
Perhaps he will be persuaded.
                                        But you, my child,
stay here by the fast ships, rage on at the Achaeans,
just keep clear of every foray in the fighting.
Only yesterday Zeus went off to the Ocean River
to feast with the Aethiopians, loyal, lordly men,

and all the gods went with him. But in twelve days
the Father returns to Olympus. Then, for your sake,
up I go to the bronze floor, the royal house of Zeus—
I'll grasp his knees, I think I'll win him over."

                                        With that vow   510
his mother went away and left him there, alone,
his heart inflamed for the sashed and lovely girl
they'd wrenched away from him against his will.
Meanwhile Odysseus drew in close to Chryse Island,
bearing the splendid sacrifice in the vessel's hold.
And once they had entered the harbor deep in bays
they furled and stowed the sail in the black ship,
they lowered the mast by the forestays, smoothly,
quickly let it down on the forked mast-crutch
and rowed her into a mooring under oars.   520
Out went the bow-stones—cables fast astern—
and the crew themselves swung out in the breaking surf,
leading out the sacrifice for the archer god Apollo,
and out of the deep-sea ship Chryseis stepped too.
Then tactful Odysseus led her up to the altar,
placing her in her loving father's arms, and said,
"Chryses, the lord of men Agamemnon sent me here
to bring your daughter back and perform a sacrifice,
a grand sacrifice to Apollo—for all Achaea's sake—
so we can appease the god   530
who's loosed such grief and torment on the Argives."

    With those words he left her in Chryses' arms
and the priest embraced the child he loved, exultant.
At once the men arranged the sacrifice for Apollo,
making the cattle ring his well-built altar,
then they rinsed their hands and took up barley.
Rising among them Chryses stretched his arms to the sky
and prayed in a high resounding voice, "Hear me, Apollo!
God of the silver bow who strides the walls of Chryse
and Cilla sacrosanct—lord in power of Tenedos!   540
If you honored me last time and heard my prayer
and rained destruction down on all Achaea's ranks,

now bring my prayer to pass once more. Now, at last,
drive this killing plague from the armies of Achaea!"

His prayer went up and Phoebus Apollo heard him.
And soon as the men had prayed and flung the barley,
first they lifted back the heads of the victims,
slit their throats, skinned them and carved away
the meat from the thighbones and wrapped them in fat,
a double fold sliced clean and topped with strips of flesh.   550
And the old man burned these over dried split wood
and over the quarters poured out glistening wine
while young men at his side held five-pronged forks.
Once they had burned the bones and tasted the organs
they cut the rest into pieces, pierced them with spits,
roasted them to a turn and pulled them off the fire.
The work done, the feast laid out, they ate well
and no man's hunger lacked a share of the banquet.
When they had put aside desire for food and drink,
the young men brimmed the mixing bowls with wine   560
and tipping first drops for the god in every cup
they poured full rounds for all. And all day long
they appeased the god with song, raising a ringing hymn
to the distant archer god who drives away the plague,
those young Achaean warriors singing out his power,
and Apollo listened, his great heart warm with joy.

Then when the sun went down and night came on
they made their beds and slept by the stern-cables . . .
When young Dawn with her rose-red fingers shone once more,
they set sail for the main encampment of Achaea.   570
The Archer sent them a bracing following wind,
they stepped the mast, spread white sails wide,
the wind hit full and the canvas bellied out
and a dark blue wave, foaming up at the bow,
sang out loud and strong as the ship made way,
skimming the whitecaps, cutting toward her goal.
And once offshore of Achaea's vast encampment
they eased her in and hauled the black ship high,

far up on the sand, and shored her up with timbers.
Then they scattered, each to his own ship and shelter.   580

But *he* raged on, grimly camped by his fast fleet,
the royal son of Peleus, the swift runner Achilles.
Now he no longer haunted the meeting grounds
where men win glory, now he no longer went to war
but day after day he ground his heart out, waiting there,
yearning, always yearning for battle cries and combat.

But now as the twelfth dawn after this shone clear
the gods who live forever marched home to Olympus,
all in a long cortege, and Zeus led them on.
And Thetis did not forget her son's appeals.   590
She broke from a cresting wave at first light
and soaring up to the broad sky and Mount Olympus,
found the son of Cronus gazing down on the world,
peaks apart from the other gods and seated high
on the topmost crown of rugged ridged Olympus.
And crouching down at his feet,
quickly grasping his knees with her left hand,
her right hand holding him underneath the chin,
she prayed to the lord god Zeus, the son of Cronus:
"Zeus, Father Zeus! If I ever served you well   600
among the deathless gods with a word or action,
bring this prayer to pass: honor my son Achilles!—
doomed to the shortest life of any man on earth.
And now the lord of men Agamemnon has disgraced him,
seizes and keeps his prize, tears her away himself. But you—
exalt him, Olympian Zeus: your urgings rule the world!
Come, grant the Trojans victory after victory
till the Achaean armies pay my dear son back,
building higher the honor he deserves!"
                                        She paused
but Zeus who commands the storm clouds answered nothing.   610
The Father sat there, silent. It seemed an eternity . . .
But Thetis, clasping his knees, held on, clinging,
pressing her question once again: "Grant my prayer,

once and for all, Father, bow your head in assent!
Or deny me outright. What have *you* to fear?
So I may know, too well, just how cruelly
I am the most dishonored goddess of them all."

Filled with anger
Zeus who marshals the storm clouds answered her at last:
"Disaster. You will drive me into war with Hera.
She will provoke me, she with her shrill abuse.   620
Even now in the face of all the immortal gods
she harries me perpetually, Hera charges *me*
that I always go to battle for the Trojans.
Away with you now. Hera might catch us here.
I will see to this. I will bring it all to pass.
Look, I will bow my head if that will satisfy you.
That, I remind you, that among the immortal gods
is the strongest, truest sign that I can give.
No word or work of mine—nothing can be revoked,
there is no treachery, nothing left unfinished   630
once I bow my head to say it shall be done."

So he decreed. And Zeus the son of Cronus bowed
his craggy dark brows and the deathless locks came pouring
down from the thunderhead of the great immortal king
and giant shock waves spread through all Olympus.

So the two of them made their pact and parted.
Deep in the sea she dove from radiant Mount Olympus.
Zeus went back to his own halls, and all the gods
in full assembly rose from their seats at once
to meet the Father striding toward them now.   640
None dared remain at rest as Zeus advanced,
they all sprang up to greet him face-to-face
as he took his place before them on his throne.
But Hera knew it all. She had seen how Thetis,
the Old Man of the Sea's daughter, Thetis quick
on her glistening feet was hatching plans with Zeus.
And suddenly Hera taunted the Father, son of Cronus:
"So, who of the gods this time, my treacherous one,

was hatching plans with you?
Always your pleasure, whenever my back is turned,   650
to settle things in your grand clandestine way.
You never deign, do you, freely and frankly,
to share your plots with me—never, not a word!"

   The father of men and gods replied sharply,
"Hera—stop hoping to fathom all my thoughts.
You will find them a trial, though you are my wife.
Whatever is right for you to hear, no one, trust me,
will know of it before you, neither god nor man.
Whatever I choose to plan apart from all the gods—
no more of your everlasting questions, probe and pry no more."   660

   And Hera the Queen, her dark eyes wide, exclaimed,
"Dread majesty, son of Cronus, what are you saying?
Now surely I've never probed or pried in the past.
Why, you can scheme to your heart's content
without a qualm in the world for me. But now
I have a terrible fear that she has won you over,
Thetis, the Old Man of the Sea's daughter, Thetis
with her glistening feet. I know it. Just at dawn
she knelt down beside you and grasped your knees
and I suspect you bowed your head in assent to her—   670
you granted once and for all to exalt Achilles now
and slaughter hordes of Achaeans pinned against their ships."

   And Zeus who marshals the thunderheads returned,
"Maddening one . . . you and your eternal suspicions—
I can never escape you. Ah but tell me, Hera,
just what can you *do* about all this? Nothing.
Only estrange yourself from me a little more—
and all the worse for you.
If what you say is true, that must be my pleasure.
Now go sit down. Be quiet now. Obey my orders,   680
for fear the gods, however many Olympus holds,

are powerless to protect you when I come
to throttle you with my irresistible hands."

He subsided
but Hera the Queen, her eyes wider, was terrified.
She sat in silence. She wrenched her will to his.
And throughout the halls of Zeus the gods of heaven
quaked with fear. Hephaestus the Master Craftsman
rose up first to harangue them all, trying now
to bring his loving mother a little comfort,
the white-armed goddess Hera: "Oh disaster . . .   690
that's what it is, and it will be unbearable
if the two of you must come to blows this way,
flinging the gods in chaos just for mortal men.
No more joy for us in the sumptuous feast
when riot rules the day.
I urge you, mother—you know that I am right—
work back into his good graces, so the Father,
our beloved Father will never wheel on us again,
send our banquets crashing! The Olympian lord of lightning—
what if he would like to blast us from our seats?   700
He is far too strong. Go back to him, mother,
stroke the Father with soft, winning words—
at once the Olympian will turn kind to us again."

    Pleading, springing up with a two-handled cup,
he reached it toward his loving mother's hands
with his own winning words: "Patience, mother!
Grieved as you are, bear up, or dear as you are,
I have to see you beaten right before my eyes.
I would be shattered—what could I do to save you?
It's hard to fight the Olympian strength for strength.   710
You remember the last time I rushed to your defense?
He seized my foot, he hurled me off the tremendous threshold
and all day long I dropped, I was dead weight and then,
when the sun went down, down I plunged on Lemnos,
little breath left in me. But the mortals there
soon nursed a fallen immortal back to life."

At that the white-armed goddess Hera smiled
and smiling, took the cup from her child's hands.
Then dipping sweet nectar up from the mixing bowl
he poured it round to all the immortals, left to right.
And uncontrollable laughter broke from the happy gods
as they watched the god of fire breathing hard
and bustling through the halls.
                                        That hour then
and all day long till the sun went down they feasted
and no god's hunger lacked a share of the handsome banquet
or the gorgeous lyre Apollo struck or the Muses singing
voice to voice in choirs, their vibrant music rising.

At last, when the sun's fiery light had set,
each immortal went to rest in his own house,
the splendid high halls Hephaestus built for each   730
with all his craft and cunning, the famous crippled Smith.
And Olympian Zeus the lord of lightning went to his own bed
where he had always lain when welcome sleep came on him.
There he climbed and there he slept and by his side
lay Hera the Queen, the goddess of the golden throne.

BOOK THREE

Helen Reviews
the Champions

Now with the squadrons marshaled, captains leading each,
the Trojans came with cries and the din of war like wildfowl
when the long hoarse cries of cranes sweep on against the sky
and the great formations flee from winter's grim ungodly storms,
flying in force, shrieking south to the Ocean gulfs, speeding
blood and death to the Pygmy warriors, launching at daybreak
savage battle down upon their heads. But Achaea's armies
came on strong in silence, breathing combat-fury,
hearts ablaze to defend each other to the death.

When the South Wind showers mist on the mountaintops,   10
no friend to shepherds, better than night to thieves—
you can see no farther than you can fling a stone—
so dust came clouding, swirling up from the feet of armies
marching at top speed, trampling through the plain.

Now closer, closing, front to front in the onset
till Paris sprang from the Trojan forward ranks,
a challenger, lithe, magnificent as a god,
the skin of a leopard slung across his shoulders,
a reflex bow at his back and battle-sword at hip
and brandishing two sharp spears tipped in bronze   20
he strode forth, challenging all the Argive best
to fight him face-to-face in mortal combat.

Soon as the warrior Menelaus marked him,
Paris parading there with his big loping strides,
flaunting before the troops, Atrides thrilled
like a lion lighting on some handsome carcass,
lucky to find an antlered stag or wild goat
just as hunger strikes—he rips it, bolts it down,
even with running dogs and lusty hunters rushing *him*.
So Menelaus thrilled at heart—princely Paris there,   30
right before his eyes. The outlaw, the adulterer . . .
"Now for revenge!" he thought, and down he leapt
from his chariot fully armed and hit the ground.

But soon as magnificent Paris marked Atrides
shining among the champions, Paris' spirit shook.
Backing into his friendly ranks, he cringed from death
as one who trips on a snake in a hilltop hollow
recoils, suddenly, trembling grips his knees
and pallor takes his cheeks and back he shrinks.
So he dissolved again in the proud Trojan lines,   40
dreading Atrides—magnificent, brave Paris.
                                        At one glance
Hector raked his brother with insults, stinging taunts:
"Paris, appalling Paris! Our prince of beauty—
mad for women, you lure them all to ruin!
Would to god you'd never been born, died unwed.
That's all I'd ask. Better that way by far
than to have you strutting here, an outrage—
a mockery in the eyes of all our enemies. Why,
the long-haired Achaeans must be roaring with laughter!

They thought *you* the bravest champion we could field,   50
and just because of the handsome luster on your limbs,
but you have no pith, no fighting strength inside you.
What?—is *this* the man who mustered the oarsmen once,
who braved the seas in his racing deep-sea ships,
trafficked with outlanders, carried off a woman
far from her distant shores, a great beauty
wed to a land of rugged spearmen?

                     You . . .
curse to your father, your city and all your people,
a joy to our enemies, rank disgrace to yourself!
So, you can't stand up to the battling Menelaus?   60
You'd soon feel his force, that man you robbed
of his sumptuous, warm wife. No use to you then,
the fine lyre and these, these gifts of Aphrodite,
your long flowing locks and your striking looks,
not when you roll and couple with the dust.
What cowards, the men of Troy—or years ago
they'd have decked you out in a suit of rocky armor,
stoned you to death for all the wrongs you've done!"

    And Paris, magnificent as a god, replied,
"Ah Hector, you criticize me fairly, yes,   70
nothing unfair, beyond what I deserve.
The heart inside you is always tempered hard,
like an ax that goes through wood when a shipwright
cuts out ship timbers with every ounce of skill
and the blade's weight drives the man's stroke.
So the heart inside your chest is never daunted.
Still, don't fling in my face the lovely gifts
of golden Aphrodite. Not to be tossed aside,
the gifts of the gods, those glories . . .
whatever the gods give of their own free will—   80
how could we ever choose them for ourselves?

                        Now, though,
if you really want me to fight to the finish here,
have all Trojans and Argives take their seats
and pit me against Menelaus dear to Ares—

right between the lines—
we'll fight it out for Helen and all her wealth.
And the one who proves the better man and wins,
he'll take those treasures fairly, lead the woman home.
The rest will seal in blood their binding pacts of friendship.
Our people will live in peace on the rich soil of Troy,   90
our enemies sail home to the stallion-land of Argos,
the land of Achaea where the women are a wonder . . ."

   When Hector heard that challenge he rejoiced
and right in the no man's land along his lines he strode,
gripping his spear mid-haft, staving men to a standstill.
But the long-haired Argive archers aimed at Hector,
trying to cut him down with arrows, hurling rocks
till King Agamemnon cried out in a ringing voice,
"Hold back, Argives! Sons of Achaea, stop your salvos!
Look, Hector with that flashing helmet of his—   100
the man is trying to tell us something now."

   They held their attack. Quickly men fell silent
and Hector pleaded, appealing to both armed camps:
"Hear me—Trojans, Achaeans geared for combat!
Hear the challenge of Paris,
the man who caused our long hard campaign.
He urges all the Trojans, all the Argives too,
to lay their fine armor down on the fertile earth
while Paris himself and the warrior Menelaus
take the field between you and fight it out   110
for Helen and all her wealth in single combat.
And the one who proves the better man and wins,
he'll take those treasures fairly, lead the woman home.
The rest will seal in blood their binding pacts of friendship."

   He stopped. A hushed silence held the ranks.
And Menelaus whose cry could marshal armies
urged both sides, "Now hear me out as well!
Such limited vengeance hurts me most of all—
but I intend that we will part in peace, at last,

Trojans and Achaeans. Look what heavy casualties   120
you have suffered just for me, my violent quarrel,
and Paris who brought it on you all. Now we'll fight—
and death to the one marked out for doom and death!
But the rest will part in peace, and soon, soon.
Bring two lambs—a white male and a black ewe
for the Sun and Earth—and we'll bring a third for Zeus.
And lead on Priam too, Priam in all his power,
so the king himself can seal our truce in blood—
his royal sons are reckless, not to be trusted:
no one must trample on the oath we swear to Zeus.   130
The minds of the younger men are always flighty,
but let an old man stand his ground among them,
one who can see the days behind, the days ahead—
that is the best hope for peace, for both our armies."

    The Achaean and Trojan forces both exulted,
hoping *this* would end the agonies of war.
They hauled their chariots up in ranks, at rest,
the troops dismounted and stripped away their arms
and laid them down on the earth, crowded together—
hardly a foot of plowland showed between them.   140
Back to the city Hector sent two heralds now
to bring the lambs at once and summon Priam
while King Agamemnon sent Talthybius off,
heading down to the ships for one more lamb.
The herald obeyed his captain's orders quickly.

    And now a messenger went to white-armed Helen too,
Iris, looking for all the world like Hector's sister
wed to Antenor's son, Helicaon's bride Laodice,
the loveliest daughter Priam ever bred.
And Iris came on Helen in her rooms . . .   150
weaving a growing web, a dark red folding robe,
working into the weft the endless bloody struggles
stallion-breaking Trojans and Argives armed in bronze
had suffered all for her at the god of battle's hands.

Iris, racing the wind, brushed close and whispered,
"Come, dear girl, come quickly—
so you can see what wondrous things they're doing,
stallion-breaking Trojans and Argives armed in bronze!
A moment ago they longed to kill each other, longed
for heartbreaking, inhuman warfare on the plain.   160
Now those very warriors stand at ease, in silence—
the fighting's stopped, they lean against their shields,
their long lances stuck in the ground beside them.
Think of it: Paris and Menelaus loved by Ares
go to fight it out with their rugged spears—
all for you—and the man who wins that duel,
you'll be called his wife!"
                                    And with those words
the goddess filled her heart with yearning warm and deep
for her husband long ago, her city and her parents.
Quickly cloaking herself in shimmering linen,   170
out of her rooms she rushed, live tears welling,
and not alone—two of her women followed close behind,
Aethra, Pittheus' daughter, and Clymene, eyes wide,
and they soon reached the looming Scaean Gates.

   And there they were, gathered around Priam,
Panthous and Thymoetes, Lampus and Clytius,
Hicetaon the gray aide of Ares, then those two
with unfailing good sense, Ucalegon and Antenor.
The old men of the realm held seats above the gates.
Long years had brought their fighting days to a halt   180
but they were eloquent speakers still, clear as cicadas
settled on treetops, lifting their voices through the forest,
rising softly, falling, dying away . . . So they waited,
the old chiefs of Troy, as they sat aloft the tower.
And catching sight of Helen moving along the ramparts,
they murmured one to another, gentle, winged words:
"Who on earth could blame them? Ah, no wonder
the men of Troy and Argives under arms have suffered
years of agony all for her, for such a woman.
Beauty, terrible beauty!   190

A deathless goddess—so she strikes our eyes!

But still,

ravishing as she is, let her go home in the long ships
and not be left behind . . . for us and our children
down the years an irresistible sorrow."

They murmured low

but Priam, raising his voice, called across to Helen,
"Come over here, dear child. Sit in front of me,
so you can see your husband of long ago,
your kinsmen and your people.
I don't blame you. I hold the gods to blame.
They are the ones who brought this war upon me,   200
devastating war against the Achaeans—

Here, come closer,

tell me the name of that tremendous fighter. Look,
who's that Achaean there, so stark and grand?
Many others afield are much taller, true,
but I have never yet set eyes on one so regal,
so majestic . . . That man must be a king!"

And Helen the radiance of women answered Priam,
"I revere you so, dear father, dread you too—
if only death had pleased me then, grim death,
that day I followed your son to Troy, forsaking   210
my marriage bed, my kinsmen and my child,
my favorite, now full-grown,
and the lovely comradeship of women my own age.
Death never came, so now I can only waste away in tears.
But about your question—yes, I have the answer.
That man is Atreus' son Agamemnon, lord of empires,
both a mighty king and a strong spearman too,
and he used to be my kinsman, whore that I am!
There was a world . . . or was it all a dream?"

Her voice broke but the old king, lost in wonder,   220
cried out, "How lucky you are, son of Atreus,
child of fortune, your destiny so blessed!
Look at the vast Achaean armies you command!

Years ago I visited Phrygia rife with vineyards,
saw the Phrygian men with their swarming horses there—
multitudes—the armies of Otreus, Mygdon like a god,
encamped that time along the Sangarius River banks.
And I took my stand among them, comrade-in-arms
the day the Amazons struck, a match for men in war.
But not even those hordes could match these hordes of yours,   230
your fiery-eyed Achaeans!"

                              And sighting Odysseus next
the old king questioned Helen, "Come, dear child,
tell me of that one too—now who is he?
Shorter than Atreus' son Agamemnon, clearly,
but broader across the shoulders, through the chest.
There, you see? His armor's heaped on the green field
but the man keeps ranging the ranks of fighters like a ram—
yes, he looks to me like a thick-fleeced bellwether ram
making his way through a big mass of sheep-flocks,
shining silver-gray."

                              Helen the child of Zeus replied,   240
"That's Laertes' son, the great tactician Odysseus.
He was bred in the land of Ithaca. Rocky ground
and he's quick at every treachery under the sun—
the man of twists and turns."

                              Helen paused
and the shrewd Antenor carried on her story:
"Straight to the point, my lady, very true.
Once in the past he came our way, King Odysseus
heading the embassy they sent for your release,
together with Menelaus dear to Ares.
I hosted them, treated them warmly in my halls   250
and learned the ways of both, their strategies, their traits.
Now, when they mingled with our Trojans in assembly,
standing side-by-side, Menelaus' shoulders
mounted over his friend's in height and spread,
when both were seated Odysseus looked more lordly.
But when they spun their appeals before us all,
Menelaus spoke out quickly—his words racing,
few but clear as a bell, nothing long-winded

or off the mark, though in fact the man was younger.
But when Odysseus sprang up, the famed tactician   260
would just stand there, staring down, hard,
his eyes fixed on the ground,
never shifting his scepter back and forth,
clutching it stiff and still like a mindless man.
You'd think him a sullen fellow or just plain fool.
But when *he* let loose that great voice from his chest
and the words came piling on like a driving winter blizzard—
then no man alive could rival Odysseus! Odysseus . . .
we no longer gazed in wonder at his looks."

Catching sight
of a third fighter, Ajax, the old king asked her next,   270
"Who's that other Achaean, so powerful, so well-built?
He towers over the Argives, his head, his massive shoulders!"

And Helen in all her radiance, her long robes, replied,
"Why, that's the giant Ajax, bulwark of the Achaeans.
And Idomeneus over there—standing with his Cretans—
like a god, you see? And the Cretan captains
form a ring around him. How often Menelaus,
my good soldier, would host him in our halls,
in the old days, when he'd sail across from Crete.
And now I see them all, the fiery-eyed Achaeans,   280
I know them all by heart, and I could tell their names . . .
but two I cannot find, and they're captains of the armies,
Castor breaker of horses and the hardy boxer Polydeuces.
My blood brothers. Mother bore them both. Perhaps
they never crossed over from Lacedaemon's lovely hills
or come they did, sailing here in the deep-sea ships,
but now they refuse to join the men in battle,
dreading the scorn, the curses hurled at me . . ."

So she wavered, but the earth already held them fast,
long dead in the life-giving earth of Lacedaemon,   290
the dear land of their fathers.

Now through Troy
the heralds brought the offerings for the gods,

sacred victims to bind and seal the oaths:
two lambs and the wine that warms the heart,
the yield of the vine, filling a goatskin sack,
and the herald Idaeus carried a gleaming bowl
and golden winecups. Reaching the old king's side
the crier roused him sharply: "Son of Laomedon, rise up!
They are calling for you now, commanders of both armies,
stallion-breaking Trojans and Argives armed in bronze—   300
come down to the plain so you can seal our oaths.
Now Paris and Menelaus, Atrides loved by Ares,
will fight it out with their rugged spears for Helen,
and Helen and all her treasures go to the man who wins.
The rest will seal in blood their binding pacts of friendship.
Our people will live in peace on the rich soil of Troy.
Our enemies sail home to the stallion-land of Argos,
the land of Achaea where the women are a wonder."

A shudder went shooting through the old man
but he told his men to yoke the team at once.   310
They promptly obeyed and Priam climbed aboard,
pulling the reins back taut. Antenor flanked him,
mounting the gleaming car, and both men drove the team
through the Scaean Gates, heading toward the plain.

Reaching the front, they climbed down from the chariot,
onto the earth that feeds us all, and into the space
between Achaean and Trojan lines they marched.
Lord Agamemnon rose at once to greet them both
with the great tactician Odysseus by his side.
The noble heralds brought on the victims   320
marked for the gods to seal and bind the oaths.
They mixed the contenders' wine in a large bowl
and rinsed the warlords' waiting hands with water.
Atreus' son drew forth the dagger always slung
at his battle-sword's big sheath, cut some tufts
from the lambs' heads, and heralds passed them round
to Achaean and Trojan captains. Then Atreus' son

Agamemnon stood in behalf of all, lifted his arms
and prayed in his deep resounding voice, "Father Zeus!
Ruling over us all from Ida, god of greatness, god of glory!   330
Helios, Sun above us, you who see all, hear all things!
Rivers! And Earth! And you beneath the ground
who punish the dead—whoever broke his oath—
be witness here, protect our binding pacts.
If Paris brings Menelaus down in blood,
he keeps Helen himself and all her wealth
and we sail home in our racing deep-sea ships.
But if red-haired Menelaus brings down Paris,
the Trojans surrender Helen and all her treasures.
And they pay us reparations fair and fitting,   340
a price to inspire generations still to come.
But if Priam and Priam's sons refuse to pay,
refuse me, Agamemnon—with Paris beaten down—
then I myself will fight it out for the ransom,
I'll battle here to the end of our long war."
                                        On those terms
he dragged his ruthless dagger across the lambs' throats
and let them fall to the ground, dying, gasping away
their life breath, cut short by the sharp bronze.
Then dipping up the wine from the mixing bowls,
brimming their cups, pouring them on the earth,   350
men said their prayers to the gods who never die.
You could hear some Trojan or Achaean calling, "Zeus—
god of greatness, god of glory, all you immortals!
Whichever contenders trample on this treaty first,
spill their brains on the ground as this wine spills—
theirs, their children's too—their enemies rape their wives!"

But Zeus would not fulfill their prayers, not yet . . .
Now Priam rose in their midst and took his leave:
"Hear me, Trojans, Achaeans geared for combat—
home I go to windy Ilium, straight home now.   360
This is more than I can bear, I tell you—
to watch my son do battle with Menelaus

loved by the War-god, right before my eyes.
Zeus knows, no doubt, and every immortal too,
which fighter is doomed to end all this in death."

And laying the victims in the chariot, noble Priam
climbed aboard, pulling the reins back taut.
Antenor flanked him, mounting the gleaming car,
and back they drove again, heading home to Troy.
But Priam's son Prince Hector and royal Odysseus   370
measured off the ground for single combat first,
then dropped two stones in a helmet, lots for casting—
who would be first to hurl his bronze-tipped spear?
The armies prayed and stretched their hands to the gods.
You could hear some Trojan or Achaean pleading, "Father Zeus!
Ruling over us all from Ida, god of greatness, glory!
Whoever brought this war on both our countries,
let him rot and sink to the House of Death—
but let our pacts of friendship all hold fast!"
                                         So they prayed
as tall Hector, eyes averted under his flashing helmet,   380
shook the two lots hard and Paris' lot leapt out.
The troops sat down by rank, each beside his horses
pawing the ground where blazoned war-gear lay. And now—
one warrior harnessed burnished armor on his back,
magnificent Paris, fair-haired Helen's consort.
First he wrapped his legs with well-made greaves,
fastened behind the heels with silver ankle-clasps,
next he strapped a breastplate round his chest,
his brother Lycaon's that fitted him so well.
Then over his shoulder Paris slung his sword,   390
the fine bronze blade with its silver-studded hilt,
and then the shield-strap and his sturdy, massive shield
and over his powerful head he set a well-forged helmet,
the horsehair crest atop it tossing, bristling terror,
and last he grasped a spear that matched his grip.
Following step by step
the fighting Menelaus strapped on armor too.

Both men armed at opposing sides of the forces,
into the no man's land between the lines they strode,
glances menacing, wild excitement seizing all who watched,   400
the stallion-breaking Trojans and Argive men-at-arms.
Striking a stand in the dueling-ground just cleared
they brandished spears at each other, tense with fury.
Suddenly Paris hurled—his spear's long shadow flew
and the shaft hit Menelaus' round shield, full center—
not pounding through, the brazen point bent back
in the tough armor.
                  But his turn next—Menelaus
reared with a bronze lance and a prayer to Father Zeus:
"Zeus, King, give me revenge, he wronged me first!
Illustrious Paris—crush him under my hand!   410
So even among the men to come a man may shrink
from wounding the host who showers him with kindness."

Shaking his spear, he hurled and its long shadow flew
and the shaft hit Paris' round shield, hit full center—
straight through the gleaming hide the heavy weapon drove,
ripping down and in through the breastplate finely worked,
tearing the war-shirt, close by Paris' flank it jabbed
but the Trojan swerved aside and dodged black death.
So now Menelaus drew his sword with silver studs
and hoisting the weapon high, brought it crashing down   420
on the helmet ridge but the blade smashed where it struck—
jagged shatters flying—it dropped from Atrides' hand
and the hero cried out, scanning the blank skies,
"Father Zeus—no god's more deadly than you!
Here I thought I'd punish Paris for all his outrage—
now my sword is shattered, right in my hands, look,
my spear flew from my grip for nothing—I never hit him!"

Lunging at Paris, he grabbed his horsehair crest,
swung him round, started to drag him into Argive lines
and now the braided chin-strap holding his helmet tight   430
was gouging his soft throat—Paris was choking, strangling.
Now he'd have hauled him off and won undying glory

but Aphrodite, Zeus's daughter quick to the mark,
snapped the rawhide strap, cut from a bludgeoned ox,
and the helmet came off empty in Menelaus' fist.
Whirling it round the fighter sent it flying
into his Argives scrambling fast to retrieve it—
back at his man he sprang, enraged with brazen spear,
mad for the kill but Aphrodite snatched Paris away,
easy work for a god, wrapped him in swirls of mist   440
and set him down in his bedroom filled with scent.
Then off she went herself to summon Helen
and found her there on the steep, jutting tower
with a troop of Trojan women clustered round her.
The goddess reached and tugged at her fragrant robe,
whispering low, for all the world like an old crone,
the old weaver who, when they lived in Lacedaemon,
wove her fine woolens and Helen held her dear.
Like her to the life, immortal Love invited,
"Quickly—Paris is calling for you, come back home!   450
There he is in the bedroom, the bed with inlaid rings—
he's glistening in all his beauty and his robes!
You'd never dream he's come from fighting a man,
you'd think he's off to a dance or slipped away
from the dancing, stretching out at ease."

                                        Enticing so
that the heart in Helen's breast began to race.
She knew the goddess at once, the long lithe neck,
the smooth full breasts and the fire in those eyes—
and she was amazed, she burst out with her name:
"Maddening one, my Goddess, oh what now?   460
Lusting to lure me to my ruin yet again?
Where will you drive me next?
Off and away to other grand, luxurious cities,
out to Phrygia, out to Maeonia's tempting country?
Have you a favorite mortal man there too?

                                        But why now?—
because Menelaus has beaten your handsome Paris
and hateful as I am, he longs to take me home?
Is that why you beckon here beside me now

with all the immortal cunning in your heart?
Well, go to him yourself—*you* hover beside him!   470
Abandon the gods' high road and be a mortal!
Never set foot again on Mount Olympus, never!—
suffer for Paris, protect Paris, for eternity . . .
until he makes you his wedded wife—that or his slave.
Not I, I'll never go back again. It would be wrong,
disgraceful to share that coward's bed once more.
The women of Troy would scorn me down the years.
Oh the torment—never-ending heartbreak!"

    But Aphrodite rounded on her in fury:
"Don't provoke me—wretched, headstrong girl!   480
Or in my immortal rage I may just toss you over,
hate you as I adore you now—with a vengeance.
I might make you the butt of hard, withering hate
from both sides at once, Trojans and Achaeans—
then your fate can tread you down to dust!"
                                            So she threatened
and Helen the daughter of mighty Zeus was terrified.
Shrouding herself in her glinting silver robes
she went along, in silence. None of her women
saw her go . . . The goddess led the way.

    And once they arrived at Paris' sumptuous halls   490
the attendants briskly turned to their own work
as Helen in all her radiance climbed the steps
to the bedroom under the high, vaulting roof.
There Aphrodite quickly brought her a chair,
the goddess herself with her everlasting smile,
and set it down, face-to-face with Paris.
And there Helen sat, Helen the child of Zeus
whose shield is storm and lightning, glancing away,
lashing out at her husband: "So, home from the wars!
Oh would to god you'd died there, brought down   500
by that great soldier, my husband long ago.
And how you used to boast, year in, year out,
that you were the better man than fighting Menelaus

in power, arm and spear! So why not go back now,
hurl your challenge at Menelaus dear to Ares,
fight it out together, man-to-man again?

                                             Wait,
take my advice and call a halt right here:
no more battling with fiery-haired Menelaus,
pitting strength against strength in single combat—
madness. *He* just might impale you on his spear!"   510

   But Paris replied at once to Helen's challenge:
"No more, dear one—don't rake me with your taunts,
myself and all my courage. This time, true,
Menelaus has won the day, thanks to Athena.
I'll bring him down tomorrow.
Even we have gods who battle on our side.

                                     But come—
let's go to bed, let's lose ourselves in love!
Never has longing for you overwhelmed me so,
no, not even then, I tell you, that first time
when I swept you up from the lovely hills of Lacedaemon,   520
sailed you off and away in the racing deep-sea ships
and we went and locked in love on Rocky Island . . .
That was nothing to how I hunger for you now—
irresistible longing lays me low!"

   He led the way to bed. His wife went with him.
And now, while the two made love in the large carved bed,
Menelaus stalked like a wild beast, up and down the lines—
where could he catch a glimpse of magnificent Paris?
Not a single Trojan, none of their famous allies
could point out Paris to battle-hungry Menelaus.   530
Not that they would hide him out of friendship,
even if someone saw him—
all of them hated him like death, black death.
But marshal Agamemnon called out to the armies,
"Hear me now, you Trojans, Dardans, Trojan allies!
Clearly victory goes to Menelaus dear to Ares.

You must surrender Helen and all her treasure with her.
At once—and pay us reparations fair and fitting,
a price to inspire generations still to come!"

So Atrides demanded. His armies roared assent.   540

BOOK SIX

Hector
Returns to Troy

So the clash of Achaean and Trojan troops was on its own,
the battle in all its fury veering back and forth,
careering down the plain
as they sent their bronze lances hurtling side-to-side
between the Simois' banks and Xanthus' swirling rapids.

That Achaean bulwark giant Ajax came up first,
broke the Trojan line and brought his men some hope,
spearing the bravest man the Thracians fielded,
Acamas tall and staunch, Eussorus' son.
The first to hurl, Great Ajax hit the ridge   10
of the helmet's horsehair crest—the bronze point
stuck in Acamas' forehead pounding through the skull
and the dark came swirling down to shroud his eyes.

A shattering war cry! Diomedes killed off Axylus,
Teuthras' son who had lived in rock-built Arisbe,
a man of means and a friend to all mankind,
at his roadside house he'd warm all comers in.
But who of his guests would greet his enemy now,
meet him face-to-face and ward off grisly death?
Diomedes killed the man and his aide-in-arms at once,   20
Axylus and Calesius who always drove his team—
both at a stroke he drove beneath the earth.

Euryalus killed Dresus, killed Opheltius,
turned and went for Pedasus and Aesepus, twins
the nymph of the spring Abarbarea bore Bucolion . . .
Bucolion, son himself to the lofty King Laomedon,
first of the line, though his mother bore the prince
in secrecy and shadow. Tending his flocks one day
Bucolion took the nymph in a strong surge of love
and beneath his force she bore him twin sons.   30
But now the son of Mecisteus hacked the force
from beneath them both and loosed their gleaming limbs
and tore the armor off the dead men's shoulders.

Polypoetes braced for battle killed Astyalus—
Winging his bronze spear Odysseus slew Pidytes
bred in Percote, and Teucer did the same
for the royal Aretaon—
                         Ablerus went down too,
under the flashing lance of Nestor's son Antilochus,
and Elatus under the lord of men Agamemnon's strength—
Elatus lived by the banks of rippling Satniois,   40
in Pedasus perched on cliffs—
                         The hero Leitus
ran Phylacus down to ground at a dead run
and Eurypylus killed Melanthius outright—
                         But Menelaus
lord of the war cry had caught Adrestus alive.
Rearing, bolting in terror down the plain
his horses snared themselves in tamarisk branches,

splintered his curved chariot just at the pole's tip
and breaking free they made a dash for the city walls
where battle-teams by the drove stampeded back in panic.
But their master hurled from the chariot, tumbling over the wheel   50
and pitching facedown in the dust, and above him now
rose Menelaus, his spear's long shadow looming.
Adrestus hugged his knees and begged him, pleading,
"Take me alive, Atrides, take a ransom worth my life!
Treasures are piled up in my rich father's house,
bronze and gold and plenty of well-wrought iron—
father would give you anything, gladly, priceless ransom
if only he learns I'm still alive in Argive ships!"

    His pleas were moving the heart in Menelaus,
just at the point of handing him to an aide   60
to take him back to the fast Achaean ships . . .
when up rushed Agamemnon, blocking his way
and shouting out, "So soft, dear brother, why?
Why such concern for enemies? I suppose you got
such tender loving care at home from the Trojans.
Ah would to god not one of them could escape
his sudden plunging death beneath our hands!
No baby boy still in his mother's belly,
not even he escape—all Ilium blotted out,
no tears for their lives, no markers for their graves!"   70

    And the iron warrior brought his brother round—
rough justice, fitting too.
Menelaus shoved Adrestus back with a fist,
powerful Agamemnon stabbed him in the flank
and back on his side the fighter went, faceup.
The son of Atreus dug a heel in his heaving chest
and wrenched the ash spear out.
                              And here came Nestor
with orders ringing down the field: "My comrades—
fighting Danaans, aides of Ares—no plunder now!
Don't lag behind, don't fling yourself at spoils   80
just to haul the biggest portion back to your ship.

Now's the time for killing! Later, at leisure,
strip the corpses up and down the plain!"

    So he ordered, spurring each man's nerve—
and the next moment crowds of Trojans once again
would have clambered back inside their city walls,
terror-struck by the Argives primed for battle.
But Helenus son of Priam, best of the seers
who scan the flight of birds, came striding up
to Aeneas and Hector, calling out, "My captains!   90
You bear the brunt of Troy's and Lycia's fighting—
you are our bravest men, whatever the enterprise,
pitched battle itself or planning our campaigns,
so stand your ground right here!
Go through the ranks and rally all the troops.
Hold back our retreating mobs outside the gates
before they throw themselves in their women's arms in fear,
a great joy to our enemies closing for the kill.
And once you've roused our lines to the last man,
we'll hold out here and fight the Argives down,   100
hard-hit as we are—necessity drives us on.
                                        But you,
Hector, you go back to the city, tell our mother
to gather all the older noble women together
in gray-eyed Athena's shrine on the city's crest,
unlock the doors of the goddess' sacred chamber—
and take a robe, the largest, loveliest robe
that she can find throughout the royal halls,
a gift that far and away she prizes most herself,
and spread it out across the sleek-haired goddess' knees.
Then promise to sacrifice twelve heifers in her shrine,   110
yearlings never broken, if only she'll pity Troy,
the Trojan wives and all our helpless children,
if only she'll hold Diomedes back from the holy city—
that wild spearman, that invincible headlong terror!
He is the strongest Argive now, I tell you.
Never once did we fear Achilles so,
captain of armies, born of a goddess too,

or so they say. But here's a maniac run amok—
no one can match his fury man-to-man!"

                                        So he urged
and Hector obeyed his brother start to finish.   120
Down he leapt from his chariot fully armed, hit the ground
and brandishing two sharp spears went striding down his lines,
ranging flank to flank, driving his fighters into battle,
rousing grisly war—and round the Trojans whirled,
bracing to meet the Argives face-to-face.
And the Argives gave way, they quit the slaughter—
they thought some god swept down from the starry skies
to back the Trojans now, they wheeled and rallied so.
Hector shouted out to his men in a piercing voice,
"Gallant-hearted Trojans and far-famed allies!   130
Now be men, my friends, call up your battle-fury!
Till I can return to Troy and tell them all,
the old counselors, all our wives, to pray to the gods
and vow to offer them many splendid victims."

    As Hector turned for home his helmet flashed
and the long dark hide of his bossed shield, the rim
running the metal edge, drummed his neck and ankles.

                                                    And now
Glaucus son of Hippolochus and Tydeus' son Diomedes
met in the no man's land between both armies:
burning for battle, closing, squaring off   140
and the lord of the war cry Diomedes opened up,
"Who are you, my fine friend?—another born to die?
I've never noticed you on the lines where we win glory,
not till now. But here you come, charging out
in front of all the rest with such bravado—
daring to face the flying shadow of my spear.
Pity the ones whose sons stand up to me in war!
But if you are an immortal come from the blue,
I'm not the man to fight the gods of heaven.
Not even Dryas' indestructible son Lycurgus,   150
not even he lived long . . .
that fellow who tried to fight the deathless gods.

He rushed at the maenads once, nurses of wild Dionysus,
scattered them breakneck down the holy mountain Nysa.
A rout of them strewed their sacred staves on the ground,
raked with a cattle prod by Lycurgus, murderous fool!
And Dionysus was terrified, he dove beneath the surf
where the sea-nymph Thetis pressed him to her breast—
Dionysus numb with fear: shivers racked his body,
thanks to the raucous onslaught of that man.   160
But the gods who live at ease lashed out against him—
worse, the son of Cronus struck Lycurgus blind.
Nor did the man live long, not with the hate
of all the gods against him.
                   No, my friend,
I have no desire to fight the blithe immortals.
But if you're a man who eats the crops of the earth,
a mortal born for death—here, come closer,
the sooner you will meet your day to die!"

    The noble son of Hippolochus answered staunchly,
"High-hearted son of Tydeus, why ask about my birth?   170
Like the generations of leaves, the lives of mortal men.
Now the wind scatters the old leaves across the earth,
now the living timber bursts with the new buds
and spring comes round again. And so with men:
as one generation comes to life, another dies away.
But about my birth, if you'd like to learn it well,
first to last—though many people know it—
here's my story . . .
                 There is a city, Corinth,
deep in a bend of Argos, good stallion-country
where Sisyphus used to live, the wiliest man alive.   180
Sisyphus, Aeolus' son, who had a son called Glaucus,
and in his day Glaucus sired brave Bellerophon,
a man without a fault. The gods gave him beauty
and the fine, gallant traits that go with men.
But Proetus plotted against him. Far stronger,
the king in his anger drove him out of Argos,
the kingdom Zeus had brought beneath his scepter.

Proetus' wife, you see, was mad for Bellerophon,
the lovely Antea lusted to couple with him,
all in secret. Futile—she could never seduce   190
the man's strong will, his seasoned, firm resolve.
So straight to the king she went, blurting out her lies:
'I wish you'd die, Proetus, if you don't kill Bellerophon!
Bellerophon's bent on dragging me down with him in lust
though I fight him all the way!'
                          All of it false
but the king seethed when he heard a tale like that.
He balked at killing the man—he'd some respect at least—
but he quickly sent him off to Lycia, gave him tokens,
murderous signs, scratched in a folded tablet,
and many of them too, enough to kill a man.   200
He told him to show them to Antea's father:
that would mean his death.
                          So off he went to Lycia,
safe in the escort of the gods, and once he reached
the broad highlands cut by the rushing Xanthus,
the king of Lycia gave him a royal welcome.
Nine days he feasted him, nine oxen slaughtered.
When the tenth Dawn shone with her rose-red fingers,
he began to question him, asked to see his credentials,
whatever he brought him from his in-law, Proetus.
But then, once he received that fatal message   210
sent from his own daughter's husband, first
he ordered Bellerophon to kill the Chimaera—
grim monster sprung of the gods, nothing human,
all lion in front, all snake behind, all goat between,
terrible, blasting lethal fire at every breath!
But he laid her low, obeying signs from the gods.
Next he fought the Solymi, tribesmen bent on glory,
roughest battle of men he ever entered, so he claimed.
Then for a third test he brought the Amazons down,
a match for men in war. But as he turned back,   220
his host spun out the tightest trap of all:
picking the best men from Lycia far and wide
he set an ambush—that never came home again!

Fearless Bellerophon killed them all.

Then, yes,
when the king could see the man's power at last,
a true son of the gods, he pressed him hard to stay,
he offered his own daughter's hand in marriage,
he gave him half his royal honors as the king.
And the Lycians carved him out a grand estate,
the choicest land in the realm, rich in vineyards   230
and good tilled fields for him to lord it over.
And his wife bore good Bellerophon three children:
Isander, Hippolochus and Laodamia. Laodamia
lay in the arms of Zeus who rules the world
and she bore the god a son, our great commander,
Sarpedon helmed in bronze.

But the day soon came
when even Bellerophon was hated by all the gods.
Across the Alean plain he wandered, all alone,
eating his heart out, a fugitive on the run
from the beaten tracks of men. His son Isander?   240
Killed by the War-god, never sated—a boy fighting
the Solymi always out for glory. Laodamia? Artemis,
flashing her golden reins, cut her down in anger.
But Hippolochus fathered me, I'm proud to say.
He sent me off to Troy . . .
and I hear his urgings ringing in my ears:
'Always be the best, my boy, the bravest,
and hold your head up high above the others.
Never disgrace the generation of your fathers.
They were the bravest champions born in Corinth,   250
in Lycia far and wide.'

There you have my lineage.
That is the blood I claim, my royal birth.''

When he heard that, Diomedes' spirits lifted.
Raising his spear, the lord of the war cry drove it home,
planting it deep down in the earth that feeds us all
and with winning words he called out to Glaucus,
the young captain, ''Splendid—you are my friend,

my guest from the days of our grandfathers long ago!
Noble Oeneus hosted your brave Bellerophon once,
he held him there in his halls, twenty whole days,   260
and they gave each other handsome gifts of friendship.
My kinsman offered a gleaming sword-belt, rich red,
Bellerophon gave a cup, two-handled, solid gold—
I left it at home when I set out for Troy.
My father, Tydeus, I really don't remember.
I was just a baby when father left me then,
that time an Achaean army went to die at Thebes.
So now I am your host and friend in the heart of Argos,
you are mine in Lycia when I visit in your country.
Come, let us keep clear of each other's spears,   270
even there in the thick of battle. Look,
plenty of Trojans there for me to kill,
your famous allies too, any soldier the god
will bring in range or I can run to ground.
And plenty of Argives too—kill them if you can.
But let's trade armor. The men must know our claim:
we are sworn friends from our fathers' days till now!"

      Both agreed. Both fighters sprang from their chariots,
clasped each other's hands and traded pacts of friendship.
But the son of Cronus, Zeus, stole Glaucus' wits away.   280
He traded his gold armor for bronze with Diomedes,
the worth of a hundred oxen just for nine.

                                    And now,
when Hector reached the Scaean Gates and the great oak,
the wives and daughters of Troy came rushing up around him,
asking about their sons, brothers, friends and husbands.
But Hector told them only, "Pray to the gods"—
all the Trojan women, one after another . . .
Hard sorrows were hanging over many.

                                    And soon
he came to Priam's palace, that magnificent structure
built wide with porches and colonnades of polished stone.   290
And deep within its walls were fifty sleeping chambers
masoned in smooth, lustrous ashlar, linked in a line

where the sons of Priam slept beside their wedded wives,
and facing these, opening out across the inner courtyard,
lay the twelve sleeping chambers of Priam's daughters,
masoned and roofed in lustrous ashlar, linked in a line
where the sons-in-law of Priam slept beside their wives.
And there at the palace Hector's mother met her son,
that warm, goodhearted woman, going in with Laodice,
the loveliest daughter Hecuba ever bred. His mother   300
clutched his hand and urged him, called his name:
"My child—why have you left the bitter fighting,
why have you come home? Look how they wear you out,
the sons of Achaea—curse them—battling round our walls!
And that's why your spirit brought you back to Troy,
to climb the heights and stretch your arms to Zeus.
But wait, I'll bring you some honeyed, mellow wine.
First pour out cups to Father Zeus and the other gods,
then refresh yourself, if you'd like to quench your thirst.
When a man's exhausted, wine will build his strength—   310
battle-weary as *you* are, fighting for your people."

    But Hector shook his head, his helmet flashing:
"Don't offer me mellow wine, mother, not now—
you'd sap my limbs, I'd lose my nerve for war.
And I'd be ashamed to pour a glistening cup to Zeus
with unwashed hands. I'm splattered with blood and filth—
how could I pray to the lord of storm and lightning?
No, mother, you are the one to pray.
Go to Athena's shrine, the queen of plunder,
go with offerings, gather the older noble women   320
and take a robe, the largest, loveliest robe
that you can find throughout the royal halls,
a gift that far and away you prize most yourself,
and spread it out across the sleek-haired goddess' knees.
Then promise to sacrifice twelve heifers in her shrine,
yearlings never broken, if only she'll pity Troy,
the Trojan wives and all our helpless children,
if only she'll hold Diomedes back from the holy city—
that wild spearman, that invincible headlong terror!

Now, mother, go to the queen of plunder's shrine   330
and I'll go hunt for Paris, summon him to fight
if the man will hear what *I* have to say . . .
Let the earth gape and swallow him on the spot!
A great curse Olympian Zeus let live and grow in him,
for Troy and high-hearted Priam and all his sons.
That man—if I could see him bound for the House of Death,
I could say my heart had forgot its wrenching grief!"

    But his mother simply turned away to the palace.
She gave her servants orders and out they strode
to gather the older noble women through the city.   340
Hecuba went down to a storeroom filled with scent
and there they were, brocaded, beautiful robes . . .
the work of Sidonian women. Magnificent Paris
brought those women back himself from Sidon,
sailing the open seas on the same long voyage
he swept Helen off, her famous Father's child.
Lifting one from the lot, Hecuba brought it out
for great Athena's gift, the largest, loveliest,
richly worked, and like a star it glistened,
deep beneath the others. Then she made her way   350
with a file of noble women rushing in her train.

    Once they reached Athena's shrine on the city crest
the beauty Theano opened the doors to let them in,
Cisseus' daughter, the horseman Antenor's wife
and Athena's priestess chosen by the Trojans. Then—
with a shrill wail they all stretched their arms to Athena
as Theano, her face radiant, lifting the robe on high,
spread it out across the sleek-haired goddess' knees
and prayed to the daughter of mighty Father Zeus:
"Queen Athena—shield of our city—glory of goddesses!   360
Now shatter the spear of Diomedes! That wild man—
hurl him headlong down before the Scaean Gates!
At once we'll sacrifice twelve heifers in your shrine,
yearlings never broken, if only you'll pity Troy,
the Trojan wives and all our helpless children!"

But Athena refused to hear Theano's prayers.
And while they prayed to the daughter of mighty Zeus
Hector approached the halls of Paris, sumptuous halls
he built himself with the finest masons of the day,
master builders famed in the fertile land of Troy.   370
They'd raised his sleeping chamber, house and court
adjoining Priam's and Hector's aloft the city heights.
Now Hector, dear to Zeus, strode through the gates,
clutching a thrusting-lance eleven forearms long;
the bronze tip of the weapon shone before him,
ringed with a golden hoop to grip the shaft.
And there in the bedroom Hector came on Paris
polishing, fondling his splendid battle-gear,
his shield and breastplate, turning over and over
his long curved bow. And there was Helen of Argos,   380
sitting with all the women of the house, directing
the rich embroidered work they had in hand.
                                        Seeing Paris,
Hector raked his brother with insults, stinging taunts:
"What on earth are you doing? Oh how wrong it is,
this anger you keep smoldering in your heart! Look,
your people dying around the city, the steep walls,
dying in arms—and all for you, the battle cries
and the fighting flaring up around the citadel.
You'd be the first to lash out at another—anywhere—
you saw hanging back from this, this hateful war.   390
                                        Up with you—
before all Troy is torched to a cinder here and now!"

    And Paris, magnificent as a god, replied,
"Ah Hector, you criticize me fairly, yes,
nothing unfair, beyond what I deserve. And so
I will try to tell you something. Please bear with me,
hear me out. It's not so much from anger or outrage
at our people that I keep to my rooms so long.
I only wanted to plunge myself in grief.
But just now my wife was bringing me round,
her winning words urging me back to battle.   400

And it strikes me, even me, as the better way.
Victory shifts, you know, now one man, now another.
So come, wait while I get this war-gear on,
or you go on ahead and I will follow—
I think I can overtake you."

                                    Hector, helmet flashing,
answered nothing. And Helen spoke to him now,
her soft voice welling up: "My dear brother,
dear to me, bitch that I am, vicious, scheming—
horror to freeze the heart! Oh how I wish
that first day my mother brought me into the light   410
some black whirlwind had rushed me out to the mountains
or into the surf where the roaring breakers crash and drag
and the waves had swept me off before all this had happened!
But since the gods ordained it all, these desperate years,
I wish I had been the wife of a better man, someone
alive to outrage, the withering scorn of men.
This one has no steadiness in his spirit,
not now, he never will . . .
and he's going to reap the fruits of it, I swear.
But come in, rest on this seat with me, dear brother.   420
You are the one hit hardest by the fighting, Hector,
you more than all—and all for me, whore that I am,
and this blind mad Paris. Oh the two of us!
Zeus planted a killing doom within us both,
so even for generations still unborn
we will live in song."

                                    Turning to go,
his helmet flashing, tall Hector answered,
"Don't ask me to sit beside you here, Helen.
Love me as you do, you can't persuade me now.
No time for rest. My heart races to help our Trojans—   430
they long for me, sorely, whenever I am gone.
But rouse this fellow, won't you?
And let him hurry himself along as well,
so he can overtake me before I leave the city.
For I must go home to see my people first,
to visit my own dear wife and my baby son.

Who knows if I will ever come back to them again?—
or the deathless gods will strike me down at last
at the hands of Argive fighters."
                              A flash of his helmet
and off he strode and quickly reached his sturdy,   440
well-built house. But white-armed Andromache—
Hector could not find her in the halls.
She and the boy and a servant finely gowned
were standing watch on the tower, sobbing, grieving.
When Hector saw no sign of his loyal wife inside
he went to the doorway, stopped and asked the servants,
"Come, please, tell me the truth now, women.
Where's Andromache gone? To my sisters' house?
To my brothers' wives with their long flowing robes?
Or Athena's shrine where the noble Trojan women   450
gather to win the great grim goddess over?"

    A busy, willing servant answered quickly,
"Hector, seeing you want to know the truth,
she hasn't gone to your sisters, brothers' wives
or Athena's shrine where the noble Trojan women
gather to win the great grim goddess over.
Up to the huge gate-tower of Troy she's gone
because she heard our men are so hard-pressed,
the Achaean fighters coming on in so much force.
She sped to the wall in panic, like a madwoman—   460
the nurse went with her, carrying your child."

    At that, Hector spun and rushed from his house,
back by the same way down the wide, well-paved streets
throughout the city until he reached the Scaean Gates,
the last point he would pass to gain the field of battle.
There his warm, generous wife came running up to meet him,
Andromache the daughter of gallant-hearted Eetion
who had lived below Mount Placos rich with timber,
in Thebe below the peaks, and ruled Cilicia's people.
His daughter had married Hector helmed in bronze.   470
She joined him now, and following in her steps

a servant holding the boy against her breast,
in the first flush of life, only a baby,
Hector's son, the darling of his eyes
and radiant as a star . . .
Hector would always call the boy Scamandrius,
townsmen called him Astyanax, Lord of the City,
since Hector was the lone defense of Troy.
The great man of war breaking into a broad smile,
his gaze fixed on his son, in silence. Andromache,   480
pressing close beside him and weeping freely now,
clung to his hand, urged him, called him: "Reckless one,
my Hector—your own fiery courage will destroy you!
Have you no pity for *him*, our helpless son? Or me,
and the destiny that weighs me down, your widow,
now so soon? Yes, soon they will kill you off,
all the Achaean forces massed for assault, and then,
bereft of you, better for me to sink beneath the earth.
What other warmth, what comfort's left for me,
once you have met your doom? Nothing but torment!   490
I have lost my father. Mother's gone as well.
Father . . . the brilliant Achilles laid him low
when he stormed Cilicia's city filled with people,
Thebe with her towering gates. He killed Eetion,
not that he stripped his gear—he'd some respect at least—
for he burned his corpse in all his blazoned bronze,
then heaped a grave-mound high above the ashes
and nymphs of the mountain planted elms around it,
daughters of Zeus whose shield is storm and thunder.
And the seven brothers I had within our halls . . .   500
all in the same day went down to the House of Death,
the great godlike runner Achilles butchered them all,
tending their shambling oxen, shining flocks.
                                                 And mother,
who ruled under the timberline of woody Placos once—
he no sooner haled her here with his other plunder
than he took a priceless ransom, set her free
and home she went to her father's royal halls
where Artemis, showering arrows, shot her down.

You, Hector—you are my father now, my noble mother,
a brother too, and you are my husband, young and warm
     and strong!   510
Pity me, please! Take your stand on the rampart here,
before you orphan your son and make your wife a widow.
Draw your armies up where the wild fig tree stands,
there, where the city lies most open to assault,
the walls lower, easily overrun. Three times
they have tried that point, hoping to storm Troy,
their best fighters led by the Great and Little Ajax,
famous Idomeneus, Atreus' sons, valiant Diomedes.
Perhaps a skilled prophet revealed the spot—
or their own fury whips them on to attack."   520

    And tall Hector nodded, his helmet flashing:
"All this weighs on my mind too, dear woman.
But I would die of shame to face the men of Troy
and the Trojan women trailing their long robes
if I would shrink from battle now, a coward.
Nor does the spirit urge me on that way.
I've learned it all too well. To stand up bravely,
always to fight in the front ranks of Trojan soldiers,
winning my father great glory, glory for myself.
For in my heart and soul I also know this well: 530
the day will come when sacred Troy must die,
Priam must die and all his people with him,
Priam who hurls the strong ash spear . . .
                              Even so,
it is less the pain of the Trojans still to come
that weighs me down, not even of Hecuba herself
or King Priam, or the thought that my own brothers
in all their numbers, all their gallant courage,
may tumble in the dust, crushed by enemies—
That is nothing, nothing beside your agony
when some brazen Argive hales you off in tears,   540
wrenching away your day of light and freedom!
Then far off in the land of Argos you must live,
laboring at a loom, at another woman's beck and call,

fetching water at some spring, Messeis or Hyperia,
resisting it all the way—
the rough yoke of necessity at your neck.
And a man may say, who sees you streaming tears,
'There is the wife of Hector, the bravest fighter
they could field, those stallion-breaking Trojans,
long ago when the men fought for Troy.' So he will say   550
and the fresh grief will swell your heart once more,
widowed, robbed of the one man strong enough
to fight off your day of slavery.
                              No, no,
let the earth come piling over my dead body
before I hear your cries, I hear you dragged away!"

    In the same breath, shining Hector reached down
for his son—but the boy recoiled,
cringing against his nurse's full breast,
screaming out at the sight of his own father,
terrified by the flashing bronze, the horsehair crest,   560
the great ridge of the helmet nodding, bristling terror—
so it struck his eyes. And his loving father laughed,
his mother laughed as well, and glorious Hector,
quickly lifting the helmet from his head,
set it down on the ground, fiery in the sunlight,
and raising his son he kissed him, tossed him in his arms,
lifting a prayer to Zeus and the other deathless gods:
"Zeus, all you immortals! Grant this boy, my son,
may be like me, first in glory among the Trojans,
strong and brave like me, and rule all Troy in power   570
and one day let them say, 'He is a better man than his father!'—
when he comes home from battle bearing the bloody gear
of the mortal enemy he has killed in war—
a joy to his mother's heart."
                              So Hector prayed
and placed his son in the arms of his loving wife.
Andromache pressed the child to her scented breast,
smiling through her tears. Her husband noticed,
and filled with pity now, Hector stroked her gently,

58

trying to reassure her, repeating her name: "Andromache,
dear one, why so desperate? Why so much grief for me?   580
No man will hurl me down to Death, against my fate.
And fate? No one alive has ever escaped it,
neither brave man nor coward, I tell you—
it's born with us the day that we are born.
So please go home and tend to your own tasks,
the distaff and the loom, and keep the women
working hard as well. As for the fighting,
men will see to that, all who were born in Troy
but I most of all."
                    Hector aflash in arms
took up his horsehair-crested helmet once again.   590
And his loving wife went home, turning, glancing
back again and again and weeping live warm tears.
She quickly reached the sturdy house of Hector,
man-killing Hector,
and found her women gathered there inside
and stirred them all to a high pitch of mourning.
So in his house they raised the dirges for the dead,
for Hector still alive, his people were so convinced
that never again would he come home from battle,
never escape the Argives' rage and bloody hands.   600

   Nor did Paris linger long in his vaulted halls.
Soon as he buckled on his elegant gleaming bronze
he rushed through Troy, sure in his racing stride.
As a stallion full-fed at the manger, stalled too long,
breaking free of his tether gallops down the plain,
out for his favorite plunge in a river's cool currents,
thundering in his pride—his head flung back, his mane
streaming over his shoulders, sure and sleek in his glory,
knees racing him on to the fields and stallion-haunts he loves—
so down from Pergamus heights came Paris, son of Priam,   610
glittering in his armor like the sun astride the skies,
exultant, laughing aloud, his fast feet sped him on.
Quickly he overtook his brother, noble Hector
still lingering, slow to turn from the spot

where he had just confided in his wife . . .
Magnificent Paris spoke first: "Dear brother,
look at me, holding you back in all your speed—
dragging my feet, coming to you so late,
and you told me to be quick!"

A flash of his helmet as Hector shot back,   620
"Impossible man! How could anyone fair and just
underrate your work in battle? You're a good soldier.
But you hang back of your own accord, refuse to fight.
And that, that's why the heart inside me aches
when I hear our Trojans heap contempt on you,
the men who bear such struggles all for you.

                                                        Come,
now for attack! We'll set all this to rights,
someday, if Zeus will ever let us raise
the winebowl of freedom high in our halls,
high to the gods of cloud and sky who live forever—   630
once we drive these Argives geared for battle out of Troy!"

Homer, *The Odyssey*
Books 9 and 11

In the One-Eyed
Giant's Cave

Odysseus, the great teller of tales, launched out on his story:
"Alcinous, majesty, shining among your island people,
what a fine thing it is to listen to such a bard
as we have here—the man sings like a god.
The crown of life, I'd say. There's nothing better
than when deep joy holds sway throughout the realm
and banqueters up and down the palace sit in ranks,
enthralled to hear the bard, and before them all, the tables
heaped with bread and meats, and drawing wine from a mixing-bowl
the steward makes his rounds and keeps the winecups flowing.   10
This, to my mind, is the best that life can offer.

                                        But now
you're set on probing the bitter pains I've borne,
so I'm to weep and grieve, it seems, still more.
Well then, what shall I go through first,

64

[14–42]

what shall I save for last?
What pains—the gods have given me my share.
Now let me begin by telling you my name . . .
so you may know it well and I in times to come,
if I can escape the fatal day, will be your host,
your sworn friend, though my home is far from here.   20
I am Odysseus, son of Laertes, known to the world
for every kind of craft—my fame has reached the skies.
Sunny Ithaca is my home. Atop her stands our seamark,
Mount Neriton's leafy ridges shimmering in the wind.
Around her a ring of islands circle side-by-side,
Dulichion, Same, wooded Zacynthus too, but mine
lies low and away, the farthest out to sea,
rearing into the western dusk
while the others face the east and breaking day.
Mine is a rugged land but good for raising sons—   30
and I myself, I know no sweeter sight on earth
than a man's own native country.
                                        True enough,
Calypso the lustrous goddess tried to hold me back,
deep in her arching caverns, craving me for a husband.
So did Circe, holding me just as warmly in her halls,
the bewitching queen of Aeaea keen to have me too.
But they never won the heart inside me, never.
So nothing is as sweet as a man's own country,
his own parents, even though he's settled down
in some luxurious house, off in a foreign land   40
and far from those who bore him.
                                        No more. Come,
let me tell you about the voyage fraught with hardship
Zeus inflicted on me, homeward bound from Troy . . .

The wind drove me out of Ilium on to Ismarus,
the Cicones' stronghold. There I sacked the city,
killed the men, but as for the wives and plunder,
that rich haul we dragged away from the place—
we shared it round so no one, not on my account,
would go deprived of his fair share of spoils.

Then I urged them to cut and run, set sail,   50
but would they listen? Not those mutinous fools;
there was too much wine to swill, too many sheep to slaughter
down along the beach, and shambling longhorn cattle.
And all the while the Cicones sought out other Cicones,
called for help from their neighbors living inland:
a larger force, and stronger soldiers too,
skilled hands at fighting men from chariots,
skilled, when a crisis broke, to fight on foot.
Out of the morning mist they came against us—
packed as the leaves and spears that flower forth in spring—   60
and Zeus presented us with disaster, me and my comrades
doomed to suffer blow on mortal blow. Lining up,
both armies battled it out against our swift ships,
both raked each other with hurtling bronze lances.
Long as morning rose and the blessed day grew stronger
we stood and fought them off, massed as they were, but then,
when the sun wheeled past the hour for unyoking oxen,
the Cicones broke our lines and beat us down at last.
Out of each ship, six men-at-arms were killed;
the rest of us rowed away from certain doom.   70

     From there we sailed on, glad to escape our death
yet sick at heart for the dear companions we had lost.
But I would not let our rolling ships set sail until the crews
had raised the triple cry, saluting each poor comrade
cut down by the fierce Cicones on that plain.
Now Zeus who masses the stormclouds hit the fleet
with the North Wind—

                    a howling, demonic gale, shrouding over
in thunderheads the earth and sea at once—

                              and night swept down
from the sky and the ships went plunging headlong on,
our sails slashed to rags by the hurricane's blast!   80
We struck them—cringing at death we rowed our ships
to the nearest shoreline, pulled with all our power.
There, for two nights, two days, we lay by, no letup,
eating our hearts out, bent with pain and bone-tired.

When Dawn with her lovely locks brought on the third day,
then stepping the masts and hoisting white sails high,
we lounged at the oarlocks, letting wind and helmsmen
keep us true on course . . .
                              And now, at long last,
I might have reached my native land unscathed,
but just as I doubled Malea's cape, a tide-rip
and the North Wind drove me way off course   90
careering past Cythera.
                        Nine whole days
I was borne along by rough, deadly winds
on the fish-infested sea. Then on the tenth
our squadron reached the land of the Lotus-eaters,
people who eat the lotus, mellow fruit and flower.
We disembarked on the coast, drew water there
and crewmen snatched a meal by the swift ships.
Once we'd had our fill of food and drink I sent
a detail ahead, two picked men and a third, a runner,   100
to scout out who might live there—men like us perhaps,
who live on bread? So off they went and soon enough
they mingled among the natives, Lotus-eaters, Lotus-eaters
who had no notion of killing my companions, not at all,
they simply gave them the lotus to taste instead . . .
Any crewmen who ate the lotus, the honey-sweet fruit,
lost all desire to send a message back, much less return,
their only wish to linger there with the Lotus-eaters,
grazing on lotus, all memory of the journey home
dissolved forever. But *I* brought them back, back   110
to the hollow ships, and streaming tears—I forced them,
hauled them under the rowing benches, lashed them fast
and shouted out commands to my other, steady comrades:
'Quick, no time to lose, embark in the racing ships!'—
so none could eat the lotus, forget the voyage home.
They swung aboard at once, they sat to the oars in ranks
and in rhythm churned the water white with stroke on stroke.

    From there we sailed on, our spirits now at a low ebb,
and reached the land of the high and mighty Cyclops,

lawless brutes, who trust so to the everlasting gods   120
they never plant with their own hands or plow the soil.
Unsown, unplowed, the earth teems with all they need,
wheat, barley and vines, swelled by the rains of Zeus
to yield a big full-bodied wine from clustered grapes.
They have no meeting place for council, no laws either,
no, up on the mountain peaks they live in arching caverns—
each a law to himself, ruling his wives and children,
not a care in the world for any neighbor.
                                                            Now,
a level island stretches flat across the harbor,
not close inshore to the Cyclops' coast, not too far out,   130
thick with woods where the wild goats breed by hundreds.
No trampling of men to start them from their lairs,
no hunters roughing it out on the woody ridges,
stalking quarry, ever raid their haven.
No flocks browse, no plowlands roll with wheat;
unplowed, unsown forever—empty of humankind—
the island just feeds droves of bleating goats.
For the Cyclops have no ships with crimson prows,
no shipwrights there to build them good trim craft
that could sail them out to foreign ports of call   140
as most men risk the seas to trade with other men.
Such artisans would have made this island too
a decent place to live in . . . No mean spot,
it could bear you any crop you like in season.
The water-meadows along the low foaming shore
run soft and moist, and your vines would never flag.
The land's clear for plowing. Harvest on harvest,
a man could reap a healthy stand of grain—
the subsoil's dark and rich.
There's a snug deep-water harbor there, what's more,   150
no need for mooring-gear, no anchor-stones to heave,
no cables to make fast. Just beach your keels, ride out
the days till your shipmates' spirit stirs for open sea
and a fair wind blows. And last, at the harbor's head
there's a spring that rushes fresh from beneath a cave
and black poplars flourish round its mouth.

                                              Well,
here we landed, and surely a god steered us in
through the pitch-black night.
Not that he ever showed himself, with thick fog
swirling around the ships, the moon wrapped in clouds   160
and not a glimmer stealing through that gloom.
Not one of us glimpsed the island—scanning hard—
or the long combers rolling us slowly toward the coast,
not till our ships had run their keels ashore.
Beaching our vessels smoothly, striking sail,
the crews swung out on the low shelving sand
and there we fell asleep, awaiting Dawn's first light.

    When young Dawn with her rose-red fingers shone once more
we all turned out, intrigued to tour the island.
The local nymphs, the daughters of Zeus himself,   170
flushed mountain-goats so the crews could make their meal.
Quickly we fetched our curved bows and hunting spears
from the ships and, splitting up into three bands,
we started shooting, and soon enough some god
had sent us bags of game to warm our hearts.
A dozen vessels sailed in my command
and to each crew nine goats were shared out
and mine alone took ten. Then all day long
till the sun went down we sat and feasted well
on sides of meat and rounds of heady wine.   180
The good red stock in our vessels' holds
had not run out, there was still plenty left;
the men had carried off a generous store in jars
when we stormed and sacked the Cicones' holy city.
Now we stared across at the Cyclops' shore, so near
we could even see their smoke, hear their voices,
their bleating sheep and goats . . .
And then when the sun had set and night came on
we lay down and slept at the water's shelving edge.
When young Dawn with her rose-red fingers shone once more   190
I called a muster briskly, commanding all the hands,
'The rest of you stay here, my friends-in-arms.

I'll go across with my own ship and crew
and probe the natives living over there.
What *are* they—violent, savage, lawless?
or friendly to strangers, god-fearing men?'

   With that I boarded ship and told the crew
to embark at once and cast off cables quickly.
They swung aboard, they sat to the oars in ranks
and in rhythm churned the water white with stroke on stroke.   200
But as soon as we reached the coast I mentioned—no long trip—
we spied a cavern just at the shore, gaping above the surf,
towering, overgrown with laurel. And here big flocks,
sheep and goats, were stalled to spend the nights,
and around its mouth a yard was walled up
with quarried boulders sunk deep in the earth
and enormous pines and oak-trees looming darkly . . .
Here was a giant's lair, in fact, who always pastured
his sheepflocks far afield and never mixed with others.
A grim loner, dead set in his own lawless ways.   210
Here was a piece of work, by god, a monster
built like no mortal who ever supped on bread,
no, like a shaggy peak, I'd say—a man-mountain
rearing head and shoulders over the world.

                                            Now then,
I told most of my good trusty crew to wait,
to sit tight by the ship and guard her well
while I picked out my dozen finest fighters
and off I went. But I took a skin of wine along,
the ruddy, irresistible wine that Maron gave me once,
Euanthes' son, a priest of Apollo, lord of Ismarus,   220
because we'd rescued him, his wife and children,
reverent as we were;
he lived, you see, in Apollo's holy grove.
And so in return he gave me splendid gifts,
he handed me seven bars of well-wrought gold,
a mixing-bowl of solid silver, then this wine . . .
He drew it off in generous wine-jars, twelve in all,
all unmixed—and such a bouquet, a drink fit for the gods!

No maid or man of his household knew that secret store,
only himself, his loving wife and a single servant.   230
Whenever they'd drink the deep-red mellow vintage,
twenty cups of water he'd stir in one of wine
and what an aroma wafted from the bowl—
what magic, what a godsend—
no joy in holding back when *that* was poured!
Filling a great goatskin now, I took this wine,
provisions too in a leather sack. A sudden foreboding
told my fighting spirit I'd soon come up against
some giant clad in power like armor-plate—
a savage deaf to justice, blind to law.   240

    Our party quickly made its way to his cave
but we failed to find our host himself inside;
he was off in his pasture, ranging his sleek flocks.
So we explored his den, gazing wide-eyed at it all,
the large flat racks loaded with drying cheeses,
the folds crowded with young lambs and kids,
split into three groups—here the spring-born,
here mid-yearlings, here the fresh sucklings
off to the side—each sort was penned apart.
And all his vessels, pails and hammered buckets   250
he used for milking, were brimming full with whey.
From the start my comrades pressed me, pleading hard,
'Let's make away with the cheeses, then come back—
hurry, drive the lambs and kids from the pens
to our swift ship, put out to sea at once!'
But I would not give way—
and how much better it would have been—
not till I saw him, saw what gifts he'd give.
But he proved no lovely sight to my companions.

    There we built a fire, set our hands on the cheeses,   260
offered some to the gods and ate the bulk ourselves
and settled down inside, awaiting his return . . .
And back he came from pasture, late in the day,
herding his flocks home, and lugging a huge load

of good dry logs to fuel his fire at supper.
He flung them down in the cave—a jolting crash—
we scuttled in panic into the deepest dark recess.
And next he drove his sleek flocks into the open vault,
all he'd milk at least, but he left the males outside,
rams and billy goats out in the high-walled yard.   270
Then to close his door he hoisted overhead
a tremendous, massive slab—
no twenty-two wagons, rugged and four-wheeled,
could budge that boulder off the ground, I tell you,
such an immense stone the monster wedged to block his cave!
Then down he squatted to milk his sheep and bleating goats,
each in order, and put a suckling underneath each dam.
And half of the fresh white milk he curdled quickly,
set it aside in wicker racks to press for cheese,
the other half let stand in pails and buckets,   280
ready at hand to wash his supper down.
As soon as he'd briskly finished all his chores
he lit his fire and spied us in the blaze and
'Strangers!' he thundered out, 'now who are you?
Where did you sail from, over the running sea-lanes?
Out on a trading spree or roving the waves like pirates,
sea-wolves raiding at will, who risk their lives
to plunder other men?'
                        The hearts inside us shook,
terrified by his rumbling voice and monstrous hulk.
Nevertheless I found the nerve to answer, firmly,   290
'Men of Achaea we are and bound now from Troy!
Driven far off course by the warring winds,
over the vast gulf of the sea—battling home
on a strange tack, a route that's off the map,
and so we've come to you . . .
so it must please King Zeus's plotting heart.
We're glad to say we're men of Atrides Agamemnon,
whose fame is the proudest thing on earth these days,
so great a city he sacked, such multitudes he killed!
But since we've chanced on you, we're at your knees   300
in hopes of a warm welcome, even a guest-gift,

the sort that hosts give strangers. That's the custom.
Respect the gods, my friend. We're suppliants—at your mercy!
Zeus of the Strangers guards all guests and suppliants:
strangers are sacred—Zeus will avenge their rights!'

'Stranger,' he grumbled back from his brutal heart,
'you must be a fool, stranger, or come from nowhere,
telling *me* to fear the gods or avoid their wrath!
We Cyclops never blink at Zeus and Zeus's shield
of storm and thunder, or any other blessed god—   310
we've got more force by far.
I'd never spare you in fear of Zeus's hatred,
you or your comrades here, unless I had the urge.
But tell me, where did you moor your sturdy ship
when you arrived? Up the coast or close in?
I'd just like to know.'
                        So he laid his trap
but he never caught me, no, wise to the world
I shot back in my crafty way, 'My ship?
Poseidon god of the earthquake smashed my ship,
he drove it against the rocks at your island's far cape,   320
he dashed it against a cliff as the winds rode us in.
I and the men you see escaped a sudden death.'

Not a word in reply to that, the ruthless brute.
Lurching up, he lunged out with his hands toward my men
and snatching two at once, rapping them on the ground
he knocked them dead like pups—
their brains gushed out all over, soaked the floor—
and ripping them limb from limb to fix his meal
he bolted them down like a mountain-lion, left no scrap,
devoured entrails, flesh and bones, marrow and all!   330
We flung our arms to Zeus, we wept and cried aloud,
looking on at his grisly work—paralyzed, appalled.
But once the Cyclops had stuffed his enormous gut
with human flesh, washing it down with raw milk,
he slept in his cave, stretched out along his flocks.
And I with my fighting heart, I thought at first

to steal up to him, draw the sharp sword at my hip
and stab his chest where the midriff packs the liver—
I groped for the fatal spot but a fresh thought held me back.
There at a stroke we'd finish off ourselves as well—   340
how could *we* with our bare hands heave back
that slab he set to block his cavern's gaping maw?
So we lay there groaning, waiting Dawn's first light.

When young Dawn with her rose-red fingers shone once more
the monster relit his fire and milked his handsome ewes,
each in order, putting a suckling underneath each dam,
and as soon as he'd briskly finished all his chores
he snatched up two more men and fixed his meal.
Well-fed, he drove his fat sheep from the cave,
lightly lifting the huge doorslab up and away,   350
then slipped it back in place
as a hunter flips the lid of his quiver shut.
Piercing whistles—turning his flocks to the hills
he left me there, the heart inside me brooding on revenge:
how could I pay him back? would Athena give me glory?
Here was the plan that struck my mind as best . . .
the Cyclops' great club: there it lay by the pens,
olivewood, full of sap. He'd lopped it off to brandish
once it dried. Looking it over, we judged it big enough
to be the mast of a pitch-black ship with her twenty oars,   360
a freighter broad in the beam that plows through miles of sea—
so long, so thick it bulked before our eyes. Well,
flanking it now, I chopped off a fathom's length,
rolled it to comrades, told them to plane it down,
and they made the club smooth as I bent and shaved
the tip to a stabbing point. I turned it over
the blazing fire to char it good and hard,
then hid it well, buried deep under the dung
that littered the cavern's floor in thick wet clumps.
And now I ordered my shipmates all to cast lots—   370
who'd brave it out with me
to hoist our stake and grind it into his eye
when sleep had overcome him? Luck of the draw:

I got the very ones I would have picked myself,
four good men, and I in the lead made five . . .

   Nightfall brought him back, herding his woolly sheep
and he quickly drove the sleek flock into the vaulted cavern,
rams and all—none left outside in the walled yard—
his own idea, perhaps, or a god led him on.
Then he hoisted the huge slab to block the door   380
and squatted to milk his sheep and bleating goats,
each in order, putting a suckling underneath each dam,
and as soon as he'd briskly finished all his chores
he snatched up two more men and fixed his meal.
But this time I lifted a carved wooden bowl,
brimful of my ruddy wine,
and went right up to the Cyclops, enticing,
'Here, Cyclops, try this wine—to top off
the banquet of human flesh you've bolted down!
Judge for yourself what stock our ship had stored.   390
I brought it here to make you a fine libation,
hoping you would pity me, Cyclops, send me home,
but your rages are insufferable. You barbarian—
how can any man on earth come visit you after *this*?
What you've done outrages all that's right!'

   At that he seized the bowl and tossed it off
and the heady wine pleased him immensely—'More'—
he demanded a second bowl—'a hearty helping!
And tell me your name now, quickly,
so I can hand my guest a gift to warm *his* heart.   400
Our soil yields the Cyclops powerful, full-bodied wine
and the rains from Zeus build its strength. But this,
this is nectar, ambrosia—this flows from heaven!'

   So he declared. I poured him another fiery bowl—
three bowls I brimmed and three he drank to the last drop,
the fool, and then, when the wine was swirling round his brain,
I approached my host with a cordial, winning word:
'So, you ask me the name I'm known by, Cyclops?

I will tell you. But you must give me a guest-gift
as you've promised. Nobody—that's my name. Nobody—   410
so my mother and father call me, all my friends.'

But he boomed back at me from his ruthless heart,
'Nobody? I'll eat Nobody last of all his friends—
I'll eat the others first! That's my gift to *you!'*
                                            With that
he toppled over, sprawled full-length, flat on his back
and lay there, his massive neck slumping to one side,
and sleep that conquers all overwhelmed him now
as wine came spurting, flooding up from his gullet
with chunks of human flesh—he vomited, blind drunk.
Now, at last, I thrust our stake in a bed of embers   420
to get it red-hot and rallied all my comrades:
'Courage—no panic, no one hang back now!'
And green as it was, just as the olive stake
was about to catch fire—the glow terrific, yes—
I dragged it from the flames, my men clustering round
as some god breathed enormous courage through us all.
Hoisting high that olive stake with its stabbing point,
straight into the monster's eye they rammed it hard—
I drove my weight on it from above and bored it home
as a shipwright bores his beam with a shipwright's drill   430
that men below, whipping the strap back and forth, whirl
and the drill keeps twisting faster, never stopping—
So we seized our stake with its fiery tip
and bored it round and round in the giant's eye
till blood came boiling up around that smoking shaft
and the hot blast singed his brow and eyelids round the core
and the broiling eyeball burst—
                                its crackling roots blazed
and hissed—
              as a blacksmith plunges a glowing ax or adze
in an ice-cold bath and the metal screeches steam
and its temper hardens—that's the iron's strength—   440
so the eye of the Cyclops sizzled round that stake!
He loosed a hideous roar, the rock walls echoed round

and we scuttled back in terror. The monster wrenched the spike
from his eye and out it came with a red geyser of blood—
he flung it aside with frantic hands, and mad with pain
he bellowed out for help from his neighbor Cyclops
living round about in caves on windswept crags.
Hearing his cries, they lumbered up from every side
and hulking round his cavern, asked what ailed him:
'What, Polyphemus, what in the world's the trouble?   450
Roaring out in the godsent night to rob us of our sleep.
Surely no one's rustling your flocks against your will—
surely no one's trying to kill you now by fraud or force!'

'*Nobody*, friends'—Polyphemus bellowed back from his cave—
'Nobody's killing me now by fraud and not by force!'

'If you're alone,' his friends boomed back at once,
'and nobody's trying to overpower you now—look,
it must be a plague sent here by mighty Zeus
and there's no escape from *that*.
You'd better pray to your father, Lord Poseidon.'   460

They lumbered off, but laughter filled my heart
to think how nobody's name—my great cunning stroke—
had duped them one and all. But the Cyclops there,
still groaning, racked with agony, groped around
for the huge slab, and heaving it from the doorway,
down he sat in the cave's mouth, his arms spread wide,
hoping to catch a comrade stealing out with sheep—
such a blithering fool he took me for!
But I was already plotting . . .
what was the best way out? how could I find   470
escape from death for my crew, myself as well?
My wits kept weaving, weaving cunning schemes—
life at stake, monstrous death staring us in the face—
till this plan struck my mind as best. That flock,
those well-fed rams with their splendid thick fleece,
sturdy, handsome beasts sporting their dark weight of wool:

I lashed them abreast, quietly, twisting the willow-twigs
the Cyclops slept on—giant, lawless brute—I took them
three by three; each ram in the middle bore a man
while the two rams either side would shield him well.   480
So three beasts to bear each man, but as for myself?
There was one bellwether ram, the prize of all the flock,
and clutching him by his back, tucked up under
his shaggy belly, there I hung, face upward,
both hands locked in his marvelous deep fleece,
clinging for dear life, my spirit steeled, enduring . . .
So we held on, desperate, waiting Dawn's first light.

                                          As soon
as young Dawn with her rose-red fingers shone once more
the rams went rumbling out of the cave toward pasture,
the ewes kept bleating round the pens, unmilked,   490
their udders about to burst. Their master now,
heaving in torment, felt the back of each animal
halting before him here, but the idiot never sensed
my men were trussed up under their thick fleecy ribs.
And last of them all came my great ram now, striding out,
weighed down with his dense wool and my deep plots.
Stroking him gently, powerful Polyphemus murmured,
'Dear old ram, why last of the flock to quit the cave?
In the good old days you'd never lag behind the rest—
you with your long marching strides, first by far   500
of the flock to graze the fresh young grasses,
first by far to reach the rippling streams,
first to turn back home, keen for your fold
when night comes on—but now you're last of all.
And why? Sick at heart for your master's eye
that coward gouged out with his wicked crew?—
only after he'd stunned my wits with wine—
that, that Nobody . . .
who's not escaped his death, I swear, not yet.
Oh if only you thought like *me*, had words like *me*   510
to tell me where that scoundrel is cringing from my rage!
I'd smash him against the ground, I'd spill his brains—

flooding across my cave—and that would ease my heart
of the pains that good-for-nothing Nobody made me suffer!'

And with that threat he let my ram go free outside.
But soon as we'd got one foot past cave and courtyard,
first I loosed myself from the ram, then loosed my men,
then quickly, glancing back again and again we drove
our flock, good plump beasts with their long shanks,
straight to the ship, and a welcome sight we were   520
to loyal comrades—we who'd escaped our deaths—
but for all the rest they broke down and wailed.
I cut it short, I stopped each shipmate's cries,
my head tossing, brows frowning, silent signals
to hurry, tumble our fleecy herd on board,
launch out on the open sea!
They swung aboard, they sat to the oars in ranks
and in rhythm churned the water white with stroke on stroke.
But once offshore as far as a man's shout can carry,
I called back to the Cyclops, stinging taunts: 530
'So, Cyclops, no weak coward it was whose crew
you bent to devour there in your vaulted cave—
you with your brute force! Your filthy crimes
came down on your own head, you shameless cannibal,
daring to eat your guests in your own house—
so Zeus and the other gods have paid you back!'

That made the rage of the monster boil over.
Ripping off the peak of a towering crag, he heaved it
so hard the boulder landed just in front of our dark prow
and a huge swell reared up as the rock went plunging under—   540
a tidal wave from the open sea. The sudden backwash
drove us landward again, forcing us close inshore
but grabbing a long pole, I thrust us off and away,
tossing my head for dear life, signaling crews
to put their backs in the oars, escape grim death.
They threw themselves in the labor, rowed on fast
but once we'd plowed the breakers twice as far,
again I began to taunt the Cyclops—men around me

trying to check me, calm me, left and right:
'So headstrong—why? Why rile the beast again?'   550

 'That rock he flung in the sea just now, hurling our ship
to shore once more—we thought we'd die on the spot!'

 'If he'd caught a sound from one of us, just a moan,
he would have crushed our heads and ship timbers
with one heave of another flashing, jagged rock!'

 'Good god, the brute can throw!'
        So they begged
but they could not bring my fighting spirit round.
I called back with another burst of anger, 'Cyclops—
if any man on the face of the earth should ask you
who blinded you, shamed you so—say Odysseus,   560
raider of cities, *he* gouged out your eye,
Laertes' son who makes his home in Ithaca!'

 So I vaunted and he groaned back in answer,
'Oh no, no—that prophecy years ago . . .
it all comes home to me with a vengeance now!
We once had a prophet here, a great tall man,
Telemus, Eurymus' son, a master at reading signs,
who grew old in his trade among his fellow-Cyclops.
All this, he warned me, would come to pass someday—
that I'd be blinded here at the hands of one Odysseus.   570
But I always looked for a handsome giant man to cross my path,
some fighter clad in power like armor-plate, but now,
look what a dwarf, a spineless good-for-nothing,
stuns me with wine, then gouges out my eye!
Come here, Odysseus, let me give you a guest-gift
and urge Poseidon the earthquake god to speed you home.
I am his son and he claims to be my father, true,
and he himself will heal me if he pleases—
no other blessed god, no man can do the work!'
           'Heal you!'—
here was my parting shot—'Would to god I could strip you   580

of life and breath and ship you down to the House of Death
as surely as no one will ever heal your eye,
not even your earthquake god himself!'

　But at that he bellowed out to lord Poseidon,
thrusting his arms to the starry skies, and prayed, 'Hear me—
Poseidon, god of the sea-blue mane who rocks the earth!
If I really am your son and you claim to be my father—
come, grant that Odysseus, raider of cities,
Laertes' son who makes his home in Ithaca,
never reaches home. Or if he's fated to see   590
his people once again and reach his well-built house
and his own native country, let him come home late
and come a broken man—all shipmates lost,
alone in a stranger's ship—
and let him find a world of pain at home!'
　　　　　　　　　　　　　　　So he prayed
and the god of the sea-blue mane, Poseidon, heard his prayer.
The monster suddenly hoisted a boulder—far larger—
wheeled and heaved it, putting his weight behind it,
massive strength, and the boulder crashed close,
landing just in the wake of our dark stern,   600
just failing to graze the rudder's bladed edge.
A huge swell reared up as the rock went plunging under,
yes, and the tidal breaker drove us out to our island's
far shore where all my well-decked ships lay moored,
clustered, waiting, and huddled round them, crewmen
sat in anguish, waiting, chafing for our return.
We beached our vessel hard ashore on the sand,
we swung out in the frothing surf ourselves,
and herding Cyclops' sheep from our deep holds
we shared them round so no one, not on my account,   610
would go deprived of his fair share of spoils.
But the splendid ram—as we meted out the flocks
my friends-in-arms made him my prize of honor,
mine alone, and I slaughtered him on the beach
and burnt his thighs to Cronus' mighty son,
Zeus of the thundercloud who rules the world.

But my sacrifices failed to move the god:
Zeus was still obsessed with plans to destroy
my entire oarswept fleet and loyal crew of comrades.
Now all day long till the sun went down we sat   620
and feasted on sides of meat and heady wine.
Then when the sun had set and night came on
we lay down and slept at the water's shelving edge.
When young Dawn with her rose-red fingers shone once more
I roused the men straightway, ordering all crews
to man the ships and cast off cables quickly.
They swung aboard at once, they sat to the oars in ranks
and in rhythm churned the water white with stroke on stroke.
And from there we sailed on, glad to escape our death
yet sick at heart for the comrades we had lost."   630

BOOK ELEVEN

The Kingdom of the Dead

"Now down we came to the ship at the water's edge,
we hauled and launched her into the sunlit breakers first,
stepped the mast in the black craft and set our sail
and loaded the sheep aboard, the ram and ewe,
then we ourselves embarked, streaming tears,
our hearts weighed down with anguish . . .
But Circe, the awesome nymph with lovely braids
who speaks with human voice, sent us a hardy shipmate,
yes, a fresh following wind ruffling up in our wake,
bellying out our sail to drive our blue prow on as we,   10
securing the running gear from stem to stern, sat back
while the wind and helmsman kept her true on course.
The sail stretched taut as she cut the sea all day
and the sun sank and the roads of the world grew dark.

    And she made the outer limits, the Ocean River's bounds
where Cimmerian people have their homes—their realm and city
shrouded in mist and cloud. The eye of the Sun can never
flash his rays through the dark and bring them light,
not when he climbs the starry skies or when he wheels
back down from the heights to touch the earth once more—   20
an endless, deadly night overhangs those wretched men.
There, gaining that point, we beached our craft
and herding out the sheep, we picked our way
by the Ocean's banks until we gained the place
that Circe made our goal.
                              Here at the spot
Perimedes and Eurylochus held the victims fast,
and I, drawing my sharp sword from beside my hip,
dug a trench of about a forearm's depth and length
and around it poured libations out to all the dead,
first with milk and honey, and then with mellow wine,   30
then water third and last, and sprinkled glistening barley
over it all, and time and again I vowed to all the dead,
to the drifting, listless spirits of their ghosts,
that once I returned to Ithaca I would slaughter
a barren heifer in my halls, the best I had,
and load a pyre with treasures—and to Tiresias,
alone, apart, I would offer a sleek black ram,
the pride of all my herds. And once my vows
and prayers had invoked the nations of the dead,
I took the victims, over the trench I cut their throats   40
and the dark blood flowed in—and up out of Erebus they came,
flocking toward me now, the ghosts of the dead and gone . . .
Brides and unwed youths and old men who had suffered much
and girls with their tender hearts freshly scarred by sorrow
and great armies of battle dead, stabbed by bronze spears,
men of war still wrapped in bloody armor—thousands
swarming around the trench from every side—
unearthly cries—blanching terror gripped me!
I ordered the men at once to flay the sheep
that lay before us, killed by my ruthless blade,   50

and burn them both, and then say prayers to the gods,
to the almighty god of death and dread Persephone.
But I, the sharp sword drawn from beside my hip,
sat down on alert there and never let the ghosts
of the shambling, shiftless dead come near that blood
till I had questioned Tiresias myself.
                                              But first
the ghost of Elpenor, my companion, came toward me.
He'd not been buried under the wide ways of earth,
not yet, we'd left his body in Circe's house,
unwept, unburied—this other labor pressed us.   60
But I wept to see him now, pity touched my heart
and I called out a winged word to him there: 'Elpenor,
how did you travel down to the world of darkness?
Faster on foot, I see, than I in my black ship.'

    My comrade groaned as he offered me an answer:
'Royal son of Laertes, Odysseus, old campaigner,
the doom of an angry god, and god knows how much wine—
they were my ruin, captain . . . I'd bedded down
on the roof of Circe's house but never thought
to climb back down again by the long ladder—   70
headfirst from the roof I plunged, my neck snapped
from the backbone, my soul flew down to Death. Now,
I beg you by those you left behind, so far from here,
your wife, your father who bred and reared you as a boy,
and Telemachus, left at home in your halls, your only son.
Well I know when you leave this lodging of the dead
that you and your ship will put ashore again
at the island of Aeaea—then and there,
my lord, remember me, I beg you! Don't sail off
and desert me, left behind unwept, unburied, don't,   80
or my curse may draw god's fury on your head.
No, burn me in full armor, all my harness,
heap my mound by the churning gray surf—
a man whose luck ran out—
so even men to come will learn my story.

Perform my rites, and plant on my tomb that oar
I swung with mates when I rowed among the living.'

   'All this, my unlucky friend,' I reassured him,
'I will do for you. I won't forget a thing.'
                      So we sat
and faced each other, trading our bleak parting words,   90
I on my side, holding my sword above the blood,
he across from me there, my comrade's phantom
dragging out his story.
                But look, the ghost
of my mother came! My mother, dead and gone now . . .
Anticleia—daughter of that great heart Autolycus—
whom I had left alive when I sailed for sacred Troy.
I broke into tears to see her here, but filled with pity,
even throbbing with grief, I would not let her ghost
approach the blood till I had questioned Tiresias myself.

   At last he came. The shade of the famous Theban prophet,   100
holding a golden scepter, knew me at once and hailed me:
'Royal son of Laertes, Odysseus, master of exploits,
man of pain, what now, what brings you here,
forsaking the light of day
to see this joyless kingdom of the dead?
Stand back from the trench—put up your sharp sword
so I can drink the blood and tell you all the truth.'

   Moving back, I thrust my silver-studded sword
deep in its sheath, and once he had drunk the dark blood
the words came ringing from the prophet in his power: 110
'A sweet smooth journey home, renowned Odysseus,
that is what you seek
but a god will make it hard for you—I know—
you will never escape the one who shakes the earth,
quaking with anger at you still, still enraged
because you blinded the Cyclops, his dear son.
Even so, you and your crew may still reach home,
suffering all the way, if you only have the power

to curb their wild desire and curb your own, what's more,
from the day your good trim vessel first puts in   120
at Thrinacia Island, flees the cruel blue sea.
There you will find them grazing,
herds and fat flocks, the cattle of Helios,
god of the sun who sees all, hears all things.
Leave the beasts unharmed, your mind set on home,
and you all may still reach Ithaca—bent with hardship,
true—but harm them in any way, and I can see it now:
your ship destroyed, your men destroyed as well.
And even if *you* escape, you'll come home late
and come a broken man—all shipmates lost,   130
alone in a stranger's ship—
and you will find a world of pain at home,
crude, arrogant men devouring all your goods,
courting your noble wife, offering gifts to win her.
No doubt you will pay them back in blood when you come home!
But once you have killed those suitors in your halls—
by stealth or in open fight with slashing bronze—
go forth once more, you must . . .
carry your well-planed oar until you come
to a race of people who know nothing of the sea,   140
whose food is never seasoned with salt, strangers all
to ships with their crimson prows and long slim oars,
wings that make ships fly. And here is your sign—
unmistakable, clear, so clear you cannot miss it:
When another traveler falls in with you and calls
that weight across your shoulder a fan to winnow grain,
then plant your bladed, balanced oar in the earth
and sacrifice fine beasts to the lord god of the sea,
Poseidon—a ram, a bull and a ramping wild boar—
then journey home and render noble offerings up   150
to the deathless gods who rule the vaulting skies,
to all the gods in order.
And at last your own death will steal upon you . . .
a gentle, painless death, far from the sea it comes
to take you down, borne down with the years in ripe old age
with all your people there in blessed peace around you.

All that I have told you will come true.'

                                    'Oh Tiresias,'
I replied as the prophet finished, 'surely the gods
have spun this out as fate, the gods themselves.
But tell me one thing more, and tell me clearly.   160
I see the ghost of my long-lost mother here before me.
Dead, crouching close to the blood in silence,
she cannot bear to look me in the eyes—
her own son—or speak a word to me. How,
lord, can I make her know me for the man I am?'

    'One rule there is,' the famous seer explained,
'and simple for me to say and you to learn.
Any one of the ghosts you let approach the blood
will speak the truth to you. Anyone you refuse
will turn and fade away.'
                        And with those words,   170
now that his prophecies had closed, the awesome shade
of lord Tiresias strode back to the House of Death.
But I kept watch there, steadfast till my mother
approached and drank the dark, clouding blood.
She knew me at once and wailed out in grief
and her words came winging toward me, flying home:
'Oh my son—what brings you down to the world
of death and darkness? You are still alive!
It's hard for the living to catch a glimpse of this . . .
Great rivers flow between us, terrible waters,   180
the Ocean first of all—no one could ever ford
that stream on foot, only aboard some sturdy craft.
Have you just come from Troy, wandering long years
with your men and ship? Not yet returned to Ithaca?
You've still not seen your wife inside your halls?'

                                    'Mother,'
I replied, 'I had to venture down to the House of Death,
to consult the shade of Tiresias, seer of Thebes.
Never yet have I neared Achaea, never once
set foot on native ground,
always wandering—endless hardship from that day   190

I first set sail with King Agamemnon bound for Troy,
the stallion-land, to fight the Trojans there.
But tell me about yourself and spare me nothing.
What form of death overcame you, what laid you low,
some long slow illness? Or did Artemis showering arrows
come with her painless shafts and bring you down?
Tell me of father, tell of the son I left behind:
do my royal rights still lie in their safekeeping?
Or does some stranger hold the throne by now
because men think that I'll come home no more?   200
Please, tell me about my wife, her turn of mind,
her thoughts . . . still standing fast beside our son,
still guarding our great estates, secure as ever now?
Or has she wed some other countryman at last,
the finest prince among them?'
                              'Surely, surely,'
my noble mother answered quickly, 'she's still waiting
there in your halls, poor woman, suffering so,
her life an endless hardship like your own . . .
wasting away the nights, weeping away the days.
No one has taken over your royal rights, not yet.   210
Telemachus still holds your great estates in peace,
he attends the public banquets shared with all,
the feasts a man of justice should enjoy,
for every lord invites him. As for your father,
he keeps to his own farm—he never goes to town—
with no bed for him there, no blankets, glossy throws;
all winter long he sleeps in the lodge with servants,
in the ashes by the fire, his body wrapped in rags.
But when summer comes and the bumper crops of harvest,
any spot on the rising ground of his vineyard rows   220
he makes his bed, heaped high with fallen leaves,
and there he lies in anguish . . .
with his old age bearing hard upon him, too,
and his grief grows as he longs for your return.
And I with the same grief, I died and met my fate.
No sharp-eyed Huntress showering arrows through the halls
approached and brought me down with painless shafts,

nor did some hateful illness strike me, that so often
devastates the body, drains our limbs of power.
No, it was my longing for *you*, my shining Odysseus—   230
you and your quickness, you and your gentle ways—
that tore away my life that had been sweet.'

And I, my mind in turmoil, how I longed
to embrace my mother's spirit, dead as she was!
Three times I rushed toward her, desperate to hold her,
three times she fluttered through my fingers, sifting away
like a shadow, dissolving like a dream, and each time
the grief cut to the heart, sharper, yes, and I,
I cried out to her, words winging into the darkness:
'Mother—why not wait for me? How I long to hold you!—   240
so even here, in the House of Death, we can fling
our loving arms around each other, take some joy
in the tears that numb the heart. Or is this just
some wraith that great Persephone sends my way
to make me ache with sorrow all the more?'

My noble mother answered me at once:
'My son, my son, the unluckiest man alive!
This is no deception sent by Queen Persephone,
this is just the way of mortals when we die.
Sinews no longer bind the flesh and bones together—   250
the fire in all its fury burns the body down to ashes
once life slips from the white bones, and the spirit,
rustling, flitters away . . . flown like a dream.
But you must long for the daylight. Go, quickly.
Remember all these things
so one day you can tell them to your wife.'

And so we both confided, trading parting words,
and there slowly came a grand array of women,
all sent before me now by august Persephone,
and all were wives and daughters once of princes.   260
They swarmed in a flock around the dark blood
while I searched for a way to question each alone,

and the more I thought, the more this seemed the best:
Drawing forth the long sharp sword from beside my hip,
I would not let them drink the dark blood, all in a rush,
and so they waited, coming forward one after another.
Each declared her lineage, and I explored them all.

And the first I saw there? Tyro, born of kings,
who said her father was that great lord Salmoneus,
said that she was the wife of Cretheus, Aeolus' son.   270
And once she fell in love with the river god, Enipeus,
far the clearest river flowing across the earth,
and so she'd haunt Enipeus' glinting streams,
till taking his shape one day
the god who girds the earth and makes it tremble
bedded her where the swirling river rushes out to sea,
and a surging wave reared up, high as a mountain, dark,
arching over to hide the god and mortal girl together.
Loosing her virgin belt, he lapped her round in sleep
and when the god had consummated his work of love   280
he took her by the hand and hailed her warmly:
'Rejoice in our love, my lady! And when this year
has run its course you will give birth to glorious children—
bedding down with the gods is never barren, futile—
and you must tend them, breed and rear them well.
Now home you go, and restrain yourself, I say,
never breathe your lover's name but know—
I am Poseidon, god who rocks the earth!'

With that he dove back in the heaving waves
and she conceived for the god and bore him Pelias, Neleus,   290
and both grew up to be stalwart aides of Zeus almighty,
both men alike. Pelias lived on the plains of Iolcos,
rich in sheepflocks, Neleus lived in sandy Pylos.
And the noble queen bore sons to Cretheus too:
Aeson, Pheres and Amythaon, exultant charioteer.

And after Tyro I saw Asopus' daughter Antiope,
proud she'd spent a night in the arms of Zeus himself

and borne the god twin sons, Amphion and Zethus,
the first to build the footings of seven-gated Thebes,
her bastions too, for lacking ramparts none could live   300
in a place so vast, so open—strong as both men were.

And I saw Alcmena next, Amphitryon's wife,
who slept in the clasp of Zeus and merged in love
and brought forth Heracles, rugged will and lion heart.
And I saw Megara too, magnanimous Creon's daughter
wed to the stalwart Heracles, the hero never daunted.

And I saw the mother of Oedipus, beautiful Epicaste.
What a monstrous thing she did, in all innocence—
she married her own son . . .
who'd killed his father, then he married *her!*   310
But the gods soon made it known to all mankind.
So he in growing pain ruled on in beloved Thebes,
lording Cadmus' people—thanks to the gods' brutal plan—
while she went down to Death who guards the massive gates.
Lashing a noose to a steep rafter, there she hanged aloft,
strangling in all her anguish, leaving her son to bear
the world of horror a mother's Furies bring to life.

And I saw magnificent Chloris, the one whom Neleus
wooed and won with a hoard of splendid gifts,
so dazzled by her beauty years ago . . .   320
the youngest daughter of Iasus' son Amphion,
the great Minyan king who ruled Orchomenos once.
She was his queen in Pylos, she bore him shining sons,
Nestor and Chromius, Periclymenus too, good prince.
And after her sons she bore a daughter, majestic Pero,
the marvel of her time, courted by all the young lords
round about. But Neleus would not give her to any suitor,
none but the man who might drive home the herds
that powerful Iphiclus had stolen. Lurching,
broad in the brow, those longhorned beasts,   330
and no small task to round them up from Phylace.

Only the valiant seer Melampus volunteered—
he would drive them home—
but a god's iron sentence bound him fast:
barbarous herdsmen dragged him off in chains.
Yet when the months and days had run their course
and the year wheeled round and the seasons came again,
then mighty Iphiclus loosed the prophet's shackles,
once he had told him all the gods' decrees.
And so the will of Zeus was done at last.   340

     And I saw Leda next, Tyndareus' wife,
who'd borne the king two sons, intrepid twins,
Castor, breaker of horses, and the hardy boxer Polydeuces,
both buried now in the life-giving earth though still alive.
Even under the earth Zeus grants them that distinction:
one day alive, the next day dead, each twin by turns,
they both hold honors equal to the gods'.

     And I saw Iphimedeia next, Aloeus' wife,
who claimed she lay in the Sea-lord's loving waves
and gave the god two sons, but they did not live long,   350
Otus staunch as a god and far-famed Ephialtes.
They were the tallest men the fertile earth has borne,
the handsomest too, by far, aside from renowned Orion.
Nine yards across they measured, even at nine years old,
nine fathoms tall they towered. They even threatened
the deathless gods they'd storm Olympus' heights
with the pounding rush and grinding shock of battle.
They were wild to pile Ossa upon Olympus, then on Ossa
Pelion dense with timber—their toeholds up the heavens.
And they'd have won the day if they had reached peak strength   360
but Apollo the son of Zeus, whom sleek-haired Leto bore,
laid both giants low before their beards had sprouted,
covering cheek and chin with a fresh crop of down.

     Phaedra and Procris too I saw, and lovely Ariadne,
daughter of Minos, that harsh king. One day Theseus tried

to spirit her off from Crete to Athens' sacred heights
but he got no joy from her. Artemis killed her first
on wave-washed Dia's shores, accused by Dionysus.

And I saw Clymene, Maera and loathsome Eriphyle—
bribed with a golden necklace   370
to lure her lawful husband to his death . . .
But the whole cortege I could never tally, never name,
not all the daughters and wives of great men I saw there.
Long before that, the godsent night would ebb away.
But the time has come for sleep, either with friends
aboard your swift ship or here in your own house.
My passage home will rest with the gods and you."

Odysseus paused . . . They all fell silent, hushed,
his story holding them spellbound down the shadowed halls
till the white-armed queen Arete suddenly burst out,   380
"Phaeacians! How does this man impress you now,
his looks, his build, the balanced mind inside him?
The stranger is my guest
but each of you princes shares the honor here.
So let's not be too hasty to send him on his way,
and don't scrimp on his gifts. His need is great,
great as the riches piled up in your houses,
thanks to the gods' good will."
                                        Following her,
the old revered Echeneus added his support,
the eldest lord on the island of Phaeacia: 390
"Friends, the words of our considerate queen—
they never miss the mark or fail our expectations.
So do as Arete says, though on Alcinous here
depend all words and action."
                                        "And so it will be"—
Alcinous stepped in grandly—"sure as I am alive
and rule our island men who love their oars!
Our guest, much as he longs for passage home,
must stay and wait it out here till tomorrow,
till I can collect his whole array of parting gifts.

His send-off rests with every noble here   400
but with me most of all:
I hold the reins of power in the realm."

Odysseus, deft and tactful, echoed back,
"Alcinous, majesty, shining among your island people,
if you would urge me now to stay here one whole year
then speed me home weighed down with lordly gifts,
I'd gladly have it so. Better by far, that way.
The fuller my arms on landing there at home,
the more respected, well received I'd be
by all who saw me sailing back to Ithaca."   410

"Ah Odysseus," Alcinous replied, "one look at you
and we know that you are no one who would cheat us—
no fraud, such as the dark soil breeds and spreads
across the face of the earth these days. Crowds of vagabonds
frame their lies so tightly none can test them. But you,
what grace you give your words, and what good sense within!
You have told your story with all a singer's skill,
the miseries you endured, your great Achaeans too.
But come now, tell me truly: your godlike comrades—
did you see any heroes down in the House of Death,   420
any who sailed with you and met their doom at Troy?
The night's still young, I'd say the night is endless.
For us in the palace now, it's hardly time for sleep.
Keep telling us your adventures—they are wonderful.
I could hold out here till Dawn's first light
if only you could bear, here in our halls,
to tell the tale of all the pains you suffered."

So the man of countless exploits carried on:
"Alcinous, majesty, shining among your island people,
there is a time for many words, a time for sleep as well.   430
But if you insist on hearing more, I'd never stint
on telling my own tale and those more painful still,
the griefs of my comrades, dead in the war's wake,
who escaped the battle-cries of Trojan armies

only to die in blood at journey's end—
thanks to a vicious woman's will.
                              Now then,
no sooner had Queen Persephone driven off
the ghosts of lovely women, scattering left and right,
than forward marched the shade of Atreus' son Agamemnon,
fraught with grief and flanked by all his comrades,   440
troops of his men-at-arms who died beside him,
who met their fate in lord Aegisthus' halls.
He knew me at once, as soon as he drank the blood,
and wailed out, shrilly; tears sprang to his eyes,
he thrust his arms toward me, keen to embrace me there—
no use—the great force was gone, the strength lost forever,
now, that filled his rippling limbs in the old days.
I wept at the sight, my heart went out to the man,
my words too, in a winging flight of pity:
'Famous Atrides, lord of men Agamemnon!   450
What fatal stroke of destiny brought you down?
Wrecked in the ships when lord Poseidon roused
some punishing blast of stormwinds, gust on gust?
Or did ranks of enemies mow you down on land
as you tried to raid and cut off herds and flocks
or fought to win their city, take their women?'

    The field marshal's ghost replied at once:
'Royal son of Laertes, Odysseus, mastermind of war,
I was not wrecked in the ships when lord Poseidon
roused some punishing blast of stormwinds, gust on gust,   460
nor did ranks of enemies mow me down on land—
Aegisthus hatched my doom and my destruction,
he killed me, he with my own accursed wife . . .
he invited me to his palace, sat me down to feast
then cut me down as a man cuts down some ox at the trough!
So I died—a wretched, ignominious death—and round me
all my comrades killed, no mercy, one after another,
just like white-tusked boars
butchered in some rich lord of power's halls

for a wedding, banquet or groaning public feast.   470
You in your day have witnessed hundreds slaughtered,
killed in single combat or killed in pitched battle, true,
but if you'd laid eyes on this it would have wrenched your heart—
how we sprawled by the mixing-bowl and loaded tables there,
throughout the palace, the whole floor awash with blood.
But the death-cry of Cassandra, Priam's daughter—
the most pitiful thing I heard! My treacherous queen,
Clytemnestra, killed her over my body, yes, and I,
lifting my fists, beat them down on the ground,
dying, dying, writhing around the sword.   480
But she, that whore, she turned her back on me,
well on my way to Death—she even lacked the heart
to seal my eyes with her hand or close my jaws.

                                                          So,
there's nothing more deadly, bestial than a woman
set on works like these—what a monstrous thing
she plotted, slaughtered her own lawful husband!
Why, I expected, at least, some welcome home
from all my children, all my household slaves
when I came sailing back again . . . But she—
the queen hell-bent on outrage—bathes in shame   490
not only herself but the whole breed of womankind,
even the honest ones to come, forever down the years!'

   So he declared and I cried out, 'How terrible!
Zeus from the very start, the thunder king
has hated the race of Atreus with a vengeance—
his trustiest weapon women's twisted wiles.
What armies of us died for the sake of Helen . . .
Clytemnestra schemed your death while you were worlds away!'

   'True, true,' Agamemnon's ghost kept pressing on,
'so even your own wife—never indulge her too far.   500
Never reveal the whole truth, whatever you may know;
just tell her a part of it, be sure to hide the rest.
Not that you, Odysseus, will be murdered by your wife.

She's much too steady, her feelings run too deep,
Icarius' daughter Penelope, that wise woman.
She was a young bride, I well remember . . .
we left her behind when we went off to war,
with an infant boy she nestled at her breast.
That boy must sit and be counted with the men now—
happy man! His beloved father will come sailing home   510
and see his son, and he will embrace his father,
that is only right. But *my* wife—she never
even let me feast my eyes on my own son;
she killed me first, his father!
I tell you this—bear it in mind, you must—
when you reach your homeland steer your ship
into port in secret, never out in the open . . .
the time for trusting women's gone forever!

    Enough. Come, tell me this, and be precise.
Have you heard news of my son? Where's he living now?   520
Perhaps in Orchomenos, perhaps in sandy Pylos
or off in the Spartan plains with Menelaus?
He's not dead yet, my Prince Orestes, no,
he's somewhere on the earth.'
                                    So he probed
but I cut it short: 'Atrides, why ask me that?
I know nothing, whether he's dead or alive.
It's wrong to lead you on with idle words.'

    So we stood there, trading heartsick stories,
deep in grief, as the tears streamed down our faces.
But now there came the ghosts of Peleus' son Achilles,   530
Patroclus, fearless Antilochus—and Great Ajax too,
the first in stature, first in build and bearing
of all the Argives after Peleus' matchless son.
The ghost of the splendid runner knew me at once
and hailed me with a flight of mournful questions:
'Royal son of Laertes, Odysseus, man of tactics,
reckless friend, what next?

What greater feat can that cunning head contrive?
What daring brought you down to the House of Death?—
where the senseless, burnt-out wraiths of mortals make their home.' 540

    The voice of his spirit paused, and I was quick to answer:
'Achilles, son of Peleus, greatest of the Achaeans,
I had to consult Tiresias, driven here by hopes
he would help me journey home to rocky Ithaca.
Never yet have I neared Achaea, never once
set foot on native ground . . .
my life is endless trouble.
                      But you, Achilles,
there's not a man in the world more blest than you—
there never has been, never will be one.
Time was, when you were alive, we Argives   550
honored you as a god, and now down here, I see,
you lord it over the dead in all your power.
So grieve no more at dying, great Achilles.'

    I reassured the ghost, but he broke out, protesting,
'No winning words about death to *me*, shining Odysseus!
By god, I'd rather slave on earth for another man—
some dirt-poor tenant farmer who scrapes to keep alive—
than rule down here over all the breathless dead.
But come, tell me the news about my gallant son.
Did he make his way to the wars,   560
did the boy become a champion—yes or no?
Tell me of noble Peleus, any word you've heard—
still holding pride of place among his Myrmidon hordes,
or do they despise the man in Hellas and in Phthia
because old age has lamed his arms and legs?
For I no longer stand in the light of day—
the man I was—comrade-in-arms to help my father
as once I helped our armies, killing the best fighters
Troy could field in the wide world up there . . .
Oh to arrive at father's house—the man I was,   570
for one brief day—I'd make my fury and my hands,

invincible hands, a thing of terror to all those men
who abuse the king with force and wrest away his honor!'

   So he grieved but I tried to lend him heart:
'About noble Peleus I can tell you nothing,
but about your own dear son, Neoptolemus,
I can report the whole story, as you wish.
I myself, in my trim ship, I brought him
out of Scyros to join the Argives under arms.
And dug in around Troy, debating battle-tactics,   580
he always spoke up first, and always on the mark—
godlike Nestor and I alone excelled the boy. Yes,
and when our armies fought on the plain of Troy
he'd never hang back with the main force of men—
he'd always charge ahead,
giving ground to no one in his fury,
and scores of men he killed in bloody combat.
How could I list them all, name them all, now,
the fighting ranks he leveled, battling for the Argives?
But what a soldier he laid low with a bronze sword: 590
the hero Eurypylus, Telephus' son, and round him
troops of his own Cetean comrades slaughtered,
lured to war by the bribe his mother took.
The only man I saw to put Eurypylus
in the shade was Memnon, son of the Morning.
Again, when our champions climbed inside the horse
that Epeus built with labor, and I held full command
to spring our packed ambush open or keep it sealed,
all our lords and captains were wiping off their tears,
knees shaking beneath each man—but not your son.   600
Never once did I see his glowing skin go pale;
he never flicked a tear from his cheeks, no,
he kept on begging me there to let him burst
from the horse, kept gripping his hilted sword,
his heavy bronze-tipped javelin, keen to loose
his fighting fury against the Trojans. Then,
once we'd sacked King Priam's craggy city,
laden with his fair share and princely prize

he boarded his own ship, his body all unscarred.
Not a wound from a flying spear or a sharp sword,   610
cut-and-thrust close up—the common marks of war.
Random, raging Ares plays no favorites.'

                                                So I said and
off he went, the ghost of the great runner, Aeacus' grandson
loping with long strides across the fields of asphodel,
triumphant in all I had told him of his son,
his gallant, glorious son.

    Now the rest of the ghosts, the dead and gone
came swarming up around me—deep in sorrow there,
each asking about the grief that touched him most.
Only the ghost of Great Ajax, son of Telamon,   620
kept his distance, blazing with anger at me still
for the victory I had won by the ships that time
I pressed my claim for the arms of Prince Achilles.
His queenly mother had set them up as prizes,
Pallas and captive Trojans served as judges.
Would to god I'd never won such trophies!
All for them the earth closed over Ajax,
that proud hero Ajax . . .
greatest in build, greatest in works of war
of all the Argives after Peleus' matchless son.   630
I cried out to him now, I tried to win him over:
'Ajax, son of noble Telamon, still determined,
even in death, not once to forget that rage
you train on me for those accursed arms?
The gods set up that prize to plague the Achaeans—
so great a tower of strength we lost when you went down!
For *your* death we grieved as we did for Achilles' death—
we grieved incessantly, true, and none's to blame
but Zeus, who hated Achaea's fighting spearmen
so intensely, Zeus sealed your doom.   640
Come closer, king, and listen to my story.
Conquer your rage, your blazing, headstrong pride!'

    So I cried out but Ajax answered not a word.

He stalked off toward Erebus, into the dark
to join the other lost, departed dead.
Yet now, despite his anger,
he might have spoken to me, or I to him,
but the heart inside me stirred with some desire
to see the ghosts of others dead and gone.

And I saw Minos there, illustrious son of Zeus,   650
firmly enthroned, holding his golden scepter,
judging all the dead . . .
Some on their feet, some seated, all clustering
round the king of justice, pleading for his verdicts
reached in the House of Death with its all-embracing gates.

I next caught sight of Orion, that huge hunter,
rounding up on the fields of asphodel those wild beasts
the man in life cut down on the lonely mountain-slopes,
brandishing in his hands the bronze-studded club
that time can never shatter.
          I saw Tityus too,   660
son of the mighty goddess Earth—sprawling there
on the ground, spread over nine acres—two vultures
hunched on either side of him, digging into his liver,
beaking deep in the blood-sac, and he with his frantic hands
could never beat them off, for he had once dragged off
the famous consort of Zeus in all her glory,
Leto, threading her way toward Pytho's ridge,
over the lovely dancing-rings of Panopeus.

And I saw Tantalus too, bearing endless torture.
He stood erect in a pool as the water lapped his chin—   670
parched, he tried to drink, but he could not reach the surface,
no, time and again the old man stooped, craving a sip,
time and again the water vanished, swallowed down,
laying bare the caked black earth at his feet—
some spirit drank it dry. And over his head
leafy trees dangled their fruit from high aloft,
pomegranates and pears, and apples glowing red,

succulent figs and olives swelling sleek and dark,
but as soon as the old man would strain to clutch them fast
a gust would toss them up to the lowering dark clouds.   680

And I saw Sisyphus too, bound to his own torture,
grappling his monstrous boulder with both arms working,
heaving, hands struggling, legs driving, he kept on
thrusting the rock uphill toward the brink, but just
as it teetered, set to topple over—
                              time and again
the immense weight of the thing would wheel it back and
the ruthless boulder would bound and tumble down to the plain again—
so once again he would heave, would struggle to thrust it up,
sweat drenching his body, dust swirling above his head.

And next I caught a glimpse of powerful Heracles—   690
his ghost, I mean: the man himself delights
in the grand feasts of the deathless gods on high,
wed to Hebe, famed for her lithe, alluring ankles,
the daughter of mighty Zeus and Hera shod in gold.
Around him cries of the dead rang out like cries of birds,
scattering left and right in horror as on he came like night,
naked bow in his grip, an arrow grooved on the bowstring,
glaring round him fiercely, forever poised to shoot.
A terror too, that sword-belt sweeping across his chest,
a baldric of solid gold emblazoned with awesome work . . .   700
bears and ramping boars and lions with wild, fiery eyes,
and wars, routs and battles, massacres, butchered men.
May the craftsman who forged that masterpiece—
whose skills could conjure up a belt like that—
never forge another!
Heracles knew me at once, at first glance,
and hailed me with a winging burst of pity:
'Royal son of Laertes, Odysseus famed for exploits,
luckless man, you too? Braving out a fate as harsh
as the fate I bore, alive in the light of day?   710
Son of Zeus that I was, my torments never ended,
forced to slave for a man not half the man I was:

he saddled me with the worst heartbreaking labors.
Why, he sent me down here once, to retrieve the hound
that guards the dead—no harder task for me, he thought—
but I dragged the great beast up from the underworld to earth
and Hermes and gleaming-eyed Athena blazed the way!'

    With that he turned and back he went to the House of Death
but I held fast in place, hoping that others might still come,
shades of famous heroes, men who died in the old days   720
and ghosts of an even older age I longed to see,
Theseus and Pirithous, the gods' own radiant sons.
But before I could, the dead came surging round me,
hordes of them, thousands raising unearthly cries,
and blanching terror gripped me—panicked now
that Queen Persephone might send up from Death
some monstrous head, some Gorgon's staring face!
I rushed back to my ship, commanded all hands
to take to the decks and cast off cables quickly.
They swung aboard at once, they sat to the oars in ranks
and a strong tide of the Ocean River swept her on downstream,   730
sped by our rowing first, then by a fresh fair wind."

Pindar,
The Odes

NEMEAN I

For Chromios of Aitna, winner in the horse-race

I

Holy place where Alpheos breathes again,
Green branch of glorious Syracuse,
Ortygia, in whom Artemis sleeps,
Sister of Delos,
From you the hymn's sweet words set out
5 To lift the strong praise of storm-footed horses
For the sake of Zeus of Aitna:
And Chromios' car and Nemea press me
To yoke a triumphant tune
To his victorious doings.

My beginnings are laid in the Gods
With that man's predestined prowess.
10 In success is the top
Of world-wide glory, and the Muse
Loves to remember great Games.
Scatter then a brightness on the island
Which Zeus, master of Olympos,
Gave to Persephona,
And to her with his locks consented
To exalt on high, surpassing the fruitful earth,

15 Sicily, teeming with wealthy peaks
Of cities.
The Son of Kronos gave her
A people of horsemen
To make love to bronze-armoured war –
And often indeed to have fastened on them

The Olympian olive's golden leaves.
I have struck a chance to say much,
And I touch nothing with falsehood.

II

I have taken my stand at the courtyard-gate
20 Of a man who welcomes strangers,
And sweet is my song.
Here a fitting feast is set; not often
Is the house without guests from over sea.
– He has found good men
To quench with water the smoke of cavil.
25   Many are the arts of men,
But we must walk on straight ways
And fight by our own blood.

Action sets strength to work,
And counsel the mind
In those who by their breed foresee what is coming.
    Son of Hagesidamos, in your nature lies
30 The use of the one and the other.
I do not lust to hide great wealth
And keep it in a store-room,
But of my stock to live well
And win a good name to my friends' delight.
For to all comes a share in the hopes

Of those who toil hard. Gladly I cling
To Herakles
On the tall peaks of prowess
And awake an ancient tale,
35 How when the son of Zeus
Came straight from his mother's womb
To the glittering daylight
And with his twin-brother escaped the pangs of birth,

NEMEAN I

III

From her golden throne Hera failed not to see him
When he was swaddled in his saffron baby-clothes.
40 The Queen of the Gods was angry at heart
And at once sent snakes,
Which passed through the open doors
Into the chamber's wide space,
Eager to writhe their quick jaws
Around the children. But *he*
Lifted his head on high and made first trial of battle.

In two unescapable hands
45 He seized the two serpents by their necks:
He strangled them, and his grip
Squeezed the life out of their unspeakable frames.
Then unbearable terror smote the women,
All who were there to help Alkmana in childbed.
Unclothed as she was,
She jumped to her feet from her blankets
And would ward off the arrogant brutes.

50 Quickly the Kadmeians' princes,
One and all,
Raced up with bronze weapons;
Amphitryon came and shook
A naked sword from its sheath.
Piercing pangs struck him; for every man
Feels the burden of what is his own,
But for another's trouble
The heart soon ceases to fret.

IV

55 He stood dumbfounded in wonder
Hard to endure but delightful.

He saw the surpassing spirit and strength of his son.
The Undying Ones had turned
The messengers' tale to falsehood.
60 He called for his neighbour,
Chief interpreter of most high Zeus,
Teiresias, prophet of truth,
Who told him and all the company
With what fortunes the boy shall consort,

How many he shall slay on dry land,
How many wicked, wild beasts in the sea,
'And one who sidles in surfeit
65 And walks the most hateful of men,'
He said, 'he shall give to his doom.
For when on Phlegra's plain
The Gods meet the Giants in battle
Bright hair shall be fouled in the dust
Under the gale of his arrows,'

He told, 'but he for the whole of time
Unending
70 Shall win calm as the choice reward of his mighty labours
In the Halls of the Blest.
He shall have tender Youth for bride,
And feast at his wedding with Zeus Kronidas
And praise the ways of the Holy.'

Nemean I was written in 476 B.C. and performed at Syracuse soon after
Pindar's arrival (19 ff.). Chromios was a veteran soldier who had served
Hieron in his wars.

1 The river Alpheos, which flows past Olympia, was believed to pass
under the sea and reappear as the fountain Arethoisa at Syracuse.

2 Ortygia is the island part of Syracuse, which was early joined to the
mainland.

4 Ortygia is sister of Delos because both have a cult of Artemis.

6 Hieron refounded Katana as Aitna and established a cult of Zeus of Aitna.

13 Sicily was the wedding-gift of Zeus to Persephona.

24 This means that Chromios has friends to protect him from slander.

33 Herakles is introduced as the subject for the myth. He was much honoured in Sicily. Pindar tells his story in the form of a prophecy made by Teiresias just after his birth.

39 Hera is jealous of Alkmana, Herakles' mother, and sends snakes to kill the child.

63–5 It is not clear who this is. Alkyoneus is a possibility.

67–8 Herakles, fighting for the Gods against the Giants, is depicted on the frieze of the Siphnian Treasury at Delphoi.

OLYMPIAN II

For Theron of Akragas, winner in the chariot-race

I

Lords of the harp, my songs,
Of what God, of what Hero,
Of what Man shall our music be?
Pisa belongs to Zeus, the Olympian feast
Herakles founded, the loot of war,
5 But of Theron let your voices ring,
For his victorious four-in-hand.
He is courteous and kind to guests,
The bulwark of Akragas;
In him his famous fathers
Flower, and the city stands.

They suffered much in their hearts to win
A holy home on the river,
10 And were the eye of Sicily;
The destined days
Came adding wealth and joy
To their trueborn nobleness.
  Son of Kronos and Rhea,
Lord of a seat on Olympos and the Hill of the Games
And the Ford of Alpheos,
Rejoice in my songs, and in friendliness
Guide still their ancestral fields

15 For the generations to come.
Of what has been done
In right or against right
Not even Time, father of everything,

Can undo the accomplishment;
In good luck and fortune
Forgetfulness will come;
For in noble delights sorrow perishes
20 Angry but overwhelmed,

II

When God's fate tips the scale of happiness high.
  This word fits the high-throned daughters of Kad-
    mos.
Greatly they suffered, but heavy grief
Falls under conquering blessings.
25 Among the Olympians she lives who died
In the thunderbolt's crash,
Long-haired Semela: Pallas
Loves her for ever, and father Zeus, and exceedingly
Her ivy-crowned boy loves her.

They say that in the sea also
Among the sea-maidens, the daughters of Nereus,
30 Unperishing life has been ordained for Ino
For the whole of time.
Truly no mark is set for the death of men,
Nor when we shall close the quiet day, the Sun's child,
With unfaltering joy.
Many are the streams that come to men,
Now with the heart's delight, and now with sorrow.

35 So Fate, who holds for them the friendly fortune
That their fathers had,
With heaven-born joy brings grief,
Itself to turn about with time;
Ever-since his doomed son encountered Laios
And killed him, fulfilling the oracle
40 Spoken in Pytho long before.

III

The sharp-eyed Fury saw
And destroyed the warrior-race
In slaughter one of another.
Polyneikes fell, but he left Thersandros,
Honoured in young men's games and in battles of war,
45 A shoot from Adrastos' stock, who succoured his house.
    With his root from that seed
It is right that Ainesidamos' son
Should find songs of praise and the harp.

For at Olympia he
Won the prize himself; at Pytho and the Isthmos
50 The impartial Graces made his brother
Share his portion in the flowers
For the chariot racing twelve times round.
(To win the game by trying
Saves a man from the name of fool.)
Truly wealth patterned with prowess
Brings the moment for this or for that,
If it rouses deep ambition to range afar,

55 A transcendent star, the truest light for a man.
    If any man has it, and knows what shall come, –
That of those who die here
The lawless souls at once pay penalty,
And sins done in this kingdom of Zeus
Are judged by one below earth
60 With harsh inexorable doom.

IV

But in nights like ours for ever,
With a like sun in their days,
The good win a life without labour,

Nor brace their hands to trouble earth
65 Or the sea's water for an empty livelihood.
Beside the most honoured of Gods
Those who delighted to keep their word
Pass unweeping days; the others
Support a burden not to be looked upon.

All who have endured three times
In a sojourn in either world,
70 To keep their souls utterly clean of wrong,
Go by God's road to the Tower of Kronos,
Where the Airs, daughters of Ocean,
Blow round the Island of the Blest,
And the flowers are of gold,
Some on land flaming from bright trees,
Others the water feeds;
They bind their hands with them and make garlands,

75 In the straight rule of Rhadamanthys,
Whom the great Father keeps at his side in counsel,
The husband of Rhea on her all-highest throne.
Peleus and Kadmos are in that number;
Achilles too was brought by his mother,
80 When she moved the heart of Zeus with prayers.

V

He overthrew Hektor, Troy's
Unconquerable, unshaken pillar,
And Kyknos he gave to death,
And the Dawn's Ethiopian son.
    In the quiver under my elbow
85 Are many swift arrows that speak to the wise,
But for the crowd they need interpreters.
He knows, whose blood tells him much;

Mere learners babble, the pair of them,
And like crows chatter vainly against

God's holy bird.
  Now keep the bow on the mark.
  Come, my heart, at whom do we aim
90 And shoot from a gentle heart our shafts of glory?
  At Akragas I draw, and I shall speak
  My words on oath with an honest mind: –
  In a hundred years this city has borne
  No man more lavish in heart to his friends,
  More open of hand,

95 Than Theron. Yet against my praise
  Surfeit advances, not companioned
  By right, but in gluttonous mouths,
  And wishes to make its prattle
  Cover up the fine doings of men.
  – Since sand escapes all counting,
  Of *his* gifts to others
100 Who could recount the tale?

Olympian II was written at about the same time as *Olympian III*, also for Theron, but possibly for a more intimate occasion.

8–10 Theron's ancestors came from Rhodes.

22 The daughters of Kadmos, Semela and Ino, are examples of ill fortune being turned to good.

25–7 Semela, mother of Dionysos, the 'ivy-crowned boy' (27), was killed by lightning.

38 The 'doomed son of Laios' is Oidipous, whose sons, Eteokles and Polyneikes (42), kill one another, but the family survives in Thersandros, who takes part in the War of the Successors after the failure of the Seven against Thebes, who included Adrastos.

49 The brother of Theron is Xenokrates, known from *Pythian VI* and *Isthmian II*.

56–83 Instead of a myth Pindar tells of life after death in language which suggests cults in Sicily and Theron's own beliefs.

59 'One below earth' is the judge of the dead, not named because he is not to be spoken of.

61–6 The abode of the good, with days and nights like ours.

68–80 The Isle of the Blest, with no clear geographical setting.

75 Rhadamanthys, the incarnation of justice, holds rule.

76 The 'great father' is Kronos, who has Rhea at his side.

83 Pindar breaks off his revelations and turns to personalities. Theron must be 'the wise', who will understand what Pindar says. The ancient commentators identify the 'crows' with the poets Simonides and Bacchylides, who were in Sicily at this time.

PYTHIAN III

For Hieron of Syracuse

I

I could wish
That Cheiron, Philyra's son,
(If with my lips I should utter all men's prayer)
Were alive, who is departed,
The lord of wide lands, the seed of Kronos Ouranidas,
– That he ruled in the glades of Pelion, the wild Centaur,
5 With a heart friendly to man:
As he was when he nursed
The gentle worker of sound-limbed painlessness,
Asklapios the hero,
Healer of every sickness.

Him the daughter of Phlegyas the great horseman
Had not brought to birth
With Eleithyia to tend her,
When she was struck by the golden arrows
10 Of Artemis: in her chamber she went down
To the house of Death
By the device of Apollo.
It is not idle, the anger of Zeus' children –
But she,
Making light of it in the folly of her soul,
Must needs wed with another, cheating her sire,
She who had lain already with long-haired Phoibos

15 And bore the God's pure seed.
She would not wait the coming of the marriage-meal
Nor for the shout of many voices,

The Bride's song, that her friends, the girls of her age,
As the night falls, will sing to their playmate.
20 – Not she: she was after what was not there,
As many have been; vain heads all the sort of them,
Who disdain home things and cast their glance afar,
Chasing the empty air, with hopes
Which they cannot attain.

II

Like that was the great blindness of the soul
25 Of lovely-robed Koronis.
For a stranger came
From Arkadia, and she lay in his bed: but the Watcher
saw her.
By the sheep-altar in Pytho, the temple's King
Loxias, standing, was aware of her.
A most instant helper made him sure,
His All-knowing Mind:
Which holds no traffic with lies: no God, no man de-
ceives it
30 Either in word or in plan.

Yea, then he perceived
How with Ischys son of Elatos,
A stranger, she lay, sinning deceitfully,
He sent his sister storming in terrible strength
To Lakereia: for there
Where the hills slope down to Boibias Lake
The girl was dwelling. Changed now was the doom
35 That turned her to evil and overcame her.
Many were they of her neighbours
Who felt that stroke and died with her:
(Much is the timber on the hillside
That fire destroys, leaping from a single seed).

But when her kinsmen set the girl
On the piled logs
40 And the hungry light of the Fire God ran around,
Then Apollo spoke:
'No more can my spirit endure
To destroy my child by this most pitiful death
After his mother's anguish.'
– He spoke, and with one stride came
And out of the dead body snatched the child:
The flaming pyre blazed either side of him.
He bore him away and gave him
45 To the Magnesian Centaur: there he should learn
To heal the divers pains of the sicknesses of men.

III

All who came
Bound fast to sores which their own selves grew,
Or with limbs wounded, by grey bronze
50 Or a far-flung stone, or wasting in body with summer
        fire, or with winter
He, loosing all from their several sorrows,
Delivered them. Some he tended with soft incantations,
Some had juleps to drink,
Or round about their limbs he laid his simples,
And for some the knife: so he set all up straight.

Yet even Wisdom
Is in bondage to gain. Him too
55 A princely wage seduced, when the gold
Gleamed in his hand,
To raise from the dead
A man whom death had taken.
But Kronos' son
Cast with his hands at the two of them:

Quickly he tore the breath out of their breasts
And the blazing thunderbolt drove death home.
– We must ask from the Gods
Things suited to hearts that shall die,
60 Knowing the path we are in, the nature of our doom.

Dear soul of mine, for immortal days
Trouble not: the help that is to be had
Drain to the last. And yet, if only
Wise Cheiron were still living in his cave,
And the honey of our songs laid a spell on his soul,
65 O surely I had moved him to send, even now,
One that should heal good men
From burning sicknesses,
One called Son of Latoïdas or of the Father.
I would have ploughed the Ionian Sea
And come by ship to the Fountain of Arethoisa,
To my friend of Aitna town;

IV

70 Who reigns in Syracuse
A King, kind to his people, not envying merit,
To strangers a marvellous father.
Could I have landed with double delight for him,
With a golden gift of health,
And a triumph to make bright the Pythian crowns,
Which Pherenikos the conqueror horse
Won at the games
In Krisa once –
75 No star in heaven, I say, had then shone farther
Than I, as I came from crossing the deep sea.

But I wish to make my vow to the Mother.
To her and Pan the Maidens sing

Before my house,
Goddess of awe, in the nights.
80 And you, Hieron,
Having the wit to know
What sayings are sharp and true, have learned the old
proverb:
'With every blessing God gives a pair of curses.'
This is what fools cannot bear with decency;
But good men can, and turn the fair part outwards.

Your portion of Felicity attends you.
85 On the Prince who rules his people, if on any,
Is the eye of mighty Fate,
Untroubled life.
Neither Peleus had, the son of Aiakos,
Nor godlike Kadmos.
These two, they say, had the utmost bliss of men:
They heard the Muses
90 Singing, with gold in their hair,
On that mountain and in seven-gated Thebes
(When one
Married soft-eyed Harmonia, and one Thetis,
Wise Nereus' golden child)

V

And with both the Gods feasted. They saw those Kings,
The sons of Kronos, sitting on golden thrones,
And took their marriage-gifts.
95 Through the favour of Zeus, they put from them
Their former sorrows, and set their hearts up straight.
– But time passed on: and from Kadmos
Three of his daughters, by their sharp anguish,
Took away his share of delight,
– Though father Zeus came to the lovely bed

Of white-armed Thyona –

100 And Peleus' son, the only son
Whom immortal Thetis bore to him in Phthia,
Killed by an arrow in battle, was burned with fire
And woke the Danaans' tears.
    If any man understands the way of truth,
When the Blessed Ones send him aught,
He must needs be happy.
105 Many are the high-flying winds, and blow many ways:
Man's bliss does not go steady for long
When it follows him with all its weight.

I will be little when little is my circumstance
And great when it is great. What doom,
Now or to come, attends me,
By that I shall set my heart, and serve it after my
    measure.
110 If God should give me the luxury of wealth,
I think surely I should know
Thenceforth the heights of fame.
    Of Nestor and the Lykian Sarpedon,
Those household names,
The loud lines speak, which craftsmen built with skill,
And thence we know them.
Greatness in noble songs
115 Endures through time: but to win this, few find easy.

Pythian III, written about 474 B.C., is not an Epinician but a poetical
epistle to Hieron, who is ill and has asked Pindar to visit him in Sicily.
Pindar, with some elaboration, refuses.

1–60 The double myth of Koronis and her child, Asklapios, illustrates
the danger of trying to pass beyond the proper limits for men, and
enforces Pindar's advice that Hieron should not indulge too strong hopes
of recovery.

124

THE ODES OF PINDAR

8 The daughter of Phlegyas is Koronis, who, when with child by Apollo, promises to marry Ischys.

26 The stranger is Ischys.

28 In earlier versions Apollo heard the news from a raven.

32 Apollo sends Artemis to kill the guilty couple.

45 The child, Asklapios, is given to Cheiron to be educated.

54 Asklapios is bribed to raise a man from the dead, and is punished for it.

61 Pindar addresses himself, but what he says is more relevant to Hieron.

74 The horse Pherenikos is celebrated in *Olympian I*.

77 Pindar explains that he cannot come to Syracuse because he is busy with the cult of Pan and the Great Mother (Kybele). This would be taken seriously.

110 Pindar suggests that he would like a handsome reward, but leaves it not very explicit. It is possible that this was prompted by the large fine inflicted on him by the Thebans for praising Athens.

PYTHIAN II

PYTHIAN II

For Hieron of Syracuse

I

Mighty City of Syracuse!
Where Ares dwells in depths of war,
Where men and horses mailed for battle
Have holy nurture, to you I come
Bringing from shining Thebes this song. I tell
5   How, where the teams of four horses made earth tremble,
Hieron and his good chariot conquered
And wreathed Ortygia with far-shining crowns,
Where the Lady of Rivers, Artemis, dwells.
She failed him not
When with light hand on the embroidered reins
He broke those young mares in.

For she, archeress maiden, with either hand,
10   And Hermes, Lord of the Games,
Put on the bright harness, when to the smooth car
And the axle that follows the rein
He yokes the strong mares,
And calls on the Trident-lifter, the far-felt God.
  For one or another king a poet makes
The clear-voiced hymn, the due of his greatness.
Often in Kypros they celebrate with song
15   Kinyras, whom Apollo the golden-haired
Delighted to love,

And Aphrodita stalled him in her temple.
Their songs are of thanks and worship
For the labours of his love.

But your name, O son of Deinomenes,
The girl of Lokris-in-the-West
Sings on her doorstep: after the toils and despairs of war
20 Because of your strength her eyes are steadfast.
    They say that Ixion, commanded by the Gods,
Speaks thus to man, on his winged wheel turning all
      ways:
'Thou shalt be zealous for him that does thee service
And pay him gentle return.'

II

25 He learned that surely. Among Kronos' kindly sons
Lapped in sweet ease, he stayed not long in bliss,
Fool in his wits!
Who loved Hera, her that is set apart
For the mighty joys of Zeus. But pride drove him
To blind presumptuous folly.
30 He suffered soon his due, getting a choice award of woe.
His two sins live and bring him misery: one
That he, a hero, first and with guile
Brought kindred blood upon men,

The other that in the great darkness of a bridal chamber
He tempted the wife of Zeus.
(Let a man, when he measures,
Remember his own size!) His lawless love
35 Cast him into great depths of evil
When he came to her bed: for he lay by the side of a
      Cloud,
Clasping a sweet lie, ignorant man.
Its shape was like the most mighty daughter of Kronos
The son of Heaven.
40 The hands of Zeus made it,
To snare him, a lovely sorrow.

And so, bound to the four spokes,

He got his own ruin.
Thrown in fetters he shall not escape, he proclaims
His universal message.
Far were the Graces when the Cloud
Bore him a monstrous issue,
She like nothing, and like nothing It;
Which found no favour among men, nor in
The company of the Gods.
She nursed It and called It Kentauros: and It lay
45   With the Magnesian mares on Pelion's foot-hills.
And a race was born
Prodigious, in the image of both parents,
Their nether parts of the mother, their father's above.

III

God reaches, as soon as thought, his ends:
50   God, who can catch the winged eagle
And overtakes the dolphin in the sea.
He can bring down any whose heart is high,
And to others he will give unaging splendour.
But I
Must keep from the sharp bites of slander:
For far in the past I see
55   Archilochos the scold in poverty,
Fattening his leanness with hate and heavy words.
Wealth, and the fortune
To be wise as well, is best.

And that, men see, is yours.
Your free heart displays it,
Sovran master of the many streets
Which crown your city, and of a host of men.
And if anyone says

That riches like that and such great glory
60 Were ever yet surpassed by the older Hellenes,
The fond fool struggles in vain.
I will climb to the flowery bows
And make noise of your greatness.
Youth asks for courage in the terrors of war:
And thence you won
Your infinite renown.

65 Fighting now in the charging cavalry,
Now with the men on foot.
Your riper age's wisdom
Gives me a theme, where without peril I sound
The whole gamut of praise.
    Good-bye. This song
I am sending, like a Phoenician merchant, over the grey
    sea.
And on the Kastoreion's Aeolian mood, so please you,
Look: turn to it, if ever
70 You liked my seven-stringed harp.
O find, and be, yourself! 'O that
Lovely ape!' cry the children, 'O how

IV

Lovely!' But Rhadamanthys has found bliss,
Because his judgement bore him fruit without cavil,
And his heart in him has no pleasure in lies,
75 The constant retinue of crafty whispering men.
    – Whom you cannot fight, and they spoil two lives,
Sly hinters of slander,
Their minds exceedingly like foxes' minds.
    Yet Lady Vixen was not so cunning for once –
Let the rest of the tackle toil in the sea's depth, I
80 Am the cork that rides the surge. I'll get no ducking!

He cannot throw his word like a man
In honest company, your twisting knave –
He fawns upon all, weaving fine threads of mischief.
My boldness is not his. Let me love my friend,
But if I must fight my foe, I'll be wolf and make for his legs,
85 I'll be here and there, and twist and turn!
And yet, whoever governs, way is made
For the straight-spoken man;
Where one is king, or when a city is overwatched
By the brute multitude, or by the wise.
No man must fight with God,

Who exalts now those, then to others anon
He will give great splendour. But that
90 Is little comfort for envious minds.
They strain at a course they cannot stay,
And the sharp wound is in their heart, or ever
Their careful schemes come right.
Let them take the yoke on their neck
And bear it lightly: it were best.
95 To kick against the goads is the way
To come sprawling. – May I have the regard
Of the noble, and be with them.

Pythian II, like *Pythian III* and *Isthmian II*, is not a true Epinician but a poetical letter, sent probably in 468 B.C. to Hieron who has just won the chariot-race at Olympia and asked not Pindar but Bacchylides to celebrate it. Pindar attributes this rebuff to slanderers at Hieron's Court and, while protesting his admiration and affection for Hieron, lets himself go in denouncing these sycophants.

3 Pindar writes the poem in Thebes and sends it to Syracuse.

4–8 To win the chariot-race at Olympia was regarded as the highest possible success.

9 The 'archeress maiden' is Artemis.

12 The 'Trident-lifter' is Poseidon.

15 Kinyras is mentioned as an example of a man whom the Gods love. He was a priest-king at Paphos in Kypros and loved alike by Apollo and Aphrodite.

18-20 Hieron has recently saved Western Lokris from Kroton.

31-2 Ixion killed his father-in-law, Eioneus, but was forgiven by the Gods.

21-48 Myth of Ixion, on the theme of ingratitude. Pindar seems to indicate with what horror he regards it and so disclaims being guilty of it. We may also detect a latent hint that Hieron is more likely to be guilty of ingratitude than Pindar.

33-4 Ixion assaults Hera, but a cloud takes her place, from which (42 ff.) a monstrous being, Kentauros, is born. From this and the mares on Pelion are born the Centaurs. Kentauros is Pindar's own invention, intended to soften the violence of the Centaurs' origin.

53 ff. Pindar does not wish to be accused of having a sharp tongue, and quotes the sad precedent of Archilochos, a poet of the early seventh century, who was renowned for his savage quarrels.

68 The song sent by Pindar 'like a Phoenician merchant' comes, as it were, on approval, to remind Hieron of what kind of poet Pindar is.

69 Pindar asks Hieron to look at some earlier song that he has written for him.

72 Hieron must be his true self on the lines of the Delphic motto 'Know thyself'.

72 The sudden break in the tone and sequence indicates the degree of Pindar's resentment. The ancient commentators say that the ape is Bacchylides, who wrote his *Ode V* for this occasion and certainly imitates Pindar in what might be thought an ape-like way.

73 Against the slanderers Pindar sets Rhadamanthys, judge of the dead, as the ideal of fairness and honesty.

78 The slanderers do themselves no good, and Pindar is untouched by them.

86 Pindar will speak his mind freely, no matter what the form of government is.

90 The slanderers again. It is not quite clear in what pursuit they hurt themselves, and the point of the words is that in Greek 'strain' and 'wound' echo the same sound.

NEMEAN X

For Theaios of Argos, a wrestler

I

The city of Danaos
And his fifty daughters on shining thrones,
Sing of it, Graces,
Of Argos, home of Hera, fit for the Gods.
It is aflame with glories past number
Because of bold doings.
Long are the tales of what Perseus did to the Gorgon
    Medoisa,
5 And many the cities of Egypt founded by Epaphos' hands;
Nor went Hypermestra astray
When she kept in its sheath
Her single, dissentient sword.

Once the fair Bright-eyed One
Made Diomedes a god undying,
And at Thebes the earth,
Thunderstruck with the bolts of Zeus,
Swallowed Oikleës' son, the battle's cloud.
10 In lovely-haired women it is first from of old;
Zeus proved the truth of this
When he came to Alkmana and to Danaä.
In Adrastos' father and in Lynkeus he grafted
The heart's fruit on upstanding right.

He nursed the spear of Amphitryon,
Who was foremost in fortune and came to kinship with
    him,

15 When in armour of bronze he spoiled the Teleboai.
In his likeness the King of Immortals came into his
    palace
And brought the unconquerable seed of Herakles,
Whose bride Youth walks on Olympus
At the side of the Mother, the Match-maker,
Most beautiful of goddesses.

II

My breath is too short to rehearse all the fine things
20 That belong to the precinct of Argos;
The boredom of men is heavy to counter.
Nevertheless, awake the fine strings of the harp
And turn your thoughts to wrestling.
The brazen struggle hurries the people
To the sacrifice of oxen to Hera
And the verdict of the Games,
Where Theaios, son of Oulias, conquered twice,
And found forgetfulness of toils he had lightly borne.

25 Once he routed the host of Hellas at Pytho,
And fortunate was his coming
To the crown at the Isthmos and Nemea.
He gave ploughland to the Muses
When he won three times in the gates of the sea,
Three times by Adrastos' rules on holy ground.
Father Zeus, on his heart's desire his lips are silent;
Every end of doing rests with thee –
30 But not with a sluggard's heart
Does he ask for favour wrongly,
But brings endurance with him.

I sing what is known to him
And to all who strive for the peaks of the highest Games.

The foremost, which Herakles founded, belongs to Pisa,
Yet in prelude sweet Athenian voices
Have twice extolled him in their festivals;
35 And in fire-baked clay the olive's fruit
Has come to Hera's people of noble men
In the pots' richly patterned walls.

III

Over the far-famed race
Of your mother's clan, Theaios,
Watches renown for success in the Games,
With the Graces often to help and Tyndareos' sons.
40 If I were kin of Thrasyklos and Antias,
I should hold it right
Not to veil the light of my eyes from Argos.
For with how many victories
Has this horse-breeding city of Proitos burst into flower
In the Gulf of Korinth,
And four times over the men of Kleonai.

From Sikyon they came silvered with wine-cups,
From Pellana with clothes of soft wool on their backs.
45 But I cannot add up the multitudinous bronze,
– It takes too long to count –
Which Kleitor and Tegea,
The Achaians' high-set towns and the Lykaian Hill,
Set in the race-track of Zeus
To be won by strong feet and hands.

Since Kastor and his brother Polydeukes
50 Came to be guests of Pamphaes,
It is no wonder that this race begets good athletes.
For they who watch over Sparta's broad places,
With Hermes and Herakles,
Make the rule of the Games to prosper,

And care for good men exceedingly. Truly
The breed of the Gods may be trusted.

IV

55 Turn and turn about they pass
One day with their loving father Zeus,
The other hidden by earth in Therapna's caverns,
And fulfil a like fate.
This life, and not to be fully a god and live in the sky,
Polydeukes chose, when Kastor was killed in war.
60 For Idas, in anger over some oxen,
Struck him with a spear's bronze point.

Lynkeus looked out from Taygetos
And saw them sitting in an oak's dry trunk;
For his eye was the sharpest of all on earth.
With racing feet they came at once and quickly
Devised a great enterprise,
And Zeus worked terrible suffering for them,
65 The sons of Aphareus.
For straightway in chase came Leda's son,
And they stood on defence by their father's tomb.

From it they ripped Death's ornament,
A polished stone,
And flung it on Polydeukes' breast.
But they did not break him or drive him back.
With his quick spear he jumped upon them
70 And drove the bronze into Lynkeus' lungs;
And on Idas Zeus threw a fiery smoking thunderbolt.

V

To his strong brother quickly came back Tyndareos' son
And found him not yet dead

But shaking with gasps in his breath.
75 He let hot tears fall and lifted his voice in lament:
'Father Kronion, what release shall there be from
    sorrows?
Give death to me also, Master, with him.
Honour goes from one who has lost his friends,
And in trouble few among men may be trusted

To share in suffering.' He spoke,
And Zeus came before him
80 And spoke this word clearly:
'You are my son,
But this man was begotten of mortal seed
By his hero father,
Who drew after me to your mother.
Yet now I give you this choice:
If you would escape from death and from hated old age
And dwell on Olympus with me
And with Athana and with black-speared Ares,

85 This lot may be yours.
But if you fight for your brother,.
And are minded to share with him in all things alike,
You may live half beneath the earth,
And half in the sky's golden palaces.'
He spoke, and Polydeukes set
No double counsel in his heart,
90 But freed the eye, and then the voice
Of bronze-belted Kastor.

Nemean X seems to have been written about 464 B.C. for an Argive who
won not at Nemea but in local games at the festival of Hera.

1–18 The first triad deals with the glories of Argos.

1 Danaos was the father of fifty daughters, of whom all but one was
forced to marry an Egyptian suitor.

NEMEAN X

4 Perseus was born in Argos.

5 Epaphos, the son of Io, founded Memphis and other Egyptian cities.

6 Hypermestra was the only daughter of Danaos who did not kill her suitor but married him.

7 Athana made Diomedes a god in the Adriatic.

8–9 Amphiaraos, son of Oikleës, was swallowed up in the earth in the war of the Seven against Thebes.

11 Alkmana, wife of Amphitryon, bears Herakles to Zeus.

12 Talaos is father of Adrastos, Lynkeus the son of Aphareus, both renowned for their wisdom.

15 Zeus begets Herakles by assuming the likeness of Amphitryon who is away fighting the Teleboai.

19–36 The second triad tells of the victories won by Theaios.

24 Oulias is father of Theaios.

28 The Adrastos games were at Argos.

35–6 The prizes at Athens were painted pots.

37–54 The third triad tells of victories won by the family of Theaios.

49–54 A connexion is made between the present victor and the Dioskouroi. In the past Pamphaes used to entertain them. With Hermes and Herakles they look after games.

55–90 The last two triads tell the story of the last fight of the Dioskouroi against the sons of Aphareus, Idas and Lynkeus.

60 Pindar hurries past the real reason for the quarrel, which included women as well as oxen.

62 Lynkeus sees the Dioskouroi from a great distance.

72 Tyndareos' son is Polydeukes, who comes to the help of Kastor.

90 Polydeukes' decision brings his brother back to life.

PYTHIAN IV

For Arkesilas of Kyrene, winner in the chariot-race

I

Today, Muse, you must stand by the side of a friend,
By the King of Kyrene, the land of good horses:
And when Arkesilas holds his triumph
Swell the gale of your songs,
Paying your debt to Lato's Twins, and to Pytho,
5 Where once, when Apollo was in his land,
The priestess – she who sits by the gold eagles of Zeus –
Ordained Battos a leader of men
Into fruitful Libya.
He must straightway leave his holy island
And build a city
Of charioteers
On a silver breast of the earth.

To bring back the word of Medeia
10 In the seventeenth generation,
Which at Thera once Aietas' terrible child
Breathed from immortal lips, the Kolchians' Queen –
And thus she spoke:
To the seed of Gods, to the sailors of Jason the fighter:
'Hear, sons of high-hearted men and of Gods!
I tell you, from this wave-beaten land shall go
A stock, and shall beteem the daughter of Epaphos,
And cities shall rise
15 And the world know it
In the place where Zeus Ammon stands.

Instead of the short-finned dolphins

They shall have swift horses, and reins for oars:
They shall drive the stormfoot chariots.
The Omen, that shall make
20 Thera mother-city of mighty cities,
Was given, where Lake Tritonis flows to the sea,
To Euphamos once
(A guest-gift from the God in a man's likeness)
A Clod. Euphamos, alighting from the bows,
Took it, and Father Zeus, the son of Kronos,
Well pleased rang out in thunder.

II

He found us slinging the bronze-jawed anchor
25 Beside the prow, swift Argo's bridle.
I had bidden them haul her, our sea-timber, ashore,
And he had borne her from Ocean
Twelve days across earth's lonely ridges.
Out of his solitudes then
The God appeared
Clothed in the bright shape of a reverend lord:
30 And friendly words he began,
As a good host when strangers come,
Begins with his offers of supper.

But we spoke of our sweet road home
And could not stay. He told us his name
Eurypylos, son of the undying
Shaker and Holder of Earth.
And he knew our hurry: and there and then
35 Took a clod in his right hand, fain to offer
What gift he could;
And the hero did not refuse it.
He leaped to the beach, and clasping hand in hand
Took the piece of earth divine, –

But a wave broke,
I hear, and washed it
Overboard into the sea

40 At evening, and it went with the waters of the deep.
O often I bade the servants we had for our ease
Keep it safe: but their souls forgot.
So now against this isle has been washed
The undying seed of Libya's wide meadows,
Out of due time.
For had he come home, and cast it
Beside Hell's mouth in the earth,
Had he come to holy Tainaros, – he
Euphamos, son of Poseidon the captain of horse,
45 Born on Kaphisos' banks of Europa, Tityos' child, –

III

Then the blood of his grandsons' grandsons after him,
With a Danaan host, had taken that wide mainland.
For then, behold!
Men coming from great Lakedaimon,
From the gulf of Argos and from Mykenai!
50 – But now, he shall lie with foreign women
And get a chosen race: who shall come to this island
(For the Gods will care for them)
And have a son to be lord
Of those dark-clouded plains.
Him one day
In that gold-stored House
Phoibos shall tell in oracles

55 (When in later days he comes down to the Pythian
       shrine)
To carry cities in ships
To the land where Neilos dwells, the son of Kronos.'

Medeia's words filed past: and the godlike heroes
Kept silent and still, and bowed their heads,
Listening to her deep wisdom.
    O happy son of Polymnastos!
To you, as was here foretold,
The oracle of the Delphic Bee gave glory
60 In her unprompted cry,
Bidding you three times 'Hail!'
Foreshown
Kyrene's King to be.

(You were asking
About your stammering tongue, might the Gods
    release you.)
And later in time, even today,
There flowers, as when spring puts out her reddest
    blossoms,
65 The eighth generation, Arkesilas.
He has got from Apollo, and from Pytho
A name for chariot-driving
Among the peoples around.
I will offer to the Muses
Him, and the Ram's Fleece of Gold.
For the Minyai sailed to find it; and from that root
Sprang up the honours of the house
About whose goings is God.

IV

70 What was the beginning of their voyage?
And what danger held them in strong adamantine bolts?
– It was appointed that Pelias
Must die by the hands of Aiolos' proud sons
Or their unrelenting counsels.
A prophecy came to him, chilling his wary heart,

Spoken at the midmost navel-stone
Of earth, fair-forested mother:
75 'Let him beware at all costs
The man with one sandal,
When he comes from the steadings in the hills
To the sunny plains of great Iolkos,

Stranger be he or townsman.' In time he came,
With two spears, a terrible man.
And he wore two kinds of clothing:
80 The garment of the Magnesian land
Fitted close on his marvellous limbs,
And a leopard-skin over it
Kept off the shivering rains.
His bright locks of hair, not cut and cast away,
Flamed all down his back.
And at once, when he came,
He stood testing his never-flinching heart
85 Where the people thronged in the main square.

None knew him: yet despite their amazement
Thus spoke one:
'This is not Apollo, I think,
No, nor Aphrodita's bronze-charioted lord,
And they say that in bright Naxos
The sons of Iphimedeia died,
Otos, and you, daring lord Ephialtas:
90 And the swift arrow of Artemis
Caught Tityos, sped from that unconquered quiver,
That a man be fain to choose
Attainable loves'

V

So they spoke
One to another in question and answer.

But then drove up, with his mules and burnished car,
95 Pelias, in headlong haste.
Amazed at once he stared and knew well
The single sandal on the right foot.
But he hid his fear in his heart, and said:
'What sort of country do you say is yours, O
        stranger?
And pray, what gutter-bred wench
Dropped you from her aged womb?
100 No loathsome, filthy lies, but tell me your race.'

And the other answered without fear and gently:
'Cheiron I name my master
And men shall see it. I come from the cave,
From Chariklo and Philyra,
The Centaur's holy daughters who nursed me.
I have brought twenty years to an end, and in them
105 Have done, nor said, nothing to shame me.
And I have come home
Claiming the ancient honour of my father
(Now against right overruled)
Which Zeus once gave
To Aiolos and his sons.

I am told that Pelias the transgressor
Gave way to his pale heart
110 And stole this by force
From my parents, who ruled of right.
When the sun first opened my eyes, they feared
That violent prince's malice:
So they darkened the house and made a keening
As if I had died,
And amongst the wailing of women
Stealthily they sent me away
In swaddling bands of purple,

115 And Night knew the secret of our road.
So they gave me to Cheiron, Kronos' son, for nurture.

VI

You have heard the sum of my story.
But where
Is the house of my fathers that rode white horses?
Good citizens, tell me clearly.
I am Aison's son, a man of the land,
Nor am I come to a strange country
Belonging to others.
By my name Jason the godlike Beast addressed me.'
120 He spoke; and when he went in, his father's eyes
Knew him, and tears welled down
From his old eyelids:
For in his soul
He was glad, seeing
His chosen son, the fairest of men.

And his two brothers came to that house
125 At the fame of the man. From near
Pheras came, leaving the fountain Hypereia,
From Messana Amythaon.
And soon Admatos came and Melampos,
For their hearts yearned to their cousin.
– With due feasting, and words honey-sweet,
Jason their host made pleasant entertainment
130 And long stretched-out delight, five nights
Without ceasing
And five days
Gathering the great luxurious hours.

But on the sixth day, with sober words
He let his kinsman know all from the beginning:
And they gave him heed,

And he leaped up quickly from his couch, and they with
    him,
And went to Pelias' hall
135 And made haste and stood within.
When the King heard them, himself came forth to them,
The son of Tyro, lovely-haired queen;
And Jason with soft voice, let smooth words fall,
Laying a foundation of wise speech:
'Son of Poseidon of the Rock,

VII

The hearts of men are perhaps too quick
140 At choosing a smart advantage rather than right
(Though the next day the taste is wry in the mouth).
But I and you must rule our wrath
And weave our future fortune.
You know as well as I, one womb
Bore Kretheus and Salmoneus hardy in cunning,
From whom in the third generation ourselves sprang,
Who look on the golden strength of the sun.
145 – The Fates recoil
When men of one blood
Hating each other, lose sight of shame.

We must not take, you and I,
Swords of biting bronze or javelins
To divide our father's honours.
The sheep and the tawny herds of oxen
I yield you, and all the fields,
150 Which you stole from my parents and live on,
Fattening your substance.
Nourish with these your house, it irks me little.
But there is the sceptre of absolute rule,
And the throne on which the son of Kretheus sat

And gave straight judgements
To a people of horsemen.
To spare both of us sorrow

155 Let me have these;
And no fresh evil come of them!'
– So he spoke: and gently too
Pelias answered him:
'I will do as you say.
But already the sere end of life attends me
And your youth bursts into flower.
You have power to lay the wrath of those in earth.
160 Phrixos is calling, that someone redeem his ghost,
And, going to the halls of Aietas, fetch
The thick-piled Fleece
Of the Ram, by whom he was saved of old
From the sea,

VIII

And from the godless knives of his step-mother.
A marvellous dream came and told me of this.
I have asked the oracle of Kastalia:
"Shall I follow this up?", and he bids me find
At once the crew for a ship.
165 – Achieve this task, so please you; and I swear
I will let you be sole ruler and king.
Let Him be our strong oath,
Zeus the Witness, the father of both our races.'
So they approved
This covenant:
And these two parted, but as for Jason, already

170 He was sending messengers everywhere
That a quest was afoot.
– And soon there came, that never tired of battle,

The sons of Zeus Kronidas,
Of Alkmana of the dancing eyelids and of Leda:
And two tall-crested men, the Earth-Shaker's seed,
In the proudness of valour,
From Pylos and Cape Tainaros:
– Fair was the fame they won,
175 Euphamos, and you, strong Periklymenos.
From Apollo's house
The lute-player came,
The father of songs, ever-worshipped Orpheus.

Hermes of the golden wand
Sent his twin sons to that long stretch of labour,
Echion one (O loud exultation of youth),
The other Erytos. Quick came two
180 Who dwelt round the roots of Pangaion:
For gladly with laughing heart and swiftly
Their father Boreas, King of Winds,
Sent Zetes and Kalaïs – men,
Yet scarlet feathers ruffled upon their backs.
And in these sons of Gods Hera kindled
That all-persuading sweet desire

IX

185 For the ship Argo, that none be left behind
To nurse at his mother's side a ventureless life,
But, even though he die,
Find in his own valour the fairest enchantment
With others young as he.
   They came to the port of Iolkos, the finest of sailors,
And Jason marshalled all, and approved them.
190 And the seer Mopsos, that watched the Gods' will for him
In birds and holy sortilege,
Bade with good heart

148

THE ODES OF PINDAR

The host be started.
They hung the anchor over the prow; and then

The Captain at the stern
Held in his hands a gold cup, and called
On the Father of the Sons of Heaven,
Zeus, whose spear is the lightning,
195 On the swift rushing of the waves, the winds,
On the nights and the paths of the sea;
For days of kind weather, and the sweet road home at
    last.
From the clouds answered back to him
The assenting voice of thunder,
And the lightnings flashed and tore the sky.
The heroes found fresh breath of courage,
For they believed
The omens of God.
200 The Seer of Signs called to them

To fall to the oars,
And he put sweet hopes into them: under their rapid
    hands
The oars insatiably fell and rose.
A south wind blew, and before it
They reached the Unwelcoming Sea.
They marked a holy acre there
For Poseidon of the Deep
205 And there was a red herd of Thracian bulls
And a hollow altar newly fashioned of stone.
    They were running toward deep danger
And prayed to the Lord of Ships

X

To escape the awful onset
Of the Clashing Rocks. Two they were, and alive,

And they rolled swifter
210 Than the howling winds charge past.
But that sailing of the sons of Gods
Brought them to an end.
    After that they came to the River Phasis
And matched their might
Among the dark-faced Kolchians,
In the very presence of Aietas.
But from Olympos the Queen of sharpest arrows
Bound past loosing
The dappled wryneck
215 To the four spokes of a wheel:

She, the Kypros-born, for the first time brought
The maddening bird to men.
She taught Aison's wise son
What sorceries he must chant, and Medeia forget
To honour those who begot her,
And her heart be all on fire for lovely Hellas
And tremble under the lash of love.
220 She showed him at once
How to achieve his father's tasks:
With olive-oil she made an enchantment against hard
    pains
And gave it to him for anointing.
And they swore to make a sweet marriage one with
    another.

But when Aietas
Dragged forth the adamantine plough in the midst of
    them
225 And the oxen who breathed from yellow nostrils
A flame of burning fire,
And hoof after bronze-shod hoof ripped up the ground –
He took them and forced them to the yoke

Alone, and straight was the furrow he ploughed as he
    drove them:
He cast up the clods, and clove earth's back
230 A fathom deep; and thus he spoke:
'Let the King do this, the captain of the ship!
Let him do this, I say,
And have for his own the immortal coverlet,

XI

The Fleece, glowing with matted skeins of gold.'
He spoke; and Jason
Threw off his saffron clothing, and trusting in God
Assayed the task.
And the fire did not make him flinch,
Through the strange woman's words, that strong
    enchantress.
He, grasping the plough,
235 Harnessed perforce the oxen's necks, and driving
In those huge flanks a steady goad
With violence he achieved the appointed distance.
And, speechless through
His grief, Aietas
Howled in amazement at his might.

To the mighty man his comrades
240 Stretched out their hands, and gathered grass to crown
    him:
With sweet words they caressed him.
Then the Sun's wondrous child
Told him where the shining Skin
Had been stretched by Phrixos' sword (and there
Was a labour where, he hoped, he yet may fail).
It lay in a snake's den,
Caught on the monster's raging teeth

245 That was thicker and longer
Than a ship
Of fifty oars
Made by the smiting iron.

The journey is long on the high road:
Time presses me, and I know a short path,
(In the wisdom of song I am the leader of many).
– He slew by cunning
The snake with glaring eyes and bright-scaled back;
250 O Arkesilas,
He stole Medeia, she willing, – she, who was Pelias'
death.
They came to the depths of Ocean, to the Red Sea,
To the Land of Lemnians,
Women the slayers of men.
There in bodily games they proved their might
(A garment for the prize)

XII

And there they wedded. Then it was, in foreign furrows
255 A day, or a night,
Received the destined seed
Of your house's sunlike fortune.
For then the race of Euphamos took root,
Growing thereafter always higher.
They mixed first in Lakedaimon's dwellings,
They went to live in the island
Once called Loveliest.
And after that Lato's son
Gave you Libya's plain, for the Gods love you,
260 To enrich and govern
The holy city
Of Kyrene on her throne of gold

Since judgement and right counsel are yours.
　Try now the Art of Oidipous.
If a man with a keen axe-blade
Lops the branches of a great oak,
Defiling the beauty that men gazed at –
265　Though its fruit has perished, yet it gives
Witness of itself, when it comes at last
In winter to the fire,
Or rests on the upright pillars of a master,
Doing sad labour in a stranger's house
While its own land is desolate.

270　– But you can heal in the very nick of time.
You give light, and Paian adds honour to it.
Stretch out a gentle hand, to tend
A sore wound.
It is easy even for weaker men than you
To shake a city, but hard indeed
To set it back in the land,
Unless a God be suddenly there, the pilot of kings.
275　For you
The web of these bright years is being woven.
Have patience for the sake of Kyrene's happiness
To give it all your care.

XIII

Remember a saying of Homer's, and cherish it –
'A good messenger,' he said, 'heightens
The honour of any errand.'
Even the Muse's stature
Is more, if she be well reported.
There was known in Kyrene
280　And to that most famous hall of Battos
A man of just heart, Damophilos,

PYTHIAN IV

Young in the eyes of boys, but in counsel
An old man with a hundred garner'd years,
He robs of loudness
The slanderous tongue.
He has learned to hate the insolent,

285 He does not strive counter to the good,
None of his purposes tarry; for very swift
Is the Moment for a man.
He has seen it: Time is his servant now, and not running
away.
– They say there is nothing more sorrowful
Than to see joy and stand perforce outside.
290 Atlas indeed still wrestles with the sky
Far from his father's country and his possessions:
Yet deathless Zeus
Set free the Titans.
In time the wind sags, and we hoist

New sails. – But now, he cries,
He has done with foul illness at last, and he sees home.
Near Apollo's fountain
295 He shall lie at the feast, and yield his heart to youth
Often, and playing his painted harp,
Where men know music, shall touch the hands of peace:
Giving sorrow to none, and having
No wrong from his fellow-townsmen.
And perhaps he will tell, Arkesilas,
What a well of immortal words he found
When lately a guest at Thebes.

Pythian IV celebrates the same victory as *Pythian V* but seems to have
been sung at the court of Arkesilas. It is by far the longest of Pindar's
surviving poems and owes something to the epic despite its formal
lyrical art.

1–8 The poem begins with recalling the occasion on which the first Battos was told by the Delphic Oracle to found a city in Africa.

9–69 The Prelude. Through a prophecy once spoken by Medeia Pindar explains why North Africa was not colonized much earlier by Greeks. Her prophecy was fulfilled much later when men from Thera, where the prophecy was given and where Battos was born, went to Africa.

14 The 'daughter of Epaphos' is Libya.

16 Zeus Ammon had an oracular temple in an oasis in the desert.

19 The omen is about to be mentioned – the clod offered to Euphamos. It is a sign that the Argonauts will rule Africa, but when it is washed away at sea (38 ff.) the prophecy is delayed. The promise comes from Eurypylos, son of Poseidon.

43 ff. If Euphamos had placed the clod in the holy cave at Tainaron, Greeks would have colonized Africa in four generations from then.

50 ff. As it is, events have had to wait for Battos to be sent by Apollo.

64 The preliminaries being finished, Pindar prepares the way for his myth – the quest of the Golden Fleece. It is told as a story for its own sake and because Arkesilas is descended from an Argonaut.

70–254 The tale of the quest.

89 Otos and Ephialtas, sons of Poseidon, renowned for their size and beauty.

119 'the godlike Beast' is Cheiron.

120 Jason's father is Aison.

135 The son of Tyro is Pelias.

152 The son of Kretheus is Aison.

159–62 Phrixos was saved by the ram with a golden fleece from being drowned at sea, as his step-mother, who was in love with him, wished. The ram's fleece was in Kolchis, strongly guarded.

208–10 The Argonauts pass safely through the Symplegades or Clashing Rocks.

214 Aphrodita uses the wryneck to work a magical spell on Medeia and make her fall in love with Jason.

247 The myth really ends with the recovery of the Fleece, but Pindar touches lightly on some later events.

250 Medeia killed Pelias by claiming to rejuvenate him by magic.

258 The island called Loveliest is Thera.

262 Pindar changes his direction and sets a riddle. It concerns a kinsman of the king, one Damophilos, who recently conspired against Arkesilas and is now in exile in Greece. There Pindar met him, and he now pleads for clemency to him. The riddle of the oak means that Damophilos can be either wasted or turned to a profitable use.

270 Now is the time to heal the wound.

277 The actual words of Homer come from *Iliad XIV*, 207, 'this too is a good thing, when a messenger says what is fitting'.

290 If Zeus relented about the Titans, Arkesilas can about Damophilos.

We do not know what happened, but Pindar's hopes were not fulfilled, since soon afterwards Arkesilas was killed by his own people.

Aeschylus,
Prometheus Bound

PROMETHEUS BOUND

*

*

A rocky mountain-top, within sight of the sea.
Enter STRENGTH *and* VIOLENCE, *dragging in* PROMETHEUS.*
HEPHAESTUS *follows.*

STRENGTH: Here we have reached the remotest region of the earth,
  The haunt of Scythians, a wilderness without a footprint.
  Hephaestus, do your duty. Remember what command
  The Father laid on you. Here is Prometheus, the rebel:
  Nail him to the rock; secure him on this towering summit
  Fast in the unyielding grip of adamantine chains.
  It was your treasure that he stole, the flowery splendour
  Of all-fashioning fire, and gave to men – an offence
  Intolerable to the gods, for which he now must suffer,
  Till he be taught to accept the sovereignty of Zeus
  And cease acting as champion of the human race.
HEPHAESTUS: For you two, Strength and Violence, the command of Zeus
  Is now performed. You are released. But how can I

  * An asterisk indicates a Note at the end of the book, p. 153 ff.

Find heart to lay hands on a god of my own race,
And cruelly clamp him to this bitter, bleak ravine?
And yet I must; heart or no heart, this I must do.
To slight what Zeus has spoken is a fearful thing.
[*to* PROMETHEUS] Son of sagacious Themis, god of moun-
    tainous thoughts,
With heart as sore as yours I now shall fasten you
In bands of bronze immovable to this desolate peak,
Where you will hear no voice, nor see a human form;
But scorched with the sun's flaming rays your skin will lose
Its bloom of freshness. Glad you will be to see the night
Cloaking the day with her dark spangled robe; and glad
Again when the sun's warmth scatters the frost at dawn.
Each changing hour will bring successive pain to rack
Your body; and no man yet born shall set you free.
Your kindness to the human race has earned you this.
A god who would not bow to the gods' anger – you,
Transgressing right, gave privileges to mortal men.
For that you shall keep watch upon this bitter rock,
Standing upright, unsleeping, never bowed in rest.
And many groans and cries of pain shall come from you,
All useless; for the heart of Zeus is hard to appease.
Power newly won is always harsh.
STRENGTH: What is the use
    Of wasting time in pity? Why do you not hate
    A god who is an enemy to all the gods,
    Who gave away to humankind your privilege?
HEPHAESTUS: The ties of birth and comradeship are strangely
    strong.
STRENGTH: True, yet how is it possible to disobey
    The Father's word? Is not that something you dread more?
HEPHAESTUS: You have been always cruel, full of aggressive-
    ness.
STRENGTH: It does no good to break your heart for him. Come
    now,

You cannot help him: waste no time in worrying.

HEPHAESTUS: I hate my craft, I hate the skill of my own hands.

STRENGTH: Why do you hate it? Take the simple view: your craft

Is not to blame for what must be inflicted now.

HEPHAESTUS: True – yet I wish some other had been given my skill.

STRENGTH: All tasks are burdensome – except to rule the gods.
No one is free but Zeus.

HEPHAESTUS: I know. All this [indicating PRO-
METHEUS] is proof
Beyond dispute.

STRENGTH: Be quick, then; put the fetters on him
Before the Father sees you idling.

HEPHAESTUS: Here, then, look!
The iron wrist-bands are ready. [he begins to fix them]

STRENGTH: Take them; manacle him;
Hammer with all your force, rivet him to the rock.

HEPHAESTUS: All right, I'm doing it! There, that iron will
not come loose.

STRENGTH: Drive it in further; clamp him fast, leave nothing
slack.

HEPHAESTUS: This arm is firm; at least he'll find no way out
there.

STRENGTH: Now nail his other arm securely. Let him learn
That all his wisdom is but folly before Zeus.

HEPHAESTUS: There! None – but he – could fairly find fault
with my work.

STRENGTH: Now drive straight through his chest with all the
force you have
The unrelenting fang of the adamantine wedge.

HEPHAESTUS: Alas! I weep, Prometheus, for your sufferings.

STRENGTH: Still shrinking? Weeping for the enemy of Zeus?
Take care; or you may need your pity for yourself.

HEPHAESTUS drives in the wedge.

HEPHAESTUS: There! Now you see a sight to pain your eyes.

STRENGTH: I see
Prometheus getting his deserts. Come, fix these girths
Around his ribs.

HEPHAESTUS: I must. Don't drive me with commands.

STRENGTH: I swear I *will* command you – yes, and hound you
on.
Come lower down now; force his legs into this ring.

HEPHAESTUS: That's quickly done.

STRENGTH: Now nail those shackles
fast. Hit hard!
Our work has a stern judge.

HEPHAESTUS: Your speech matches your looks.

STRENGTH [*jeering*]: Be soft, then. But if I am hard and pitiless,
Don't cast it at me.

HEPHAESTUS: Come, his legs are safe; let's go.
                    Exit HEPHAESTUS.

STRENGTH [*to* PROMETHEUS]: Stay there, and swell with
upstart arrogance; and steal
The privileges of gods to give to mortal men.
How are your mortals going to cut *this* knot for you?
You're wrongly named, Prometheus, Wise-before-the-event!
Wisdom is just the thing you want, if you've a mind
To squirm your way out of this blacksmith's masterpiece!
              Exeunt STRENGTH *and* VIOLENCE.

PROMETHEUS: O divinity of sky, and swift-winged winds, and
leaping streams,
O countless laughter of the sea's waves,
O Earth, mother of all life!
On you, and on the all-seeing circle of the sun, I call:
See what is done by gods to me, a god!

See with what outrage
Racked and tortured
I am to agonize

For a thousand years!
See this shameful prison
Invented for me
By the new master of the gods!
I groan in anguish
For pain present and pain to come:
Where shall I see rise
The star of my deliverance?

What am I saying? I know exactly every thing
That is to be; no torment will come unforeseen.
My appointed fate I must endure as best I can,
Knowing the power of Necessity is irresistible.
Under such suffering, speech and silence are alike
Beyond me. For bestowing gifts upon mankind
I am harnessed in this torturing clamp. For I am he
Who hunted out the source of fire, and stole it, packed
In pith of a dry fennel-stalk. And fire has proved
For men a teacher in every art, their grand resource.
That was the sin for which I now pay the full price,
Bared to the winds of heaven, bound and crucified.

Ah! Who is there?
What sound, what fragrant air
Floats by me – whence, I cannot see?
From god, or man, or demigod?
Have you come to this peak at the world's end
To gaze at my torment? Or for what?
See me, a miserable prisoner,
A god, the enemy of Zeus,
Who have earned the enmity of all gods
That frequent the court of Zeus
Because I was too good a friend to men.

Ah, ah! I hear it again, close to me!
A rustling – is it of birds?
And the air whispering with the light beat of wings!

Whatever comes, brings fear.
> *Enter the* CHORUS *in a winged ship or carriage.*

CHORUS: Fear nothing. We are all your friends.
We have flown to this mountain on racing wings,
Winning reluctant leave from our father;
And the winds carried us swiftly along.
For the echo of ringing steel
Shivered through the depths of our cave,
Shaking quiet bashfulness out of our thoughts;
And barefoot as we were
We came at once in our winged carriage.

PROMETHEUS: Alas, alas! Children of fertile Tethys,
Daughters of Oceanus, whose unsleeping tide
Encircles the whole earth, look at me.
See in how cruel a grip,
Pinned on the craggy peak of this ravine,
I must endure my fearful watch.

CHORUS: I look, Prometheus; and sudden fear fills my eyes
To see your body withering on this rock,
Outraged with fetters of adamant.
A new master holds the helm of Olympus;
These are new laws indeed
By which Zeus tyrannically rules;
And the great powers of the past he now destroys.

PROMETHEUS: Would that Zeus had sunk me under the earth,
Down below Hades, haven of the dead,
Into the immensity of Tartarus,
Fastening me in cruel fetters inextricably,
That no god or any other creature
Might feel glad to see me suffer.
Instead I am the miserable sport of every wind,
And my torments bring joy to my enemies.

CHORUS: What god is cruel-hearted enough
To find joy in such a sight?
Who does not suffer with you in your pain –

Save Zeus? He, firm in inflexible anger,
Treads down the race of Ouranos, and will not relent
Till his passion is sated, or till some cunning plot
Wrests from his hand his impregnable empire.
PROMETHEUS: I swear to you that I, humiliated as I am,
Bound hand and foot in these strong straps,
Shall yet be needed by the lord of immortals
To disclose the new design, tell him who it is
Shall rob him of his power and his glory.
The honied spells of his persuasive tongue shall not enchant me,
Nor shall I cower under his fierce threats, or tell this secret,
Until he free me from these brutal bonds
And consent to compensate me for his outrage.
CHORUS: You are defiant, Prometheus, and your spirit,
In spite of all your pain, yields not an inch.
But there is too much freedom in your words.
My heart is shaken with a piercing terror;
I tremble at your fate: how are you to reach
The end of these troubles and rest in a safe port?
For the son of Cronos is unapproachable in temper,
And no words can soften his heart.
PROMETHEUS: Zeus, I know, is ruthless,
And keeps law within his own will.
Nevertheless his temper shall in time turn mild,
When my words come true and he is broken.
Then at last he will calm his merciless anger,
And ask for a pact of friendship with me;
And I shall welcome him.
CHORUS: Now disclose everything and explain to us
Upon what charge Zeus had you seized
And treated with such ignominy and brutality.
Tell us, if telling involves no harm for you.
PROMETHEUS: To speak of this is painful for me; to keep
    silence
Is no less pain. On every side is suffering.

When first among the immortal gods anger broke out
Dividing them into two factions, of which one
Resolved to unseat the power of Cronos, and make Zeus
Absolute king – mark that! – while the opposing side
Resolved no less that Zeus should never rule the gods –
At that time I, offering the best of all advice,
Tried to convince the Titan sons of Heaven and Earth,
And failed. They despised cunning; in their pride of strength
They foresaw easy victory and the rule of might.
I knew the appointed course of things to come. My mother,
Themis, or Earth (one person, though of various names),
Had many times foretold to me, that not brute strength,
Not violence, but cunning must give victory
To the rulers of the future. This I explained to them,
With reasons – which they found not worth one moment's
    heed.

Then, of the courses open to me, it seemed best
To take my stand – my mother with me – at the side
Of Zeus, willing and welcome. It was I who gave
That counsel through which ancient Cronos and his crew
Lie buried now in the black abyss of Tartarus.
That was the help I gave the king of the gods; and this
Is my reward – this is his black ingratitude.
To look on all friends with suspicion – this disease
Would seem to be inherent in a tyrant's soul.

Now, for your question, on what charge Zeus tortures me,
I'll tell you. On succeeding to his father's throne
At once he appointed various rights to various gods,
Giving to each his set place and authority.
Of wretched humans he took no account, resolved
To annihilate them and create another race.
This purpose there was no one to oppose but I:
I dared. I saved the human race from being ground
To dust, from total death.

For that I am subjected to these bitter pains* –
Agony to endure, heart-rending to behold.
I pitied mortal men; but being myself not thought
To merit pity, am thus cruelly disciplined –
A sight to fix dishonour on the name of Zeus.

CHORUS: Only a heart of iron, a temper carved from rock,
Prometheus, could refuse compassion for your pains.
Had I known, I could have wished never to see this sight;
Now I have seen, sorrow and anger rack my heart.

PROMETHEUS: Indeed my friends feel pity at the sight of me.

CHORUS: Did your offence perhaps go further than you have said?

PROMETHEUS: Yes: I caused men no longer to foresee their death.

CHORUS: What cure did you discover for their misery?

PROMETHEUS: I planted firmly in their hearts blind hopeful-ness.

CHORUS: Your gift brought them great blessing.

PROMETHEUS: I did more than that:
I gave them fire.

CHORUS: What? Men, whose life is but a day,
Possess already the hot radiance of fire?

PROMETHEUS: They do; and with it they shall master many crafts.

CHORUS: This then was the offence for which you suffer here –

PROMETHEUS: Suffer the unrelenting savagery of Zeus.

CHORUS: And is no end of this ordeal appointed you?

PROMETHEUS: No, none; until such time as he sees fit to choose.

CHORUS: He never will. What hope is there? Oh, you were wrong –
Do you not see? To say that you were wrong grieves me,
And tortures you. So let us talk no more of it.
Instead, try now to think of some deliverance.

PROMETHEUS: Oh, it is easy for the one who stands outside

The prison-wall of pain to exhort and teach the one
Who suffers. All you have said to me I always knew.
Wrong? I accept the word. I willed, willed to be wrong!
And helping humans I found trouble for myself.
Yet I did not expect such punishment as this —
To be assigned an uninhabited desert peak,
Fastened in mid-air to this crag, and left to rot!

      Listen: stop wailing for the pain I suffer now.
Step to the ground; I'll tell you what the future holds
For me; you shall know everything from first to last.
Do what I ask you, do it! Share the suffering
Of one whose turn is now. Grief is a wanderer
Who visits many, bringing always the same gift.
CHORUS: Your appeal falls on willing ears, Prometheus.
Come, sisters, leave your seats
In the ship that flies on the holy highway of birds;
Step lightly down to the rocky ground.
— We are eager to hear to the end
The story of all you have undergone, Prometheus.
    The CHORUS *leave their ship. As they group themselves on the*
      ground OCEANUS *arrives seated on a winged four-footed*
      creature.
OCEANUS: Here at last!
Prometheus, I have come a long way to visit you,
Guiding this swift-winged creature
By will, without any bridle.
Believe me, I am sorry for your misfortunes.
Being related to you, I suppose,
Makes me sympathize with you;
But apart from relationship, there is no one
Whom I hold in greater respect.
That is true, and I will prove it to you:
For I am incapable of mere flattery.
Come, now, tell me what I should do to help you.

You shall never say, Prometheus,
That you have any firmer friend than Oceanus.
PROMETHEUS: What's that? Who is it? Ah! So you too have
    come
To observe my torment? How was it you dared to leave
Your Ocean-river and your rock-roofed natural caves
To visit Earth, mother of iron? Are you here
To gaze at what I suffer, and add your grief to mine?
Behold a spectacle – me here, the friend of Zeus,
By whose help he established his sole sovereignty:
See with what pains I am now disciplined by him.
OCEANUS: I see, Prometheus; and although your mind is subtle
I want at least to give you the best advice I can.
A new king rules among the gods. Then know yourself,
And take upon yourself new ways to suit the time.
If in this way you fling out edged and angry speeches,
It may be Zeus – throned though he is so far above –
Will hear you; and, for result, your present load of troubles
Will seem a childish trifle. Oh, my unhappy friend,
Throw off your angry mood and seek deliverance
From all your suffering. What I say may seem perhaps
Well worn; but your plight is the inescapable
Reward, Prometheus, of a too proud-speaking tongue.
You still will not be humble, will not yield to pain;
You mean to add new sufferings to those you have.
Come now, accept my guidance: we are ruled by one
Whose harsh and sole dominion none may call to account.
Acknowledge this, and cease to kick against the goad.
Now I will go and try if there is any way
Within my power to set you free. Meanwhile, keep quiet,
Don't rage and storm. You are intelligent: full well
You know that punishment falls on the unruly tongue.
PROMETHEUS: I envy you your luck in not being under censure
Even for having dared to sympathize with me.
Now leave it, give it no more thought. Do what you may,

You never will persuade him; he is immovable.
Look out yourself, lest you meet trouble on your way.
OCEANUS: You are a far more prudent counsellor of others
  Than of yourself; experience makes this plain to me.
  But I'm resolved to go, so say no more against it.
  I'm sure – yes, sure that Zeus will grant me what I ask,
  And for my sake will loose your bonds and set you free.
PROMETHEUS: I thank you, and shall always thank you. Your
    goodwill
  Is all that one could ask. But stir no hand for me;
  Your trouble will be wasted, and bring me no good,
  Whatever you intend to try. Do nothing, and
  Keep clear of danger. If I suffer, I do not therefore
  Wish that as many as possible should suffer too;
  Far from it. The fate of Atlas grieves me – my own brother,
  Who in the far West stands with his unwieldy load
  Pressing upon his back, the pillar of heaven and earth.
  I pity Typhon, that earth-born destroying giant,
  The hundred-headed, native of the Cilician caves;
  I saw him, all his fiery strength subdued by force.
  Against the united gods he stood, his fearful jaws
  Hissing forth terror; from his eyes a ghastly glare
  Flashed, threatening to annihilate the throne of Zeus.
  But Zeus's sleepless weapon came on him; he felt
  The fiery vapour of the crashing thunderbolt,
  Which blasted him out of his lofty boasts, and struck
  His very heart, and burnt his strength to sulphurous ash.
  Now, crushed under Mount Etna's roots, near the sea-strait,
  He lies, a helpless sprawling hulk; while on the peak
  Hephaestus hammers red-hot iron; and thence one day
  Rivers of flame shall burst forth, and with savage jaws
  Devour the bright smooth fields of fertile Sicily;
  Such rage shall Typhon, though charred with the bolt of Zeus,
  Send boiling out in jets of fierce, fire-breathing spume
  Unquenchable. But you are not without experience;

You have no need of my instruction. Save yourself
As you know how. Meanwhile I'll drink my painful cup
To the dregs, till Zeus relaxes from his angry mood.

OCEANUS: Have you not learnt, Prometheus, anger's a disease
Which words can heal?

PROMETHEUS: Yes, if you soothe the spirit when
The moment's ripe – not roughly baulk a swelling rage.

OCEANUS: Tell me, Prometheus: do you see some risk entailed
Even in my having dared to sympathize with you?

PROMETHEUS: Superfluous labour and light-minded foolishness.

OCEANUS: Let me be guilty then of foolishness. Sometimes
A wise man gains his point by being thought not wise.

PROMETHEUS: In this case it is I who will be thought not wise.

OCEANUS: Your way of speaking plainly sends me home again.

PROMETHEUS: Why, yes. In pitying me I fear you may well gain
An enemy.

OCEANUS: Who? The new-enthroned almighty lord?

PROMETHEUS: Take care; he may turn angry.

OCEANUS: Your fate is a lesson
To me, Prometheus.

PROMETHEUS: Go! Get out! Be what you are!

OCEANUS: I'm anxious to be going; there's no need to shout.
This four-legged beast's already beating with his wings
The smooth path of the air. Yes, he'll be pleased enough
To lie down comfortably in his own stall at home.

                         Exit OCEANUS.

CHORUS: I weep, Prometheus, for your deadly plight.
Tears flow from my eyes,
Fall in a gentle stream,
And wash my cheek like a spring of water.
In this pitiful sight
Zeus, ruling by laws of his own invention,
Provides an example
Of his proud power over the gods of the past.

Now every country cries aloud in grief:
The peoples of Europe mourn*
For you and the Titan race,
Your glorious, ancient rule and honour;
And all the settled tribes
That graze the fields of holy Asia
Weep loudly for you and share your suffering;

The Amazons of the land of Colchis,
Virgins fearless in battle,
The Scythian hordes who live at the world's end
On the shores of Lake Maeotis;
The warlike princes of Arabia,
Holding their cliff-perched fortress near Mount Caucasus,*
Whose battle-cry strikes terror
In the ranks of sharpened spears, weep for you.

Only once before have I seen
A Titan god so tormented,
Vanquished in bonds invincible;
Atlas, alone in excellence of strength,
Who holds the vault of the sky upon his back, and groans;*

And the wave of the wide Ocean
Roars in unison with him,
The depths of waters weep,
The cavernous darkness of the dead world mutters under,
and the holy fountains of flowing rivers
Weep in pity for his pain.

PROMETHEUS: You must not think it is through pride or
    stubbornness
That I am silent; thought and anger gnaw my heart,
To see myself so outraged. Why, who else but I
Assigned to these new gods their honours, first and last?
All that you know, and I'll not speak of. What I did

For mortals in their misery, hear now. At first
Mindless, I gave them mind and reason. – What I say
Is not in censure of mankind, but showing you
How all my gifts to them were guided by goodwill. –
In those days they had eyes, but sight was meaningless;
Heard sounds, but could not listen; all their length of life
They passed like shapes in dreams, confused and purposeless.
Of brick-built, sun-warmed houses, or of carpentry,
They had no notion; lived in holes, like swarms of ants,
Or deep in sunless caverns; knew no certain way
To mark off winter, or flowery spring, or fruitful summer;
Their every act was without knowledge, till I came.
I taught them to determine when stars rise or set –
A difficult art. Number, the primary science, I
Invented for them, and how to set down words in writing –
The all-remembering skill, mother of many arts.
I was the first to harness beasts under a yoke
With trace or saddle as man's slaves, to take man's place
Under the heaviest burdens; put the horse to the chariot,
Made him obey the rein, and be an ornament
To wealth and greatness. No one before me discovered
The sailor's waggon – flax-winged craft that roam the seas.
Such tools and skills I found for men: myself, poor wretch,
Lack even one trick to free me from this agony.
CHORUS: Humiliation follows pain; distraught in mind
      You have lost your way; like a bad doctor fallen ill
      You now despair of finding drugs to cure yourself.
PROMETHEUS: Now hear the rest of what I have to tell, what
         crafts,
      What methods I devised – and you will wonder more.
      First in importance: if a man fell ill, he had
      No remedy, solid or liquid medicine,
      Or ointment, but for lack of drugs they pined away;
      Until I showed them how to mix mild healing herbs
      And so protect themselves against all maladies.

Then I distinguished various modes of prophecy,
And was the first to tell from dreams what Fate ordained
Should come about; interpreted the hidden sense
Of voices, sounds, sights met by chance upon the road.
The various flights of crook-clawed vultures I defined
Exactly, those by nature favourable, and those
Sinister; how each species keeps its mode of life;
What feuds, friendships, associations kind with kind
Preserves; how to interpret signs in sacrifice,
Smoothness of heart and lights, what colours please the gods
In each, the mottled shapeliness of liver-lobes.
The thigh-bones wrapped in fat, and the long chine, I burnt,
Leading men on the highway of an occult art;
And signs from flames, obscure before, I now made plain.

So much for prophecy. Next the treasures of the earth,
The bronze, iron, silver, gold hidden deep down – who else
But I can claim to have found them first? No one, unless
He talks like a fool. So, here's the whole truth in one word:
All human skill and science was Prometheus' gift.
CHORUS: Then do not, after helping men to your own hurt,
    Neglect to save yourself from torment. I have hopes
    That you will yet be freed and rival Zeus in power.
PROMETHEUS: Fate fulfils all in time; but it is not ordained
    That these events shall yet reach such an end. My lot
    Is to win freedom only after countless pains.
    Cunning is feebleness beside Necessity.
CHORUS: And whose hand on the helm controls Necessity?
PROMETHEUS: The three Fates; and the Furies, who forget
    nothing.
CHORUS: Has Zeus less power than they?
PROMETHEUS: He cannot fly from Fate.
CHORUS: What fate is given to Zeus, but everlasting power?
PROMETHEUS: This is a thing you may not know; so do not ask.
CHORUS: It is some holy truth you cloak in mystery.

PROMETHEUS: Turn your thoughts elsewhere; now is not the
    time to speak
  Of that; it is a secret which by every means
  Must be kept close. By keeping it I shall escape
  This ignominious prison and these fearful pains.
CHORUS: May Zeus, who disposes all things,
  Never exert his power to crush my will;
  May I never grow weary
  In worshipping the gods with pure offerings of bulls
  Beside the inexhaustible stream of my father Oceanus.
  May I not offend in word; but let this resolve
  Remain unfading in my heart.

  It is a pleasant thing to spend the length of life
  In confidence and hope,
  And to nourish the soul in light and cheerfulness.
  But I shudder when I see you, Prometheus,
  Racked by infinite tortures.
  For you have no fear of Zeus,
  But pursuing your own purpose
  You respect too highly the race of mortals.

  See, my friend, how thankless were all your benefits.
  Tell me, what strength is there, and where,
  What help to be found in men who live for a day?
  Did you not note the helpless infirmity,
  Feeble as a dream,
  Which fetters the blind tribes of men?
  For human purposes shall never trespass
  Outside the harmony of Zeus's government.

  This is the truth I have learnt from your downfall, Prometheus.
  What strikes my ear is the difference
  Between today's sounds of sorrow
  And the songs we sang to grace your marriage,

The song for the bath and the song for the bed,
When you wooed and won with gifts
My sister Hesione for your wedded bride.

Enter Io.

Io: What land is this? What race lives here?
Who is this that I see held in fetters of rock
At the mercy of wind and storm?
For what sin do you suffer such a death?
Tell me, where has my miserable wandering brought me?
                [*suddenly she shrieks in pain and terror*]
The gadfly stings me again. Oh, oh!
I see the ghost of Argus,
The earth-born herdsman with a thousand eyes —
Gods! Keep him away!
He was killed, but no earth can hide him;
He follows me with his crafty gaze;
He escapes from his grave to hound me without mercy,
And drives me starving along the sandy shores;
While the clear music of wax-bound pipes*
Fills my ears with a tune that longs for sleep.

Where, where, where
Will my endless, endless journeys bring me?
Son of Cronos, what have I done?
What sin did you find in me,
To put on me such a yoke of torment,
Plague me to misery and madness
With this driving, stinging terror?
Burn me with fire, let the earth swallow me,
Throw me as food for sea-serpents —
Lord God, will you grudge me this prayer?
I have wandered so far,
I have been punished enough with wandering;
I cannot tell how to escape from pain.
Do you hear my voice? It is Io, the girl with horns!

PROMETHEUS: I hear indeed the frenzied daughter of Inachus
 Who fired the heart of Zeus with love, and suffers now
 Through Hera's hate her long ordeal of cruel pursuit.
IO: You spoke my father's name: how do you know it?
 Tell me who you are – you, as pitiable as I.
 You know who I am, and you named truly
 The heaven-sent tormentor
 Which ravages and drives me with stings.
 I have run without rest
 In a leaping frenzy of pain and hunger,
 The victim of Hera's calculating resentment.
 Are there any in all this suffering world
 Who endure what I endure?
 Tell me clearly what remains for me to suffer,
 What resource, what cure can save me.
 Speak, if you know; give help and guidance
 To the tortured exiled virgin.
PROMETHEUS: I'll tell you plainly everything you wish to
    learn,
 Not weaving mysteries, but in such simple speech
 As one should use in speaking to a friend. I am
 Prometheus, who bestowed on man the gift of fire.
IO: O universal benefactor of mankind,
 Ill-starred Prometheus, why are you thus crucified?
PROMETHEUS: I was lamenting all my pains. I have ceased now.
IO: Will you not tell me –
PROMETHEUS: Ask; I can tell everything.
IO: Who was it, then, that clamped you fast in this ravine?
PROMETHEUS: The will of Zeus decreed; Hephaestus' hand
    obeyed.
IO: What were the sins for which you suffer punishment?
PROMETHEUS: What I have told you is enough.
IO: Then reveal this:
 Where is the end of my cursed wandering, and when?
PROMETHEUS: Not to know this is better for you than to know.

Io: Do not hide from me what it is my doom to suffer.

PROMETHEUS: It is not that I grudge you what you ask of me.

Io: Why then do you hesitate to tell me the whole truth?

PROMETHEUS: Not from ill will. I shrink from shattering your
   heart.

Io: Come, do not take more thought for me than I would wish.

PROMETHEUS: Since you're determined, I must tell you.
   Listen then.

CHORUS: Not yet. Let us too share this pleasure. Let us ask
   Io to tell us first the story of her affliction,
   And hear the ruin of her life from her own lips.
   Then let her learn from you what she must yet endure.

PROMETHEUS: It is for you, Io, to grant them their request;
   And more especially, since they are your father's sisters.
   Tears and lamenting find their due reward when those
   Who listen are ready too with tears of sympathy.

Io: I cannot disobey; you shall hear everything
   You want to know, in plain words; though even to speak
   Of those events from which my troubles first arose,
   And my unhappy transformation, makes me weep.

   At night in my own room visions would visit me,
   Repeating in seductive words, 'Most blessed maid,
   Why live a virgin for so long? Love waits for you –
   The greatest: Zeus, inflamed with arrows of desire,
   Longs to unite with you in love. Do not reject,
   My child, the bed of Zeus. Go out to the deep grass
   Of Lerna, where your father's sheep and cattle graze,
   That the eye of Zeus may rest from longing and be satisfied'.

   By such dreams every troubled night I was beset,
   Until I dared to tell my father. Then he sent
   Messengers many times to Pytho and Dodona
   To learn what he must do or say to please the gods.
   They came back with reports of riddling oracles,

178   [662–697]

Obscurely worded, hard to interpret. But at last
Was given a clear utterance unmistakably
Commanding Inachus to turn me from his house
And city, to wander homeless* to the ends of the earth;
If he refused, the fiery thunderbolt of Zeus
Would fall and extirpate his race to the last man.

      Such was the oracle of Loxias. My father
Yielded, and sent me forth, and locked his door against me –
He as unwilling as myself; but he was forced
To do this by the cruel bridle-rein of Zeus.
At once my shape was changed, my mind distorted. Horned,
As you now see, stung by the gadfly's stabbing goad,
Convulsed and mad, I rushed on, to the crystal stream
Of Cerchnea and the spring of Lerna; I was followed
By Argus, a giant herdsman of ungoverned rage,
Who watched my every step with his ten thousand eyes.
A sudden, unexpected stroke robbed him of life.
I, gadfly-maddened, still am driven from land to land,
Lashed by this God-appointed scourge.

                                        That is my story.
If you can say what still remains to be endured,
Tell me; and do not out of pity comfort me
With lies. I count false words the foulest plague of all.
CHORUS: What a pitiful, terrible fate!
    Never did I dream that so strange a story
    Would ever come to my ears;
    That anguish, cruelty, terror,
    So bitter to see and to endure,
    Would ever chill my spirit with a wound so sharp.
    Alas, Fate, Fate!
    I see the lot of Io, and tremble.
PROMETHEUS: You shed your tears too early, like a frightened
      woman.
    Keep them until you hear what is to follow now.

CHORUS: Speak, then, and tell her all. It comforts those in
    pain
    To know beforehand all the pain they still must bear.
PROMETHEUS: Your first request to me was easily obtained;
    You wished to hear Io's ordeal from her own lips.
    Now hear the rest – what sufferings at Hera's hands
    Are yet in store for this young maid. Now lay to heart
    My words, daughter of Inachus, and learn the goal
    Of all your journeys.

        From this place turn first toward the rising sun, and pass
    Over the unploughed plains until you reach the land
    Of nomad Scythians, living high above the ground
    In houses built on strong-wheeled carts, with wattled roofs.
    They are armed with powerful bows; keep well away from
        them,
    And take your path by the loud-roaring rocky shore,
    And so pass through that country. Next, on your left hand,
    Is the country of the Chalybes, craftsmen in iron.
    Beware of them; they are savage, and no stranger can
    Approach them safely. After this you reach the river
    Hybristes, whose wild torrent justifies its name.
    Do not attempt to cross – it is too dangerous –
    Until you come to Caucasus itself, the peak
    Of all that range, where from the very brows the river
    Floods forth its fury. You must cross the topmost ridge
    Close to the stars, and take the pathway leading south.
    There you will find the warlike race of Amazons,
    Haters of men. This race in time to come shall found
    The city of Themiscyra, on the Thermodon,
    Where the rough jaw of Salmydessus fronts the sea,
    An enemy to sailors, stepmother to ships.
    The Amazons will most gladly guide you on your way.
    Next, where a narrow creek gives entrance to a lake,
    You will come to the Cimmerian Isthmus. Boldly then

Leave land, and cross the Maeotic Strait. Ages to come
Shall tell the story of your passage, and the place
Shall be called Bosporus to commemorate you. Thus
From Europe you will reach the Asian continent.

Does it not seem to you that this king of the gods
In all matters alike is given to violence?
A god, lusting for union with this mortal maid,
He dooms her to such journeys! You are unfortunate,
Io, in your lover. All that I have told so far
Hardly begins – believe me! – all there is to tell.

Io [*weeping*]: Oh, oh! I cannot bear it!

PROMETHEUS: More cries and groans? When you shall hear
the rest, what then?

CHORUS: Have you still more to tell her of distress and pain?

PROMETHEUS: I have, a stormy sea of deadly misery.

Io: Why should I go on living? Why not hurl myself
At once down from this rocky cliff, be dashed in pieces,
And find relief from all my pain? Better to die
Once, than to suffer torment all my living days.

PROMETHEUS: Then you would find it hard to bear *my* agonies,
Since I am fated not to die. Death would have brought
Release; but now no end to suffering is in sight
For me, until Zeus be deposed from sovereignty.

Io: What? Is it possible that Zeus should be deposed?

PROMETHEUS: You would be glad, I think, to see that come
about.

Io: How could I help it, after all he has made me suffer?

PROMETHEUS: Learn it as truth: it shall be so.

Io: By whom shall Zeus
Be stripped of power?

PROMETHEUS: By his own foolish purposes.

Io: How will it happen? Tell me, if it does no harm.

PROMETHEUS: He plans a union that will turn to his undoing.

Io: With mortal or immortal? Tell me, if you may.

PROMETHEUS: Why ask with whom? That is a thing I may not tell.

IO: Then is it she who will unseat him from his throne?

PROMETHEUS: She is to bear a son more powerful than his father.

IO: Is there no way by which Zeus can escape this fate?

PROMETHEUS: None, but with my help. I could save him, once set free.

IO: But if Zeus be unwilling, who can set you free?

PROMETHEUS: A child of yours is named as my deliverer.

IO: What do you say? My child shall free you from these chains?

PROMETHEUS: Yes, in the thirteenth generation after you.

IO: I find it hard to interpret this last prophecy.

PROMETHEUS: Then do not seek to learn your own appointed lot.

IO: You offered me this favour; do not now refuse.

PROMETHEUS: I'll grant you one or other of two prophecies.

IO: What are they? Offer me my choice.

PROMETHEUS: Then choose between
The remainder of your journey, and my deliverer.

CHORUS: Of these two favours, if you please, grant one to her,
And one to me, Prometheus; do not grudge the telling.
Reveal to Io all her future wandering,
And tell me who shall set you free. I long to know.

PROMETHEUS: Since you are eager, I will not refuse to tell
Everything you desire. First, Io, I will name
The many lands where Fate will toss you in your journey;
Write what I tell you in your book of memory.

When you have crossed the stream that bounds two
    continents
Press on, over the surge of the sea, towards the east
Where the sun stalks in flame, to the Gorgonean land,
Cisthene. There live Phorcys' aged virgin daughters,
In shape like swans, possessing one eye and one tooth

Between the three; beings on whom no ray of sun
Ever looks down, nor moon at night. And close to them
Their three winged sisters, loathed enemies of humankind,
The snake-haired Gorgons, whom no man can see and live.
This is but the beginning. Now hear yet another
Grim sight you must encounter: beware the silent hounds
Of Zeus, the sharp-beaked griffins; and beware the tribe
Of one-eyed Arimaspian horsemen, on the banks
Of the Plutonian river whose waters wash down gold.
Do not go near them. Then you will reach a remote region
Where near the sun's bright fountains live a dark-skinned race.
There is the Ethiopian river; follow its course
Down, till you reach the cataract where from the Bybline hills
The Nile pours forth his holy stream to quench men's thirst.
And he will guide you to the delta of the Nile
Where, Io, you and your descendants shall at last
By Fate's appointment found your far-off colony.

    If any point is indistinct or hard to follow
Ask further, and make sure that you have understood.
I have more time to spare than I would wish to have.
CHORUS: If anything passed over still remains to tell
Of Io's painful journeys, speak. If not, grant now
To us the favour which, you remember, we asked of you.
PROMETHEUS: Io has heard the whole course of her wandering.
And, lest she think I may have given her idle words,
I'll speak of what she suffered before coming here,
To prove my words. Most of the details I'll omit,
And come directly to your recent wanderings.

    On reaching the Molossian plains, and the rock-wall
Which towers above Dodona, where Thesprotian Zeus
Has his oracular seat, where grow the speaking oaks –
A marvel past belief – by which you were addressed
Plainly and unambiguously as the destined bride

Of Zeus – does that truth touch you? – from that place you
   rushed,
Plagued by the gadfly's sting, along the sea-shore path
To the wide Adriatic,* whence back yet again
The storm of frenzy drove you on your wild flight here.
And that bay of the sea shall for all future time –
Mark this – be called Ionian, to perpetuate
For all mankind the story of Io's wanderings.
I tell you this as proof that my prophetic mind
Sees more than meets the eye. Now to you all I'll tell
The rest, resuming at the point where I broke off.

Where the Nile's outflow lays its bank of silt, there
   stands
On the last edge of land the city of Canopus;
And here at last Zeus shall restore your mind, and come
Upon you, not with terror, with a gentle touch;
His hand laid on you shall put life into your womb,
And you shall bear a dark-skinned son to Zeus, and name him
From his begetting, 'Child of a touch', Epaphos.
He shall possess the harvest-wealth of all those lands
Watered by the broad-flowing Nile. Five generations
From him, a family of fifty sisters shall return
Against their will to Argos, desperate to escape
From kindred marriage with their cousins. The young men
Follow in passionate pursuit close on their track,
As hawks hunt doves; lusting for an unlawful love.*
But God shall grudge them the enjoyment of their brides.
And Argive soil shall welcome them, when in the night
Bold resolution goes on guard, and women's hands
Make war and slaughter, and male pride is overthrown.
For each shall plunge her sharp sword in his throat, and kill
Her husband. May such love come to my enemies!
But sweet desire shall charm one girl, and blunt the edge
Of her resolve, and she shall spare her husband's life,

And choose to be called coward, but not murderess;
And she shall live in Argos and give birth to kings.

    And from her children's children shall be born in time
(To trace each step would take too long) a fearless hero
Famed as an archer, who shall free me from these bonds.
Such is the oracle as my mother told it me,
Titanian Themis, born in the old time. But how
All this shall come about, would take me long to tell,
And you in listening would gain nothing.
          Io interrupts with a wild cry of pain.
Io: The stroke of madness burns me again,
  My brain is convulsed, the gadfly
  Stings me with his immortal arrow.
  My heart beats wildly in my body;
  My eyeballs roll and turn;
  Insanity falls on me like a raging storm
  And drives me off course;
  I can't govern my tongue; words rush out at random,
  Beating against waves of deadly ruin!*
          Exit Io.
CHORUS: He was a wise man indeed
  Who first weighed this thought in his mind
  And gave it utterance in speech,
  That the best rule by far
  Is to marry in your own rank;
  That a man who works with his hands should never crave
  To marry either a woman pampered by wealth
  Or one who prides herself on her noble family.

  O Fates, who bring all things to fulfilment,
  May you never see me sharing the bed of Zeus;
  May I never be joined in marriage with any god!
  For I tremble when I look at the girlhood of Io,
  Denied the love of a man,

Tormented in ever-restless exile
By the cruelty of Hera.

When marriage is with an equal
For me it holds no fear or danger.
But may the love of the greater gods
Never cast on me its irresistible glance.
That is a fight which cannot be fought,
The straight road to despair.
What would become of me I cannot say;
For I see no way to escape the design of Zeus.

PROMETHEUS: I swear that Zeus, for all his obstinacy, shall yet
Be humbled, so disastrous shall this marriage prove
Which he proposes – a marriage that shall hurl him out
Of throne and sovereignty into oblivion.
And then the curse his father Cronos cursed him with,
The day he lost his ancient throne, shall all come true.
There is no god but I who can reveal to him
The way to avert this ignominy. I know it all.
So now let him sit on, serenely confident
In his celestial thunders, brandishing in his hand
His fierce fire-breathing thunderbolt – that will not save him:
His fall will be sure, shameful, unendurable!
Such an antagonist he is even now himself
Preparing against himself, a wonder irresistible,
One who will find a flame hotter than lightning-strokes,
A crash to overwhelm the thunder; one whose strength
Shall split Poseidon's trident-spear, that dreaded scourge
That shakes both sea and land. This is the reef on which
His power shall strike and founder, till he learns how great
A chasm lies between ruling and being ruled.

CHORUS: These threats against Zeus surely voice but your own
wish.

PROMETHEUS: I speak what shall prove true – and my own
wish as well.

CHORUS: Must we expect one who shall bring Zeus to his knees?

PROMETHEUS: Yes; Zeus's neck shall bow beneath worse pains than mine.

CHORUS: Why are you not afraid to fling such taunting words?

PROMETHEUS: Why should I fear? My destiny is not to die.

CHORUS: Zeus might invent for you some still worse agony.

PROMETHEUS: Then let him do it! I am prepared for everything.

CHORUS: A wise man will speak humbly, and fear Nemesis.*

PROMETHEUS: Bow! Pray! As always, fawn upon the powerful hand!

For great Zeus I care less than nothing. Let him do
And govern as he wills, for the short time he has.
He will not govern long among the gods. – Why, look!
Here comes his runner, the new tyrant's lickspittle.
No doubt he brings some message.

Enter HERMES.

HERMES: I speak to you – the master-mind, with heart more sour

Than sourness; you who honoured creatures of a day
And sinned against immortals; you, the thief of fire:
The Father bids you tell him what this marriage is
Through which you boast that he shall fall from power. Now speak
No clever riddles, but set forth the detailed truth.
Do not, Prometheus, make me travel all this way
Again; Zeus is not mollified by such replies.

PROMETHEUS: This underling of gods makes a high-sounding speech

Crammed with importance. – You and all your crew are young;
So is your power; and you imagine that you hold
An unassailable citadel. But I have seen

Two dynasties already hurled from those same heights;
And I shall see the third, today's king, fall to earth
More shamefully than his precursors, and more soon.
Do you think I quake and cower before these upstart gods?
Not much, nor little – not one slightest thought! Now you
Trot back the way you came; you'll find out nothing here.

HERMES: Conduct like this, both obstinate and insolent,
Has once already brought you to a painful plight.

PROMETHEUS: Understand this: I would not change my painful plight,
On any terms, for your servile humility.

HERMES: Being bondslave to this rock is preferable, no doubt,
To being the trusted messenger of Father Zeus.

PROMETHEUS: You use the fitting language of the insolent.

HERMES: It seems you find your present state a luxury.

PROMETHEUS: You think so? May I one day see my enemies,
And you among them, in such luxury as this!

HERMES: What, I? Do you blame me too for your sufferings?

PROMETHEUS: In one word, I detest all gods who could repay
My benefits with such outrageous infamy.

HERMES: It's plain that your insanity is far advanced.

PROMETHEUS: Perhaps – if to hate enemies is insanity.

HERMES: Now you, free and in power, would be unbearable.

PROMETHEUS: Alas!

HERMES: Alas? That word is one which Zeus has never known.

PROMETHEUS: But Time, as he grows older, teaches everything.

HERMES: Time has not taught *you* self-control or prudence –
yet.

PROMETHEUS: No – or I would not argue with an underling.

HERMES: It seems you'll tell nothing of what Zeus wants to
know.

PROMETHEUS: And yet I owe him much – that I would gladly
pay.

HERMES: You banter with me – do you think I am a child?

PROMETHEUS: Are you not then a child, or worse than child-
    ish, if
You still expect to get an answer out of me?
There is no torture, no ingenuity, by which
Zeus can persuade me to reveal my secret, till
The injury of these bonds is loosed from me. Therefore
Let scorching flames be flung from heaven; let the whole earth
With white-winged snowstorms, subterranean thunderings,
Heave and convulse: nothing will force me to reveal
By whose hand Fate shall hurl Zeus from his tyranny.
HERMES: Consider now whether this course seems profitable.
PROMETHEUS: I have long ago considered all this, and re-
    solved.
HERMES: Come, bring yourself, perverse fool, while there is
    still time,
To weigh your situation, and so turn to sense.
PROMETHEUS: You waste your breath; you may as well exhort
    the waves.
Never persuade yourself that I, through fear of what
Zeus may intend, will show a woman's mind, or kneel
To my detested enemy, with womanish hands
Outspread in supplication for release. No, never!
HERMES: My words lead only to more words, without effect;
Beg as I may, nothing can soothe or soften you.
Like an unbroken colt you try your strength, and take
The bit between your teeth, and fight against the reins.
Yet all your violence springs from feeble reckoning;
For obstinacy in a fool has by itself
No strength at all. Consider now what punishments
Will burst inevitably upon you like a storm
Of mountainous waves, if you refuse to listen to me.

    First, Zeus will split this rugged chasm with the shock
And flame of lightning, and entomb you underground
Still clamped on this embracing rock. When a long age

Has passed, you will return into the light; and then
The dark-winged hound of Zeus will come, the savage eagle,
An uninvited banqueter, and all day long
Will rip your flesh in rags and feast upon your liver,
Gnawing it black. And you may hope for no release
From such a torment, till some god be found* to take
Your pains upon him, and of his own will descend
To sunless Hades and the black depths of Tartarus.

So think again; this is no fabricated boast,
But truth as Zeus has spoken it, who cannot lie,
But will accomplish every word his mouth has uttered.
Look every way; consider; and be sure of this:
Wise counsel always is worth more than stubbornness.
CHORUS: To us it seems that Hermes' words are sensible.
He bids you quit resistance and seek good advice.
Do so; a wise man's folly forfeits dignity.
PROMETHEUS: I knew what Hermes had to say
Before he made his brag. It is no dishonour
For an enemy to suffer at his enemy's hands.
So let the pronged locks of lightning be launched at me,
Let the air be roused with thunder and convulsion of wild
    winds,
Let hurricanes upheave by the roots the base of the earth,
Let the sea-waves' roaring savagery
Confound the courses of the heavenly stars;
Let him lift me high and hurl me to black Tartarus
On ruthless floods of irresistible doom:
I am one whom he cannot kill.
HERMES: Thoughts and words like these
Are what one may hear from lunatics.
This prayer of his shows all the features of frenzy;
And I see no sign of improvement.
[to the CHORUS] You, however, who sympathize with his
    sufferings,

Get away quickly from this place,
Lest the intolerable roar of thunder stun your senses.
CHORUS: If you want to persuade me, use a different tone
And give other advice. You speak too hastily,
Bidding me do what I could not think of doing.
Would you have me practise cowardice?
I will stay with Prometheus, come what must.
I was taught to hate those who desert their friends;
And there is no infamy I more despise.
HERMES: Then remember my warning;
And when you are caught by calamity
Don't lay the blame on Fortune, or say that Zeus
Plunged you in suffering unforeseen;
Not Zeus but yourselves will be to blame.
You know what is coming; it is neither sudden nor secret.
Only your own folly will entangle you
In the inextricable net of destruction.

Exit HERMES.

PROMETHEUS: Now it is happening: threat gives place to
  performance.
The earth rocks; thunder, echoing from the depth,
Roars in answer; fiery lightnings twist and flash.
Dust dances in a whirling fountain;
Blasts of the four winds skirmish together,
Set themselves in array for battle;
Sky and sea rage indistinguishably.
The cataclysm advances visibly upon me,
Sent by Zeus to make me afraid.

O Earth, my holy mother,
O sky, where sun and moon
Give light to all in turn,
You see how I am wronged!

The rock collapses and disappears, as the
CHORUS *scatter in all directions.*

Sophocles,
Women of Trachis

Preface to Women of Trachis

THE TRADITION

Sophocles' audience would have been very familiar with the many stories of the strong man Heracles, the son of Zeus and Alcmena, persecuted throughout his life by Zeus' wife, Hera, and subjected to his famous labours by Eurystheus, king of Tiryns. In these and other exploits, he was seen as the great liberator of Greece from various beasts and monsters. Tradition told how Heracles died by wearing a poisoned robe sent to him by his wife Deïanira, whom he had originally won in a fight with the river god Acheloüs. Sophocles also drew on an epic poem, *The Capture of Oechalia*, in which Heracles enslaved Iole, the daughter of King Eurytus, and brought her home as his concubine. In historic times, Heracles was accorded status as a hero who (uniquely) went on to become a god. There were numerous cults of him in Attica, and the myth of his cremation on a pyre at the top of Mt Oeta in Thessaly may have been created to explain the existence of an early cult there also. There was another tradition current in Sophocles' time that Heracles was transported to join the gods on Olympus, and it is very possible that this apotheosis was associated with the story of the pyre on Mt Oeta.

SYNOPSIS

Heracles has left home on his final journey, and Deïanira, now approaching middle age, anxiously awaits his return. News is brought by a messenger of the sack of Oechalia by Heracles, who has sent ahead a group of captive women. The captives, who include the beautiful princess Iole, arrive. The herald Lichas who leads them at first disguises the truth that Iole is Heracles' concubine, but is later persuaded to admit the facts. Deïanira, determined to regain Heracles' love, sends him a present she believes will act as a love-charm: a robe anointed with the preserved blood of the centaur Nessus, whom Heracles had killed many years before with an arrow tipped with the venom of the Hydra of Lerna. When Heracles dons the robe, it sticks to his flesh with horrifying results. On learning from her son Hyllus that she has destroyed her husband, Deïanira herself commits suicide. The dying Heracles finally returns home in agony and gives Hyllus instructions to cremate his body on Mt Oeta and to marry Iole.

INTERPRETATION

Women of Trachis is the least well known and possibly the most puzzling of Sophocles' extant tragedies. It appears to fall into two unequal, apparently disjointed parts: the first and much longer part with Deïanira as the central character, and the second, which concentrates on Heracles' agony in the throes of death. There is a further strange disparity between the domestic, civil-ized milieu associated with Deïanira, the faithful wife who seeks to regain her erring husband's love, and the primitive, violent fairy-tale world of beasts and monsters that Heracles inhabits. Another difficulty is that there is no external evidence for dating the play in the sequence of Sophocles' oeuvre.[1] Modern criticism, however, has done a great deal to demonstrate the unity of the piece and to make it a great deal more accessible to the modern reader or theatre audience.[2]

In the first place, it is clear that the drama shows primitive emotions impinging on civilized society. The river-god Acheloüs and the centaur Nessus are explicitly associated with the power of sexual passion, which has such a disruptive influence on the marriage of Heracles and Deïanira. This motif lies at the play's very centre and is an important aspect of its unity.

Furthermore, there is no point in debating whether Deïanira or Heracles is the leading character in the tragedy. In the ancient theatre, the two roles were performed by the same actor, and the play takes its title from neither but from the Chorus, presumably because the two characters are to be seen equally as integral to a single tragic movement. Structurally, the plot follows the 'return home' pattern of a king or hero.[3] Although Heracles himself does not come on until the last quarter of the play, his return is being anticipated and spoken about almost from the outset; his actions and behaviour are very much in the forefront as the drama proceeds. Among the other characters, Hyllus and Lichas are important in relation to both Heracles and Deïanira, and there is a crucial visual link in the play's sole prop: the casket containing the poisoned robe, which leads to the death of both characters played by the lead actor.

No less significant are the themes that bind the fates of Heracles and Deïanira together. First, as we have already noted, is the power of sexual love, *erôs*, which motivates the actions of them both. Twice the Chorus refers to the presiding agency of the 'Cyprian goddess', Aphrodite, who is not portrayed on stage but who is powerfully present in the background of the play's imagery. Moreover, the 'sickness' language associated with sexual passion at several points links it with the poisoned robe. A second idea at the heart of the play is that of mutability in a natural cycle of change in human life. This theme is articulated in the imagery and rhythmical patterning of the Chorus' entrance song (see note 9) and reflected as much in the reversals of mood and expectation as in the tragedy's actual events. Lastly there is the theme of partial and complete knowledge, of learning the truth in the end. This first comes to the fore when Deïanira, after being deceived by Lichas into believing that Iole is someone of no importance, discovers that she in fact has a young and attractive rival for Heracles' affections. Her next dreadful discovery occurs when she realizes that the 'love-charm' of the anointed robe may be a trick of Nessus (deceit again) to avenge his own death on Heracles – partial knowledge made complete when she hears Hyllus' terrible description of what happened when Heracles actually put the robe on. The final recognition is that of Heracles himself when he perceives the meaning of the oracles about the end of his labours and changes from his mood of agonized rage and vindictive indignation to a resigned and much calmer acceptance of his destiny. His death can thus be seen not as an unwelcome appendage to Deïanira's tragedy, but as an integral progression from it: his wife can only respond to the knowledge she has acquired by killing herself, while he, though facing death, is able to confront it with heroic courage.

It seems very possible, if not certain, that the traditional view of Deïanira (her name means 'husband-killer') represented her as deliberately killing Heracles; she was the human agent of Hera's hatred in punishing him for bringing home Iole as his concubine.[4] That would make her like Clytemnestra, who kills her husband Agamemnon, as the embodiment of justice for the sacrifice of their daughter Iphigenia, on his return from Troy in Aeschylus' *Oresteia*. If that is right, Sophocles' portrayal of Heracles' wife as a gentle, compassionate and diffident character is a crucial innovation. Her situation is a great deal more tragic if she kills her husband unintentionally, with the aim of recovering his love. Sophocles may also have been the first poet to have linked the centaur Nessus with the death of Heracles[5] and to have introduced the detail of the arrow steeped in the Hydra's venom[6] as the basis of the supposed love-charm which Deïanira sends to her husband. This certainly adds to the sympathy we feel for her, as she can also be seen as the unwitting instrument of the centaur's revenge.[7] In any event, she emerges as one of the most attractive of Greek tragedy's heroines – no villainess, but a faithful and devoted wife, married to a husband who is constantly absent, and never free from fear and apprehension on his behalf.

Heracles, by contrast, is anything but sympathetic, even if he is 'the greatest man in the world' (177). His insensitivity is evident before he appears in the introduction of Iole into his house and in his brutal treatment of the wretched Lichas, who has brought him the poisoned robe.[8] When he is onstage, the line (1133) in which he regrets that Deïanira has taken her death out of his own hands by suicide is perhaps the most dreadful moment in the play. In some ways he is as much of a beast as the monsters he has destroyed. And yet there is a kind of magnificence in Deïanira's imagined picture (607–9) and Hyllus' description of Heracles standing in the splendid golden robe as he prepares to sacrifice to Zeus at Cenaeum. There is enough greatness established to arouse some compassion for the shattered column of a man whom we see and hear 'sobbing . . . like a girl' (1071–2) in his frightful pain. The great moment of recognition when Hyllus mentions Nessus and Heracles sees the meaning of the paradoxical or ambiguous oracles about himself is deeply moving. After that, despite his self-centred (though very Greek) insistence on Hyllus marrying Iole (see note 83), we are bound to admire the way in which he takes control of all the arrangements for his passing and the heroic courage of his closing lines, before he is carried off to die in the pyre on Mt Oeta.

Scholars have been divided on whether Sophocles expected his audience to watch the closing scene with the perspective of Heracles' eventual apotheosis implicitly in the background. Some have argued that if the poet had intended this point to be borne in mind, he would have made it more explicit, or else that the portrayal of Heracles is too repellent for him to be imagined as becoming a god. The prevailing view now seems to be that apotheosis was so embedded in all the traditions and cult practices to do with Heracles that it could not possibly be left altogether out of account. Indeed, there would be no point in the constant references to Mt Oeta and the drama's conclusion in the march to the pyre unless the apotheosis were implied. As for Heracles' vices, these, like those of other Sophoclean heroes, are to be accepted along with his virtues as two sides of the same coin. His courage and resolution cannot be separated from his selfishness and pride; heroic greatness is not to be submerged beneath civilized refinement. If we ask why apotheosis is never mentioned, the artistic reason is not far to seek: it enhances Heracles' heroism in the face of the pyre, and so the irony of the situation, if he is himself ignorant of the fact (although the audience knows it) that this will lead him not to Hades but to Olympus.

Where, then, does this horrific but strangely beautiful play lead us? The divine perspective has lifted the drama well above the level of human domestic tragedy. The concluding lines of the Chorus summarize the suffering they have witnessed and add, 'And all this story is great Zeus.' Aphrodite is not the only deity presiding over the action. The name of Zeus is invoked again and again in the text, and his will is expressed in the oracles and written tablets of prophecy which the plot shows being fulfilled. In the end, Zeus was not blind and indifferent to his own son (cf. 140). All this suggests an outlook that human life, in all its instability, may be cruelly hard and unpredictable, but there is still an underlying meaning and purpose to it. The gods have knowledge where mortals are ignorant. That message is what makes *Women of Trachis* so peculiarly powerful. The play is not merely saying, 'Even the greatest men can be brought down by the power of sex.' It also grapples philosophically with the mystery of human suffering.

CASTING

The first actor must have played both Deïanira and Heracles in a doubling almost inconceivable in the modern theatre, which could well have emphasized the continuity and progression between the earlier and later parts of the drama. The second actor probably took the roles of Hyllus and Lichas; the third combined the Nurse, the Messenger and the Old Man. Mutes required were: Iole (no doubt distinctively masked) among the group of captive women, soldiers guarding them, Deïanira's attendant and men bearing Heracles' litter.

STAGING

There are no technical problems in this play. The stage-building would have represented the house associated with Deïanira. One of the *eisodoi* (see Appendix) could have served for almost all entrances from elsewhere, the other, perhaps, being reserved for the solemn exit to Mt Oeta at the very end. Opportunities for spectacle were there in the choral dances, the entry and grouping of the captives, and the processions on and off with the dying Heracles on his litter. The moment when Heracles reveals his body with the poisoned robe clinging to him would have been the visual high point in the long closing scene.

DRAMATIC TECHNIQUE

Women of Trachis and *Ajax* are regarded as the earlier two among the four plays of Sophocles in this volume, but neither can be exactly dated. The former is printed first, as it seems the closest in technique to the extant plays of Sophocles' predecessor, Aeschylus. The drama of that earlier poet, though outstandingly powerful, does not hang in the main on what is actually *done* onstage. The carefully contrived dynamic thrust depends above all else on what is *said*. This may include some description of past events, but words are also conceived and employed as having *power* to control the fate of the persons or communities with which the plot is concerned, either favourably or adversely. Thus prayers for good or expressions of hope are 'performative utterances' felt to carry the drama forward in a positive kind of way, while curses or expressions of fear are assumed to have a contrary effect. Sometimes language can be used ambiguously or contain resonances of which the character speaking may or may not be aware, but which the audience (or some of it) has the knowledge to pick up. This last phenomenon is known as dramatic (or tragic) irony and often regarded as an artistic device that lends a kind of spice to the drama. Irony, however, runs more deeply than that, if words are seen as a form of *action*, including action of which the characters performing it may not be fully in control and which implies the existence of forces, personified by the gods or fate, mysteriously operating in the background and contributing to the drama's momentum towards a conclusion, whether sad, joyful or strangely enigmatic.

Thus in Aeschylus' *Agamemnon* (with which *Women of Trachis* has certain things in common) the issue of Agamemnon's homecoming to be murdered by his wife Clytemnestra is shaped not by showing the queen plotting with her lover Aegisthus, but by ominous words spoken by the Chorus and solo-speaking characters, which inspire an overwhelming sense that when Agamemnon returns to Argos victorious after the sack of Troy, he is completely doomed. The Chorus and principals favourable to Agamemnon keep trying to say the right, well-omened thing, but their train of thought and utterance always leads them to a dismal conclusion, while the malevolent Clytemnestra indulges in a sinister kind of wordplay, like a witch's spell, full of double meanings, to hammer verbal nails into Agamemnon's coffin.

Sophocles dramatizes the return of Heracles in a similar way. In the play's very first words, Deïanira begins by quoting an 'old saying': 'Call no man happy until he is dead.' Now one might explain this opening quite simply, by saying that Deïanira is using a commonplace maxim in order to contradict it. She goes on to tell the audience that she knows already before *she* dies (as in fact happens in the play) that her own life is *un*happy. But the chief issue in the play as it unfolds is to be the death of Heracles. Did *he* die happy or unhappy? The *visual* climax of the play is excruciatingly frightful: we see the dying, but still alive, Heracles tortured by the most appalling physical agony, displaying the wounds on his mangled body, which is being eaten away by the 'shirt of Nessus'. But Heracles' final speech (1262) speaks of a *joyful* ending to his travail. He means the release that death will bring him, but his words also convey the resonance of the apotheosis in the Athenian cult of the hero. As note 3 on the text points out, this specific conclusion may also be implicit in the resonances of Deïanira's initial quotation.

Deïanira is not, of course, malevolent to her husband like Clytemnestra. Indeed, in this respect, Sophocles seems to have departed from tradition (see p. 6). However, her constant expressions of fear and her modifications of positive statements by qualifying 'if' or 'unless' clauses[9] may be seen, in themselves, as words of bad omen. Moreover, if we know, as the ancient audience would have done, what will happen to Heracles when he puts on the poisoned robe, Deïanira's words about a gift 'in *fitting* response' to the ones that Heracles sent (494) are a fine example of the sort of unconscious irony which Aeschylus liked to put into the mouths of his characters – as is Lichas' promise at 623 to deliver the robe to Heracles and 'tell him about your vow, to *clinch* the matter'.

In a similar way, what happens in this play is determined by the oracles and prophecies, which keep recurring, though always in a slightly different form – a ploy that has the effect of enhancing the mystery and maintaining suspense. Sophocles makes play with oracles in almost all his extant dramas, and their ambiguous or paradoxical quality is part of the magical power of words that also lies at the root of dramatic irony.

Not all of the language in Sophocles is ominous or ambivalent. Nevertheless, it is remarkable how much of what *happens* in *Women of Trachis* is not enacted onstage, but described in long narrative speeches. The 'messenger speech' convention was, of course, part of the Greek tragedy recipe from its very outset, but the most striking formal characteristic of this play is that Deïanira, Lichas, Hyllus and the Nurse are all given graphic stories to tell in 'messenger mode'. All of these speeches, except for Lichas' narrative at 248–90 (which is strangely confused in its arrangement and entails a major suppression of the truth), either anticipate or describe the disasters to which the drama is leading, and so can legitimately be regarded as parts of the play's *action*.

Paradoxically, the one character actually called a messenger has a comparatively short speech. His function as a foil and counterweight to Lichas is as important as his news-bearing role. In general, there is much less in the way of stichomythic exchange in this play than in the rest of Sophocles' extant output. This makes the exchanges we *do* get all the more exciting: the altercation between the Messenger and Lichas (with Deïanira in between, turning from one to the other as they volley their shots), and the two important verbal tussles between the dying Heracles and his son Hyllus in the closing scenes.

Although the Chorus bears the title of this play, it is nothing like so prominent as in Aeschylus' surviving plays.[10] The women still play a significant part in the drama's dynamic. The imagery of their beautiful songs highlights the general themes of *erós* / Aphrodite, the mutability of human life and oracles as an expression of its ordered pattern. They are also used to identify with Deïanira's joys and hopes or (more often) her sorrows and fears. In so doing they contribute much to the play's continuity through Sophocles' choral technique of backward and forward reference. In their sympathy with Deïanira, the Trachiniae are characterized as *young* women, unaffected so far by the stresses of marriage and parenthood. This is important for the one moment when they become involved in the action in a practical way, rather than responding to it as witnesses. When Deïanira, with her characteristic diffidence, asks them if they think it foolish of her to send Heracles the anointed robe before she has tested the ointment out, they advise her to act regardless, with the naive comment that 'you'll never know [whether it's safe] unless you try.' And so Deïanira hands over the casket to Lichas, with disastrous consequences.

The point just mentioned about continuity needs reinforcing. Far from composing a 'broken-backed' play, something Sophocles has been accused of in the past, his technique keeps the drama moving forward, within its formal conventions, with the inexorable logic of a musical composition. The notes to the play aim to show how this is done, particularly in the use of 'dovetailed' entrances as an alternative to introducing new arrivals by formal announcements. No less important, of course, are the sudden changes and reversals of mood, which illustrate the suddenness of change in human life.

Finally, I have suggested in my discussion of the play's interpretation that Sophocles' public entered the theatre with expectations of a vengeful Deïanira, and that the different characterization of Heracles' wife in this play may well be innovative. It is also highly likely that the audience assumed that Heracles was going to his deification at the end, even if this was only suggested by an association of ideas. This 'discrepant awareness' on the audience's part is not simply an incidental point of technique. As in other Sophocles plays, it is a crucial factor in his peculiar brand of irony, integral to the way in which his drama works in the theatre and the kind of pleasure it will have inspired in its original audience. With a minimum of supplementary information, it can inspire a similar pleasure in a spectator or reader today.

NOTES

1. Any date between 457 and 430 is possible.
2. I am particularly indebted here to the important work of Pat Easterling and to articles by Jenny March, Philip Holt, Robert L. Fowler and Barbara Goward.
3. Two obvious examples are Homer's *Odyssey* and *Agamemnon*, the first play of Aeschylus' Orestean trilogy.
4. Homer (*Iliad* 18.117–19) refers to Heracles being 'subdued by fate and the cruel wrath of Hera'. The Hesiodic *Catalogue of Women* (sixth century BC) mentions Deïanira's anointing of a robe, which she gave to Lichas. Iole was known from *The Capture of Oechalia*.
5. This story also occurs in a dithyramb by the lyric poet Bacchylides (fifth century BC), but it is not possible to establish whether he derived it from Sophocles or vice versa.
6. Representations in art show Heracles killing Nessus, who had tried to rape Deïanira, with his club or a sword.
7. It also gives Sophocles the opportunity for the tragic paradox of 'the dead killing the living', of which he was so fond (see note 77). Heracles himself becomes the victim of the monsters (the Hydra and Nessus) whom he has rid the world of by his heroic prowess.
8. Not to mention his imputed murder of Iphitus in Lichas' narrative (269–73), which we have no reason to doubt on this particular point.
9. For example, at 27, 228, 243 and especially 586–7.
10. Except in *Prometheus Bound*, which many scholars today believe to be the work of another hand.

Characters

DEÏANIRA, *wife of Heracles*
NURSE
HYLLUS, *son of Deïanira and Heracles*
CHORUS *of women of Trachis*
MESSENGER
LICHAS, *a herald*
OLD MAN
IOLE, *daughter of King Eurytus*
CAPTIVE WOMEN, GUARDS, ATTENDANT, BEARERS

[*Scene: Before the palace of Ceyx in Trachis.*][1]

SCENE 1[2]

[*Enter* DEÏANIRA *from the palace.*]
DEÏANIRA:
An old saying goes: 'You can never know for sure
Whether a mortal's life has been good or bad
Until his death.'[3] You can in my case. I know
Too well, this side of the grave, how hard and unlucky   5
My life has been. When I lived in Pleuron,
In my father Oeneus' house, I dreaded the thought
Of marriage more than any girl in the land.
My hand was sought by the river god Acheloüs,
Who took three shapes when he asked my father to make   10
Me his: first, he revealed himself as a bull,
Then as a serpent with shimmering[4] coils, and last
As a monster in human form with the horns of an ox
And rivulets streaming over his tangled beard.
Waiting in terror, I kept on praying to die   15
Before I yielded to such a lover's embrace.

At last, to my huge relief and joy, he arrived –
Heracles, Zeus' and Alcmena's glorious son.
He closed in combat with the river god   20
And set me free. How the battle was fought
I could not tell, as I do not know. Some brave,

Intrepid spectator might be able to say.
For me, I sat apart, benumbed with terror,
25 Shuddering to think of the pain my beauty could win.
But Zeus, the god of battles, brought about
A happy ending – if happy it was. I became
Heracles' bride, but still I'm haunted by one fear
After another, in endless fretting for him.
30 Night follows night, and worry succeeds to worry.
We did have children, but Heracles rarely saw them,
Like a farmer who only visits a distant field
At seed-time and harvest. That was my husband's life,
35 Coming and going from home in endless servitude.
          [*Enter* NURSE *from palace.*]⁵
And now when he has surmounted all these labours,
I feel more frightened than ever I did before.
The killing of Iphitus⁶ meant we had to uproot
40 Ourselves and live as guests with the king of Trachis.
But where my husband is not a soul can tell.
I only know the bitter pains that his absence
Inflicts on *me*. He's in some danger now,
I am almost certain. Fifteen months have gone by
45 And still no news. He *must* be in terrible danger.
That tablet he left for me when he went away –
How often I pray to the gods it bodes no harm!
NURSE:
Deïanira, mistress, I've often watched you
50 Sobbing and shedding tears in long lament
For Heracles' never-ending absence abroad.
I'm only a slave, but may I presume to advise you?
Why aren't you sending one of your many sons
To search him out? Hyllus would be the best,
55 If he's at all concerned for auspicious news
Of his father's welfare. Look now, here he is,
Racing towards the house just when we need him.
So if you believe that my advice is sound,
60 You can take advantage of his arrival too.
          [*Enter* HYLLUS *by a side entrance.*]

DEÏANIRA:

My dearest boy! Listen, it doesn't take breeding
To talk good sense. This woman's only a slave,
But you wouldn't think it, to judge by her words just now.

HYLLUS:

What has she said? Please tell me, Mother.

DEÏANIRA:

You haven't inquired about your father. He's been   65
Abroad for such a time. It does you shame.

HYLLUS:

I know where he is, if report can be trusted.

DEÏANIRA:

Exactly where have you heard, my boy?

HYLLUS:

For all of the past twelve months they say
He has worked as a slave for a Lydian woman.[7]   70

DEÏANIRA:

Heracles work as a slave? No, no!

HYLLUS:

At least he's released from *that*, I hear.

DEÏANIRA:

Where is he now, alive or dead?

HYLLUS:

He's in Euboea,[8] marching an army
Against King Eurytus' city, Oechalia –   75
Or just about to invade.

DEÏANIRA:

Euboea! My son, you know he left me
An oracle about that very place?

HYLLUS:

I don't know, Mother. What did it say?

DEÏANIRA:

That 'either Heracles would end his days,
Or else this exploit would be followed by   80
A life of happiness for ever after.'
His fate lies in the balance, my dear son.
So won't you go to help? His life and safety

85 Mean *our* safety, or we're lost with him.

HYLLUS:
Mother, of course I'll go. If I'd only known
About this prophecy, I'd have been there long since.
I trusted my father's usual luck, and never
Allowed myself to fret or be over-anxious
90 On his behalf. But now I've heard those words,
I'll spare no effort to learn the truth behind them.

DEÏANIRA:
Be off, then, son. However late you arrive,
News of success is always a source of gain.

[*Exit* HYLLUS, *by a side entrance;* DEÏANIRA *and* NURSE *go back into the palace.*]

CHORAL ENTRANCE SONG[9]

[*Enter* CHORUS *of young Trachinian women.*]
CHORUS:
      O Sún whom Night, spóiled of her shímmering
          stárs,   [*Strophe 1*]
95   Brings forth and puts to sleep in a cradle of flame,[10]
      Helios, Helios, help us!
      Cry aloud your answer, tell me
      Where is the son of Alcmena,
      Heracles, thou lord of the burning ray?
100   To eastward near the Pontus' straits?
      Or westward, straddling continents?[11]
      Speak out, O Sun, all-seeing master!

      I héard it said, Deïaníra, the príze   [*Antistrophe 1*]
      He fought for, weeps and waits in her longing desire,
105   Cries like a bird in bereavement,
      Always longing, always weeping,
      Never closing her eyelids
      Fast in sleep; but feeding a fear that recalls
      Her man who's gone, she watches, anxious,
110   Racked upon her lonely bed,
      Distraught with grief and grim foreboding.

See, on the breadths of the ocean   [*Strophe* 2]
Roller on roller advancing,
Driven by blasts of the tireless
Winds from the south or the north.   115
So Héracles tósses on life's
Stórmy seas. Nów he's submerged,
Nów upraised; nów in a trough,
Nów on the crést. Yet sóme divíne
Spirit prevents his toppling down,   120
Down to the house of Hades.[12]

[DEÏANIRA *re-enters from the palace.*][13]
Lady, I love and respect you,   [*Antistrophe* 2]
Yet must I fault you for grieving.
Do not despair in your sorrow,
Hold to your hopes for the good.   125
King Zeús, the ordaíner supreme,
Rúled that life cánnot remain
Freé from all páin and distress.[14]
No, in a cycle of joy and pain,
Fortune revolves from day to day,   130
Órbiting líke the Gréat Bear.

The shimmering night yields to dawn,   [*Epode*]
Man's disasters pass away;
A flash, and golden wealth is lost.
It soon becomes our neighbour's turn   135
For dáys of jóy or leán tímes.
So nów I bíd you, lády, keép this ín your héart
And líft your hópes hígh. For whó behéld Zeús
So blínd, cóld, hárd towárds his ówn sóns?[15]   140

SCENE 2[16]

DEÏANIRA:
You're here, I suppose, because you've heard about
My unhappy plight. I hope you never know
For yourselves the pain I feel deep down inside me.

Young plants are grown in sheltered places, untroubled
145 By sun's strong heat, the rain or stormy winds.
A girl's like a sapling, happy and carefree,
Until her girlhood's ended and she's now
A wife. We start to lie awake at night
150 And fret about our husbands or our children.
You'll learn then from your own changed way of life
The kind of misery that is torturing me.

Well, I've had many reasons for distress,
But here is something absolutely new.
155 When Heracles went from here on his last journey,
He left behind an ancient tablet,[17] inscribed
With mystic letters. He'd never mentioned it
Before, when he'd gone off on one of his labours.
160 His thoughts were on success, never on death.
This time he spoke as though his end had come.
He gave instructions, first for what he'd settled
On me as his wife, and then on how he willed
His estate should be divided among his children.
165 He specified a time and said to me,
'When I have been abroad for fifteen months,
The moment will have come when I shall either
Have to die, or else survive to live
A life that's free from pain for ever after.'
170 This, he declared, Fate had ordained should mark
The last of Heracles' labours. So Dodona's
Ancient oak had spoken, through the mouth
Of the twin priestesses[18] at Zeus' oracle.

The moment's now. Those words are coming true.
175 That's why, dear friends, when I'm asleep at night,
The nightmare startles me out of bed in terror.
To stay bereft of the greatest man in the world!
CHORUS LEADER:
No more ill-omened words![19] I see a man coming,
His head crowned with a wreath. He bears good news.
    [*Enter* MESSENGER.]

MESSENGER:
My lady Deïanira, allow me to be   180
The first to give you tidings and calm your fears.
Heracles is alive, victorious, bearing
The battle spoils' first fruits to the gods of Malis.
DEÏANIRA:
Amazing news, old sir! Please tell me again.
MESSENGER:
I say your glorious husband will soon be coming   185
Home to your house, in all the might of victory.
DEÏANIRA:
How and where on earth did you find this out?
MESSENGER:
In a field where the oxen graze in summer, Lichas
The herald's addressing a crowd. As soon as I heard him,
I darted away, in order, of course, to bring   190
The news to you first and so ensure my reward.
DEÏANIRA:
Why isn't he here himself with his joyful tidings?
MESSENGER:
Madam, it's hardly easy. The whole population
Of Malis is thronging round and interrogating him.
He can't move an inch. They all have their own questions   195
To ask and won't let him go till they've had their answers.
So, willy-nilly, he's trapped. But it won't be long
Before he arrives and you can see him yourself.
DEÏANIRA:
O Zeus, god of the sacred meadow on Oeta's   200
Heights![20] At last, at last you have brought us joy!
Raise the cry, you women within the house,
And you who stand without. This comforting news
Is a rising sun I never thought to see!
CHORUS:
    Now sing a sóng of jóy![21]   205
    Now let the héarth resóund
    Álalalaí!
    The hoúse awaíts the bríde and groóm. So lét the chóir
    Of mén crý stróng for óur Deféndér,

210   Apólló, árcher gód.
        And wíth them, ó maídens, ráise
        Víctory's páean, the tríumph hýmn,
        And shóut his síster's náme alóud,
        Délian Ártemis, tórch goddess, shóoter of déer.
215   Práise the nýmphs of Málís!
        I sóar to héaven, enthrálled to héar
        The jóyful, skírling pípe,[22] O máster óf my sóul.
        Oh sée, hów it transpórts mé –
        Euhói! –
        My ívy crówn, which whírls me róund
220   In frénzied Bácchus' wíld dánce!
        [The CHORUS dances round, as LICHAS and some soldiers
        enter with a group of captive women, including IOLE.]
        Ió, ió, Paián!
        Lóok, oh lóok, my lády déar,
        The néws is trúe, the shíp's come ín,
        Befóre your éyes in fúll víew!
    DEÏANIRA:
225 Yes, yes, dear women. I have watched it all.
    I see the whole procession. Herald, at last
    You've come, and I wish you joy – if your news is joyful.
    LICHAS:
    My coming here's auspicious. So is your welcome.
230 The occasion merits it, madam. When fortune's fair,
    Fair greetings are the order of the day.
    DEÏANIRA:
    You are the best of friends! First questions first.
    Is Heracles coming home to me alive?
    LICHAS:
    Yes, surely. When I left him, he was alive
235 And strong as ever, in the best of health.
    DEÏANIRA:
    And where was that? In Greece or farther abroad?
    LICHAS:
    You know Euboea. There on Cape Cenaeum
    Your lord is consecrating ground to Zeus,
    For altars and for tribute-bearing soil.[23]

DEÏANIRA:
Fulfilling a vow, or on some oracle's orders?
LICHAS:
He made a vow when he planned to take and uproot 240
The country of these women you see before you.
DEÏANIRA:
Who are these women? Who's their master? Tell me.
Their plight, if I'm not deceived, is worth some pity.
LICHAS:
When Heracles sacked Oechalia, these were the ones
He chose for his household slaves or temple servants. 245
DEÏANIRA:
Was it to take that city he stayed away
Those countless days, so unforeseeably long?
LICHAS:[24]
No, most of the time he was detained in Lydia.
He wasn't a free man – so he says himself –
As he'd been sold as a slave. (Madam, no need 250
To take offence, where Zeus is clearly at work.)
Yes, he was Omphale's slave and freely admits
He served the Lydian queen for one whole year.
He was so incensed at suffering this disgrace
That he bound himself with a solemn oath to act: 255
'I swear I'll make a slave of the man who caused me
All this shame – along with his wife and children!'
His words weren't spoken in vain. Once purified,
He formed a private army and marched against
The city of Eurytus, who he claimed was the person 260
Solely to blame for his recent humiliation.

Why so? When he was staying at Eurytus' house
As a guest and family friend, his host had treated
Him to a load of malicious and foolish insults.
'Your arrows may be unerring,' he'd jeered, 'but you're still 265
A less good archer than my own sons.' He then
Exclaimed, 'Eurystheus' slave! You're being broken
By all those labours.' Last, when Heracles got himself
Drunk at a banquet, he'd thrown him out of the house.

270   Your husband took his revenge when Eurytus' young son
      Iphitus later came to the hill of Tiryns,
      Following in the tracks of some straying horses.
      The youth was looking distractedly over the plain,
      When Heracles pushed him over the citadel walls.

275   This incident made Olympian Zeus, the royal
      Father of all, extremely angry. He sent
      The hero out to be sold as a slave. The reason?
      Iphitus was the only person he'd ever
      Chosen to murder by stealth, and this was not
      To be borne. If he'd taken revenge in an open way,
      Zeus would have forgiven a just reprisal. The gods,
280   No less than men, dislike insulting behaviour.
      Eurytus, then, and his sons have paid the price
      For their arrogant rudeness, and all have gone to the grave.
      What's more, their city's enslaved. These women you see here,
      After a sorry change of fortune, now
285   Are assigned to you. Those were your husband's orders,
      Which I, as his faithful servant, am carrying out.
      As for himself, as soon as he's offered the sacrifice
      Due to his father Zeus for Oechalia's fall,
      You can reckon that he'll be here. Of all the auspicious
290   News I've brought, you'll be best pleased with that.
      CHORUS LEADER:
      My lady, now your joy is assured. These captives
      Are here already, and Heracles soon will arrive.
      DEÏANIRA:
      Yes, in conscience, I must be glad to hear
295   That all is well with my husband. It has to follow.
      And yet, when I think about it, there's still the fear
      That our good luck may suddenly be reversed.
      I, my friends, feel deeply sorry to see
      Those ill-starred prisoners, here in a foreign land,
300   Exiles who've lost their fathers and lost their homes,
      The daughters of free men, maybe, but now condemned
      To a life as slaves. O Zeus, who turns the tide
      Of battle, may I never see you strike

A child of mine like this, or if you must,
I pray you do it when I'm not here to see!   305
Seeing these women fills me with such foreboding.
  [*She approaches one of the women.*]
Unhappy girl,[25] please tell me who you are.
Have you a husband? Children? You look as if
You're still too young – though nobly born, I'd say.
Lichas, who is this girl? Who were her father   310
And mother? Tell me; I feel more sorry for her
Than all the others. She shows great dignity.
LICHAS:
How would *I* know? Why should you ask? Perhaps
She comes from one of Oechalia's better families.   315
DEÏANIRA:
The royal house? Eurytus' child, maybe?
LICHAS:
Can't say. I didn't go out of my way to ask.
DEÏANIRA:
Did you hear her name from one of her friends on the road?
LICHAS:
No, I was quietly getting on with my job.
DEÏANIRA:
Well, poor child, you tell me your name yourself.   320
It's really sad that I don't know who you are.
LICHAS:
You won't get very much out of her, I fear.
You know, ever since she left her ruined country,
We haven't heard her utter a single word.
She has been in misery over her wretched lot,   325
Endlessly crying her eyes out. Certainly she's come
Down in the world, but we shouldn't press her too far.
DEÏANIRA:
Very well, we had better leave her alone and allow her
To pass indoors in peace. I wouldn't want   330
To add to her pain myself. It is bad enough
As it is. Let's all go in. You'll want to be busy
For your return, while I arrange things here.
  [*The prisoners, soldiers and* LICHAS *start to move towards*

the house and gradually pass offstage. The MESSENGER
advances and stops DEÏANIRA.]

MESSENGER:

335   Wait here a moment first! A word in private.
       You need to learn what people you're taking indoors,
       And be made aware of things that you ought to know
       But haven't been told. *I* know the whole of the truth.

DEÏANIRA:

       What is it? Why are you trying to stop me?

MESSENGER:

340   Just wait and listen. My earlier news
       Was worth your attention. This will be too.

DEÏANIRA:

       Do you want me to call the others back,
       Or simply to speak with me and these women?

MESSENGER:

       With you and them I can be quite open.
       Forget the others.

DEÏANIRA:

345   They've gone now. Speak.

MESSENGER:

       All the information that fellow gave
       Just now was totally wrong. Either he lied,
       Or else he wasn't telling the truth before.

DEÏANIRA:

       What? You must explain what you mean.

350   I don't understand a word you've said.

MESSENGER:

       I heard that man declaring, before a host
       Of witnesses, this: It was all for that beautiful girl
       That Heracles sacked Oechalia's lofty towers
       And conquered Eurytus. Love was the only god

355   To charm him into this warlike expedition,
       Nothing to do with penal servitude out
       In Lydia, under Omphale, nothing to do
       With Iphitus' death when he hurled him down from the walls.
       Lichas has changed his story, omitting Love.

In fact, when Heracles failed to persuade her father
To let him have the girl as his secret bedmate,   360
He trumped up some excuse or other, and then
Invaded her land and sacked her city. Now,
As you see, he has come back home with the lass in tow.   365
It has all been carefully planned, my lady. She
Won't be a slave – you mustn't imagine that.
It's hardly likely, given that furnace of lust.

That's why, dear madam, I felt you had to know
The facts, as I chanced to hear them from Lichas' lips.   370
What's more, there were plenty of others who heard him
   speaking,
Right at the heart of Trachis' meeting place.
They could challenge him, too. If my news isn't welcome,
I'm sorry for that – but still I've told you the truth!

DEÏANIRA:
Oh god, what's happening to me? I'm so distressed!   375
What lurking pest am I harbouring under
My own roof? God, oh god! Can she be so lacking
In all distinction, as Lichas who brought her swore?

MESSENGER:
I'll say! Her birth is just as illustrious
As her beautiful face. She's Eurytus' daughter, once   380
Called Iole. Lichas never chose to inform
You so – he didn't go out of his way to ask!

CHORUS LEADER:
What underhand behaviour! A lie like that
Deserves more condemnation than other wrongs.

DEÏANIRA:
Oh women, what should I do?   385
This news – I'm cut to the quick!

CHORUS LEADER:
Go to Lichas; demand the truth. Perhaps
He'll give you an explanation, if you press him.

DEÏANIRA:
You're right. I'll go at once.

MESSENGER:

390   What about me? Should I go or stay?

DEÏANIRA:

Please stay. Here's Lichas in person,
Leaving the house of his own accord.

    [*Re-enter* LICHAS *from the palace.*]

LICHAS:

Madam, what message may I take Heracles?
Tell me, I'm on my way, as you see.

DEÏANIRA:

395   You took so long to arrive, and now how quickly
You're rushing off, before we've spoken again!

LICHAS:

If you wish to ask any questions, I'm at your service.

DEÏANIRA:

Will you really give me the honest truth?

LICHAS:

Zeus be my witness, I shall, if I know.

DEÏANIRA:

400   Who, then, is the woman you came with here?

LICHAS:

She's from Euboea. I've no idea
Who her parents are.

MESSENGER [*coming forward*]:

                You! Look here!
Who do you think you're talking to, man?

LICHAS:

Why on earth should you ask me that?

MESSENGER:

Come on, reply, if you have the wit!

LICHAS:

405   I'm addressing the lady Deïanira,
Daughter of Oeneus, Heracles' wife,
My mistress – unless my sight is deceived.

MESSENGER:

Just what I wanted to hear you say.
Your mistress – yes?

LICHAS:
That's quite correct.

MESSENGER:
Well, then, what do you think the correct reward   410
If your treatment of her is found to be incorrect?

LICHAS:
How incorrect? What are you quibbling about?

MESSENGER:
Quibbling! It's you who are doing that.

LICHAS:
I'm going. I've been a fool
To listen to you so long.

MESSENGER:
You won't until you have answered one brief question.   415

LICHAS:
Ask what you wish. You have a tongue in your head.

MESSENGER:
That female prisoner you've taken into the house –
I suppose you know who I mean?

LICHAS:
Of course, why ask?

MESSENGER:
Didn't you say this girl, whom you pretend   420
To know nothing about, was Iole, Eurytus' daughter?

LICHAS:
Said it to whom, and where? Your witnesses, please.
Who'll testify to hearing me make that statement?

MESSENGER:
You said it in public. A huge great crowd in the middle
Of Trachis' meeting place heard that much from you.

LICHAS:
Very well.   425
They *said* they heard it. Giving a rough impression
Is not the same as an accurate statement of fact.

MESSENGER:
A rough impression! Didn't you claim on oath
That you were bringing the girl to be Heracles' woman?

LICHAS:

430 On oath? His woman? For god's sake, my dear lady,
Tell me, who on earth is this interloper?

MESSENGER:

A witness, who heard you say it was lust for her
That caused Oechalia's ruin. It wasn't destroyed
By Lydia's queen, but Heracles' flagrant passion.

LICHAS:

Tell this fellow to go, my lady. No sane
435 Person bandies words with a man who's sick!

DEÏANIRA:

No, I beg you,[26] by Zeus whose lightnings flash
Atop Mt Oeta, don't cheat me or hide the truth.
You know I'm not a hard, ungenerous woman.
I understand the ways of the world, and human
440 Nature is never constant in its desires.
You can't engage in a boxing match with Love.[27]
Who'd be such a fool? Love governs even the gods
At his own sweet will. He certainly governs *me*.
Why not another woman just like myself?
445 Love is a sickness. If I get angry with my own
Husband for having caught it, I'm utterly mad.
There's no sense either in being angry with *her*.
She's doing nothing to be ashamed of or harmful
To me. I can't be jealous. No, if you're telling
450 Lies on my man's instructions, you've learned a bad lesson.
Perhaps you're teaching yourself to lie. In that case,
People will doubt your word when you want to be trusted.
Please tell me the whole truth. Look, you're not a slave!
For a freeborn person like you to be called a liar
455 Is real disgrace. And you won't get away with your lie.
There are many to whom you've talked who'll talk to me.
If you're afraid, your fear's misguided. Indeed,
Not learning the truth is what would give me distress.
But *knowing* – what's so dreadful in that?[28] Hasn't Heracles
460 Taken dozens of other women to bed?
None of them ever received hard words or reproaches
From *me*. Neither would Iole, even if

She were pining away with love herself. Didn't
I pity her more than the others as soon as I saw her?
Her beauty's ruined her life, and she was the poor   465
Unwitting cause of her home town's sack and enslavement.
Well, blow wind! But to you I'll say: If you must
Tell lies, then tell them to others, but never to me!
CHORUS LEADER:
Do as she says. She's right. You'll have no cause   470
To fault her kindness, and I shall be grateful, too.
LICHAS:
Well, dear lady, I see you think as a mortal
Should and show some feeling for human weakness.
I'll hide the truth no longer and tell you all.
Yes, it is just as this man says: the girl   475
Inspired the terrible passion that shot through Heracles.
She was the cause that led to her father's desolate
Realm, Oechalia, facing capture and ruin.
I need to add, in my master's defence, that he never
Denied his love or ordered me to conceal it.   480
No, I took it upon myself to lie, because
I felt afraid this story would give you pain.
If you account this wrong, then I was at fault.

Since, however, you *are* aware of the whole truth,
Please, for Heracles' sake and your own no less,   485
Accept this girl in your house and try to act
On the tolerant words you used just now towards her.
Your husband's prowess may be supreme in everything
    else,
But his love for her has proved his utter defeat.[29]
DEÏANIRA:
Yes, be sure, that is what I'm minded to do.   490
No point in nursing a sickness that's self-imposed
By fighting a losing battle against the gods.
Let's go inside now. You must be given my message
And also carry a gift,[30] in fitting response
To the ones he sent. You must not leave empty-handed   495
After arriving here so richly attended.

[*Exeunt* DEÏANIRA *and* LICHAS *into the palace, the* MESS-
ENGER *by a side entrance.*[31]]

CHORAL SONG 1

CHORUS:
What a víctory the Cýprian góddess[32] will álways béar
    awáy!   [*Strophe*]
Bést be sílent
500   Of the góds, and of hów she beguíled the Olýmpian lórd of
    áll,
Hádes the kíng of the dárkness,
Ór Poseídon[33] sháker of eárth with his trídent.
Síng we of Déïaníra
And the méttlesome rívals who stróve for her hánd,
505   Of stróng blóws, clóuds of dúst that fílled the lísts,
Áfter the fíghters éntered.

One a ríver god stróng in the fórm of a foúr-legg'd búll,
    with hórns   [*Antistrophe*]
Shárp and tówering,
510   Acheloüs from Óeniadáe. And he fáced the són of Zéus,
Héracles, wíelding his cúrved bow,
Brándishíng two spéars and the clúb he had bórne from
Thébes. Then uniting in óne mass,
They attácked and they lócked in the héat of desíre;
515   While Lóve's gréat quéen alóne, with stáff in hánd,
Júdged the dispúte betwéen them.

And thén there were póunding fists,[34] twángings
    of bów,   [*Epode*]
Cláshing hórns in a whírl of confúsion.
520   Then wréstlers' grápplings ládder-like,[35] blóws from the
    bull's báttering fórehead,
Groánings and grúntings on bóth sides.
Whíle that lóvely maiden
Crówned a dístant híllside,

Sítting in fear. Whó should bé her máster?   525
For mé, I téll the tále as thóugh I'd wátched thére.[36]
But shé, the fáir príze they sóught to táke hóme,
Could ónly wáit with thróbbing héart –
Góne her móther, her lífe uptúrned,
Lóst like a cálf abándoned.   530

SCENE 3[37]

[DEÏANIRA *re-enters from the palace accompanied by an*
attendant holding a casket.]
DEÏANIRA:
My friends, while Lichas is bidding farewell indoors
To the captive women, I've slipped outside to you,
Partly to say what I have contrived[38] to do,
But also to claim your sympathy in my plight.   535

This girl, no longer an *innocent* girl, I think,
Is now installed. I've allowed her to come on board,
As a merchant accepts an extra item of freight,[39]
To destroy my peace of mind. Now there are two of us,
Under a single blanket, awaiting the arms
Of a single lover. That's the wages Heracles –   540
Faithful, noble man as I thought – has sent me
For looking after his home in his lengthy absence.
I can't be *angry*. This malady strikes him far
Too often for that. But living together in one house,
Sharing the self-same partner – what woman could stand
For that? Her beauty, I see, is fast approaching   545
Its full perfection, while mine is fading away.
A man's eye's greedy to pluck the flower of youth,
But cast on an older woman, it turns away.
This makes me afraid that Heracles will be called   550
'Deïanira's husband, Iole's man.'
Yet, as I've said, resentment isn't a course
For a sensible woman. Friends, I have found a way
To rid myself of this fear. I'll tell it you now.

555 Long years ago, in days gone by, I received
     A gift which I hid away in a brazen urn.
     I was still a girl, and it came from the centaur[40] Nessus,
     A horse with the shaggy front of a man. As he
     Was dying, I took my gift from his bleeding wound.
     Nessus was running a ferry across a river,
560 The deep Evenus, and charging a fare. His passengers
     Didn't cross in a rowing- or sailing-boat.
     He carried them all in his arms. He carried me too,
     When my father, Oeneus, sent me away from home
     And I first accompanied Heracles as his bride.
     I was riding on Nessus' shoulders, but when we'd reached
565 Midstream, he started to fondle my body. I screamed
     For help, and at once Zeus' son turned round and shot
     An arrow, which whistled its way to the centaur's chest
     And lodged in his lungs. With his dying breath, the beast
     Gasped out, 'Now listen, Deïanira! This
570 Is how you will gain from being ferried by me
     As my final passenger, if you'll do what I say.
     Take the clotted blood from around my wound,
     Where Heracles' arrow, dipped in the Hydra of Lerna's[41]
     Murky venom, struck. That blood will give you
575 A charm for Heracles' heart, and he'll never look
     At another woman to love her more than yourself.

     Since Nessus' death, dear friends, I've kept it locked
     Away in my house, and I've remembered it now.
580 I've smeared the blood on this tunic, applying it all
     Just as the centaur told me while he lived.
     Everything's ready. I wouldn't wish to become
     An expert or take lessons in evil magic –
     I hate all women who try it. But if, by a gentle
     Charm, I'm somehow able to overcome
585 This beautiful girl and win back Heracles' love,
     The remedy's now prepared – unless you think
     I am being foolish. If so, I'll leave it alone.
     CHORUS LEADER:
     Well, if you firmly trust your charm will work,

Your plan, in my opinion, is not unsound.
DEÏANIRA:
All I'm certain about is this: it *seems*   590
A good idea, though I haven't tested it out.
CHORUS LEADER:
You'll only know by acting. Whatever you think,
You'll have no means of judging, unless you try.[42]
DEÏANIRA:
We'll know before very long. Here's Lichas, now
At the door already. He'll soon be off. Just keep   595
My plan a secret. Even a shameful act,
If carried out in the dark, won't lead to shame.
        [LICHAS *re-enters from the palace.*]
LICHAS:
Please give me your orders, lady Deïanira.
This long delay now means that I am late.
DEÏANIRA:
I've been attending to the matter, Lichas,   600
While you were speaking with the women indoors.
This casket holds a full-length robe for Heracles.
Take it to him and say it's a present from me,
With these instructions: Nobody else should wear it
Before he does, nor should it be exposed   605
To the shining sun or the heat of a fire in a sacred
Precinct or household shrine, till Heracles stands
In the public gaze and displays this robe to the gods
On a solemn day when bulls are slain on the altar.
I made a vow that, if ever I saw or heard   610
He was safely home, I'd dress him up in this robe
And show him off to the gods in new attire
For a grand new rite. In proof that it comes from me,
I've put my seal on the box. He'll know it at once.   615

Now be on your way, and first observe the messenger's
Rule: Don't strain to overdo your duty,
And then make sure you perform my errand as well
As you have done his, to earn our thanks twice over.

LICHAS:

620 By Hermes, god of heralds, as I discharge
My duties fairly, I promise I shan't fail *you*.
I'll bring this casket to Heracles as it is,
And tell him about your vow, to clinch the matter.[43]

DEÏANIRA:

Be on your way at once. You understand
625 Quite well, I think, the way things are at home.

LICHAS:

I do, and will say that all is safe and sound.

DEÏANIRA:

And then, about the girl. You know because
You saw, how very warmly I made her welcome.

LICHAS:

Yes, yes, I was amazed and truly delighted.

DEÏANIRA:

630 What else is there to tell? I fear it would be
Too soon to add how much I'm longing for him,
Before I'm certain that he is longing for me.[44]

[*Exeunt* LICHAS *by a side entrance, and* DEÏANIRA, *followed
by her attendant, into the palace.*]

CHORAL SONG 2[45]

CHORUS:

O hárbours and rócks of Tráchis,   [*Strophe 1*]
Óeta's héights, and áll who dwéll
635 Close bý to Thermópylae's hót springs,
Bý the círcling márgin of Mális' láke,
Where Ártemis' spírit háunts the báy,
And fár-famed cóuncils of Gréeks
Assémble neár the Gréat Gates.[46]

640 The glórious sóund of píping   [*Antistrophe 1*]
Sóon shall ríse alóng these cóasts
Once móre in a sóng of good ómen,
Jóyous líke the stráins of the lýre divíne.

For Zéus' and Alcména's míghty són
Is hástening báck to his hóme
With spóils of pérfect prówess.   645

He was lóst on the ócean, góne from hóme,   [Strophe 2]
As we wáited in féar a wéary twélve-month,[47]
While nó one knéw where he míght be stráying.
Áll the while, his lóving wífe   650
In hársh, crúel gríef and néver-énding wóe,
Bewáiled her fáte and píned awáy.
Now Wár crazed with lúst has
Fréed her from sádness and páinful dáys.

Bring him hóme, bring him hóme and rést   655
     not, oárs,   [Antistrophe 2]
Of the ship that cárry the héro wéstward,
Until you sét him ashóre in Tráchis,
Báck from Cápe Cenáeum's héarth,
Where mán's vóice cláims he óffers thánks to Zéus.
We práy he cómes in hót desíre,   660
Inflámed by that lóve-charm,
Mélted by Néssus' sweet dýing gíft.[48]

SCENE 4[49]

[Re-enter DEÏANIRA from the palace.]
DEÏANIRA:
Women, I'm so afraid! Perhaps I have gone
Too far in all I have just being doing.
CHORUS LEADER:
Dear lady, Deïanira, tell us why.   665
DEÏANIRA:
I cannot say. My hopes were all for the best,
But I fear I shall soon be shown to have done great harm.
CHORUS LEADER:
Not harm in the gift you sent to Heracles?

DEÏANIRA:
Yes, my friends! I must warn you all.
670   Don't act in haste when the way is dark.
CHORUS LEADER:
Why are you frightened? Please explain, if you can.
DEÏANIRA:
A curious thing has happened. If I describe it,
Women, you'll be completely amazed. The stuff
I used just now to anoint the festal robe,
675   A pad of wool from a fleecy sheep – it has vanished!
It wasn't consumed by anything from indoors,
But simply devoured itself. It crumbled to dust
On top of a slab in the court. So you know exactly
How it occurred, I'll tell you at greater length.

680   I disregarded none of the careful instructions
The centaur gave me, when Heracles' poisoned barb
Was painfully trapped in his side. They could have been
Graven in letters of bronze on my memory's tablets.[50]
685   He told me to keep the ointment safe in a secret
Corner, away from fire and the sun's hot rays,
Until the time when I came to apply it fresh.
I did as he said; and now, when the need arrived,
I plucked a tuft of wool from one of our sheep,
690   Then went indoors on my own and spread the charm.
Next, I folded the present up and placed it,
Away from the sun, inside the box that I handed
Over to Lichas, as you observed. But while
I was going inside again, I saw an omen
Too strange for words, beyond all comprehension.
695   I must have thrown the tuft of wool right into
A patch of sunlight. And as it started to heat,
The whole of it shrivelled up and crumbled to powder
There on the ground, just like the sawdust you see
700   In a workman's shop. Then from the earth where it lay
Exposed, blisters of foam came bubbling up,
Like the purple juice of luscious grapes, new-cut
From the vine and drenching the ground at pressing-time.

Oh, how wretched I am! My mind's in a whirl!   705
I only see I've done the most dreadful thing.
Now, I ask you, why would the dying centaur
Have shown any kindness to *me*, because of whom
He was dying? No, he wanted to kill the man
Who shot him, and so bewitched me into believing him.   710
I have learned the truth too late, when it's no more use.
If I'm not somehow wrong, I'll prove my husband's
Death and destruction – none but I, heaven help me!
I know the arrow which wounded Nessus could even
Harm old Chiron,[51] and he was a god. Whatever   715
Creatures on earth it touches die. Black poison
There in the blood! It passed through Nessus' wound
And must kill Heracles too – so *I* believe.

Howbeit, I am resolved, if Heracles falls,
Then Deïanira's death must follow, too.   720
For a woman who prides herself on her noble birth,
Life with a ruined name is not worth living.
CHORUS LEADER:
Such fearful sights must needs give cause for alarm,
But don't foresee the worst before it happens.
DEÏANIRA:
In such mistakes what else can one foresee?   725
There is no hope of good to reassure us.
CHORUS LEADER:
When we go wrong without intending it,
Allowance can be made – and so for you.
DEÏANIRA:
Only an innocent could argue that.
Find trouble for yourself, and then you'll know.   730
    [*Enter* HYLLUS *from a side entrance.*]
CHORUS LEADER:
Better to say no more for now – unless
You want to speak to your own son. Hyllus,
Who went in search of his father, has now returned.
HYLLUS:
Oh Mother! Grant me a wish – just one of three!

735 I wish you were dead, or alive but not my mother,
Or else that you'd change to a woman with more of a heart!⁵²

DEÏANIRA:
Hyllus, what have *I* done to make you hate me?

HYLLUS:
He was your husband, my father!
740 You've murdered him – today!

DEÏANIRA:
My boy! What does this outburst mean?

HYLLUS:
No less than the truth. It's there.
You cannot undo what's done.

DEÏANIRA:
Hyllus, how do you know? Who told you?
745 How can you say I've done such a hideous deed?

HYLLUS:
No one told me. I saw it myself
With my own eyes – Father dying in agony!

DEÏANIRA:
Where did you find him? How were you with him?

HYLLUS:
Right! If you have to know, I must tell it all.
750 After the sack of Eurytus' glorious city,
He left with the arms he'd captured and spoils for sacrifice.
Euboea ends in a sea-washed headland, Cape
Cenaeum. There, to my great delight, I first
Caught sight of him, tracing the line of a grove
755 With an altar precinct to honour his father Zeus.
He was making ready to cut the throats of numerous
Beasts, when Lichas, his trusty herald, came
From home, bearing your present, the fatal robe.
My father put on the garment, precisely as you
Instructed, and then began the slaughter of twelve
760 Unblemished bulls, the pick of the spoil reserved
For starting the rite – though in all he'd gathered a
    hundred
Victims of various kinds before the altar.

At first the doomed man uttered the prayers serenely,
Proudly displaying his richly embroidered robe.
But when the bleeding flesh of the bulls grew hot   765
In the flames, which were also fed by the resinous logs,
The sweat broke out on his skin, and the tunic clung
To his sides, as tightly as if a craftsman had glued it
To all his joints. A convulsive pain came over
His limbs and gnawed right into his bones. A deadly,   770
Malignant viper's poison was eating him up.
At once he shouted out for the wretched Lichas,
Who had no part in the crime which *you* committed.
'What is this trick?' he yelled at him. 'How did you come
To bring this robe?' Bewildered, the poor man stammered   775
It came as a gift from you, which he'd delivered
Intact. When his master heard him, a tearing pain
Seized hold of his lungs. He grasped his servant's foot
By the ankle and flung him out to a lonely rock
Which rose from the sea. The herald's skull was broken   780
In splinters, his blood was sprinkled over the crag,
And globules of milky brain seeped out through his hair.
The crowd broke silence[53] in a groan of horror,
Seeing them both, one sick and the other destroyed.
No one would dare come close to the stricken man,   785
As he fell to the ground or leapt to the sky in his wild
Convulsions, shouting and howling. The cliffs all round,
The mountains of Locris and capes of Euboea resounded.
At last he gave up. He'd fallen to earth so often
And raised such cries to the heavens, bemoaning his ill-starred 790
Choice of a fiend like you for his bride and the proud
Alliance with Oeneus' house that had wrecked his life.
Then, through the clouds of smoke that were swirling round
    him,
He raised his rolling eyes, and he saw me weeping,   795
There in the crowd of people. He looked towards me
And called, 'Come here, my son! Don't run away
From this horror, even if you must die beside me.
No, lift me up and take me away, I hope
Where no one else can see me. If pity prevents   800

Your doing that, at least you can ship me out
Of Euboea as soon as you can. I can't die here.'
That charge was enough. We put him on board a boat
And managed somehow to bring him ashore, still racked
805   And roaring, in Trachis. You all shall see him soon –
Alive, maybe, if he isn't already dead.

That is the crime you planned and committed against
My father, Mother. You're now convicted. I pray
The avenging spirit of Justice will make you suffer
No less – if my prayer is right. And it *must* be right.
810   The right to curse you is granted to me by *you*.
You've murdered the very greatest man in the world,[54]
The like of whom you never shall see again.
        [*Exit* DEÏANIRA *into the palace.*]
CHORUS LEADER:
Going without a word? You surely know
Your silence argues your accuser's case.
HYLLUS:
815   Oh, let her go – and a fair wind blow her
Far from my sight! Why should a woman
Pride herself on a mother's name,
If she never acts as a mother should?
No, let her go, and luck go with her. I wish her
820   All the joy and pleasure she's giving my father!
        [*Exit* HYLLUS *into the palace.*]

CHORAL SONG 3[55]

CHORUS:
        Behold, O maidens, suddenly brought to our door,   [*Strophe 1*]
        That word of the oracle, spoken
        Long ago in deep foreknowledge,
        The message of fortune that after the twelfth long year[56]
              had spanned
825   Its number of months, there would come to the true-born
              son of Zeus

Rest from his painful labours.
Trúe the wórd now,
Wafted home into harbour.
Hów could ányone lónger
Obey a týrannous máster
When once his eyes are darkened?   830

For íf a clóud of múrder is swírling aróund,   [*Antistrophe 1*]
Through Nessus' insidious scheming,
Íf his sídes are stéeped in póison,
The poison which issued from death and the shimmering
    serpent reared,
This day that he looks on the sunlight must surely be his   835
    last,
Locked in the Hydra's monstrous
Grip of terror,
Wildly goaded and tortured.
Words of guile are erupting
In red sóres on his bódy,
As Black Hair wreaks his vengeance.   840

All this pain poor Deïanira   [*Strophe 2*]
Had never foreseen, but an onrush
Of mischief, when that rival
Came to bed in her own house.
She herself did the fatal deed,
But nów bewáils hávoc wróught by a stránger's wíles,   845
Rues that ominous meeting.
Nów the déw of her pále tears
Is moistening her fair cheeks,
While Fáte as she advánces reveals tréacherous,
Tempéstuous destrúction.   850

Break, break forth, you fountains of tears!   [*Antistrophe 2*]
The disease has infested the hero.
Alas! He never suffered
Súch great hárm from a déadly
Foe or roused such pity before.   855

Oh cúrse the black-póinted spéar in the frónt of wár,
Spear which prodded the fair girl
Down Oechalia's mountains
And brought her to Trachis' walls!
860 While Cýpris, the gods' hándmaid who says néver a word
Póints to her new tríumph.

SCENE 5[57]

[*A cry of lamentation is heard offstage.*][58]
CHORUS I:
Is it my foolish fancy, or did I hear
A cry of grief, echoing through the house?
CHORUS 2:
865 What is it?
It surely has a meaning – that sound of dismal
Lamentation. It speaks of trouble within.
CHORUS LEADER:
Now look! Our lady's nurse, with downcast eyes
870 And furrowed brow, is coming to give us news.
       [*Enter* NURSE *from the palace.*]
NURSE:
Children! What fearful sorrow it was doomed
To bring us – the present sent to Heracles!
CHORUS LEADER:
       Oh Nurse! What fresh mischance is this?
NURSE:
Deïanira's gone on her final journey –
875 Without stirring a foot!
CHORUS LEADER:
You cannot mean – her death?
NURSE:
                               It's true.
CHORUS LEADER:
She's *dead*, poor lady?
NURSE:
                          Yes, she's dead.

CHORUS LEADER:
The poor, lost soul! How, oh, how did she die?

NURSE:
It was cruel, so horribly cruel!

CHORUS LEADER:
But tell us,
What was the fate she met? 880

NURSE:
She killed herself – with a two-edged sword!

CHORUS:
  What passion, or what sickness, struck,
  Drove the point of a sharpened blade
  Into her heart? A second death,
  Now by a weapon of iron! 885
  Do you say that she did it alone, then?
  Tell us how she planned it.
  It cán't be trúe! You sáw thís víolent áct?[59]

NURSE:
Oh yes, I saw it. I was standing there.

CHORUS:
  Saw what? How? Please tell us. 890

NURSE:
She dealt the blow herself, with her own hand.

CHORUS:
  You méan thát?

NURSE:
                    Beyónd dóubt.

CHORUS:
  Oh, what a deadly child she bore,
  That cáptive gírl, the néw bríde!
  She bóre the hóuse a fóul fiend![60] 895

NURSE:
Too true. If you'd been there close by to see
What Mistress did, you'd have pitied her all the more.

CHORUS LEADER:
And could a weak woman's hand have dared this thing?

NURSE:
With dreadful daring. I'll tell you all that happened,

900 Then you can witness it too. She'd gone alone
    Inside the house, and when she saw that her son
    Was making ready a loose-strung stretcher before
    He left to meet his father, she hid herself
    Where no one else could see her. Then falling down
    Before the household altars, she loudly wailed
905 They'd all be left untended. She wept to touch
    The old familiar objects she had used,
    And while she wandered through the different rooms,
    She'd spy a servant who'd been close to her,
    And weep again, poor lady, as she looked
910 Into his eyes, lamenting her own fate,
    And for the family hearth, now fatherless.[61]

    But when she'd finished walking round, I saw her
    Suddenly heading straight into Heracles' chamber.
    I quietly watched in the shadows, where I couldn't
915 Be seen myself, and then observed her carefully
    Spreading covers on to her husband's bed.
    That task completed, she suddenly sprang on top
    And sat there in the middle of the bed.
    A flood of burning tears burst out once more
920 As I heard her say, 'My bed,[62] my bridal chamber,
    Farewell for ever now. You'll never welcome
    Me again, to sleep here in this room.'

    With these sad words, she clutched the golden pin
    That held her dress at the shoulder over her breasts
925 And wrenched it out, to expose her arm and the whole
    Of her left side. I ran as fast as I could
    To tell her son what his mother was trying to do.
    There and back we hurried, but during that while,
    We found she had stabbed her side with a two-edged sword,[63]
930 Right through to her heart. When Hyllus saw her, he uttered
    A cry of terrible grief. He knew, poor boy,
    That his own great anger had driven her to this act.
    He'd learned the truth too late from one of the servants:
    The centaur was all to blame; his mother had sent

The robe with no idea what harm she was doing. 935

At that the wretched boy abandoned himself
To every kind of lament, as he mourned his mother.
He covered her lips with kisses, clung with his body
Close to her side[64] and lay there, sobbing his heart out.
'Oh, what I fool I was! My harsh reproach 940
Was false!' he wailed. 'I've lost my father and mother,
Both at a single blow. They're gone forever!'

That's how things are in the house. I have to say,
If you try to plan your life two days ahead
Or further, you're a simple fool. You cannot 945
Count on tomorrow until you've survived today.[65]
    [*Exit* NURSE *into the palace.*]

CHORAL SONG 4[66]

CHORUS:
    Whose sórrow should Í be laménting fírst?   [*Strophe 1*]
    Whose súffering hóld for a dírge to cóme?
    Áll that I knów is bóundless gríef.

    One hórror is hére to be séen withín,   [*Antistrophe 1*] 950
    Anóther disáster will sóon appéar,
    Présent and fúture bóth one wóe.

    Ah, would that a wind might blow,   [*Strophe 2*]
    A wind with power to waft me from my homeland,
    Away to dwell in far-off climes, and spare my eyes. 955
    The sudden sight of Zeus' great son
    Alone would awaken terror,
    Make me faint and gazing die.
    For they sáy that in páin that can nót be assuáged
    He's coming before the house here –   960
    Wonder past all speaking!

So soon they're arrived! I raised   [*Antistrophe* 2]
My piercing song, my nightingale, so near them!
A band of strangers, all unknown, is marching here.
965   And what must this procession bode?
Such silent yet heavy footsteps
Speak a care for one they love.
Aiái! Their appróach is quíet as the gráve.
What cán I belíeve? Is Héracles
970   Dead, or peacefully sleeping?
[*During Antistrophe* 2, HERACLES *enters, carried on a litter
by bearers led by an* OLD MAN. *At the end,* HYLLUS *enters
from the palace.*]

CLOSING SCENE[67]

HYLLUS:
Oímoí![68] Dear Father, how wretched I am!
Oh, what will become of me? *Óimoi?*
OLD MAN:[69]
Silence, boy! You mustn't stir up
975   Your father's pain in his cruel, wild state.
He is barely alive. Now curb your tongue
And be quiet!
HYLLUS:
                    Do you mean, old sir, that he still lives?
OLD MAN:
Do not wake him up when he's fast asleep
Or rouse his sickness out of its lair!
It is constantly coming
And going, my son.
HYLLUS:
980   This blow is far
Too heavy to bear. My mind's in a frenzy!
    [HERACLES *wakes.*]
HERACLES:
O Zeus![70]
Where have I come? Who are these people

I see, as I lie tormented by pain   985
Unceasingly. Help me, god! The fiend
Is starting to gnaw me again. Ah!

OLD MAN:

Didn't I warn you? Far, far better
To hide your feelings and not to scatter
The mist of sleep   990
From his head and his eyes!

HYLLUS:

                    How else can I bear
To look on this vision of horror?

HERACLES:

Cenaeum, where my altars stood,
I wish I had never set eyes on you! Such,
Zeus knows, were the gracious   995
Thanks you returned for my offerings!
What cruel wrong you have done me, wrong!
To face this eruption
Of madness which cannot be charmed away!
What worker of spells or of healing skills   1000
Will calm this torturing plague but Zeus?
I never could see such a marvel.
    É! É!⁷¹   [Strophe]
    O god, lét me bé!
    Mercy, be merciful!
    Leave me to sleep in peace!   1005
    How to endure such pain?
      [OLD MAN *tries to move him.*]
    Don't touch me, man, don't try to turn me,
    You'll kill me, you'll kill me!
    You've now disturbed what was lulled to rest.
Ambushed, pounced on again! It's attacking me! Where do   1010
    you think you've
Sprung from, Greeks, you vilest of men in the world, for
    whose sáke I
Laboured, purging the sea of monsters, purging the
    woodlands,

Wearing my poor life out? And now, when I'm helplessly
  stricken,
No one will burn my body or draw his sword to relieve me.
  É! É!
  All unwilling to come?
1015 Cut off my head, I say!
  Stifle this cruel pain!
  Finish my life! God, god!

OLD MAN:

Hyllus, you are his son. What he asks is a task too hard for a
Weak old man like me. You must help him yourself. You are
  younger
And stronger than I.

HYLLUS:

1020   My hands are here, but I haven't the
  power,
Power within or outside myself, to inflict the blow that will
Make him forget his agony. That is for Zeus to accord him.

HERACLES:

  Oh, where, whére's my són?   [*Antistrophe*]
  Come to me, come to me!
1025 Lift me and hold me close.
  Mercy, O god, I pray!
  It's rearing up once more, this pain.
  It will tear me apart,
1030 This angry, dangerous, deadly beast!
Help me, Pallas Athena![72] Again it's destroying me! Dear son,
Pity your father and draw your sword on me – no one will
  blame you.
1035 Strike me below my neck and heal this torment with which
  your
Godless mother has driven me mad. I wish I could see her,
1040 Próstrate, rúined as shé ruined mé, like thís! God of mércy,
  Hades, brother of Zeus,
  Put me to sleep, to sleep!
  Finish my wretched life,
  Grant me a speedy end.

CHORUS LEADER:
I shudder to hear[73] our master in such distress.
So great a hero, racked by such great pain!   1045
HERACLES:
How many burning labours,[74] cruel indeed,
My hands, this back, have painfully undergone!
Yet neither Zeus' wife, Hera, nor the vile
Eurystheus ever imposed such a fierce ordeal
On me – this woven robe, the devilish net
Which Deïanira, with her treacherous eyes,   1050
Has fastened to my shoulders, and now I'm dying.
Plastered against my sides, it has gnawed its way
Right into my flesh, it is sucking out the breath
Inside my lungs, and now it has drained my fresh
Life-blood to the final drop. The whole of my body's   1055
Wasted, crushed in these unspeakable chains.
Those warriors on the plain, that host of earth-born
Giants,[75] those savage beasts, and all the lands
I came to, Greek or barbarian, purging monsters –   1060
None of them ever did this much; but a feeble
Woman, without a drop of masculine blood,
Alone and swordless, managed to bring me down.

Hyllus, my son, now prove you are indeed   1065
My true-born son. Don't honour your mother's name
Above your father's. Fetch that woman from home
And pass her into my clutches with your own hands.
I need to know if it hurts you more to see
My mangled frame or hers, when I've fairly punished her.
Come on, my boy, don't shrink! Show me some pity,   1070
As others pity me. Here I am, sobbing
And crying away like a girl. No one could say
He ever saw great Heracles weeping before.
I faced my hardships without so much as a whimper.
But now, instead, I'm found a feeble woman.   1075

My son, come here, stand close beside your father,
And see how I've been brought to this dreadful pass.

I'll take these coverings off and show you. Look!
Look all of you! Gaze on my tortured body,
1080   Observe the wretched Heracles' pitiful state!
            Aiaí, áh the páin! *Aiaí*!
That burning spasm once again! It has pierced me
Through my sides. It won't allow me to rest,
It seems – this wretched, racking, gnawing plague!
1085   O king of the underworld, take me!
            Lightning of Zeus, now strike!
Brandish your bolt, lord! Father, launch it powerfully
Down on my head. It's eating me up once more;
It has bloomed, it has broken out. Oh hands, my hands,
1090   My sturdy back and chest, my loyal old arms!
You were the famous arms whose strength subdued
The lion that haunted Nemea and scourged the flocks,
A creature none would dare to approach or face.
You slew the Hydra of Lerna; you overcame
1095   Those wild half-men who walked on horses' legs,
The violent, lawless, super-mighty centaurs.
You killed the Erymanthian boar, and fetched
The monster dog[76] up from the underworld,
The dread Echidna's invincible whelp, with three
Fierce heads. You slew the dragon who closely watched
1100   The golden apples away in the farthest west.
I braved all these and countless other labours,
And no man claimed a victory over you.
But now my limbs are useless; I'm torn to rags,
Unseen disaster's ransacked my whole being,
1105   Though I was called the child of a peerless mother,
The son of Zeus who reigns among the stars.
But be assured of this: though I am nothing
And have no power to move, even as I am
I'll get my hands on that woman. Just bring her here.
1110   She must learn her lesson and cry this truth to the world:
In death, as in life, I punished evil-doers.
CHORUS LEADER:
Unhappy Greece, what sorrow I see ahead
For you – to lose so great a man as this!

HYLLUS:
Father, you're silent now, and I can reply.
Ill though you are, please listen to what I say.   1115
I ask of you no more than you ought to give.
Just hear me out and allow your anger to cool,
Else you will never learn how wrong you are
In both your wishes and the rage you feel.
HERACLES:
Say what you like and then have done. I'm ill,   1120
And can't make out a word of all your riddles.
HYLLUS:
I want to tell you about my mother – how
She is, and how she unwittingly went astray.
HERACLES:
You treacherous cur! Those words to my face? How can you
Dare to mention the mother who killed your father?   1125
HYLLUS:
You have to know how she is. I can't say nothing.
HERACLES:
You can't, when I think of all the harm she's done.
HYLLUS:
You'll understand when you know what she's done today.
HERACLES:
Go on. But take good care not to prove disloyal.
HYLLUS:
Very well. My mother's dead. She has just been killed.   1130
HERACLES:
Who did it? Ill-omened words! The gods are at work.
HYLLUS:
She wasn't murdered. She killed herself.
HERACLES:
Too early! *I* should have killed that woman!
HYLLUS:
Even you would relent if you knew the whole truth.
HERACLES:
Knew what? You puzzle me. Say what you mean.   1135
HYLLUS:
Her mistake was fatal, but her intentions were good.

HERACLES:

You call that *good* – to kill your father?

HYLLUS:

She saw the girl you'd taken and thought a love-charm
Would win you back. But her plan completely failed.

HERACLES:

1140 Love-charms in Trachis? Who dispenses *them*?

HYLLUS:

The centaur Nessus convinced her long ago
That a charm like that would drive you mad with love.

HERACLES:

I see! I see![77] Heracles' end has come.
No more to live, no more to feel the sun!

1145 At last I have some inkling where I stand.
Now go, my son. You've lost your father now.
Summon your brothers and sisters to me here,
And call Alcmena, my poor mother, who slept
With Zeus for nothing. I want you all to hear

1150 My final words and share the oracles I know.

HYLLUS:

I fear your mother is not in Trachis. She's living
Close to the sea at Tiryns. Some of your children
She's taken with her; the rest are still in Thebes.
But all of us who are here will do whatever

1155 Is needed, Father, and help you as best we may.

HERACLES:

Well, then, my son, here's what you have to do.
You're mine, and now's the time for you to show
The stuff you're made of.

                                    Many years ago
It was foretold me from my father Zeus,

1160 No living person should ever cause my death,
But one already dead who lived below
In Hades. So, the centaur-beast has made
That prophecy true: the dead has killed the living.[78]

1165 And this accords with later oracles,
Which I'll reveal – the new chimes with the old.
Up at Dodona,[79] I once visited

Zeus' mountain shrine and met the Selli,
Priests who sleep upon bare earth. I heard
My father's talking oak and wrote the words
Down on a tablet. They said that at this time,
This present time, I'd be at last released   1170
From all the labours laid on me. I thought
That meant fair days. But all it signified
Was death – my death. The dead are labour-free.
These prophecies are coming true, my son.
Your task is now to stand at Heracles' side.   1175
Don't raise my curses by a long delay.
Give me your willing help and show you've learned
That best of rules, obedience to your father.
HYLLUS:
I'm frightened, Father. Such blind promises
Are hard to give, but still I'll do as you ask.   1180
HERACLES:
First place your hand in mine to give your pledge.
HYLLUS:
What promise are you forcing me to make?
HERACLES:
Obey me, boy! Give me your hand now, quickly!
HYLLUS:
It's here, then; take it. I shan't oppose your wish.
HERACLES:
Swear by the head of Zeus, whose seed I am . . .   1185
HYLLUS:
What must I swear? You have to tell me that.
HERACLES:
Swear that you will perform the task I give you.
HYLLUS:
I, Hyllus, swear this oath. Zeus be my witness!
HERACLES:
And pray for punishment[80] if you break your oath.
HYLLUS:
I'll need no punishment, as I'll keep my oath.
But still I make that prayer.   1190

HERACLES:

                                So then.
You've been to Oeta and Zeus' holy place,
High on the mountain top?

HYLLUS:

                                I have.
I've often sacrificed at the altar there.

HERACLES:

That is the place[81] where you must bear me now.
Do it yourself, with any friends you choose.
1195   Erect a pyre of branches cut from the strong,
Deep-rooted oak and wild male olive trees
Felled to the ground, and on that lay my body.
Then take a torch of burning pine and set
The pyre alight. I want to see no tears
Of mourning. If you're Heracles' son, you'll do
1200   My bidding without one tear or cry of lament.
Or else I'll still be there, beneath the earth,
Waiting to haunt you with my curse forever.

HYLLUS:

No, Father, no! How can you be so cruel?

HERACLES:

It's what has to be done. If not, you'd better
1205   Find a new father. You're my son no more.

HYLLUS:

I say again, you're cruel. You're asking me
To be your murderer and defile myself.

HERACLES:

No, no, not I. You'll be my healer, son,
Since you alone can cure me of all this pain.

HYLLUS:

1210   How can I cure you by setting fire to your body?

HERACLES:

Well, if you shrink from that, do all the rest.[82]

HYLLUS:

Yes, Father. I shan't refuse to carry you there.

HERACLES:

And will you prepare my pyre, as I've instructed?

HYLLUS:
So long as my own hands play no part in the work,
I'll see to it all. You can rely on me.   1215
HERACLES:
That will be good enough – a generous gift.
Now promise me one more favour, small this time.
HYLLUS:
However great it is, I promise to do it.
HERACLES:
Well, then, you know the girl, King Eurytus' daughter?
HYLLUS:
It's Iole whom you mean, if I take you right.   1220
HERACLES:
Yes, Iole. This is my firm instruction, Hyllus:
When I have died, if you wish to do your duty
And to fulfil the oath you've sworn your father,
Take this girl as your wife. You can't refuse me.
No other man must be allowed to wed   1225
The woman who lay in Heracles' arms but you.[83]
You, son, must be the one to marry her.
Now say you will. You'll meet my chief demands;
Don't spoil that gift by refusing one small thing.
HYLLUS:
Oh god!
I know that anger's wrong with a man who's sick.   1230
But how could anyone sane agree to that?
HERACLES:
You sound as though you'll not do a thing I say.
HYLLUS:
Look! Iole, no one else, must be held to blame
For my mother's death and for bringing you in turn
To this terrible pass. Only a man who suffered   1235
From some demonic sickness could choose to do
As you ask. Oh Father, I'd rather die myself
Beside you than make a home with my deadliest foe.
HERACLES:
It seems this fellow won't even show respect
For his father's dying wish. Be careful, though!

1240 The curse of heaven awaits your disobedience.
HYLLUS:
Oh god! Your crazing sickness
Must soon be plain to the world.
HERACLES:
Yes, it had gone to sleep,
And you're waking it up once more.
HYLLUS:
I wish I knew what to do!
HERACLES:
Obey your father. That's all.
HYLLUS:
1245 But what you are teaching me now is wickedness.
HERACLES:
Wickedness? Not if you'll make me happy.
HYLLUS:
Is this your final, solemn command?
HERACLES:
Yes, I command it, and call the gods
To witness my word.
HYLLUS:
I cannot refuse you, then. The gods will know
1250 My action's yours. I'll do my duty, Father,
To you and prove my noble nature.
HERACLES:
The way to end. And please, my son, perform
Your service quickly. Lay me upon the pyre
Before the tearing, stinging pain returns.
1255 Make haste, men, lift me up. This is release
From toil. It signals Heracles' final end.
HYLLUS:
Yes, nothing prevents your wishes being fulfilled.
Your orders, Father, leave me without a choice.
HERACLES:
Come then,[84] my unyielding soul, do not wait
1260 To awaken the fearful demon again.
Put a curb of steel, stone-set, on my lips.
No cries of ill omen! The struggle ahead

Will be hard, but the end will be joyful.[85]
[*During the following lines, the litter carrying* HERACLES *is
raised and borne off by the bearers down a side entrance in
a cortège, led by the* OLD MAN.]

HYLLUS:
Followers, lift him! I ask you to show
Your hearts' understanding for me in this task.   1265
For you know that the hearts of the callous gods
Feel nothing in all these sorry events.
They beget their sons and are called our fathers,
Yet look down calmly on our great pain.
No man has a vision of what is to come.[86]   1270
But the present is fraught with sorrow for us here,
Shame for those hard gods,
Torment exceeding all for the hero
Who braves this fire of destruction.
[HYLLUS *follows the cortège.*]

CHORUS LEADER:
Women, you need not stay by the house.   1275
We have witnessed a strange apparition of death,
Now matched by a picture of pain unknown.
And all this story is great Zeus.[87]
[*The* CHORUS *follows.*]

Euripides,
The Bacchae

THE BACCHAE

*

Characters:

DIONYSUS
CHORUS *of Oriental women, devotees of Dionysus*
TEIRESIAS, *a blind Seer*
CADMUS, *founder of Thebes, and formerly king*
PENTHEUS, *his grandson, now king of Thebes*
A GUARD *attending Pentheus*
A HERDSMAN
A MESSENGER
AGAUË, *daughter of Cadmus and mother of Pentheus*

*

Scene: Before the palace of Pentheus in Thebes. At one side of the stage is the monument of Semele; above it burns a low flame, and around it are the remains of ruined and blackened masonry.

DIONYSUS *enters on stage right. He has a crown of ivy, a thyrsus in his hand, and a fawnskin draped over his body. He has long flowing hair and a youthful, almost feminine beauty.*
DIONYSUS:
I am Dionysus, son of Zeus. My mother was
Semele, Cadmus' daughter. From her womb the fire
Of a lightning-flash delivered me. I have come here
To Thebes and her two rivers, Dirce and Ismenus,
Veiling my godhead in a mortal shape. I see
Here near the palace my mother's monument, that records
Her death by lightning. Here her house stood; and its
        ruins
Smoulder with the still living flame of Zeus's fire –
The immortal cruelty Hera wreaked upon my mother.
Cadmus does well to keep this ground inviolable,
A precinct consecrated in his daughter's name;

And I have decked it round with sprays of young vine-
    leaves.
From the fields of Lydia and Phrygia, fertile in gold,
I travelled first to the sun-smitten Persian plains,
The walled cities of Bactria, the harsh Median country,
Wealthy Arabia, and the whole tract of the Asian coast
Where mingled swarms of Greeks and Orientals live
In vast magnificent cities; and before reaching this,
The first city of Hellas I have visited,
I had already, in all those regions of the east,
Performed my dances and set forth my ritual
To make my godhead manifest to mortal men.
   The reason why I have chosen Thebes as the first place
To raise my Bacchic shout, and clothe all who respond
In fawnskin habits, and put my thyrsus in their hands –
The weapon wreathed with ivy-shoots – my reason is
    this:
My mother's sisters said – what they should have been
    the last
To say – that I, Dionysus, was not Zeus's son;
That Semele, being with child – they said – by some
    mortal,
Obeyed her father's prompting, and ascribed to Zeus
The loss of her virginity; and they loudly claimed
That this lie was the sin for which Zeus took her life.
   Therefore I have driven those same sisters mad, turned
    them
All frantic out of doors; their home now is the mountain;
Their wits are gone. I have made them bear the emblem of
My mysteries; the whole female population of Thebes,
To the last woman, I have sent raving from their homes.
Now, side by side with Cadmus' daughters, one and all
Sit roofless on the rocks under the silver pines.
For Thebes, albeit reluctantly, must learn in full
This lesson, that my Bacchic worship is a matter

As yet beyond her knowledge and experience;
And I must vindicate my mother Semele
By manifesting myself before the human race
As the divine son whom she bore to immortal Zeus.
  Now Cadmus has made over his throne and kingly
      honours
To Pentheus, son of his eldest daughter Agauë. He
Is a fighter against gods, defies me, excludes me from
Libations, never names me in prayers. Therefore I will
Demonstrate to him, and to all Thebes, that I am a god.
  When I have set all in order here, I will pass on
To another place, and manifest myself. Meanwhile
If Thebes in anger tries to bring the Bacchants home
By force from the mountain, I myself will join that army
Of women possessed and lead them to battle. That is
      why
I have changed my form and taken the likeness of a man.
  Come, my band of worshippers, women whom I have
      brought
From lands of the east, from Tmolus, bastion of Lydia,
To be with me and share my travels! Raise the music
Of your own country, the Phrygian drums invented by
Rhea the Great Mother and by me. Fill Pentheus' palace
With a noise to make the city of Cadmus turn and look!
– And I will go to the folds of Mount Cithaeron, where
The Bacchants are, and join them in their holy dance.

  DIONYSUS *goes out towards the mountain. The* CHORUS
enter where Dionysus entered, from the road by which they
have travelled.

CHORUS:
  From far-off lands of Asia,   [*Strophe* I
  From Tmolus the holy mountain,
  We run with the god of laughter;
  Labour is joy and weariness is sweet,
  And our song resounds to Bacchus!

Who stands in our path?   [*Antistrophe* 1
Make way, make way!
Who in the house? Close every lip,
Keep holy silence, while we sing
The appointed hymn to Bacchus!

Blest is the happy man   [*Strophe* 2
Who knows the mysteries the gods ordain,
And sanctifies his life,
Joins soul with soul in mystic unity,
And, by due ritual made pure,
Enters the ecstasy of mountain solitudes;
Who observes the mystic rites
Made lawful by Cybele the Great Mother;
Who crowns his head with ivy,
And shakes aloft his wand in worship of Dionysus.

On, on! Run, dance, delirious, possessed!
Dionysus comes to his own;
Bring from the Phrygian hills to the broad streets of Hellas
The god, child of a god,
Spirit of revel and rapture, Dionysus!

Once, on the womb that held him   [*Antistrophe* 2
The fire-bolt flew from the hand of Zeus;
And pains of child-birth bound his mother fast,
And she cast him forth untimely,
And under the lightning's lash relinquished life;
And Zeus the son of Cronos
Ensconced him instantly in a secret womb
Chambered within his thigh,
And with golden pins closed him from Hera's sight.

So, when the Fates had made him ripe for birth,
Zeus bore the bull-horned god

And wreathed his head with wreaths of writhing snakes;
Which is why the Maenads catch
Wild snakes, nurse them and twine them round their hair.

O Thebes, old nurse that cradled Semele,   [*Strophe* 3
Be ivy-garlanded, burst into flower
With wreaths of lush bright-berried bryony,
Bring sprays of fir, green branches torn from oaks,
Fill soul and flesh with Bacchus' mystic power;
Fringe and bedeck your dappled fawnskin cloaks
With woolly tufts and locks of purest white.
There's a brute wildness in the fennel-wands –
Reverence it well. Soon the whole land will dance
   When the god with ecstatic shout
   Leads his companies out
   To the mountain's mounting height
   Swarming with riotous bands
   Of Theban women leaving
   Their spinning and their weaving
   Stung with the maddening trance
     Of Dionysus!

O secret chamber the Curetes knew!   [*Antistrophe* 3
O holy cavern in the Cretan glade
Where Zeus was cradled, where for our delight
The triple-crested Corybantes drew
Tight the round drum-skin, till its wild beat made
Rapturous rhythm to the breathing sweetness
Of Phrygian flutes! Then divine Rhea found
The drum could give her Bacchic airs completeness;
   From her, the Mother of all,
   The crazy Satyrs soon,
   In their dancing festival
   When the second year comes round,
   Seized on the timbrel's tune

    To play the leading part
    In feasts that delight the heart
      Of Dionysus.

O what delight is in the mountains!   [*Epode*
There the celebrant, wrapped in his sacred fawnskin,
Flings himself on the ground surrendered,
While the swift-footed company streams on;
There he hunts for blood, and rapturously
Eats the raw flesh of the slaughtered goat,
Hurrying on to the Phrygian or Lydian mountain heights.
Possessed, ecstatic, he leads their happy cries;
The earth flows with milk, flows with wine,
Flows with nectar of bees;
The air is thick with a scent of Syrian myrrh.
The celebrant runs entranced, whirling the torch
That blazes red from the fennel-wand in his grasp,
And with shouts he rouses the scattered bands,
Sets their feet dancing,
As he shakes his delicate locks to the wild wind.
And amidst the frenzy of song he shouts like thunder:
'On, on! Run, dance, delirious, possessed!
You, the beauty and grace of golden Tmolus,
Sing to the rattle of thunderous drums,
Sing for joy,
Praise Dionysus, god of joy!
Shout like Phrygians, sing out the tunes you know,
While the sacred pure-toned flute
Vibrates the air with holy merriment,
In time with the pulse of the feet that flock
To the mountains, to the mountains!'
And, like a foal with its mother at pasture,
Runs and leaps for joy every daughter of Bacchus.
      Enter THEIRESIAS. *Though blind, he makes his way*
        unaided to the door, and knocks.

TEIRESIAS:

Who keeps the gate? Call Cadmus out, Agenor's son,
Who came from Sidon here to build these walls of
    Thebes.
Go, someone, say Teiresias is looking for him.
He knows why; I'm an old man, and he's older still –
But we agreed to equip ourselves with Bacchic wands
And fawnskin cloaks, and put on wreaths of ivy-shoots.

Enter CADMUS.

CADMUS:

Dear friend, I knew your voice, although I was indoors,
As soon as I heard it – the wise voice of a wise man.
I am ready. See, I have all that the god prescribes.
He is my daughter's son; we must do all we can
To exalt and honour him. Where shall we go to dance
And take our stand with others, tossing our grey heads?
You tell me what to do, Teiresias. We're both old,
But you're the expert.
[*He stumps about, beating his thyrsus on the ground.*]
                        I could drum the ground all night
And all day too, without being tired. What joy it is
To forget one's age!

TEIRESIAS: I feel exactly the same way,
Bursting with youth! I'll try it – I'll dance with the rest.

CADMUS: You don't think we should go to the mountain in
a coach?

TEIRESIAS: No, no. That would not show the god the
same respect.

CADMUS: I'll take you there myself then – old as we both are.

TEIRESIAS: The god will guide us there, and without weariness.

CADMUS: Are we the only Thebans who will dance to him?

TEIRESIAS: We see things clearly; all the others are perverse.

CADMUS: We're wasting time; come, take my hand.

TEIRESIAS: Here, then; hold tight.

CADMUS: I don't despise religion. I'm a mortal man.

TEIRESIAS:

We have no use for theological subtleties.
The beliefs we have inherited, as old as time,
Cannot be overthrown by any argument,
Not by the most inventive ingenuity.
It will be said, I lack the dignity of my age,
To wear this ivy-wreath and set off for the dance.
Not so; the god draws no distinction between young
And old, to tell us which should dance and which should
    not.
He desires equal worship from all men: his claim
To glory is universal; no one is exempt.

CADMUS:

Teiresias, I shall be your prophet, since you are blind.
Pentheus, to whom I have resigned my rule in Thebes,
Is hurrying here towards the palace. He appears
Extremely agitated. What news will he bring?

Enter PENTHEUS. *He addresses the audience, without at first
noticing* CADMUS *and* TEIRESIAS, *who stand at the opposite
side of the stage.*

PENTHEUS:

I happen to have been away from Thebes; reports
Of this astounding scandal have just been brought to me.
Our women, it seems, have left their homes on some
    pretence
Of Bacchic worship, and are now gadding about
On the wooded mountain-slopes, dancing in honour of
This upstart god Dionysus, whoever he may be.
Amidst these groups of worshippers, they tell me, stand
Bowls full of wine; and our women go creeping off
This way and that to lonely places and give themselves
To lecherous men. They are Maenad priestesses, if you
    please!
Aphrodite supplants Bacchus in their ritual.

Well, those I've caught, my guards are keeping safe;
   we've tied
Their hands, and lodged them at state expense. Those
   still at large
On the mountain I am going to hunt out; and that
Includes my own mother Agaue and her sisters
Ino and Autonoë. Once they're fast in iron fetters,
I'll put a stop to this outrageous Bacchism.
   They tell me, too, some oriental conjurer
Has come from Lydia, a magician with golden hair
Flowing in scented ringlets, his face flushed with wine,
His eyes lit with the charm of Aphrodite; and he
Entices young girls with his Bacchic mysteries,
Spends days and nights consorting with them. Once let
   me
Get that fellow inside my walls – I'll cut his head
From his shoulders; that will stop him drumming with
   his thyrsus,
Tossing his long hair. *He*'s the one – this foreigner –
Who says Dionysus is a god; who says he was
Sewn up in Zeus's thigh. The truth about Dionysus
Is that he's dead, burnt to a cinder by lightning
Along with his mother, because she said Zeus lay with
   her.
Whoever the man may be, is not his arrogance
An outrage? Has he not earned a rope around his neck?
[PENTHEUS *turns to go, and sees* CADMUS *and* TEIRESIAS.]
Why, look! Another miracle! Here's Teiresias
The prophet – in a fawnskin; and my mother's father –
A Bacchant with a fennel-wand! Well, there's a sight
For laughter! [*But he is raging, not laughing.*]
        Sir, I am ashamed to see two men
Of your age with so little sense of decency.
Come, you're my grandfather: throw down that ivy-
   wreath,

Get rid of that thyrsus! – *You* persuaded him to this,
Teiresias. By introducing a new god, you hope
To advance your augurer's business, to collect more fees
For inspecting sacrifices. Listen: your grey hairs
Are your protection; otherwise you'd be sitting now
In prison with all these crazy females, for promoting
Pernicious practices. As for women, I tell you this:
Wherever the sparkle of sweet wine adorns their feasts,
No good will follow from such Bacchic ceremonies.

CHORUS:

Have you no reverence, Sir, no piety? Do you mock
Cadmus, who sowed the dragon-seed of earth-born men?
Do you, Echion's son, dishonour your own race?

TEIRESIAS:

When a good speaker has a sound case to present,
Then eloquence is no great feat. Your fluent tongue
Promises wisdom; but the content of your speech
Is ignorant. Power and eloquence in a headstrong man
Spell folly; such a man is a peril to the state.

This new god, whom you ridicule – no words of mine
Could well express the ascendancy he will achieve
In Hellas. There are two powers, young man, which are
    supreme
In human affairs: first, Demeter – the same goddess
Is also Earth; give her which name you please – and she
Supplies mankind with solid food. After her came
Dionysus, Semele's son; the blessing he procured
And gave to men is counterpart to that of bread:
The clear juice of the grape. When mortals drink their fill
Of wine, the sufferings of our unhappy race
Are banished, each day's troubles are forgotten in sleep.
There is no other cure for sorrow. Dionysus,
Himself a god, is thus poured out in offering
To the gods, so that through him come blessings on
    mankind.

And do you scorn this legend, that he was sewn up
In Zeus's thigh? I will explain the truth to you.
When Zeus snatched Dionysus from the lightning-flame
And took the child up to Olympus as a god,
Hera resolved to cast him out of heaven. But Zeus
Found such means to prevent her as a god will find.
He took a fragment of the ether that surrounds
The earth, fashioned it like a child, presented it
To Hera as a pledge to soothe her jealousy,
And saved Dionysus from her. Thus, in time, because
The ancient words for 'pledge' and 'thigh' are similar,
People confused them, and the 'pledge' Zeus gave to
        Hera
Became transformed, as time went on, into the tale
That Dionysus was sewn up in Zeus's thigh.
    And this god is a prophet; the Bacchic ecstasy
And frenzy hold a strong prophetic element.
When he fills irresistibly a human body
He gives those so possessed power to foretell the future.
In Ares' province too Dionysus has his share;
Sometimes an army, weaponed and drawn up for battle,
Has fled in wild panic before a spear was raised.
This too is an insanity sent by Dionysus.
    Ay, and the day will come when, on the very crags
Of Delphi, you shall see him leaping, amidst the blaze
Of torches, over the twin-peaked ridge, waving aloft
And brandishing his Bacchic staff, while all Hellas
Exalts him. Pentheus, pay heed to my words. You rely
On force; but it is not force that governs human affairs.
Do not mistake for wisdom that opinion which
May rise from a sick mind. Welcome this god to Thebes,
Offer libations to him, celebrate his rites,
Put on his garland. Dionysus will not compel
Women to be chaste, since in all matters self-control
Resides in our own natures. You should consider this;

For in the Bacchic ritual, as elsewhere, a woman
Will be safe from corruption if her mind is chaste.
Think of this too: when crowds stand at the city gates
And Thebes extols the name of Pentheus, you rejoice;
So too, I think, the god is glad to receive honour.

   Well, I at least, and Cadmus, whom you mock, will
     wear
The ivy-wreath and join the dancing – we are a pair
Of grey heads, but this is our duty; and no words
Of yours shall lure me into fighting against gods.
For a most cruel insanity has warped your mind;
While drugs may well have caused it, they can bring no
     cure.

CHORUS:

What you have said, Teiresias, shows no disrespect
To Apollo; at the same time you prove your judgement
     sound
In honouring Dionysus as a mighty god.

CADMUS:

My dear son, Teiresias has given you good advice.
Don't stray beyond pious tradition; live with us.
Your wits have flown to the winds, your sense is
     foolishness.
Even if, as you say, Dionysus is no god,
Let him have *your* acknowledgement; lie royally,
That Semele may get honour as having borne a god,
And credit come to us and to all our family.

   Remember, too, Actaeon's miserable fate –
Torn and devoured by hounds which he himself had
     bred,
Because he filled the mountains with the boast that he
Was a more skilful hunter than Artemis herself.
Don't share his fate, my son! Come, let me crown your
     head
With a wreath of ivy; join us in worshipping this god.

PENTHEUS:

    Keep your hands off! Go to your Bacchic rites, and don't
Wipe off your crazy folly on me. But I will punish
This man who has been your instructor in lunacy.
Go, someone, quickly to his seat of augury,
Smash it with crowbars, topple the walls, throw all his
    things
In wild confusion, turn the whole place upside down,
Fling out his holy fripperies to the hurricane winds!
This sacrilege will sting him more than anything else.
The rest of you – go, comb the country and track down
That effeminate foreigner, who plagues our women with
This new disease, fouls the whole land with lechery;
And once you catch him, tie him up and bring him here
To me; I'll deal with him. He shall be stoned to death.
He'll wish he'd never brought his Bacchic rites to Thebes.

                  Exit PENTHEUS.

TEIRESIAS:

    Foolhardy man! You do not know what you have said.
Before, you were unbalanced; now you are insane.
Come, Cadmus; let us go and pray both for this man,
Brutish as he is, and for our city, and beg the god
To show forbearance. Come, now, take your ivy staff
And let us go. Try to support me; we will help
Each other. It would be scandalous for two old men
To fall; still, we must go, and pay our due service
To Dionysus, son of Zeus. – Cadmus, the name
Pentheus means *sorrow*. God grant he may not bring
    sorrow
Upon your house. Do not take that as prophecy;
I judge his acts. Such foolish words bespeak a fool.

        Exeunt TEIRESIAS *and* CADMUS.

CHORUS:

    Holiness, Queen of heaven,   [*Strophe* 1
    Holiness, golden-winged ranging the earth,

Do you hear his blasphemy?
Pentheus dares – do you hear? – to revile the god of joy,
The son of Semele, who when the gay-crowned feast is
    set
Is named among gods the chief;
Whose gifts are joy and union of soul in dancing,
Joy in music of flutes,
Joy when sparkling wine at feasts of the gods
Soothes the sore regret,
Banishes every grief,
When the reveller rests, enfolded deep
In the cool shade of ivy-shoots,
On wine's soft pillow of sleep.

The brash unbridled tongue,   [*Antistrophe* 1
The lawless folly of fools, will end in pain.
But the life of wise content
Is blest with quietness, escapes the storm
And keeps its house secure.
Though blessed gods dwell in the distant skies,
They watch the ways of men.
To know much is not to be wise.
Pride more than mortal hastens life to its end;
And they who in pride pretend
Beyond man's limit, will lose what lay
Close to their hand and sure.
I count it madness, and know no cure can mend
The evil man and his evil way.

O to set foot on Aphrodite's island,   [*Strophe* 2
On Cyprus, haunted by the Loves, who enchant
Brief life with sweetness; or in that strange land
Whose fertile river carves a hundred channels
To enrich her rainless sand;
Or where the sacred pastures of Olympus slant

Down to Pieria, where the Muses dwell —
Take me, O Bromius, take me and inspire
Laughter and worship! There our holy spell
And ecstasy are welcome; there the gentle band
Of Graces have their home, and sweet Desire.

Dionysus, son of Zeus, delights in banquets;   [*Antistrophe* 2
And his dear love is Peace, giver of wealth,
Saviour of young men's lives — a goddess rare!
In wine, his gift that charms all griefs away,
Alike both rich and poor may have their part.
His enemy is the man who has no care
To pass his years in happiness and health,
His days in quiet and his nights in joy,
Watchful to keep aloof both mind and heart
From men whose pride claims more than mortals may.
The life that wins the poor man's common voice,
His creed, his practice — this shall be my choice.

Some of the guards whom PENTHEUS *sent to arrest* DIONYSUS
now enter with their prisoner. PENTHEUS *enters from the palace.*

GUARD:

Pentheus, we've brought the prey you sent us out to
     catch;
We hunted him, and here he is. But, Sir, we found
The beast was gentle; made no attempt to run away,
Just held his hands out to be tied; didn't turn pale,
But kept his florid colour, smiling, telling us
To tie him up and run him in; gave us no trouble
At all, just waited for us. Naturally I felt
A bit embarrassed. 'You'll excuse me, Sir,' I said,
'I don't want to arrest you; it's the king's command.'
     Another thing, Sir — those women you rounded up
And put in fetters in the prison, those Bacchants;
Well, they're all gone, turned loose to the glens; and
     there they are,

Frisking about, calling on Bromius their god.
The fetters simply opened and fell off their feet;
The bolts shot back, untouched by mortal hand; the doors
Flew wide. Master, this man has come here with a load
Of miracles. Well, what happens next is your concern.

PENTHEUS:
Untie this man's hands. [*The* GUARD *does so.*] He's
    securely in the trap.
He's not so nimble-footed as to escape me now.
    Well, friend: your shape is not unhandsome – for the
        pursuit
Of women, which is the purpose of your presence here.
You are no wrestler, I can tell from these long curls
Cascading most seductively over your cheek.
Your skin, too, shows a whiteness carefully preserved;
You keep away from the sun's heat, walk in the shade,
So hunting Aphrodite with your lovely face.
    Ah, well; first tell me who you are. What is your
        birth?

DIONYSUS:
Your question's easily answered, it is no secret.
Perhaps you have heard of Tmolus, a mountain decked
    with flowers.

PENTHEUS: A range that curves round Sardis? Yes, I know
    of it.

DIONYSUS: That is my home. I am a Lydian by birth.

PENTHEUS: How comes it that you bring these rituals to
    Hellas?

DIONYSUS: Dionysus, son of Zeus, himself instructed me.

PENTHEUS: Is there a Lydian Zeus, then, who begets new
    gods?

DIONYSUS: I speak of Zeus who wedded Semele here in
    Thebes.

PENTHEUS: Did he possess you in a dream, or visibly?

DIONYSUS: Yes, face to face; he gave these mysteries to me.

PENTHEUS: These mysteries you speak of: what form do they take?

DIONYSUS: To the uninitiated that must not be told.

PENTHEUS: And those who worship – what advantage do they gain?

DIONYSUS: It is not for you to learn; yet it is worth knowing.

PENTHEUS: You bait your answer well, to arouse my eagerness.

DIONYSUS: His rituals abhor a man of impious life.

PENTHEUS: You say you saw him face to face: what was he like?

DIONYSUS: Such as he chose to be. I had no say in that.

PENTHEUS: Still you side-track my question with an empty phrase.

DIONYSUS: Just so. A prudent speech sleeps in a foolish ear.

PENTHEUS: Is Thebes the first place where you have introduced this god?

DIONYSUS: No; every eastern land dances these mysteries.

PENTHEUS: No doubt. Their moral standards fall far below ours.

DIONYSUS: In this they are superior; but their customs differ.

PENTHEUS: Do you perform these mysteries by night or day?

DIONYSUS: Chiefly by night. Darkness promotes religious awe.

PENTHEUS: For women darkness is deceptive and impure.

DIONYSUS: Impurity can be pursued by daylight too.

PENTHEUS: You must be punished for your foul and slippery tongue.

DIONYSUS: And you for blindness and impiety to the god.

PENTHEUS: How bold this Bacchant is! A practised pleader too.

DIONYSUS: Tell me my sentence. What dread pain will you inflict?

PENTHEUS: I'll start by cutting off your delicate long hair.

DIONYSUS: My hair is sacred; I preserve it for the god.

PENTHEUS: And next, that thyrsus in your hand – give it to
   me.

DIONYSUS: Take it from me yourself; it is the god's emblem.

PENTHEUS: I'll lock you up in prison and keep you there.

DIONYSUS: The god
   Himself, whenever I desire, will set me free.

PENTHEUS: Of course – when you, with all your Bacchants,
   call to him!

DIONYSUS: He is close at hand here, and sees what is done
   to me.

PENTHEUS: Indeed? Where is he, then? Not visible to my
   eyes.

DIONYSUS: Beside me. You, being a blasphemer, see nothing.

PENTHEUS [to the GUARDS]: Get hold of him; he's mocking
   me and the whole city.

DIONYSUS [to the GUARDS]: Don't bind me, I warn you.
   [To PENTHEUS] I am sane, and you are mad.

PENTHEUS: My word overrules yours. [To the GUARDS] I
   tell you, bind him fast.

DIONYSUS: You know not what you are saying, what you
   do, nor who
   You are.

PENTHEUS: Who? Pentheus, son of Echion and Agauë.

DIONYSUS: Your name points to calamity. It fits you well.

PENTHEUS:
   Take him away and shut him in my stables, where
   He can stay staring at darkness. – You can dance in there!
   As for these women you've brought as your accomplices,
   I'll either send them to the slave-market to be sold,
   Or keep them in my own household to work the looms;
   And that will stop their fingers drumming on
      tambourines!

DIONYSUS:
   I'll go. Nothing can touch me that is not ordained.

But I warn you: Dionysus, who you say is dead,
Will come in swift pursuit to avenge this sacrilege.
You are putting *him* in prison when you lay hands on
  me.

GUARDS *take* DIONYSUS *away to the stables;* PENTHEUS
follows.

CHORUS:

Dirce, sweet and holy maid,   [*Strophe*
Acheloüs' Theban daughter,
Once the child of Zeus was made
Welcome in your welling water,
When the lord of earth and sky
Snatched him from the undying flame,
Laid him safe within his thigh,
Calling loud the infant's name:
'Twice-born Dithyrambus! Come,
Enter here your father's womb;
Bacchic child, I now proclaim
This in Thebes shall be your name.'
Now, divine Dirce, when my head is crowned
And my feet dance in Bacchus' revelry –
Now you reject me from your holy ground.
Why should you fear me? By the purple fruit
That glows in glory on Dionysus' tree,
His dread name yet shall haunt your memory!

Oh, what anger lies beneath   [*Antistrophe*
Pentheus' voice and sullen face –
Offspring of the dragon's teeth,
And Echion's earth-born race,
Brute with bloody jaws agape,
God-defying, gross and grim,
Slander of his human shape!
Soon he'll chain us limb to limb –
Bacchus' servants! Yes, and more:
Even now our comrade lies

Deep on his dark prison floor.
  Dionysus! Do your eyes
See us? O son of Zeus, the oppressor's rod
Falls on your worshippers; come, mighty god,
Brandish your golden thyrsus and descend
From great Olympus; touch this murderous man,
And bring his violence to a sudden end!

Where are you, Dionysus? Leading your dancing   [*Epode*
  bands
Over the mountain slopes, past many a wild beast's lair,
Or on Corycian crags, with the thyrsus in their hands?
Or in the wooded coverts, maybe, of Olympus, where
Orpheus once gathered the trees and mountain beasts,
Gathered them with his lyre, and sang an enchanting air.
Happy vale of Pieria! Bacchus delights in you;
He will cross the flood and foam of the Axius river, and
  there
He will bring his whirling Maenads, with dancing and
  with feasts,
Cross the father of waters, Lydias, generous giver
Of wealth and luck, they say, to the land he wanders
  through,
Whose famous horses graze by the rich and lovely river.
  Suddenly a shout is heard from inside the building –
  the voice of DIONYSUS.

DIONYSUS:
  Io, Io! Do you know my voice, do you hear?
  Worshippers of Bacchus! Io, Io!
CHORUS:
  Who is that? Where is he?
  The shout of Dionysus is calling us!
DIONYSUS:
  Io, Io! Hear me again:
  I am the son of Semele, the son of Zeus!

CHORUS:

Io, Io, our lord, our lord!

Come, then, come to our company, lord of joy!

DIONYSUS: O dreadful earthquake, shake the floor of the
world!

CHORUS [*with a scream of terror*]:

Pentheus' palace is falling, crumbling in pieces! [*They
continue severally*]

− Dionysus stands in the palace; bow before him!

− We bow before him. − See how the roof and pillars

Plunge to the ground! − Bromius is with us,

He shouts from prison the shout of victory!

The flame on Semele's tomb grows and brightens.

DIONYSUS:

Fan to a blaze the flame the lightning lit;

Kindle the conflagration of Pentheus' palace!

CHORUS:

Look, look, look!

Do you see, do you see the flame of Semele's tomb,

The flame that lived when she died of the lightning-stroke?

A noise of crashing masonry is heard.

Down, trembling Maenads! Hurl yourselves to the ground.

Your god is wrecking the palace, roof to floor;

He heard our cry − he is coming, the son of Zeus!

The doors open and DIONYSUS *appears.*

DIONYSUS:

Women of Asia, why do you cower thus, prostrate and
terrified?

Surely you could hear Dionysus shattering Pentheus'
palace? Come,

Lift yourselves up, take good courage, stop this trembling
of your limbs!

CHORUS:

We are saved! Oh, what a joy to hear your Bacchic call
ring out!

We were all alone, deserted; you have come, and we
   rejoice.

DIONYSUS:

Were you comfortless, despondent, when I was escorted
   in,

Helpless, sentenced to be cast in Pentheus' murky prison-
   cell?

CHORUS:

Who could help it? What protector had we, once
   deprived of you?

Tell us now how you escaped the clutches of this wicked
   man.

DIONYSUS: I alone, at once, unaided, effortlessly freed myself.

CHORUS: How could that be? Did not Pentheus bind your
   arms with knotted ropes?

DIONYSUS:

There I made a mockery of him. He thought he was
   binding me;

But he neither held nor touched me, save in his deluded
   mind.

Near the mangers where he meant to tie me up, he
   found a bull;

And he tied his rope round the bull's knees and hooves,
   panting with rage,

Dripping sweat, biting his lips; while I sat quietly by and
   watched.

It was then that Dionysus shook the building, made the
   flame

On his mother's tomb flare up. When Pentheus saw this,
   he supposed

The whole place was burning. He rushed this way, that
   way, calling out

To the servants to bring water; every slave about the
   place

Was engaged upon this futile task. He left it presently,

Thinking I had escaped; snatched up his murderous
　　sword, darted indoors.
Thereupon Dionysus – as it seemed to me; I merely
　　guess –
Made a phantom hover in the courtyard. Pentheus flew
　　at it,
Stabbing at the empty sunlight, thinking he was killing
　　me.
Yet a further humiliation Bacchus next contrived for
　　him:
He destroyed the stable buildings. Pentheus sees my
　　prison now
Lying there, a heap of rubble; and the picture grieves his
　　heart.
　　Now he's dazed and helpless with exhaustion. He has
　　dropped his sword.
He, a man, dared to take arms against a god. I quietly
　　walked
Out of the palace here to join you, giving Pentheus not
　　a thought.
But I hear his heavy tread inside the palace. Soon, I think,
He'll be out here in the forecourt. After what has
　　happened now,
What will he have to say? For all his rage, he shall not
　　ruffle *me*.
It's a wise man's part to practise a smooth-tempered
　　self-control.
Enter PENTHEUS.
PENTHEUS:
This is outrageous. He has escaped – that foreigner.
Only just now I had him locked up and in chains.
　　He sees DIONYSUS *and gives an excited shout.*
He's there! Well, what's going on now? How did you
　　get out?
How dare you show your face here at my very door?

DIONYSUS: Stay where you are. You are angry; now control
  yourself.
PENTHEUS: You were tied up inside there. How did you
  escape?
DIONYSUS: I said – did you not hear? – that I should be set
  free –
PENTHEUS: By whom? You're always finding something
  new to say.
DIONYSUS: By him who plants for mortals the rich-
  clustered vine.
PENTHEUS: The god who frees his worshippers from every
  law.*
DIONYSUS: Your insult to Dionysus is a compliment.
PENTHEUS [to attendant GUARDS]: Go round the walls and
  tell them to close every gate.
DIONYSUS: And why? Or cannot gods pass even over walls?
PENTHEUS: Oh, you know everything – save what you
  ought to know.
DIONYSUS:
  The things most needful to be known, those things I
    know.
  But listen first to what this man has to report;
  He comes from the mountain, and he has some news for
    you.
  I will stay here; I promise not to run away.
                    Enter a HERDSMAN.
HERDSMAN:
  Pentheus, great king of Thebes! I come from Mount
    Cithaeron,
  Whose slopes are never free from dazzling shafts of snow.
PENTHEUS: And what comes next? What urgent message do
  you bring?
HERDSMAN:
  I have seen the holy Bacchae, who like a flight of spears
  * This is conjecturally supplied in place of a missing line.

Went streaming bare-limbed, frantic, out of the city gate.
I have come with the intention of telling you, my lord,
And the city, of their strange and terrible doings – things
Beyond all wonder. But first I would learn whether
I may speak freely of what is going on there, or
If I should trim my words. I fear your hastiness,
My lord, your anger, your too potent royalty.

PENTHEUS:

From me fear nothing. Say all that you have to say;
Anger should not grow hot against the innocent.
The more dreadful your story of these Bacchic rites,
The heavier punishment I will inflict upon
This man who enticed our women to their evil ways.

HERDSMAN:

At dawn today, when first the sun's rays warmed the
        earth,
My herd of cattle was slowly climbing up towards
The high pastures; and there I saw three separate
Companies of women. The leader of one company
Was Autonoë; your mother Agauë was at the head
Of the second, Ino of the third; and they all lay
Relaxed and quietly sleeping. Some rested on beds
Of pine-needles, others had pillows of oak-leaves.
They lay just as they had thrown themselves down on
        the ground,
But modestly, not – as you told us – drunk with wine
Or flute-music, seeking the solitary woods
For the pursuit of love.

                                When your mother Agauë
Heard the horned cattle bellowing, she stood upright
Among the Bacchae, and called to them to stir themselves
From sleep; and they shook off the strong sleep from
        their eyes
And leapt to their feet. They were a sight to marvel at
For modest comeliness; women both old and young,

Girls still unmarried. First they let their hair fall free
Over their shoulders; some tied up the fastenings
Of fawnskins they had loosened; round the dappled fur
Curled snakes that licked their cheeks. Some would have
    in their arms
A young gazelle, or wild wolf-cubs, to which they gave
Their own white milk – those of them who had left at
    home
Young children newly born, so that their breasts were
    full.
And they wore wreaths of ivy-leaves, or oak, or flowers
Of bryony. One would strike her thyrsus on a rock,
And from the rock a limpid stream of water sprang.
Another dug her wand into the earth, and there
The god sent up a fountain of wine. Those who desired
Milk had only to scratch the earth with finger-tips,
And there was the white stream flowing for them to
    drink,
While from the thyrsus a sweet ooze of honey dripped.
Oh! if you had been there and seen all this, you would
Have offered prayers to this god whom you now
    condemn.
    We herdsmen, then, and shepherds gathered to
        exchange
Rival reports of these strange and extraordinary
Performances; and one, who had knocked about the
    town,
And had a ready tongue, addressed us: 'You who live
On the holy mountain heights,' he said, 'shall we hunt
    down
Agauë, Pentheus' mother, and bring her back from these
Rituals, and gratify the king? What do you say?'
This seemed a good suggestion; so we hid ourselves
In the leafy bushes, waiting. When the set time came,
The women began brandishing their wands, preparing

To dance, calling in unison on the son of Zeus,
'Iacchus! Bromius!' And with them the whole mountain,
And all the creatures there, joined in the mystic rite
Of Dionysus, and with their motion all things moved.
   Now, Agauë as she danced passed close to me; and I
At once leapt out from hiding, bent on capturing her.
But she called out, 'Oh, my swift-footed hounds, these
    men
Are hunting us. Come follow me! Each one of you
Arm herself with the holy thyrsus, and follow me!'
   So we fled, and escaped being torn in pieces by
Those possessed women. But our cattle were there,
    cropping
The fresh grass; and the women attacked them, with
    their bare hands.
You could see one take a full-uddered bellowing young
    heifer
And hold it by the legs with her two arms stretched
    wide;
Others seized on our cows and tore them limb from limb;
You'd see some ribs, or a cleft hoof, tossed high and low;
And rags of flesh hung from pine-branches, dripping
    blood.
Bulls, which one moment felt proud rage hot in their
    horns,
The next were thrown bodily to the ground, dragged
    down
By hands of girls in thousands; and they stripped the flesh
From the bodies faster than you could wink your royal
    eyes.
   Then, skimming bird-like over the surface of the
    ground,
They scoured the plain which stretches by Asopus' banks
And yields rich crops for Thebes; and like an enemy
    force

They fell on Hysiae and Erythrae, two villages
On the low slopes of Cithaeron, and ransacked them
    both;
Snatched babies out of the houses; any plunder which
They carried on their shoulders stayed there without
    straps –
Nothing fell to the ground, not bronze or iron; they
    carried
Fire on their heads, and yet their soft hair was not burnt.
  The villagers, enraged at being so plundered, armed
Themselves to resist; and then, my lord, an amazing
    sight
Was to be seen. The spears those men were throwing
    drew
No blood; but the women, hurling a thyrsus like a spear,
Dealt wounds; in short, those women turned the men to
    flight.
There was the power of a god in that. Then they went
    back
To the place where they had started from, to those
    fountains
The god had caused to flow for them. And they washed
    off
The blood; and snakes licked clean the stains, till their
    cheeks shone.
  So, master, whoever this divinity may be,
Receive him in this land. His powers are manifold;
But chiefly, as I hear, he gave to men the vine
To cure their sorrows; and without wine, neither love
Nor any other pleasure would be left for us.
CHORUS:
  I shrink from speaking freely before the king; yet I
  Will say it: there is no greater god than Dionysus.
PENTHEUS:
  This Bacchic arrogance advances on us like

A spreading fire, disgracing us before all Hellas.
We must act now. [*To the* HERDSMAN] Go quickly to
    the Electran gate;
Tell all my men who carry shields, heavy or light,
All riders on fast horses, all my archers with
Their twanging bows, to meet me there in readiness
For an onslaught on these maniacs. This is beyond
All bearing, if we must let women so defy us.

DIONYSUS:

You refuse, Pentheus, to give heed to what I say
Or change your ways. Yet still, despite your wrongs to me,
I warn you: stay here quietly; do not take up arms
Against a god. Dionysus will not tolerate
Attempts to drive his worshippers from their holy hills.

PENTHEUS:

I'll not have you instruct me. You have escaped your
    chains;
Now be content – or must I punish you again?

DIONYSUS:

I would control my rage and sacrifice to him
If I were you, rather than kick against the goad.
Can you, a mortal, measure your strength with a god's?

PENTHEUS:

I'll sacrifice, yes – blood of women, massacred
Wholesale, as they deserve, among Cithaeron's glens.

DIONYSUS:

Your army will be put to flight. What a disgrace
For bronze shields to be routed by those women's wands!

PENTHEUS:

How can I deal with this impossible foreigner?
In prison or out, nothing will make him hold his tongue.

DIONYSUS: My friend, a happy settlement may still be
    found.

PENTHEUS: How? Must I be a slave to my own slave-
    women?

DIONYSUS: I will, using no weapons, bring those women here.

PENTHEUS: Hear that, for the gods' sake! You're playing me some trick.

DIONYSUS: What trick? – if I am ready to save you by my skill.

PENTHEUS: You've planned this with them, so that the rituals can go on.

DIONYSUS: Indeed I have planned this – not with them, but with the god.

PENTHEUS: Bring out my armour, there! – That is enough from you.

DIONYSUS [with an authoritative shout]:
Wait! [Then quietly] Do you want to see
Those women, where they sit together, up in the hills?

PENTHEUS: Why, yes; for that, I'd give a weighty sum of gold.

DIONYSUS: What made you fall into this great desire to see?

PENTHEUS: It would cause me distress to see them drunk with wine.

DIONYSUS: Yet you would gladly witness this distressing sight?

PENTHEUS: Of course – if I could quietly sit under the pines.

DIONYSUS: They'll track you down, even if you go there secretly.

PENTHEUS: Openly, then. Yes, what you say is very true.

DIONYSUS: Then shall I lead you? You will undertake to go?

PENTHEUS: Yes, lead me there at once; I am impatient.

DIONYSUS: Then,
You must first dress yourself in a fine linen gown.

PENTHEUS: Why in a linen gown? Must I then change my sex?

DIONYSUS: In case they kill you, if you are seen there as a man.

PENTHEUS: Again you are quite right. How you think of everything!

DIONYSUS: It was Dionysus who inspired me with that thought.

PENTHEUS: Then how can your suggestion best be carried out?

DIONYSUS: I'll come indoors with you myself and dress you.

PENTHEUS: What? Dress me? In woman's clothes? But I would be ashamed.

DIONYSUS: Do you want to watch the Maenads? Are you less eager now?

PENTHEUS: What kind of dress did you say you would put on me?

DIONYSUS: First I'll adorn your head with locks of flowing hair.

PENTHEUS: And after that? What style of costume shall I have?

DIONYSUS: A full-length robe; and on your head shall be a snood.

PENTHEUS: Besides these, is there anything else you'll put on me?

DIONYSUS: A dappled fawnskin round you, a thyrsus in your hand.

PENTHEUS: I could not bear to dress myself in woman's clothes.

DIONYSUS: If you join the battle with the Maenads, blood will flow.

PENTHEUS: You are right; I must first go to spy on them.

DIONYSUS: That way Is better than inviting force by using it.

PENTHEUS: And how shall I get through the town without being seen?

DIONYSUS: We'll go by empty streets; I will show you the way.

PENTHEUS:
   The Maenads must not mock me; better anything
   Than that. Now I'll go in, and think how best to act.
DIONYSUS: You may do so. My preparations are all made.
PENTHEUS:
   I'll go in, then; and either I'll set forth at the head
   Of my armed men – or else I'll follow your advice.

                Exit PENTHEUS.

DIONYSUS:
   Women, this man is walking into the net. He will
   Visit the Bacchae; and there death shall punish him.
     Dionysus! – for you are not far distant – all is now
   In your hands. Let us be revenged on him! And first
   Fill him with wild delusions, drive him out of his mind.
   While sane, he'll not consent to put on woman's clothes;
   Once free from the curb of reason, he will put them
      on.
   I long to set Thebes laughing at him, as he walks
   In female garb through all the streets; to humble him
   From the arrogance he showed when first he threatened
      me.
     Now I will go, to array Pentheus in the dress
   Which he will take down with him to the house of
      Death,
   Slaughtered by his own mother's hands. And he shall
      know
   Dionysus, son of Zeus, in his full nature God,
   Most terrible, although most gentle, to mankind.

        DIONYSUS *follows* PENTHEUS *into the palace.*

CHORUS:
    O for long nights of worship, gay   [*Strophe*
    With the pale gleam of dancing feet,
    With head tossed high to the dewy air –
    Pleasure mysterious and sweet!
    O for the joy of a fawn at play

In the fragrant meadow's green delight,
Who has leapt out free from the woven snare,
Away from the terror of chase and flight,
And the huntsman's shout, and the straining pack,
And skims the sand by the river's brim
With the speed of wind in each aching limb,
To the blessed lonely forest where
The soil's unmarked by a human track,
And leaves hang thick and the shades are dim.

What prayer should we call wise?   [*Refrain*
What gift of Heaven should man
Count a more noble prize,
A prayer more prudent, than
To stretch a conquering arm
Over the fallen crest
Of those who wished us harm?
And what is noble every heart loves best.

Slow, yet unfailing, move the Powers   [*Antistrophe*
Of heaven with the moving hours.
When mind runs mad, dishonours God,
And worships self and senseless pride,
Then Law eternal wields the rod.
Still Heaven hunts down the impious man,
Though divine subtlety may hide
Time's creeping foot. No mortal ought
To challenge Time – to overbear
Custom in act, or age in thought.
All men, at little cost, may share
The blessing of a pious creed;
Truths more than mortal, which began
In the beginning, and belong
To very nature – these indeed
Reign in our world, are fixed and strong.

What prayer should we call wise?
What gift of heaven should man
Count a more noble prize,
A prayer more prudent, than
To stretch a conquering arm
Over the fallen crest
Of those who wished us harm?
And what is noble every heart loves best.

Blest is the man who cheats the stormy sea   [*Epode*
And safely moors beside the sheltering quay;
So, blest is he who triumphs over trial.
One man, by various means, in wealth or strength
Outdoes his neighbour; hope in a thousand hearts
Colours a thousand different dreams; at length
Some find a dear fulfilment, some denial.
    But this I say,
    That he who best
    Enjoys each passing day
    Is truly blest.
        Enter DIONYSUS. *He turns to call* PENTHEUS.
DIONYSUS:
  Come, perverse man, greedy for sights you should not
    see,
  Eager for deeds you should not do – Pentheus! Come
    out
  Before the palace and show yourself to me, wearing
  The garb of a frenzied Bacchic woman, and prepared
  To spy on your mother and all her Bacchic company.
    Enter PENTHEUS *dressed as a Bacchic devotee. He is dazed*
          and entirely subservient to DIONYSUS.
  You are the very image of one of Cadmus' daughters.
PENTHEUS:
  Why, now! I seem to see two suns; a double Thebes;
  Our city's wall with seven gates appears double.

Dionysus takes Pentheus by the hand and leads
him forward.

You are a bull I see leading me forward now;
A pair of horns seems to have grown upon your head.
Were you a beast before? You have become a bull.

DIONYSUS:
The god then did not favour us; he is with us now,
We have made our peace with him; you see as you
    should see.

PENTHEUS:
How do I look? Tell me, is not the way I stand
Like the way Ino stands, or like my mother Agauë?

DIONYSUS:
Looking at you, I think I see them both. Wait, now;
Here is a curl has slipped out of its proper place,
Not as I tucked it carefully below your snood.

PENTHEUS:
Indoors, as I was tossing my head up and down
Like a Bacchic dancer, I dislodged it from its place.

DIONYSUS:
Come, then; I am the one who should look after you.
I'll fix it in its place again. There; lift your head.

PENTHEUS: You dress me, please; I have put myself in your
hands now.

DIONYSUS:
Your girdle has come loose; and now your dress does not
Hang, as it should, in even pleats down to the ankle.

PENTHEUS:
That's true, I think – at least by the right leg, on this
    side;
But on the other side the gown hangs well to the heel.

DIONYSUS:
You'll surely count me chief among your friends, when
    you
Witness the Maenads' unexpected modesty.

PENTHEUS:
Ought I to hold my thyrsus in the right hand – so,
Or in the left, to look more like a Bacchanal?
DIONYSUS:
In the right hand; and raise it at the same time as
Your right foot. I am glad you are so changed in mind.
PENTHEUS:
Could I lift up on my own shoulders the whole weight
Of Mount Cithaeron, and all the women dancing there?
DIONYSUS:
You could, if you so wished. The mind you had before
Was sickly; now your mind is just as it should be.
PENTHEUS:
Shall we take crowbars? Or shall I put my shoulder under
The rocks, and heave the mountain up with my two arms?
DIONYSUS:
Oh, come, now! Don't destroy the dwellings of the
     nymphs,
And the quiet places where Pan sits to play his pipes.
PENTHEUS:
You are right. We ought not to use force to overcome
Those women. I will hide myself among the pines.
DIONYSUS:
Hide – yes, you'll hide, and find the proper hiding-place
For one who comes by stealth to spy on Bacchic rites.
PENTHEUS:
Why yes! I think they are there now in their hidden nests,
Like birds, all clasped close in the sweet prison of love.
DIONYSUS:
What you are going to watch for is this very thing;
Perhaps you will catch them – if you are not first
     caught yourself.
PENTHEUS:
Now take me through the central streets of Thebes; for I
Am the one man among them all that dares do this.

DIONYSUS:

   One man alone, you agonize for Thebes; therefore
   It is your destined ordeal that awaits you now.
   Come with me; I will bring you safely to the place;
   Another shall conduct you back.

PENTHEUS: My mother – yes?

DIONYSUS: A sight for all to witness.

PENTHEUS: To this end I go.

DIONYSUS: You will return borne high –

PENTHEUS: Royal magnificence!

DIONYSUS: In your own mother's arms.

PENTHEUS: You insist that I be spoiled.

DIONYSUS: One kind of spoiling.

PENTHEUS: Yet I win what I deserve.

Exit PENTHEUS.

DIONYSUS:

   Pentheus, you are a man to make men fear; fearful
   Will be your end – an end that shall lift up your fame
   To the height of heaven.
   Agauë, and you her sisters, daughters of Cadmus,
   Stretch out your hands! See, I am bringing this young man
   To his great battle; and I and Bromius shall be
   Victors. What more shall happen, the event will show.

Exit DIONYSUS.

CHORUS:

   Hounds of Madness, fly to the mountain, fly   [*Strophe*
   Where Cadmus' daughters are dancing in ecstasy!
   Madden them like a frenzied herd stampeding,
   Against the madman hiding in woman's clothes
   To spy on the Maenads' rapture!
   First his mother shall see him craning his neck
   Down from a rounded rock or a sharp crag,
   And shout to the Maenads, 'Who is the man, you Bacchae,
   Who has come to the mountain, come to the mountain
      spying

On the swift wild mountain-dances of Cadmus' daughters?
Which of you is his mother?
No, that lad never lay in a woman's womb;
A lioness gave him suck, or a Libyan Gorgon!'

Justice, now be revealed! Now let your sword
Thrust – through and through – to sever the throat
Of the godless, lawless, shameless son of Echion,
Who sprang from the womb of Earth!

See! With contempt of right, with a reckless   [*Antistrophe*
    rage
To combat your and your mother's mysteries, Bacchus,
With maniac fury out he goes, stark mad,
For a trial of strength against *your* invincible arm!
His proud purposes death shall discipline.
He who unquestioning gives the gods their due,
And knows that his days are as dust, shall live untouched.
I have no wish to grudge the wise their wisdom;
But the joys *I* seek are greater, outshine all others,
And lead our life to goodness and loveliness:
The joy of the holy heart
That night and day is bent to honour the gods
And disown all custom that breaks the bounds of right.

Justice, now be revealed! Now let your sword
Thrust – through and through – to sever the throat
Of the godless, lawless, shameless son of Echion,
Who sprang from the womb of Earth!
        [*Then with growing excitement, shouting in unison, and
                dancing to the rhythm of their words*]
                Come, Dionysus!   [*Epode*
                Come, and appear to us!
                Come like a bull or a
                Hundred-headed serpent,
                Come like a lion snorting

> Flame from your nostrils!
> Swoop down, Bacchus, on the
> Hunter of the Bacchae;
> Smile at him and snare him;
> Then let the stampeding
> Herd of the Maenads
> Throw him and throttle him,
> Catch, trip, trample him to death!
> *Enter a* MESSENGER.

MESSENGER:

O house that once shone glorious throughout Hellas, home
Of the old Sidonian king who planted in this soil
The dragon's earth-born harvest! How I weep for you!
Slave though I am, I suffer with my master's fate.

CHORUS: Are you from the mountain, from the Bacchic rites? What news?

MESSENGER: Pentheus, son of Echion, is dead.

CHORUS: Bromius, lord! Your divine power is revealed!

MESSENGER:

What, woman? What was that you said? Do you exult
When such a cruel fate has overtaken the king?

CHORUS: I am no Greek.
          I sing my joy in a foreign tune.
          Not any more do I cower in terror of prison!

MESSENGER: Do you think Thebes has no men left who can take command?

CHORUS: Dionysus commands *me*;
               Not Thebes, but Dionysus.

MESSENGER:

Allowance must be made for you; yet, to rejoice
At the accomplishment of horrors, is not right.

CHORUS: Tell us everything, then: this tyrant king
          Bent on cruelty – how did he die?

MESSENGER:

When we had left behind the outlying parts of Thebes
And crossed the river Asopus, we began to climb
Toward the uplands of Cithaeron, Pentheus and I –
I went as his attendant – and the foreigner
Who was our guide to the spectacle we were to see.
Well, first we sat down in a grassy glade. We kept
Our footsteps and our talk as quiet as possible,
So as to see without being seen. We found ourselves
In a valley full of streams, with cliffs on either side.
There, under the close shade of branching pines, the
        Maenads
Were sitting, their hands busy at their happy tasks;
Some of them twining a fresh crown of ivy-leaves
For a stripped thyrsus; others, gay as fillies loosed
From painted yokes, were singing holy Bacchic songs,
Each answering other. But the ill-fated Pentheus saw
None of this; and he said, 'My friend, from where we
        stand
My eyes cannot make out these so-called worshippers;
But if I climbed a towering pine-tree on the cliff
I would have a clear view of their shameful practices.'
    And then I saw that foreigner do an amazing thing.
He took hold of a pine-tree's soaring, topmost branch,
And dragged it down, down, down to the dark earth.
    It was bent
In a circle as a bow is bent, as a wheel's curve,
Drawn with a compass, bends the rim to its own shape;
The foreigner took that mountain-pine in his two hands
And bent it down – a thing no mortal man could do.
Then seating Pentheus on a high branch, he began
To let the tree spring upright, slipping it through his
        hands
Steadily, taking care he should not be flung off.
The pine-trunk, straightened, soared into the soaring sky,

Bearing my master seated astride, so that he was
More visible to the Maenads than they were to him.
He was just coming into view on his high perch,
When out of the sky a voice – Dionysus, I suppose;
That foreigner was nowhere to be seen – pealed forth:
'Women, here is the man who made a mock of you,
And me, and of my holy rites. Now punish him.'
And in the very moment the voice spoke, a flash
Of dreadful fire stretched between earth and the high
    heaven.
    The air fell still. The wooded glade held every leaf
Still. You could hear no cry of any beast. The women,
Not having caught distinctly what the voice uttered,
Stood up and gazed around. Then came a second word
Of command. As soon as Cadmus' daughters recognized
The clear bidding of Bacchus, with the speed of doves
They darted forward, and all the Bacchae after them.
Through the torrent-filled valley, over the rocks,
    possessed
By the very breath of Bacchus they went leaping on.
Then, when they saw my master crouched high in the
    pine,
At first they climbed the cliff which towered opposite,
And violently flung at him pieces of rocks, or boughs
Of pine-trees which they hurled as javelins; and some
Aimed with the thyrsus; through the high air all around
Their wretched target missiles flew. Yet every aim
Fell short, the tree's height baffled all their eagerness;
While Pentheus, helpless in this pitiful trap, sat there.
Then, with a force like lightning, they tore down
    branches
Of oak, and with these tried to prize up the tree's roots.
When all their struggles met with no success, Agauë
Cried out, 'Come, Maenads, stand in a circle round the
    tree

And take hold of it. We must catch this climbing beast,
Or he'll disclose the secret dances of Dionysus.'
They came; a thousand hands gripped on the pine and
    tore it.
Out of the ground. Then from his high perch plunging,
    crashing
To the earth Pentheus fell, with one incessant scream
As he understood what end was near.
                                 His mother first,
As priestess, led the rite of death, and fell upon him.
He tore the headband from his hair, that his wretched
    mother
Might recognize him and not kill him. 'Mother,' he
    cried,
Touching her cheek, 'It is I, your own son Pentheus,
    whom
You bore to Echion. Mother, have mercy; I have sinned,
But I am still your own son. Do not take my life!'
   Agauë was foaming at the mouth; her rolling eyes
Were wild; she was not in her right mind, but possessed
By Bacchus, and she paid no heed to him. She grasped
His left arm between wrist and elbow, set her foot
Against his ribs, and tore his arm off by the shoulder.
It was no strength of hers that did it, but the god
Filled her, and made it easy. On the other side
Ino was at him, tearing at his flesh; and now
Autonoë joined them, and the whole maniacal horde.
A single and continuous yell arose – Pentheus
Shrieking as long as life was left in him, the women
Howling in triumph. One of them carried off an arm,
Another a foot, the boot still laced on it. The ribs
Were stripped, clawed clean; and women's hands, thick
    red with blood,
Were tossing, catching, like a plaything, Pentheus' flesh.
   His body lies – no easy task to find – scattered

Under hard rocks, or in the green woods. His poor head –
His mother carries it, fixed on her thyrsus-point,
Openly over Cithaeron's pastures, thinking it
The head of a young mountain-lion. She has left her
    sisters
Dancing among the Maenads, and herself comes here
Inside the walls, exulting in her hideous prey,
Shouting to Bacchus, calling him her fellow-hunter,
Her partner in the kill, comrade in victory.
But Bacchus gives her bitter tears for her reward.
    Now I will go. I must find some place far away
From this horror, before Agauë returns home.
A sound and humble heart that reverences the gods
Is man's noblest possession; and the same virtue
Is wisest too, I think, for those who practise it.

Exit the MESSENGER.

CHORUS:
Let us dance a dance to Bacchus, shout and sing
For the fall of Pentheus, heir of the dragon's seed,
Who hid his beard in a woman's gown,
And sealed his death with the holy sign
Of ivy wreathing a fennel-reed,
When bull led man to the ritual slaughter-ring.
Frenzied daughters of Cadmus, what renown
Your victory wins you – such a song
As groans must stifle, tears must drown!
Emblem of conquest, brave and fine! –
A mother's hand, defiled
With blood and dripping red
Caresses the torn head
Of her own murdered child!

But look! I see her – there, running towards the palace –
Agauë, Pentheus' mother, her eyes wildly rolling.
Come, welcome them – Dionysus' holy company.

AGAUË *appears, frenzied and panting, with* PENTHEUS' *head
held in her hand. The rest of her band of devotees, whom the*
CHORUS *saw approaching with her, do not enter; but a few are
seen standing by the entrance, where they wait until the end of the
play.*

AGAUË: Women of Asia! Worshippers of Bacchus!

> AGAUË *tries to show them* PENTHEUS' *head; they shrink
> from it.*

CHORUS: Why do you urge me? Oh!

AGAUË: I am bringing home from the mountains
A vine-branch freshly cut,
For the gods have blessed our hunting.

CHORUS: We see it ... and welcome you in fellowship.

AGAUË: I caught him without a trap,
A lion-cub, young and wild.
Look, you may see him: there!

CHORUS: Where was it?

AGAUË: On Cithaeron;
The wild and empty mountain –

CHORUS: Cithaeron!

AGAUË: ... spilt his life-blood.

CHORUS: Who shot him?

AGAUË: I was first;
All the women are singing,
'Honour to great Agauë!'

CHORUS: And then – who next?

AGAUË: Why, Cadmus' ...

CHORUS: What – Cadmus?

AGAUË: Yes, his daughters –
But after me, after me –
Laid their hands to the kill.
Today was a splendid hunt!
Come now, join in the feast!

CHORUS: What, wretched woman? *Feast?*

AGAUË [*tenderly stroking the head as she holds it*]:

This calf is young: how thickly
The new-grown hair goes crisping
Up to his delicate crest!

CHORUS: Indeed, his long hair makes him
Look like some wild creature.

AGAUË: The god is a skilled hunter;
And he poised his hunting women,
And hurled them at the quarry.

CHORUS: True, our god is a hunter.

AGAUË: Do you praise me?

CHORUS: Yes, we praise you.

AGAUË: So will the sons of Cadmus ...

CHORUS: And Pentheus too, Agauë?

AGAUË: Yes, he will praise his mother
For the lion-cub she killed.

CHORUS: Oh, fearful!

AGAUË: Ay, fearful!

CHORUS: You are happy?

AGAUË: I am enraptured;
Great in the eyes of the world,
Great are the deeds I've done,
And the hunt that I hunted there!

CHORUS:

Then show it, poor Agauë – this triumphant spoil
You've brought home; show it to all the citizens of
    Thebes.

AGAUË:

Come, all you Thebans living within these towered walls,
Come, see the beast we, Cadmus' daughters, caught and
    killed;
Caught not with nets or thonged Thessalian javelins,
But with our own bare arms and fingers. After this
Should huntsmen glory in their exploits, who must buy
Their needless tools from armourers? We with our hands
Hunted and took this beast, then tore it limb from limb.

Where is my father? Let old Cadmus come. And where
Is my son Pentheus? Let him climb a strong ladder
And nail up on the cornice of the palace wall
This lion's head that I have hunted and brought home.

Enter CADMUS *with attendants bearing the body of*
PENTHEUS.

CADMUS:

Come, men, bring your sad burden that was Pentheus.
  Come,
Set him at his own door. By weary, endless search
I found his body's remnants scattered far and wide
About Cithaeron's glens, or hidden in thick woods.
I gathered them and brought them here.

                                    I had already
Returned with old Teiresias from the Bacchic dance,
And was inside the walls, when news was brought me of
My daughters' terrible deed. I turned straight back; and
  now
Return, bringing my grandson, whom the Maenads killed.
I saw Autonoë, who bore Actaeon to Aristaeus,
And Ino with her, there among the trees, still rapt
In their unhappy frenzy; but I understood
That Agauë had come dancing on her way to Thebes –
And there indeed she is, a sight for misery!

AGAUË:

Father! Now you may boast as loudly as you will
That you have sired the noblest daughters of this age!
I speak of all three, but myself especially.
I have left weaving at the loom for greater things,
For hunting wild beasts with my bare hands. See this prize,
Here in my arms; I won it, and it shall be hung
On your palace wall. There, father, take it in your hands.
Be proud of my hunting; call your friends to a feast; let
  them
Bless you and envy you for the splendour of my deed.

CADMUS:

Oh, misery unmeasured, sight intolerable!
Oh, bloody deed enacted by most pitiful hands!
What noble prize is this you lay at the gods' feet,
Calling the city, and me, to a banquet? Your wretchedness
Demands the bitterest tears; but mine is next to yours.
Dionysus has dealt justly, but pursued justice
Too far; born of my blood, he has destroyed my house.

AGAUË:

What an ill-tempered creature an old man is! How full
Of scowls! I wish my son were a great hunter like
His mother, hunting beasts with the young men of Thebes;
But *he* can only fight with gods. Father, you must
Correct him. – Will not someone go and call him here
To see me, and to share in my great happiness?

CADMUS:

Alas, my daughters! If you come to understand
What you have done, how terrible your pain will be!
If you remain as you are now, though you could not
Be happy, at least you will not feel your wretchedness.

AGAUË: Why not happy? What cause have I for wretchedness?

CADMUS: Come here. First turn your eyes this way. Look
at the sky.

AGAUË: I am looking. Why should you want me to look at it?

CADMUS: Does it appear the same to you, or is it changed?

AGAUË: Yes, it is clearer than before, more luminous.

CADMUS: And this disturbance of your mind – is it still there?

AGAUË:

I don't know what you mean; but – yes, I feel a change;
My mind is somehow clearer than it was before.

CADMUS: Could you now listen to me and give a clear reply?

AGAUË: Yes, father. I have forgotten what we said just now.

CADMUS: When you were married, whose house did you
go to then?

300   [1274-

AGAUË: You gave me to Echion, of the sown race, they said.
CADMUS: Echion had a son born to him. Who was he?
AGAUË: Pentheus. His father lay with me; I bore a son.
CADMUS: Yes; and whose head is that you are holding in
   your arms?
AGAUË: A lion's – so the women said who hunted it.
CADMUS: Then look straight at it. Come, to look is no great
   task.

               AGAUË *looks; and suddenly screams.*

AGAUË: What am I looking at? What is this in my hands?
CADMUS: Look at it steadily; come closer to the truth.
AGAUË: I see – O gods, what horror! Oh, what misery!
CADMUS: Does this appear to you to be a lion's head?
AGAUË: No! I hold Pentheus' head in my accursed hand.
CADMUS: It is so. Tears have been shed for him, before you
   knew.
AGAUË: But who killed him? How did he come into my
   hands.
CADMUS: O cruel hour, that brings a bitter truth to light!
AGAUË: Tell me – my heart is bursting, I must know the rest.
CADMUS: It was you, Agauë, and your sisters. You killed
   him.
AGAUË: Where was it done? Here in the palace? Or where
   else?
CADMUS: Where, long ago, Actaeon was devoured by
   hounds.
AGAUË: Cithaeron! But what evil fate took Pentheus there?
CADMUS: He went to mock Dionysus and your Bacchic
   rites.
AGAUË: Why were we on Cithaeron? What had brought us
   there?
CADMUS: You were possessed. All Thebes was in a Bacchic
   trance.
AGAUË: Dionysus has destroyed us. Now I understand.
CADMUS: He was insulted. You refused to call him god.

AGAUË: Father, where is the beloved body of my son?
CADMUS: Here. It was I who brought it, after painful search.
AGAUË: And are his limbs now decently composed?
CADMUS: Not yet.*
    We came back to the city with all possible haste.
AGAUË: How could I touch his body with these guilty hands?
CADMUS: Your guilt, my daughter, was not heavier than his.
AGAUË: What part did Pentheus have, then, in my insanity?
CADMUS:
    He sinned like you, refusing reverence to a god.
    Therefore the god has joined all in one ruin – you,
    Your sisters, Pentheus – to destroy my house and me.
    I have no son; and now, my unhappy child, I see
    This son of yours dead by a shameful, hideous death.
    You were the new hope of our house, its bond of
        strength,
    Dear grandson. And Thebes feared you; no one dared
        insult
    Your old grandfather if he saw you near; you would
    Teach him his lesson. But now I shall live exiled,
    Dishonoured – I, Cadmus the great, who planted here,
    And reaped, that glorious harvest of the Theban race.
    O dearest son – yes, even in death you shall be held
    Most dear – you will never touch my beard again, and
        call
    Me Grandfather, and put your arm round me and say,
    'Who has wronged you or insulted you? Who is unkind,
    Or vexes or disturbs you? Tell me, Grandfather,
    That I may punish him.' Never again. For me
    All that remains is pain; for you, the pity of death;
    For your mother, tears; torment for our whole family.
    If any man derides the unseen world, let him
    Ponder the death of Pentheus, and believe in gods.

    * This and the three following lines are missing in the text, and are
here conjecturally supplied.

CHORUS:

I grieve for your fate, Cadmus; though your grandson's
  death
Was justly merited, it falls cruelly on you.

AGAUË:

Father, you see how one disastrous day has shattered
My whole life,* *turned my pride to shame, my happiness*
To horror. Now my only wish is to compose
My son's body for burial, and lament for him;
And then die. But this is not lawful; for my hands
Are filthy with pollution of their own making.
When I have spilt the blood I bore, and torn the flesh
That grew in my own womb, how can I after this
Enfold him to my breast, or chant his ritual dirge?
And yet, I beg you, pity me, and let me touch
My son, and say farewell to that dear body which
I cherished, and destroyed unknowing. It is right
That you should pity, for your hands are innocent.

CADMUS:

My daughter, you and I and our whole house are crushed
And broken by the anger of this powerful god.
It is not for me to keep you from your son. Only
Be resolute, and steel your heart against a sight

* At this point the two MSS on which the text of this play depends
show a lacuna of considerable extent; it covers the end of this scene, in
which Agauë mourns over Pentheus' body, and the appearance of
Dionysus manifested as a god. The MSS resume in the middle of a
speech by Dionysus. A number of quotations by ancient authors,
together with less than twenty lines from *Christus Patiens* (an anonymous
fourth century A.D. work consisting largely of lines adapted from
Greek tragedies) make it possible to attempt a guess at the content of
the missing lines. Since this play is often performed, it seems worth
while to provide here a usable text. In the lines that follow, the words
printed in italics are mere conjecture, and have no value except as a
credible completion of the probable sense; while those in Roman type
represent the sources available from *Christus Patiens* and elsewhere.

Which must be fearful to any eyes, but most of all
To a mother's. [*To attendants*] *Men, put down your burden on*
   the ground
Before Agaue, and remove the covering.

AGAUË:

Dear child, how cruel, how unnatural are these tears,
Which should have fallen from your eyes on my dead face.
Now I shall die with none to mourn me. This is just;
For in my pride I did not recognize the god,
Nor understand the things I ought to have understood.
You too are punished for the same impiety;
·But which is the more terrible, your fate or mine,
I cannot tell. Since you have suffered too, you will
Forgive both what I did, not knowing what I did,
And what I do now, touching you with unholy hands –
At once your cruellest enemy and your dearest friend.

 I place your limbs as they should lie; I kiss the flesh
That my own body nourished and my own care reared
To manhood. Help me, father; lay his poor head here.
Make all exact and seemly, with what care we can.
O dearest face, O young fresh cheek; O kingly eyes,
Your light now darkened! O my son! See, with this veil
I now cover your head, your torn and bloodstained limbs.

 Take him up, carry him to burial, a king
Lured to a shameful death by the anger of a god.

Enter DIONYSUS.

CHORUS:

But look! Who is this, rising above the palace door?
It is he – Dionysus comes himself, no more disguised
As mortal, but in the glory of his divinity!

DIONYSUS:

Behold me, a god great and powerful, Dionysus,
The son whom Theban Semele bore to immortal Zeus.
I come to the city of seven gates, to famous Thebes,
Whose people slighted me, denied my divinity,

*Refused my ritual dances. Now they reap the fruit
Of impious folly. The royal house is overthrown;
The city's streets tremble in guilt, as every Theban
Repents too late his blindness and his blasphemy.
Foremost in sin was Pentheus, who not only scorned
My claims, but* put me in fetters and insulted me.
Therefore death came to him in the most shameful way,
At his own mother's hands. This fate he justly earned;
*No god can see his worship scorned, and hear his name
Profaned, and not take vengeance to the utmost limit.
Thus men may learn that gods are more powerful than they.*

Agauë and her sisters must immediately
Depart from Thebes; their exile will be just penance
For the pollution which this blood has brought on them.
Never again shall they enjoy their native land;
*That such defilement ever should appear before
The city's altars,* is an offence to piety.

Now, Cadmus, hear what suffering Fate appoints for you.
You* shall transmute your nature, and become a serpent.
Your wife Harmonia, whom her father Ares gave
To you, a mortal, likewise shall assume the nature
Of beasts, and live a snake. The oracle of Zeus
Foretells that you, at the head of a barbaric horde,
Shall with your wife drive forth a pair of heifers yoked,
And with your countless army destroy many cities;
But when they plunder Loxias' oracle, they shall find
A miserable homecoming. However, Ares shall
At last deliver both you and Harmonia,
And grant you immortal life among the blessed gods.

I who pronounce these fates am Dionysus, begotten
Not by a mortal father, but by Zeus. If you
Had chosen wisdom, when you would not, you would have lived
In wealth and safety, having the son of Zeus your friend.

* Here the MSS resume.

CADMUS: Have mercy on us, Dionysus. We have sinned.

DIONYSUS: You know too late. You did not know me when you should.

CADMUS: We acknowledge this; but your revenge is merciless.

DIONYSUS: And rightly; I am a god, and you insulted me.

CADMUS: Gods should not be like mortals in vindictiveness.

DIONYSUS: All this my father Zeus ordained from the beginning.

AGAUË: No hope, father. Our harsh fate is decreed: exile.

DIONYSUS: Then why put off a fate which is inevitable?

Exit DIONYSUS.

CADMUS:
Dear child, what misery has overtaken us all –
You, and your sisters, and your old unhappy father!
I must set forth from home and live in barbarous lands;
Further than that, it is foretold that I shall lead
A mixed barbarian horde to Hellas. And my wife,
Harmonia, Ares' daughter, and I too, must take
The brutish form of serpents; and I am to lead her thus
At the head of an armed force, to desecrate the tombs
And temples of our native land. I am to reach
No respite from this curse; I may not even cross
The downward stream of Acheron to find peace in death.

AGAUË: And I in exile, father, shall live far from you.

CADMUS:
Poor child, why do you cling to me, as the young swan
Clings fondly to the old, helpless and white with age?

AGAUË: Where can I turn for comfort, homeless and exiled?

CADMUS: I do not know. Your father is little help to you.

AGAUË:
Farewell, my home; farewell the land I know.
Exiled, accursed and wretched, now I go
Forth from this door where first I came a bride.

CADMUS:

> Go, daughter; find some secret place to hide
> Your shame and sorrow.

AGAUË: Father, I weep for you.

CADMUS: I for your suffering, and your sisters' too.

AGAUË:

> There is strange tyranny in the god who sent
> Against your house this cruel punishment.

CADMUS:

> Not strange: our citizens despised his claim,
> And you, and they, put him to open shame.

AGAUË: Father, farewell.

CADMUS: Poor child! I cannot tell
> How you can *fare well*; yet I say, Farewell.

AGAUË:

> I go to lead my sisters by the hand
> To share my wretchedness in a foreign land.
> *She turns to the Theban women who have been waiting at*
> *the edge of the stage.*
> Come, see me forth.
>   Gods, lead me to some place
> Where loath'd Cithaeron may not see my face,
> Nor I Cithaeron. I have had my fill
> Of mountain-ecstasy; now take who will
> My holy ivy-wreath, my thyrsus-rod,
> All that reminds me how I served this god!
>   *Exit, followed by* CADMUS.

CHORUS:

> Gods manifest themselves in many forms,
> Bring many matters to surprising ends;
> The things we thought would happen do not happen;
> The unexpected God makes possible:
> And that is what has happened here today.
>   *Exeunt.*

Catullus,
The Poems

64

In old days
                    driving through soft waters
to the River of Pheasants
                    to the end of the Euxine Lake
pines sprung from Pelion
                    carrying picked men
Argives each like a tree
                    hearts set on the Colchian pelt
of gold, daring to track
                    salt deserts in a fast ship
cutting blue waves with firwood blades
for whom the indweller of the arx
                    the queen of hill-castles
had made hull poop & sail
                    – volatile under light winds –
binding firmly the pine-plaits to the curved underprow
the first boat to experience innocent sea –
Amphitrite.
                    As the moving waves took the keel
the water, chopped with oars, grew white
and from the runnels of foam faces peered
of Nereids, wondering. Then
and not since
                    men with their own eyes
 saw the bare bodies of nymphs
                    in broad daylight
caught in the marbled runnels of foam
as far down as the nipples. . . .
So Peleus was stirred towards Thetis
 so Thetis came to a woman's bridal

and Jove gave his blessing.

       O heroes

brides nymphs oreads

    born in a golden time

before the tribe of gods had gone from earth

I call on you in my poem

     standing with Peleus

Pillar of Thessaly

     blest beyond most in their bride-torches

whom Jove himself

     author of gods and goddesses

has given one of his girls,

     and Thetis

prettiest of mermaids

     touched as her own,

whom Tethys & old Ocean

     girdling all that we stand on –

have yielded a granddaughter.

     On the day

the longed-for light leaps up

Thessaly gathers in concourse

     gift-bearing guests

a laughing crowd

     their hearts in their faces

converge on the Palace.

     Cieros is empty

Phthiotic Tempe deserted

     the houses in Crannon

Larissa's walls

     abandoned –

flocking into Pharsalia

     packed under Pharsalian roofs

the crowds gather.
              No man tills the field
the bullock's neck grows soft.
              Not for many days shall the pronged hoe
rake among the vine-roots,
              or the pruning hook lessen
the olive tree's deep shade.
              Oxen do not turn the lumps of loam,
              red rust flakes the neglected plough.
But in the royal halls
              wherever you look
as room unfolds into room
              silver & gold gleam
an effulgence of ivory,
              carved thrones,
glittering cups on the long tables
the whole building thrums with the splendour of royal
   goods,
and there, in the middle,
              inlaid with Indian tooth
and quilted with arras,
              the divan of the small goddess
              the arras ochred with rock-lichen &
              tinctured with stain of rose shell-fish.

This quilt is pricked
              with figures of gods & men
sketches of antiquity in *petit point*!
Here are the never-silent sands of Naxos
here Theseus vanishes towards the north,

a woman watches from the empty beach
   unflagging grief in her heart,
Ariadne doesn't yet believe, quite,
    she is witnessing what her eyes see –
she's only just woken from a trap
(of sleep)
   found herself alone on the island.
And Theseus, heedless as storm & wind
    carves up the waves as he goes
and throws their love-words overboard.
    But the Minoan girl
with seaweed on her legs
   goes on looking from the shallow water
with tragic eyes
   she goes on looking from a long way
frozen in the statuary of grief,
   like a Maenad,
until waves of her own shake her
   her hair shakes loose of her yellow snood
her thin bodice flaps open at her breasts
her breasts, the colour of milk,
   push through her torn brassière,
snood skirt bra
   the shallows take her torn clothes
swirling the silk in eddies at her ankles
the clothes do not matter:
   her body is lost in you
Theseus –
   Ariadne!
Venus has kept for you her best thorn of love
love-fated girl
   love-fated from the hour Theseus

steered from the curved breakwater of the Piraeus
set course for the iron city of the iron king
Minoan Knossos.

        A blight lay over the narrow streets of Athens. . . .
The story goes that to absolve herself
of the murder of the bull-king's son
                          Androgeos
at the games at the Panathenaea
        Athens yielded
yearly ten of her best men
yearly ten nubile girls (unmarried)
        food for the bull-king
until Prince Theseus one day
        proffered himself for his sweet city,
"The shipments of the dead not dead
from here to Crete shall stop".
He sailed in a good ship, before fine winds,
coming to the rock-hewn halls of Knossos.
From her window
        the royal girl looked down
with a girl's lust,
        whom the women's quarters enfolded
in her chaste bed
        as petals the scented stamen
who was like the myrtle buds on the banks of the Eurotas
or the coloured breath of springtime
not lifting her hot eyes
            till fire ran in her womb –
            the girl's body swathed in fire.
Remorseless Cupid

THE POEMS OF CATULLUS

Holy Child
       – who stirs hate & love in one cup!
Venus of Eryx
       – a girl who will drown in your floods
      whispering at a blond stranger!
Venus of Golgos
       – and expectations breaking in the heart!
Venus of leafy Idalia
       – how often the girl's cheeks – sallow, like gold!
As Theseus walked out to meet the beast
poised between death and celebrity
Ariadne addressed herself to her prayers
                 with firm lips
making her small offerings to the gods,
who acted.
      For as on the top of Mount Taurus
in Turkey
      where the great oaks shake out their boughs
and the pine trees drip resin
      a high wind contorting the trunk
can pluck out a tree by its roots
      so that the monster upended
comes down beamwise
      splintering what's in its path
so Theseus capsized the bull-monster
      and the quelled body lay in a heap
its fruitless horns sticking up.
      Then fingering the thread
he turned his feet back,
      along the delusive maze
of palace corridors,
      stepped out of the labyrinth

a hero, unharmed
          and made off with the girl
– prizing sweet love & Theseus
          before the lot of them
eluding her father's watch
forgoing her three sisters' embraces
                              her mother's,
tearful for a lost daughter
whom the wind blew to white-ringed Naxos
whom sleep took in the night
whom yesterday's bridegroom
                              forsworn
left, before morning.

                    And now scared at her own grief
scattering her screams broadside
                    she runs to the top of the cliffs
looks at the waves rolling northwards
then runs out into the sea
                    holding her silk petticoat above her knees,
glass-cheeked,
          at the end of tears,
          and frozen with tears,
the words well from the pit of her bride's stomach:

"Why did you lift me from Cretan bower
"dumping me here on an empty beach,
"shrugging off Heaven, her plans for us,
"heedless of freighting home snapped pledges?
"Nowhere the means to flex steel

"no appeal that could touch you.
"You did not tell me to look for seduction
"but for bride-ale & wedding torches,
"for the increments of Hymen,
"– waste words shredded now on wind.
"Now no woman listen to man's love-words
"or look to find there his love-bond:
"as long as they itch for it
"they will say anything
                    do anything,
"but with lust slaked
            "the soft words are forgotten
            "the promises null.
"I caught you from the back coil of your fate
"happy to exchange a half-brother for love's need
"and you leave me – scavenge for island birds & beasts:
            "no tumulus for me dead
            "no death-dust as cover.
"You are flint
            where the bitch-cat whelps under desert rock,
"or spume
        when brine-water sickens with sea-spawn,
"you are the kindless issue of the twin gulfs
                            – storm-ridden Syrtes –
"of the octopus & the maelstrom,
                        epitomes of ruin.
"Is this your guerdon for a life saved?
"If you did not want to marry me
"because of your father (who is prejudiced)
"you could have taken me home with you
"and I should have tended you
"got your bath ready for you,

"washing your arms & feet with spring water,
"each day smoothing the coloured bedspread in your
   room.
"But why should I give my tears
"to this wind? In this state?
"Wind is deaf as well as dumb.
"And he's wind-driven in the middle distance.
"There's nothing here but rocks & seaweed.
"In the hubris of indifference Fate
"deprives me even of an ear to listen.
"If only the Athenian sloop
"had never entered the bay
"at Knossos, with its grim cargo
"for the bull, fixed hawsers to the quay,
"captained by an attractive sailor . . .
"with a soul like a trap-door
"whom we took in out of pity –

                his name was Theseus.

"Where can I go?

            What is left for me?

"Our Cretan hills?

           There's bitter water between.

"A father?

         Whom I abandoned in blood guilt.

"Or the love-purpose of a husband?
"Who makes the rowlocks creak
"in his hurry to get away from me.
"And inland on Naxos?

             Derelict

"no roof-tree

         no escape

"the surcingle of sea-water

THE POEMS OF CATULLUS

"no hope
            no reason for refuge
"all is dumb
            all is alone
                        all is nothing
"but these lids won't grow grubby with death
"till from the gods I've wrung amercement –
"on Olympus someone tips back the scales.
"Listen:
            raveners of men's evil
                                    Erinyes
"upon whose scalps
                        as images of hate
"snakes feed,
            Tisiphone!
                        Megaera!
"Alecto!
            these moans are forced
"from a feverish body,
"as blind as epilepsy,
"they are the truth of Ariadne's heart.
"Don't waste what galls,
"make Theseus deal
"as brutally as he dealt me
"himself & someone loved."

As the voice poured from the tragic mouth
crying for revenge on the ill dealt her
Jove's brow bent in assent
so that land and wild sea shook,
the gleaming stars shivered in the sky

and a mist fell on Theseus
who at once forgot the strict words,
till then locked in his heart,
that he signal careworn Aegeus
by hoisting the glad-omened sails
when the home port hove in sight.
For before Theseus slipped anchor
dropping beneath the city's ramparts
his father had kissed him
yielding his son to sea-winds
with the words:

"Restored at the tail-end of my life
"from Troezene, my only Theseus
"dearer than years to your father
"of whom Fate & your own zest
"would rob him a second time,
"even before his failing eyes
"had gotten used to your face,
"I despatch you without happiness
"banning bravado of flags & auguries.
"I make public grief
"with dust & ash on my grey hair
"and the dark canvas hung
"from your voyaging mast:
"Hibernian dyed purple
"signal of foreboding.
                              But should Athene
"shield of Athens & of Athenians
"stoop to sprinkle your right hand
"with the bull's blood, enact closely

"heart-kept, unflecked by time
"this mandate:
                        On sight of Attic hills
"to strip ship of purple
"& hoist white sails from the plaited cords
"so Aegeus, at the first, may see
"with carefree heart his son safe,
"Theseus bent homeward in bright-omened hour."

But these words locked in intention
drifted from Theseus' head
as the wind imperceptibly lifts
the snow-mist from the hill-tops.
For Aegeus posted himself in the watch-tower,
his eyes tear-gutted,
he saw the dark shrouds
he read the false news of death
and the old king cast himself from the battlements,
while the boy, fresh from the bull-killing
'came home' – entered a stricken palace
victim of deceit as grim
as he off Naxos coast had sprung
bewildered Ariadne –

                . . . who still gazes where the hull has dwindled,
who revolves in her bride's heart a maze of sorrow.

                                And elsewhere on the quilt
flushed with desire for the Minoan bride

         Bacchus his crew
of Satyrs & Silenes
           descend about the glittering god,
from Ethiopia, from Ind, from Thrace
          with tossing heads
with frenzied 'Evoes!'
          they are shaking the thyrsus
shaking the vine leaves round it,
          they catch the torn bits of bullock
the snake belt writhes at their hips
          and the secret *cartouche*
hiding the sacred objects
          objects no common sight profanes
passes to the hand-slap drum beat,
          bagpipe, horn & cymbals
sprinkle the hillside with discordant music.

Such the stitches worked in the wedding quilt,
such the splendid figures embracing the divan.
The young guests from Thessaly
their eyes filled with the tapestry
gradually ebb
         from courts & corridors,
the demi-gods are due:
         it is a dawn figure,
Aurora climbs
         to the threshold of the day-sojourning sun,
Zephyr
         flicks the flat water into ridges
with a morning puff,
         the sloped waves

loiter musically,
        later the wind rises
& they rise,
        they multiply,
they shed the sun's sea purple as they flee.
In this way
        the crowd scatters from the royal crannies,
the mortal guests disperse to their own homes.

And now, Chiron,
        first to arrive,
carrying from Mount Pelion
        green gifts
of Thessalian buds
        from fields & alps
from river banks
        where the light west wind
has unsealed them.
        It is the centaur's *potpourri*.
They luxuriate
        through the wedding rooms
with a confused fragrance.
        And behind Chiron,
Peneus
        bearded with rushes
from Tempe
        whose girdling woods
are a river roof.
        He brings
store of beech
        dripping roots,

& laurel
        like a girl's flanks,
he brings the plane tree
        that is restless,
the piercing cypress
        & the poplar
supple in the wind,
        its tears of amber
for flame-shrouded Phaeton.
        The river god
heaps the foliage
        outside & in
until the house
        is dressed
for a bride's bower-bed.
        Next, Prometheus
patron of crafts
        & seer
still showing
        the faint cicatrices
Jove's penance
        paid on the cliff-face
in Caucasus,
        rock-chained
arms & legs
        thirty years. . . .
And then follows Jove,
        Juno,.
their issue –
        only Apollo
the archer
        & his twin sister, Artemis,

323

have spurned
       the bride-ale & wedding torches
and are left to haunt Heaven.

The gods have disposed
       their white forms
at the wedding tables.
       It is bride-hymn time.
The Parcae prepare
       to intone
the prophetic song.
       The white shift
wrapping their palsy
       is alive,
it is red-hemmed
       at the ankles,
and their white hair
       is bound
with a red cloth.
       Their deft fingers
manipulate
       the eternal thread,
one hand on the distaff
       the other carding
with upturned fingers
       the spindle wool,
drawing the thread
       downwards,
twirling the whorl
       as the thread lengthens,

and stooping
        with mauve lips
to bite the rough ends off
        so that the bits hang
from the withered skin.
        An osier basket bulges
with new-shorn fleece . . .
        the wool whirrs
and the clear voices ring
        in Epithalamion
for Thetis,
        her bride-doom
time-sealed.

"Emathian bulwark, son of Jove,
whose acts augment his born worth,
accept the sisters' wedding truth.

Inexorably, fate follows thread,
from spindle to the shuttle running.

Fair-fortuned star that draws the bride
to groom, that yields the longed-for wife
whose mastery of love will drown
his heart, who settling to the drawn-
out marriage sleep will make her arms
light cushions for his heavy neck.

Inexorably, fate follows thread,
from spindle to the shuttle running.

THE POEMS OF CATULLUS

Not yet such love as Peleus
for Thetis holds (& she for him)
has been – or such a grove of love.

Inexorably, fate follows thread,
from spindle to the shuttle running.

A child, Achilles, void of fear:
foe known face-on not fleeing, first
in racing, in hunt fleeter than
the fleet-foot stag, whose hooves strike flame.

Inexorably, fate follows thread,
from spindle to the shuttle running.

No warrior dare confront Achilles
where the Trojan rivers stream with
Trojan blood, and the Greeks raze stone
from stone of Troy, ten years consumed.

Inexorably, fate follows thread,
from spindle to the shuttle running.

The women at the gravesides weep
his deeds, their hair is loose, coated
with ash-dust, their ageing bosoms
showing fist marks of their sorrow.

Inexorably, fate follows thread,
from spindle to the shuttle running.

As the farmer's scythe in close-packed
cornstalks, stripping the yellow field,
his fierce blade crops Troy's men-at-arms.

Inexorably, fate follows thread,
from spindle to the shuttle running.

Scamander by quick Hellespont
will watch his valour swell, its width
shrink with slaughter-stooks, while its deep
course warms with the issuing blood.

Inexorably, fate follows thread,
from spindle to the shuttle running.

And Polyxena, death-given,
too shall watch . . . and watch the earth-tomb
rise, where her maiden limbs will fall.

Inexorably, fate follows thread,
from spindle to the shuttle running.

Once Chance lets slip the Greeks inside
the sea-born belt of stone, the young
girl's blood will soak the barrow mound,
who crouches to the two-edged sword
& pitches, a headless trunk, forward.

Inexorably, fate follows thread,
from spindle to the shuttle running.

But now the joining of their loves,
as Peleus accepts his nymph, &
Thetis lightly yields to wedlock.

Inexorably, fate follows thread,
from spindle to the shuttle running.

And dawn light finds the nurse who tries
today's neck fillet, her mother reads
the sign & smiles: the goddess was
not coy in love – young fruit will follow.

Inexorably, fate follows thread,
from spindle to the shuttle running."

This song
          of happy wedding-fates
the Parcae sang
          to Peleus
 in old days.
          For once
when piety had place on earth
          the gods themselves
stood at our chaste doors
          or drank at the bride-ales
of mortal heroes.
          On Holy Feasts
Jove from his bright throne
saw the earth littered with a hundred bulls.
The wine-god on Parnassus
          goading his dishevelled troop

was hailed
>with altar smoke
from happy Delphos
>where the rasping Thyiades
had emptied street & square.
>Athene, Mars or Artemis
appeared
>in the death-tussle
and lit men's hearts.
>To-day ill wreaking rules.
Man's piety is fled.

The loveless child neglects its parent's death
a brother's blood trickles from brothers' hands
the first son's girl attracts the father's lust
who seeks a step-dame & a son's demise
unwittingly the youngster mounts his mother
her vicious incest spurning the house-kin
spirits: laws bouleversé, and the welter
such, those of Hill-Heaven have withdrawn their care.

No longer do they deign
to keep our bride-ales, or
reveal themselves to us
in the light of common day.

Virgil, *The Aeneid*
Books 2, 4, and 6

BOOK II

🔲

The Fall of Troy

THEY all were silent, watching. From his couch
Aeneas spoke: "A terrible grief, O Queen,
You bid me live again, how Troy went down
Before the Greeks, her wealth, her pitiful kingdom,
Sorrowful things I saw myself, wherein
I had my share and more. Even Ulysses,
Even his toughest soldiery might grieve
At such a story.[1] And the hour is late
Already; night is sliding down the sky
And setting stars urge slumber. But if you long
To learn our downfall, to hear the final chapter
Of Troy, no matter how I shrink, remembering,
And turn away in grief, let me begin it.

Broken in war, set back by fate,[2] the leaders
Of the Greek host, as years went by, contrived,

[1] Ulysses is the Greek Odysseus, a prominent warrior in Homer's *Iliad* and the protagonist of his *Odyssey*, which tells of Odysseus' ten years of struggle to return after the war to his home, the island of Ithaca west of Greece. Homer presents Odysseus as bold, courageous, tough-minded, pragmatic, and, above all, ingeniously resourceful, a master of strategy. It was typical of him that, having originally resisted joining the expedition against Troy, he served with single-minded zeal once he was committed to the campaign. The Romans took a dimmer view of Odysseus, however: as despicable, treacherous, even cowardly.

[2] Tradition calls for epics to leap *in medias res*, "into the middle of things," supplying earlier events through long flashback narratives such as the story Aeneas here begins to relate. Virgil's main model is the long account of Odysseus' Mediterranean adventures that the hero narrates to the Phaeacians in Books IX through XII of Homer's *Odyssey*.

With Pallas' help, a horse as big as a mountain.
They wove its sides with planks of fir, pretending
This was an offering for their safe return,
At least, so rumor had it. But inside
20   They packed, in secret, into the hollow sides
The fittest warriors; the belly's cavern,
Huge as it was, was filled with men in armor.
There is an island, Tenedos, well-known,
Rich in the days of Priam; now it is only
A bay, and not too good an anchorage
For any ship to trust.³ They sailed there, hid
On the deserted shore. We thought they had gone,
Bound for Mycenae,⁴ and Troy was very happy,
Shaking off grief, throwing the gates wide open.
30   It was a pleasure, for a change, to go
See the Greek camp, station and shore abandoned;
Why, this was where Achilles camped, his minions,
The Dolopes, were here; and the fleet just yonder,
And that was the plain where we used to meet in battle.
Some of us stared in wonder at the horse,
Astounded by its vastness, Minerva's gift,
Death from the virgin goddess, had we known it.
Thymoetes, whether in treachery,⁵ or because
The fates of Troy so ordered, was the first one
40   To urge us bring it in to the heart of the city,
But Capys, and some others, knowing better,
Suspicious of Greek plotting, said to throw it
Into the sea, to burn it up with fire,
To cut it open, see what there was inside it.
The wavering crowd could not make up its mind.

And, at that point, Laocoön came running,
With a great throng at his heels, down from the hilltop

---

³ Ancient Troy was located on the eastern shore of the Aegean Sea, in
what is now Turkey, at the southwestern end of the Dardanelles strait.
Tenedos was an island near the mainland a little to the south.
    ⁴ The home of Agamemnon, the Greek commander-in-chief; by exten-
sion, Greece.
    ⁵ Thymoetes nursed a grudge against Priam, the Trojan king.

As fast as ever he could, and before he reached us,
Cried in alarm: 'Are you crazy, wretched people?
Do you think they have gone, the foe? Do you think that
          any   50
Gifts of the Greeks lack treachery? Ulysses,—
What was his reputation? Let me tell you,
Either the Greeks are hiding in this monster,
Or it's some trick of war, a spy, or engine,
To come down on the city. Tricky business
Is hiding in it. Do not trust it, Trojans,
Do not believe this horse. Whatever it may be,
I fear the Greeks, even when bringing presents.'
With that, he hurled the great spear at the side
With all the strength he had. It fastened, trembling,   60
And the struck womb rang hollow, a moaning sound.
He had driven us, almost, to let the light in
With the point of the steel, to probe, to tear, but something
Got in his way, the gods, or fate, or counsel,
Ill-omened, in our hearts; or Troy would be standing
And Priam's lofty citadel unshaken.

Meanwhile, some Trojan shepherds, pulling and hauling,
Had a young fellow, with his hands behind him,
Tied up, and they were dragging him to Priam.
He had let himself be taken so, on purpose,   70
To open Troy to the Greeks, a stranger, ready
For death or shifty cunning, a cool intriguer,
Let come what may. They crowd around to see him,
Take turns in making fun of him, that captive.
Listen, and learn Greek trickiness; learn all
Their crimes from one.
He stopped in the middle, frightened and defenceless,
Looked at the Trojan ranks,—'What land, what waters,
Can take me now?' he cried, 'There is nothing, nothing
Left for me any more, no place with the Greeks,   80
And here are the Trojans howling for my blood!'
Our mood was changed. We pitied him, poor fellow,
Sobbing his heart out. We bade him tell his story,
His lineage, his news: what can he count on,

The captive that he is? His fear had gone
As he began: 'O King, whatever happens,
I will tell the truth, tell all of it; to start with,
I own I am a Greek. Sinon is wretched,
Fortune has made him so, but she will never
90   Make him a liar. You may perhaps have heard
Rumors of Palamedes, son of Belus,[6]
A man of glorious fame. But the Greeks killed him,—
He was against the war, and so they killed him,
An innocent man, by perjury and lying
False witness. Now that he is dead they mourn him.
My father, his poor relative, had sent me
To soldier in his company; I was then
Scarcely beyond my boyhood. Palamedes
Held, for some time, some influence and standing
100   In royal councils, and we shared his glory,
But, and all men know this, Ulysses' hatred,
His cunning malice, pulled him down; thereafter
I lived in darkness, dragging out a lifetime
In sorrow for my innocent lord, and anger,
And in my anger I was very foolish,
I talked; I vowed, if I got home to Argos,
I would have vengeance: so I roused Ulysses
To hate me in his turn, and that began it,
Downfall and evil, Ulysses always trying
110   To frighten me with hint and accusation,
With rumors planted where the crowd would listen;
Oh yes, Ulysses knew what he was doing,
He never stopped, until with Calchas[7] working
Hand in glove with him—why am I telling this,
And what's the use? I am stalling. All the Greeks,
You think, are all alike; what more do you want?
Inflict the punishment. That would be something
Ulysses would rejoice in, and some others
Pay handsome money for!'

[6] Not to be confused with the Belus (Dido's father) mentioned in I.658.
Palamedes was hated by Ulysses because he had seen through and exposed
Ulysses' attempts to pose as mad and thus avoid the war.
[7] As a Greek prophet and priest, Calchas was expected to discover and
reveal the will of the gods.

But we were all on fire to hear him further.   120
Pelasgian[8] craft meant nothing to our folly.
Trembling and nervous, he resumed his lying:
'The Greeks were tired of the long war; they often
Wanted to sail from Troy for home. Oh, would
That they had only done it! But a storm
Would cut them off, or the wrong wind terrify them.
Especially, just after the horse was finished,
With the joined planks of maple, all the heaven
Roared loud with storm-clouds. In suspense and terror
We sent Eurypylus to ask Apollo   130
What could be done; the oracle was gloomy,
Foreboding: "Blood, O Greeks, and a slain virgin
Appeased the winds when first you came here; blood
Must pay for your return, a life be given,
An Argive life."[9] The word came to our ears
With terror in it, our blood ran cold in our veins,
For whom was fate preparing? who would be
The victim of Apollo? Then Ulysses
Dragged Calchas into our midst, with a great uproar,
Trying his best to make the prophet tell us   140
What the gods wanted. And there were many then
Who told me what was coming, or kept silent
Because they saw, and all too well, the scheme
Ulysses had in mind. For ten days Calchas
Said nothing at all, hid in his tent, refusing
To have a word of his pronounce the sentence,
And all the time Ulysses kept on shouting,
Till Calchas broke, and doomed me to the altar.
And all assented; what each man had feared
In his own case, he bore with great composure   150
When turned another way.
The terrible day was almost on me; fillets[10]

---

[8] Here a synonym for *Greek*.

[9] Apollo was the prophet-god; the main center of prophecy for the Greeks
was his temple at Delphi, where his oracles were pronounced. The "slain
virgin" was Agamemnon's daughter Iphigenia, who was sacrificed to appease divine anger and thus gain for the Greeks favorable winds when
they first set out for Troy. *Argive* here means *Greek*.

[10] Headbands, worn by the sacrificial victim.

Were ready for my temples, the salted meal
Prepared, the altars standing. But I fled,
I tore myself away from death, I admit it,
I hid all night in sedge and muddy water
At the edge of the lake, hoping, forever hoping,
They might set sail. And now I hope no longer
To see my home, my parents, or my children,
160   Poor things, whom they will kill because I fled them,
Whom they will murder for my sacrilege.
But oh, by the gods above, by any power
That values truth, by any uncorrupted
Remnant of faith in all the world, have pity,
Have pity on a soul that bears such sorrow,
More than I ever deserved.'
He had no need to ask us. Priam said,
Untie him, and we did so with a promise
To spare his life. Our king, with friendly words,
170   Addressed him, saying, 'Whoever you are, forget
The Greeks, from now on. You are ours; but tell me
Why they have built this monstrous horse? who made it,
Who thought of it? What is it, war-machine,
Religious offering?' And he, instructed
In every trick and artifice, made answer,
Lifting his hands, now free: 'Eternal fires,
Inviolable godhead, be my witness,
You altars, you accursèd swords, you fillets
Which I as victim wore, I had the right
180   To break those solemn bonds, I had the right
To hate those men, to bring whatever they hide
Into the light and air; I am bound no longer
To any country, any laws, but, Trojans,
Keep to the promise, if I tell the truth,
If I pay back with interest.
All the Greek hope, since first the war began,
Rested in Pallas, always. But Ulysses,
The crime-contriver, and the son[11] of Tydeus

---

[11] Diomedes.

Attacked Minerva's temple, stole her image
Out of the holy shrine, and slew the guards,   190
And laid their bloody hands upon the goddess,[12]
And from that time the Danaan[13] hopes were broken,
Faltered and failed. It was no doubtful anger
Pallas revealed; she gave them signs and portents.
From her image in the camp the upraised eyes
Shot fire, and sweat ran salty down the limbs,
Thrice from the ground she seemed to flash and leap
With vibrant spear and clashing shield. The priest,
Calchas, made prophecy: they must take to flight
Over the sea, and Troy could not be taken   200
Without new omens; they must go to Argos,
Bring back the goddess again, whom they have taken
In curved ships over the sea. And if they have gone,
They are bound for home, Mycenae, for new arms,
New gods, new soldiers; they will be here again
When least expected. Calchas' message warned them,
And so they built this image, to replace
The one they had stolen, a gigantic offering
For a tremendous sacrilege. It was Calchas,
Again, who bade them build a mass so mighty   210
It almost reached the stars, too big to enter
Through any gate, or be brought inside the walls.
For if your hands should damage it, destruction,
(May God avert it) would come upon the city,
But if your hands helped bring it home, then Asia
Would be invading Greece, and doom await
Our children's children.'
                            We believed him, we
Whom neither Diomede nor great Achilles
Had taken, nor ten years, nor that armada,
A thousand ships of war. But Sinon did it   220

---

[12] That is, upon the statue of Pallas Athena, or Minerva, which the two
men thus defiled. It was believed that the security of Troy depended on
the preservation of this statue.
[13] Greek (From *Danaus*, the name of a legendary ruler of Argos, in
Greece).

By perjury and guile.
                              Then something else,
Much greater and more terrible, was forced
Upon us, troubling our unseeing spirits.
Laocoön, allotted priest of Neptune,
Was slaying a great bull beside the altars,
When suddenly, over the tranquil deep
From Tenedos,—I shudder even now,
Recalling it—there came a pair of serpents
With monstrous coils, breasting the sea, and aiming
230   Together for the shore. Their heads and shoulders
Rose over the waves, upright, with bloody crests,
The rest of them trailing along the water,
Looping in giant spirals; the foaming sea
Hissed under their motion. And they reached the land,
Their burning eyes suffused with blood and fire,
Their darting tongues licking the hissing mouths.
Pale at the sight, we fled. But they went on
Straight toward Laocoön, and first each serpent
Seized in its coils his two young sons, and fastened
240   The fangs in those poor bodies. And the priest
Struggled to help them, weapons in his hand.
They seized him, bound him with their mighty coils,
Twice round his waist, twice round his neck, they squeezed
With scaly pressure, and still towered above him.
Straining his hands to tear the knots apart,
His chaplets[14] stained with blood and the black poison,
He uttered horrible cries, not even human,
More like the bellowing of a bull when, wounded,
It flees the altar, shaking from the shoulder
250   The ill-aimed axe. And on the pair went gliding
To the highest shrine, the citadel of Pallas,
And vanished underneath the feet of the goddess
And the circle of her shield.
                              The people trembled
Again; they said Laocoön deserved it,

---

[14] Bands or garlands for the head; part of the priest's ritual dress. There
is a famous statue, in the Vatican, depicting the struggle of Laocoön with
the two serpents.

Having, with spear, profaned the sacred image.
It must be brought to its place, they cried, the goddess
Must be appeased. We broke the walls, exposing
The city's battlements, and all were busy
Helping the work, with rollers underfoot
And ropes around the neck. It climbed our walls, 260
The deadly engine. Boys, unwedded girls
Sang alleluias round it, all rejoicing
To have a hand on the tow-rope. It came nearer,
Threatening, gliding, into the very city.
O motherland! O Ilium,[15] home of gods,
O walls of Troy! Four times it stopped, four times
The sound of arms came from it, and we pressed on,
Unheedful, blind in madness, till we set it,
Ill-omened thing, on the citadel we worshipped.
And even when Cassandra gave us warning, 270
We never believed her; so a god had ordered.[16]
That day, our last, poor wretches, we were happy,
Garlanding the temples of the gods
All through the town.
                          And the sky turned, and darkness
Came from the ocean, the great shade covering earth
And heaven, and the trickery of the Greeks.
Sprawling along the walls, the Trojans slumbered,
Sleep holding their weary limbs, and the Greek armada,
From Tenedos, under the friendly silence
Of a still moon, came surely on. The flagship 280
Blazed at the masthead with a sudden signal,
And Sinon, guarded by the fates, the hostile
Will of the gods, swung loose the bolts; the Greeks
Came out of the wooden womb. The air received them,
The happy captains, Sthenelus, Ulysses,
Thessandrus, Acamas, Achilles' son
Called Neoptolemus, Thoas, Machaon,
Epeos, who designed the thing,—they all
Came sliding down the rope, and Menelaus

[15] Another name for Troy.
[16] Cassandra was a daughter of the Trojan royal family; Apollo gave her powers to prophesy the truth but, in revenge for her rejection of his love, doomed her to be always disbelieved.

290   Was with them in the storming of a city
        Buried in sleep and wine. The watch was murdered,
        The open doors welcome the rush of comrades,
        They marshal the determined ranks for battle.
            It was the time when the first sleep begins
        For weary mortals, heaven's most welcome gift.
        In sleep, before my eyes, I seemed to see
        Hector, most sorrowful, black with bloody dust,
        Torn, as he had been, by Achilles' car,
        The thong-marks on his swollen feet.[17] How changed
300   He was from that great Hector who came, once,
        Triumphant in Achilles' spoil, from hurling
        Fire at the Grecian ships. With ragged beard,
        Hair matted with his blood, wearing the wounds
        He earned around the walls of Troy, he stood there.
        It seemed that I spoke first:—'O light of Troy,
        Our surest hope, we have long been waiting for you,
        What shores have kept you from us? Many deaths,
        Much suffering, have visited our city,
        And we are tired. Why do I see these wounds?
310   What shame has caused them?' Those were foolish questions;
        He made no answer but a sigh or a groan,
        And then: 'Alas, O goddess-born! Take flight,
        Escape these flames! The enemy has the walls,
        Troy topples from her lofty height; enough
        Has been paid out to Priam and to country.
        Could any hand have saved them, Hector's would have.
        Troy trusts to you her household gods, commending
        Her holy things to you; take them, companions
        Of destiny; seek walls for them, and a city
320   To be established, a long sea-wandering over.'
        From the inner shrine he carried Vesta's chaplets
        In his own hands, and her undying fire.[18]

            Meanwhile, the city is all confusion and sorrow;
        My father Anchises' house, remote and sheltered

_____

[17] For the death of Hector, see I.507–12.

[18] The hearth-fire (of which Vesta is goddess) is to be transported to a new city.

Among its trees, was not so far away
But I could hear the noises, always clearer,
The thickening din of war. Breaking from sleep,
I climb to the roof-top, listening and straining
The way a shepherd does on the top of a mountain
When fire goes over the corn, and the winds are roaring,   330
Or the rush of a mountain torrent drowns the fields
And the happy crops and the work of men and oxen
And even drags great trees over. And then I knew
The truth indeed; the craft of the Greeks was hidden
No longer from my sight. The house of a neighbor,
Deiphobus, went up in flames; next door,
Ucalegon was burning. Sigeum's water
Gave back the glow.[19] Men shouted, and the trumpets
Blared loud. I grab my arms, with little purpose,
There was no sense in it, but my heart was burning   340
To mass a band for war, rush to the hilltop
With comrades at my side. Anger and frenzy
Hurry me on. A decent death in battle
Is a helpful thought, sometimes.

        And here came Panthus, running from the weapons,
Priest of Apollo, and a son of Othrys,
With holy relics in his hands, and dragging
His little grandson, here came Panthus, running
In madness to my door. 'How goes it, Panthus?
What stronghold still is ours?' I had hardly spoken,   350
When he began, with a groan: 'It has come, this day
Will be our last, and we can not escape it.
Trojans we have been, Troy has been, and glory
Is ours no more. Fierce Jupiter has taken
Everything off to Argos, and Greeks lord it
In a town on fire. The horse, high in the city,
Pours out armed men, and Sinon, arrogant victor,
Lights up more fires. The gates are standing open,
And men are there by the thousands, ever as many
As came once from Mycenae; others block   360

---

[19] The death of Deiphobus, who succeeded Paris as Helen's husband,
is described more fully, in his own words, in VI.518–61. Ucalegon was
one of the king Priam's advisors. Sigeum was a cape near Troy.

The narrow streets, with weapons drawn; the blades
Flash in the dark; the point is set for murder.
A few of the guards are trying, striking blindly,
For all the good it does.'

His words, or the gods' purpose, swept me on
Toward fire and arms, where the grim furies call,
And the clamor and confusion, reaching heaven.
Ripheus joined me, Epytus, mighty in arms,
Came to my side in the moonlight, Hypanis, Dymas,
370   And young Coroebus, Mygdon's son, poor youngster,
Mad with a hopeless passion for Cassandra,
He wanted to help Priam, but never heeded
The warnings of his loved one.
                                As they ranged
Themselves for battle, eager, I addressed them:
'O brave young hearts, it will do no good; no matter.
Even if your will is fixed, to follow a leader
Taking the final risk, you can't help seeing
The fortune of our state. The gods have gone,
They have left their shrines and altars, and the power
380   They once upheld is fallen. You are helping
A town already burnt. So let us die,
Rush into arms. One safety for the vanquished
Is to have hope of none.
                                They were young, and angry.
Like wolves, marauders in black mist, whom hunger
Drives blindly on, whose whelps, abandoned, wait them
Dry-jawed, so we went on, through foes, through weapons,
To certain death; we made for the heart of the city,
Black night around us with its hollow shadow.
Who could explain that night's destruction, equal
390   Its agony with tears? The ancient city,
A power for many years, comes down, and corpses
Lie littering the streets and homes and altars.
Not only Trojans die. The old-time valor
Returns to the vanquished heart, and the Greek victors
Know what it is to fall. Everywhere sorrow,
Everywhere panic, everywhere the image
Of death, made manifold.

Out of a crowd of Greeks comes one Androgeos,
Thinking us allies, hailing us as friendly:
'Why men, where have you been, you dawdling fellows?   400
Hurry along! Here is plunder for the taking,
Others are busy at it, and you just coming
From the high ships!' And then he knew he had blundered;
He had fallen in with foes, who gave no answer.
He stopped, stepped back, like a man who treads on a serpent
Unseen in the rough brush, and then in panic
Draws back as the purple neck swells out in anger.
Even so, Androgeos pulled away in terror.
We rush them, swarm all over them; they are frightened,
They do not know their ground, and fortune favors   410
Our first endeavor. Coroebus, a little crazy
With nerve and luck, cries out: 'Comrades, where fortune
First shows the way and sides with us, we follow.
Let us change our shields, put on the Grecian emblems!
All's fair in war: we lick them or we trick them,
And what's the odds?' He takes Androgeos' helmet,
Whose plume streams over his head, takes up the shield
With proud device, and fits the sword to his side.
And Ripheus does the same, and so does Dymas,
And all the others, happily, being armed   420
With spoil, new-won. We join the Greeks, all going
Under no gods of ours, in the night's darkness
Wade into many a fight, and Greeks by the dozens
We send to hell. And some of them in panic
Speed to the ships; they know that shore, and trust it,
And some of them—these were the abject cowards—
Climb scrambling up the horse's sides, again
Take refuge in the womb.

   It is not for men to trust unwilling gods.
Cassandra was being dragged from Pallas' temple,   430
Her hair loosed to the wind, her eyes turned upward
To heaven for mercy; they had bound her hands.
Coroebus could not bear that sight; in madness
He threw himself upon them, and he died.
We followed, all of us, into the thick of it,
And were cut down, not only by Greeks; the rooftops,

Held by our friends, rained weapons: we were wearing
Greek crests and armor, and they did not know us.
And the Greeks came on, shouting with anger, burning
440   To foil that rescue; there was Menelaus,
And Agamemnon, and the savage Ajax,
And a whole army of them. Hurricanes
Rage the same way, when winds from different quarters
Clash in the sky, and the forest groans, and Neptune
Storms underneath the ocean. Those we routed
Once in the dark came back again from the byways
And alleys of the town; they mark our shields,
Our lying weapons, and our foreign voices.
Of course we are outnumbered. Peneleus
450   It was, who slew Coroebus, at the altar
Sacred to Pallas. Ripheus fell, a man
Most just of all the Trojans, most fair-minded.
The gods thought otherwise. Hypanis, Dymas,
Were slain by their own men, and Panthus' goodness
Was no protection, nor his priestly office.
I call to witness Troy, her fires, her ashes,
And the last agonies of all our people
That in that hour I ran from no encounter
With any Greek, and if the fates had been
460   For me to fall in battle, there I earned it.
The current swept me off, with two companions,
One, Iphitus, too slow with age, the other,
Pelias, limping from Ulysses' wound.
The noise kept calling us to Priam's palace.

There might have been no fighting and no dying
Through all the city, such a battle raged
Here, from the ground to roof-top. At the threshold
Waves of assault were breaking, and the Greeks
Were climbing, rung by rung, along the ladders,
470   Using one hand, the right one up and forward
Over the battlements, the left one thrust
In the protecting shield. And over their heads
The Trojans pried up towers and planking, wrecking
The building; gilded beams, the spoils of their fathers,

Were ample weapons for the final moment.
Some had the doorways blocked, others, behind them,
Were ready with drawn swords. We had a moment
When help seemed possible: new reinforcement
Might yet relieve the palace.
There was a secret entrance there, a passage   480
All the way through the building, a postern gate,
Where, while the kingdom stood, Andromache
Would go, alone, or bring the little boy,
Astyanax, to Hector's father and mother.[20]
I climbed to the top of the roof, where the poor Trojans
Were hurling down their unavailing darts.
A tower stood on the very edge, a look-out
Over all Troy, the ships and camp of the Greeks.
This we attacked with steel, where the joints were weakest,
And pried it up, and shoved it over. It crashed,   490
A noisy ruin, over the hostile columns;
But more kept coming up; the shower of stones
And darts continued raining.
Before the entrance, at the very threshold,
Stood Pyrrhus,[21] flashing proudly in bronze light,
Sleek as a serpent coming into the open,
Fed on rank herbs, wintering under the ground,
The old slough cast, the new skin shining, rolling
His slippery length, reaching his neck to the sun,
While the forked tongue darts from the mouth. Automedon   500
Was with him, Periphas, Achilles' driver,
A giant of a man, and the host from Scyros,[22]
All closing in on the palace, and hurling flames.
Among the foremost, Pyrrhus, swinging an axe,
Burst through, wrenched the bronze doors out of their
        hinges,
Smashed through the panelling, turned it into a window.
The long halls came to view, the inner chambers
Of Priam and the older kings; they see

[20] Andromache was the wife of Hector and mother of Astyanax. Hector's parents were Priam and Hecuba, king and queen of Troy.
[21] Achilles' son, fierce like his war-loving father.
[22] An island east of Greece; the home of Pyrrhus.

Armed warriors at the threshold.
510 Within, it is all confusion, women wailing,
Pitiful noise, groaning, and blows; the din
Reaches the golden stars. The trembling mothers
Wander, not knowing where, or find a spot
To cling to; they would hold and kiss the doors.
Pyrrhus comes on, aggressive as his father;
No barrier holds him back; the gate is battered
As the ram[23] smashes at it; the doors come down.
Force finds a way: the Greeks pour in, they slaughter
The first ones in their path; they fill the courtyard
520 With soldiery, wilder than any river
In flood over the banks and dikes and ploughland.
I saw them, Pyrrhus, going mad with murder,
And Atreus' twin sons,[24] and Hecuba
I saw, and all her daughters, and poor old Priam,
His blood polluting the altars he had hallowed.
The fifty marriage-chambers,[25] the proud hope
Of an everlasting line, are violated,
The doors with the golden spoil are turned to splinters.
Whatever the fire has spared the Greeks take over.
530   You would ask, perhaps, about the fate of Priam?
When he saw the city fall, and the doors of the palace
Ripped from the hinge, and the enemy pouring in,
Old as he was, he went and found his armor,
Unused so many years, and his old shoulders
Shook as he put it on. He took his sword,
A useless weapon, and, doomed to die, went rushing
Into the midst of the foe. There was an altar
In the open court-yard, shaded by a laurel
Whose shadow darkened the household gods, and here
540 Hecuba and her daughters had come thronging,
Like doves by a black storm driven. They were praying
Here at the altar, and clinging to the gods,
Whatever image was left. And the queen saw Priam

[23] The battering-ram.
[24] Agamemnon and Menelaus.
[25] The quarters of Priam's fifty sons and their wives. Priam also had
fifty daughters.

In the arms of his youth. 'O my unhappy husband,'
She cried, 'have you gone mad, to dress yourself
For battle, so? It is all no use; the time
Needs better help than yours; not even my Hector
Could help us now. Come to me, come to the altar;
It will protect us, or at least will let us
Die all together.' And she drew him to her.   550
　　Just then through darts, through weapons, came Polites,
A son of Priam, fleeing deadly Pyrrhus,
Down the long colonnades and empty hallways,
Wounded, and Pyrrhus after him, vicious, eager
For the last spear-thrust, and he drives it home;
Polites falls, and his life goes out with his blood,
Father and mother watching. And then Priam,
In the very grip of death, cried out in anger:—
'If there is any righteousness in heaven,
To care about such wickedness, the gods   560
Will have the right reward and thanks to offer
A man like this, who has made a father witness
The murder of his son, the worst pollution!
You claim to be Achilles' son. You liar!
Achilles had some reverence, respected
A suppliant's right and trust; he gave me back
My Hector's lifeless body for the tomb,
And let me go to my kingdom.'[26] With the word
He flung a feeble spear, which dropped, deflected
From the rough bronze; it had hung there for a moment.   570
And Pyrrhus sneered: 'So, go and tell my father
The latest news: do not forget to mention,
Old messenger-boy, my villainous behavior,
And what a bastard Pyrrhus is. Now die!'
He dragged the old man, trembling, to the altar,
Slipping in his son's blood; he grabbed his hair
With the left hand, and the right drove home the sword
Deep in the side, to the hilt. And so fell Priam,

---

[26] In *The Iliad*, Book XXIV, Homer tells how Achilles, after slaying Hector, agreed to return the corpse to his father Priam. Achilles himself was later slain, by an arrow from Paris' bow.

Who had seen Troy burn and her walls come down, once
    monarch,
580   Proud ruler over the peoples and lands of Asia.
He lies, a nameless body, on the shore,
Dismembered, huge, the head torn from the shoulders.
    Grim horror, then, came home to me. I saw
My father when I saw the king, the life
Going out with the cruel wound. I saw Creusa[27]
Forsaken, my abandoned home, Iulus,
My little son. I looked around. They all
Had gone, exhausted, flung down from the walls,
Or dead in the fire, and I was left alone.
590   And I saw Helen,[28] hiding, of all places,
At Vesta's shrine,[29] and clinging there in silence,
But the bright flames lit the scene. That hated woman,
Fearing both Trojan anger and Greek vengeance,
A common fury to both lands, was crouching
Beside the altar. Anger flared up in me
For punishment and vengeance. Should she then,
I thought, come home to Sparta safe, uninjured
Walk through Mycenae,[30] a triumphant queen?
See husband, home, parents and children, tended
600   By Trojan slave-girls? This, with Priam fallen
And Troy burnt down, and the shore soaked in blood?
Never! No memorable name, I knew,
Was won by punishing women, yet, for me,
There might be praise for the just abolition

[27] Aeneas' wife.

[28] There is some question about the authenticity of the Helen episode in lines 590–607, which are absent from the earliest manuscripts of *The Aeneid* and were provided by Servius, an ancient commentator. According to him, the lines were deleted from Virgil's manuscript by the men directed to edit the poem (which Virgil never put into finished form) after the poet died—their reasons, Servius argued, being that Aeneas' wrath toward a woman is unchivalrous and that the passage is inconsistent with the description of Helen in VI.538–59. The lines may well be the work of Virgil, but how he meant to work them into the poem is uncertain.

[29] It is ironic that the adulteress Helen should seek safety in the temple of Vesta, goddess of the hearth and thus the symbol of home and family.

[30] That is, Greece, signified here by the home city of Agamemnon, the Greek commander and Helen's brother-in-law. Helen's own home was Sparta, the city of her husband Menelaus.

Of this unholiness, and satisfaction
In vengeance for the ashes of my people.
All this I may have said aloud, in frenzy,
As I rushed on, when to my sight there came
A vision of my lovely mother, radiant
In the dark night, a goddess manifest,   610
As tall and fair as when she walks in heaven.
She caught me by the hand and stopped me:—'Son,
What sorrow rouses this relentless anger,
This violence?[31] Do you care for me no longer?
Consider others first, your aged father,
Anchises; is your wife Creusa living?
Where is Iulus? Greeks are all around them,
Only my love between them, fire and sword.
It is not for you to blame the Spartan woman,
Daughter of Tyndareus, or even Paris.   620
The gods are the ones, the high gods are relentless,
It is they who bring this power down, who topple
Troy from the high foundation. Look! Your vision
Is mortal dull, I will take the cloud away,—
Fear not a mother's counsel. Where you see
Rock torn from rock, and smoke and dust in billows,
Neptune is working, plying the trident, prying
The walls from their foundations. And see Juno,
Fiercest of all, holding the Scaean gates,[32]
Girt with the steel, and calling from the ships   630
Implacable companions. On the towers,—
Turn, and be certain—Pallas takes command
Gleaming with Gorgon and storm-cloud.[33] Even Jove,
Our father, nerves the Greeks with fire and spirit,
And spurs the other gods against the Trojans.
Hasten the flight, my son; no other labor
Waits for accomplishment. I promise safety
Until you reach your father's house.' She had spoken

---

[31] Although she is Aeneas' mother, Venus as goddess of love naturally protects Helen, the most beautiful of all women.

[32] The principal gates of Troy, which had faced the Greek besiegers.

[33] On the *aegis,* the shield or breastplate of Pallas Athena (Minerva), was depicted the head of Medusa, one of the female monsters known as Gorgons; Medusa turned to stone anyone who gazed on her.

And vanished in the thickening night of shadows.
640   Dread shapes come into vision, mighty powers,
Great gods at war with Troy, which, so it seemed,
Was sinking as I watched, with the same feeling
As when on mountain-tops you see the loggers
Hacking an ash-tree down, and it always threatens
To topple, nodding a little, and the leaves
Trembling when no wind stirs, and dies of its wounds
With one long loud last groan, and dirt from the ridges
Heaves up as it goes down with roots in air.
Divinity my guide, I leave the roof-top,
650   I pass unharmed through enemies and blazing,
Weapons give place to me, and flames retire.

At last I reached the house, I found my father,
The first one that I looked for. I meant to take him
To the safety of the hills, but he was stubborn,
Refusing longer life or barren exile,
Since Troy was dead. 'You have the strength,' he told me,
'You are young enough, take flight. For me, had heaven
Wanted to save my life, they would have spared
This home for me. We have seen enough destruction,
660   More than enough, survived a captured city.
Speak to me as a corpse laid out for burial,
A quick farewell, and go. Death I shall find
With my own hand;[34] the enemy will pity,
Or look for spoil. The loss of burial
Is nothing at all.[35] I have been living too long
Hated by gods and useless, since the time
Jove blasted me with lightning wind and fire.'[36]
He would not move, however we wept, Creusa,
Ascanius, all the house, insistent, pleading
670   That he should not bring all to ruin with him.
He would not move, he would not listen. Again
I rush to arms, I pray for death; what else

[34] Anchises means that he will go down fighting.
[35] Failure to receive proper burial was in fact considered a calamitous misfortune; see the Palinurus episode in Books V and VI.
[36] The god took revenge because Anchises boasted of Venus' love for him.

Was left to me? 'Dear father, were you thinking
I could abandon you, and go? what son
Could bear a thought so monstrous? If the gods
Want nothing to be left of so great a city,
If you are bound, or pleased, to add us all
To the wreck of Troy, the way is open for it—
Pyrrhus will soon be here; from the blood of Priam
He comes; he slays the son before the father,   680
The sire at the altar-stone; O my dear mother,
Was it for this you saved me, brought me through
The fire and sword, to see our enemies
Here in the very house, and wife and son
And father murdered in each other's blood?
Bring me my arms; the last light calls the conquered.
Let me go back to the Greeks, renew the battle,
We shall not all of us die unavenged.'
    Sword at my side, I was on the point of going,
Working the left arm into the shield. Creusa   690
Clung to me on the threshold, held my feet,
And made me see my little son:—'Dear husband,
If you are bent on dying, take us with you,
But if you think there is any hope in fighting,
And you should know, stay and defend the house!
To whom are we abandoned, your father and son,
And I, once called your wife?' She filled the house
With moaning outcry. And then something happened,
A wonderful portent. Over Iulus' head,
Between our hands and faces, there appeared   700
A blaze of gentle light; a tongue of flame,
Harmless and innocent, was playing over
The softness of his hair, around his temples.
We were afraid, we did our best to quench it
With our own hands, or water, but my father
Raised joyous eyes to heaven, and prayed aloud:—
'Almighty Jupiter, if any prayer
Of ours has power to move you, look upon us,
Grant only this, if we have ever deserved it,
Grant us a sign, and ratify the omen!'   710
He had hardly spoken, when thunder on the left
Resounded, and a shooting star from heaven

Drew a long trail of light across the shadows.
We saw it cross above the house, and vanish
In the woods of Ida,[37] a wake of gleaming light
Where it had sped, and a trail of sulphurous odor.
This was a victory: my father rose
In worship of the gods and the holy star,
Crying: 'I follow, son, wherever you lead;
720   There is no delay, not now; Gods of my fathers,
Preserve my house, my grandson; yours the omen,
And Troy is in your keeping. O my son,
I yield, I am ready to follow.' But the fire
Came louder over the walls, the flames rolled nearer
Their burning tide. 'Climb to my shoulders, father,
It will be no burden, so we are together,
Meeting a common danger or salvation.
Iulus, take my hand; Creusa, follow
A little way behind. Listen, you servants!
730   You will find, when you leave the city, an old temple
That once belonged to Ceres;[38] it has been tended
For many years with the worship of our fathers.
There's a little hill there, and a cypress tree;
And that's where we shall meet, one way or another.
And one thing more: you, father, are to carry
The holy objects and the gods of the household,
My hands are foul with battle and blood, I could not
Touch them without pollution.
                            I bent down
And over my neck and shoulders spread the cover
740   Of a tawny lion-skin, took up my burden;
Little Iulus held my hand, and trotted,
As best he could, beside me; Creusa followed.
We went on through the shadows. I had been
Brave, so I thought, before, in the rain of weapons
And the cloud of massing Greeks. But now I trembled
At every breath of air, shook at a whisper,
Fearful for both my burden and companion.
    I was near the gates, and thinking we had made it,

[37] A mountain near Troy.
[38] Goddess of grain and the harvest (hence our word *cereal*).

But there was a sound, the tramp of marching feet,
And many of them, it seemed; my father, peering   750
Through the thick gloom, cried out:—'Son, they are coming!
Flee, flee! I see their shields, their gleaming bronze.'
Something or other took my senses from me
In that confusion. I turned aside from the path,
I do not know what happened then. Creusa
Was lost; she had missed the road, or halted, weary,
For a brief rest. I do not know what happened,
She was not seen again; I had not looked back,
Nor even thought about her, till we came
To Ceres' hallowed home. The count was perfect,   760
Only one missing there, the wife and mother.
Whom did I not accuse, of gods and mortals,
Then in my frenzy? What worse thing had happened
In the city overthrown? I left Anchises,
My son, my household gods, to my companions,
In a hiding-place in the valley; and I went back
Into the city again, wearing my armor,
Ready, still one more time, for any danger.
I found the walls again, the gate's dark portals,
I followed my own footsteps back, but terror,   770
Terror and silence were all I found. I went
On to my house. She might, just might, have gone there.
Only the Greeks were there, and fire devouring
The very pinnacles. I tried Priam's palace;
In the empty courtyards Phoenix and Ulysses
Guarded the spoils piled up at Juno's altar.[39]
They had Trojan treasure there, loot from the altars,
Great drinking-bowls of gold, and stolen garments,
And human beings. A line of boys and women
Stood trembling there.   780
I took the risk of crying through the shadows,
Over and over, 'Creusa!' I kept calling,
'Creusa!' and 'Creusa!' but no answer.
No sense, no limit, to my endless rushing
All through the town; and then at last I saw her,
Or thought I did, her shadow a little taller

---

[39] Phoenix had been a friend and mentor of Achilles.

Than I remembered. And she spoke to me
Beside myself with terror:—'O dear husband,
What good is all this frantic grief? The gods
790   Have willed it so, Creusa may not join you
Out of this city; Jupiter denies it.
Long exile lies ahead, and vast sea-reaches
The ships must furrow, till you come to land
Far in the West; rich fields are there, and a river
Flowing with gentle current; its name is Tiber.[40]
And happy days await you there, a kingdom,
A royal wife. Banish the tears of sorrow
Over Creusa lost. I shall never see
The arrogant houses of the Myrmidons,[41]
800   Nor be a slave to any Grecian woman;
I am a Dardan[42] woman; I am the wife
Of Venus' son; it is Cybele who keeps me
Here on these shores.[43] And now farewell, and love
Our son.' I wept, there was more to say; she left me,
Vanishing into empty air. Three times
I reached out toward her, and three times her image
Fled like the breath of a wind or a dream on wings.
The night was over; I went back to my comrades.

    I was surprised to find so many more
810   Had joined us, ready for exile, pitiful people,
Mothers, and men, and children, streaming in
From everywhere, looking for me to lead them
Wherever I would. Over the hills of Ida
The morning-star was rising; in the town
The Danaans held the gates, and help was hopeless.
I gave it up, I lifted up my father,
Together we sought the hills.

---

[40] The river of Rome.

[41] The Greek soldiers who had been led by Achilles.

[42] Trojan (From *Dardanus*, the name of the founder of the Trojan royal line).

[43] Cybele was a goddess associated with the region of Troy. She was called the "mother of the gods," being identified with Rhea, mother of Jupiter by Cronos (the Roman Saturn). Creusa apparently has not died a normal death but rather has been inducted into the heavenly service of the goddess.

BOOK IV

◧

Aeneas and Dido

B
UT the queen finds no rest. Deep in her veins
The wound is fed; she burns with hidden fire.
His manhood, and the glory of his race,
Are an obsession with her, like his voice,
Gesture and countenance. On the next morning,
After a restless night, she sought her sister:
"I am troubled, Anna, doubtful, terrified,
Or am I dreaming? What new guest is this
Come to our shores? How well he talks, how brave
He seems in heart and action! I suppose   10
It must be true; he does come from the gods.
Fear proves a bastard spirit. He has been
So buffeted by fate. What endless wars
He told of! Sister, I must tell you something:
Were not my mind made up, once and for all,
Never again to marry, having been
So lost when Sychaeus left me for the grave,
Slain by my murderous brother at the altar,[1]
Were I not sick forever of the torch[2]
And bridal bed, here is the only man   20
Who has moved my spirit, shaken my weak will.

---

[1] The story of what took place in Tyre between Dido's late husband, Sychaeus, and her murderous brother, Pygmalion, and of Dido's flight to Carthage, is told in I.351–85.

[2] Carried in wedding processions; an emblem of marriage. The image of fire climaxes in Dido's funeral pyre at the end of Book IV.

I might have yielded to him. I recognize
The marks of an old fire. But I pray, rather,
That earth engulf me, lightning strike me down
To the pale shades and everlasting night,
Before I break the laws of decency.
My love has gone with Sychaeus; let him keep it,
Keep it with him forever in the grave."
She ended with a burst of tears. "Dear sister,
30   Dearer than life," Anna replied, "why must you
Grieve all your youth away in loneliness,
Not know sweet children, or the joys of love?
Is that what dust demands, and buried shadows?
So be it. You have kept your resolution
From Tyre to Libya, proved it by denying
Iarbas and a thousand other suitors
From Africa's rich kingdoms. Think a little.
Whose lands are these you settle in? Getulians,
Invincible in war, the wild Numidians,
40   Unfriendly Syrtes, ring us round, and a desert
Barren with drought, and the Barcaean rangers.[3]
Why should I mention Tyre, and wars arising
Out of Pygmalion's threats? And you, my sister,
Why should you fight against a pleasing passion?
I think the gods have willed it so, and Juno
Has helped to bring the Trojan ships to Carthage.
What a great city, sister, what a kingdom
This might become, rising on such a marriage!
Carthage and Troy together in arms, what glory
50   Might not be ours? Only invoke the blessing
Of the great gods, make sacrifice, be lavish
In welcome, keep them here while the fierce winter
Rages at sea, and cloud and sky are stormy,
And ships still wrecked and broken."
                                        So she fanned
The flame of the burning heart; the doubtful mind
Was given hope, and the sense of guilt was lessened.

---

[3] The idea is that Dido is dangerously isolated on all sides: hemmed
in on land by potentially hostile peoples and on the north by the treacherous Syrtes, the shoals off the coast.

And first of all they go to shrine and altar
Imploring peace; they sacrifice to Ceres,
Giver of law, to Bacchus, to Apollo,
And most of all to Juno, in whose keeping   60
The bonds of marriage rest. In all her beauty
Dido lifts up the goblet, pours libation
Between the horns of a white heifer, slowly,
Or, slowly, moves to the rich altars, noting
The proper gifts to mark the day, or studies
The sacrificial entrails for the omens.
Alas, poor blind interpreters! What woman
In love is helped by offerings or altars?
Soft fire consumes the marrow-bones, the silent
Wound grows, deep in the heart.   70
Unhappy Dido burns, and wanders, burning,
All up and down the city, the way a deer
With a hunter's careless arrow in her flank
Ranges the uplands, with the shaft still clinging
To the hurt side. She takes Aeneas with her
All through the town, displays the wealth of Sidon,[4]
Buildings projected; she starts to speak, and falters,
And at the end of the day renews the banquet,
Is wild to hear the story, over and over,
Hangs on each word, until the late moon, sinking,   80
Sends them all home. The stars die out, but Dido
Lies brooding in the empty hall, alone,
Abandoned on a lonely couch. She hears him,
Sees him, or sees and hears him in Iulus,
Fondles the boy, as if that ruse might fool her,
Deceived by his resemblance to his father.
The towers no longer rise, the youth are slack
In drill for arms, the cranes and derricks rusting,
Walls halt halfway to heaven.
                                And Juno saw it,
The queen held fast by this disease, this passion   90
Which made her good name meaningless. In anger
She rushed to Venus:—"Wonderful!—the trophies,

[4] Of Carthage (from Sidon, a great city in Dido's former homeland).

The praise, you and that boy of yours[5] are winning!
Two gods outwit one woman—splendid, splendid!
What glory for Olympus! I know you fear me,
Fear Carthage, and suspect us. To what purpose?
What good does all this do? Is there no limit?
Would we not both be better off, to sanction
A bond of peace forever, a formal marriage?
100 You have your dearest wish; Dido is burning
With love, infected to her very marrow.
Let us—why not?—conspire to rule one people
On equal terms; let her serve a Trojan husband;
Let her yield her Tyrian people as her dowry."
     This, Venus knew, was spoken with a purpose,
A guileful one, to turn Italian empire
To Libyan shores: not without reservation
She spoke in answer: "Who would be so foolish
As to refuse such terms, preferring warfare,
110 If only fortune follows that proposal?
I do not know, I am more than a little troubled
What fate permits: will Jupiter allow it,
One city for the Tyrians and Trojans,
This covenant, this mixture? You can fathom
His mind, and ask him, being his wife. I follow
Wherever you lead." And royal Juno answered:
"That I will tend to. Listen to me, and learn
How to achieve the urgent need. They plan,
Aeneas, and poor Dido, to go hunting
120 When sunlight floods the world to-morrow morning.
While the rush of the hunt is on, and the forest shaken
With beaters[6] and their nets, I will pour down
Dark rain and hail, and make the whole sky rumble
With thunder and threat. The company will scatter,
Hidden or hiding in the night and shadow,
And Dido and the Trojan come for shelter
To the same cave. I will be there and join them
In lasting wedlock; she will be his own,
His bride, forever; this will be their marriage."

---

[5] Cupid, who for a time had taken the form of Iulus.
[6] Men assigned to flush the game animals from cover.

Venus assented, smiling, not ungracious—   130
The trick was in the open.[7]
    Dawn, rising, left the ocean, and the youth
Come forth from all the gates, prepared for hunting,
Nets, toils, wide spears, keen-scented coursing hounds,
And Dido keeps them waiting; her own charger
Stands bright in gold and crimson; the bit foams,
The impatient head is tossed. At last she comes,
With a great train attending, gold and crimson,
Quiver of gold, and combs of gold, and mantle
Crimson with golden buckle. A Trojan escort   140
Attends her, with Iulus, and Aeneas
Comes to her side, more lordly than Apollo
Bright along Delos' ridges in the springtime
With laurel in his hair and golden weapons
Shining across his shoulders. Equal radiance
Is all around Aeneas, equal splendor.
    They reach the mountain heights, the hiding-places
Where no trail runs; wild goats from the rocks are started,
Run down the ridges; elsewhere, in the open,
Deer cross the dusty plain, away from the mountains.   150
The boy Ascanius, in the midst of the valley,
Is glad he has so good a horse, rides, dashing
Past one group or another: deer are cowards
And wild goats tame; he prays for some excitement,
A tawny lion coming down the mountain
Or a great boar with foaming mouth.
                                        The heaven
Darkens, and thunder rolls, and rain and hail
Come down in torrents. The hunt is all for shelter,
Trojans and Tyrians and Ascanius dashing
Wherever they can; the streams pour down the mountains.   160
To the same cave go Dido and Aeneas,
Where Juno, as a bridesmaid, gives the signal,[8]
And mountain nymphs wail high their incantations,

---

[7] Having been told by Jupiter (I.268–311) of the destined future of Trojans and Romans, Venus is aware that Juno's plan will fail.

[8] Juno provides the ceremonial wedding torch, in the form of lightning flashes.

First day of death, first cause of evil. Dido
Is unconcerned with fame, with reputation,
With how it seems to others. This is marriage
For her, not hole-and-corner guilt; she covers
Her folly with this name.
                                Rumor goes flying
At once, through all the Libyan cities, Rumor
170   Than whom no other evil was ever swifter.
She thrives on motion and her own momentum;
Tiny at first in fear, she swells, colossal
In no time, walks on earth, but her head is hidden
Among the clouds. Her mother, Earth, was angry,
Once, at the gods, and out of spite produced her,
The Titans' youngest sister, swift of foot,
Deadly of wing, a huge and terrible monster,
With an eye below each feather in her body,
A tongue, a mouth, for every eye, and ears
180   Double that number; in the night she flies
Above the earth, below the sky, in shadow
Noisy and shrill; her eyes are never closed
In slumber; and by day she perches, watching
From tower or battlement, frightening great cities.
She heralds truth, and clings to lies and falsehood,
It is all the same to her. And now she was going
Happy about her business, filling people
With truth and lies: Aeneas, Trojan-born,
Has come, she says, and Dido, lovely woman,
190   Sees fit to mate with him, one way or another,
And now the couple wanton out the winter,
Heedless of ruling, prisoners of passion.
They were dirty stories, but the goddess gave them
To the common ear, then went to King Iarbas
With words that fired the fuel of his anger.

This king was Ammon's son, a child of rape
Begotten on a nymph from Garamantia;[9]
He owned wide kingdoms, had a hundred altars
Blazing with fires to Jove, eternal outposts

[9] Iarbas, a rejected African suitor of Dido's (line 36), is son of Jupiter,
whom the Romans equated with the Egyptian and Libyan god Ammon.
The Garamantes were an African tribe.

In the gods' honor; the ground was fat with blood,   200
The temple portals blossoming with garlands.
He heard the bitter stories, and went crazy,
Before the presences of many altars
Beseeching and imploring:—"Jove Almighty,
To whom the Moorish[10] race on colored couches
Pours festive wine, do you see these things, or are we
A pack of idiots, shaking at the lightning
We think you brandish, when it is really only
An aimless flash of light, and silly noises?
Do you see these things? A woman, who used to wander   210
Around my lands, who bought a little city,
To whom we gave some ploughland and a contract,
Disdains me as a husband, takes Aeneas
To be her lord and master, in her kingdom,
And now that second Paris,[11] with his lackeys,
Half-men, I call them, his chin tied up with ribbons,
With millinery on his perfumed tresses,
Takes over what he stole, and we keep bringing
Gifts to your temples, we, devout believers,
Forsooth, in idle legend."
                                And Jove heard him   220
Making his prayer and clinging to the altars,
And turned his eyes to Carthage and the lovers
Forgetful of their better reputation.
He summoned Mercury:[12] —"Go forth, my son,
Descend on wing and wind to Tyrian Carthage,
Speak to the Trojan leader, loitering there
Unheedful of the cities given by fate.
Take him my orders through the rapid winds:
It was not for this his lovely mother saved him
Twice from Greek arms;[13] she promised he would be   230
A ruler, in a country loud with war,
Pregnant with empire; he would sire a race

[10] The word here means, simply, *African*.
[11] That is, another effeminate playboy and seducer come from Troy.
[12] Mercury (Roman equivalent of the Greek god Hermes) was the messenger of the gods.
[13] First in a combat with Diomedes (Homer's *Iliad*, Book V), then at the sack of Troy.

From Teucer's[14] noble line; he would ordain
Law for the world. If no such glory moves him,
If his own fame and fortune count as nothing,
Does he, a father, grudge his son the towers
Of Rome to be? What is the fellow doing?
With what ambition wasting time in Libya?
Let him set sail. That's all; convey the message."
240   Before he ended, Mercury made ready
To carry out the orders of his father;
He strapped the golden sandals on, the pinions[15]
To bear him over sea and land, as swift
As the breath of the wind; he took the wand, which summons
Pale ghosts from Hell, or sends them there, denying
Or giving sleep, unsealing dead men's eyes,
Useful in flight through wind and stormy cloud,
And so came flying till he saw the summit
And towering sides of Atlas,[16] rugged giant
250   With heaven on his neck, whose head and shoulders
Are dark with fir, ringed with black cloud, and beaten
With wind and rain, and laden with the whiteness
Of falling snow, with rivers running over
His agèd chin, and the rough beard ice-stiffened.
Here first on level wing the god paused briefly,
Poised, plummeted to ocean, like a bird
That skims the water's surface, flying low
By shore and fishes' rocky breeding-ground,
So Mercury darted between earth and heaven
260   To Libya's sandy shore, cutting the wind
From the home of Maia's[17] father.
Soon as the winged sandals skim the rooftops,
He sees Aeneas founding towers, building
New homes for Tyrians; his sword is studded
With yellow jasper; he wears across his shoulders
A cloak of burning crimson, and golden threads
Run through it, the royal gift of the rich queen.

[14] Original ancestor of the Trojans; father-in-law of Dardanus.
[15] Wings.
[16] The mountain in Africa, here personified as the giant (who, in mythology, held up the sky).
[17] Daughter of Atlas and mother of Mercury.

Mercury wastes no time:—"What are you doing,
Forgetful of your kingdom and your fortunes,
Building for Carthage? Woman-crazy fellow,   270
The ruler of the gods, the great compeller
Of heaven and earth, has sent me from Olympus
With no more word than this: what are you doing,
With what ambition wasting time in Libya?
If your own fame and fortune count as nothing,
Think of Ascanius at least, whose kingdom
In Italy, whose Roman land, are waiting
As promise justly due." He spoke, and vanished
Into thin air. Appalled, amazed, Aeneas
Is stricken dumb; his hair stands up in terror,   280
His voice sticks in his throat. He is more than eager
To flee that pleasant land, awed by the warning
Of the divine command. But how to do it?
How get around that passionate queen? What opening
Try first? His mind runs out in all directions,
Shifting and veering. Finally, he has it,
Or thinks he has: he calls his comrades to him,
The leaders, bids them quietly prepare
The fleet for voyage, meanwhile saying nothing
About the new activity; since Dido   290
Is unaware, has no idea that passion
As strong as theirs is on the verge of breaking,
He will see what he can do, find the right moment
To let her know, all in good time. Rejoicing,
The captains move to carry out the orders.
   Who can deceive a woman in love? The queen
Anticipates each move, is fearful even
While everything is safe, foresees this cunning,
And the same trouble-making goddess, Rumor,
Tells her the fleet is being armed, made ready   300
For voyaging. She rages through the city
Like a woman mad, or drunk, the way the Maenads
Go howling through the night-time on Cithaeron[18]
When Bacchus' cymbals summon with their clashing.

[18] A mountain in Greece where the Maenads (female worshippers of
Bacchus, god of wine) conducted their orgiastic rites.

She waits no explanation from Aeneas;
She is the first to speak: "And so, betrayer,
You hoped to hide your wickedness, go sneaking
Out of my land without a word? Our love
Means nothing to you, our exchange of vows,
310   And even the death of Dido could not hold you.
The season is dead of winter, and you labor
Over the fleet; the northern gales are nothing—
You must be cruel, must you not? Why, even,
If ancient Troy remained, and you were seeking
Not unknown homes and lands, but Troy again,
Would you be venturing Troyward in this weather?
I am the one you flee from: true? I beg you
By my own tears, and your right hand—(I have nothing
Else left my wretchedness)—by the beginnings
320   Of marriage, wedlock, what we had, if ever
I served you well, if anything of mine
Was ever sweet to you, I beg you, pity
A falling house; if there is room for pleading
As late as this, I plead, put off that purpose.
You are the reason I am hated; Libyans,
Numidians, Tyrians, hate me; and my honor
Is lost, and the fame I had, that almost brought me
High as the stars, is gone. To whom, O guest—
I must not call you husband any longer—
330   To whom do you leave me? I am a dying woman;
Why do I linger on? Until Pygmalion,
My brother, brings destruction to this city?
Until the prince Iarbas leads me captive?
At least if there had been some hope of children
Before your flight, a little Aeneas playing
Around my courts, to bring you back, in feature
At least, I would seem less taken and deserted."
    There was nothing he could say. Jove bade him keep
Affection from his eyes, and grief in his heart
340   With never a sign. At last, he managed something:—
"Never, O Queen, will I deny you merit,
Whatever you have strength to claim; I will not
Regret remembering Dido, while I have
Breath in my body, or consciousness of spirit.

I have a point or two to make. I did not,
Believe me, hope to hide my flight by cunning;
I did not, ever, claim to be a husband,
Made no such vows. If I had fate's permission
To live my life my way, to settle my troubles
At my own will, I would be watching over   350
The city of Troy, and caring for my people,
Those whom the Greeks had spared, and Priam's palace
Would still be standing; for the vanquished people
I would have built the town again. But now
It is Italy I must seek, great Italy,
Apollo orders, and his oracles
Call me to Italy. There is my love,
There is my country. If the towers of Carthage,
The Libyan citadels, can please a woman
Who came from Tyre, why must you grudge the Trojans   360
Ausonian[19] land? It is proper for us also
To seek a foreign kingdom. I am warned
Of this in dreams: when the earth is veiled in shadow
And the fiery stars are burning, I see my father,
Anchises, or his ghost, and I am frightened;
I am troubled for the wrong I do my son,
Cheating him out of his kingdom in the west,
And lands that fate assigns him. And a herald,
Jove's messenger—I call them both to witness—
Has brought me, through the rush of air, his orders;   370
I saw the god myself, in the full daylight,
Enter these walls, I heard the words he brought me.
Cease to inflame us both with your complainings;
I follow Italy not because I want to."
    Out of the corner of her eye she watched him
During the first of this, and her gaze was turning
Now here, now there; and then, in bitter silence,
She looked him up and down; then blazed out at him:—
"You treacherous liar! No goddess was your mother,
No Dardanus the founder of your tribe,   380
Son of the stony mountain-crags, begotten
On cruel rocks, with a tigress for a wet-nurse!

[19] Italian.

Why fool myself, why make pretense? what is there
To save myself for now? When I was weeping
Did he so much as sigh? Did he turn his eyes,
Ever so little, toward me? Did he break at all,
Or weep, or give his lover a word of pity?
What first, what next? Neither Jupiter nor Juno
Looks at these things with any sense of fairness.
390   Faith has no haven anywhere in the world.
He was an outcast on my shore, a beggar,
I took him in, and, like a fool, I gave him
Part of my kingdom; his fleet was lost, I found it,
His comrades dying, I brought them back to life.
I am maddened, burning, burning: now Apollo
The prophesying god, the oracles
Of Lycia,[20] and Jove's herald, sent from heaven,
Come flying through the air with fearful orders,—
Fine business for the gods, the kind of trouble
400   That keeps them from their sleep. I do not hold you,
I do not argue, either. Go. And follow
Italy on the wind, and seek the kingdom
Across the water. But if any gods
Who care for decency have any power,
They will land you on the rocks; I hope for vengeance,
I hope to hear you calling the name of Dido
Over and over, in vain. Oh, I will follow
In blackest fire, and when cold death has taken
Spirit from body, I will be there to haunt you,
410   A shade, all over the world. I will have vengeance,
And hear about it; the news will be my comfort
In the deep world below." She broke it off,
Leaving the words unfinished; even light
Was unendurable; sick at heart, she turned
And left him, stammering, afraid, attempting
To make some kind of answer. And her servants
Support her to her room, that bower of marble,
A marriage-chamber once; here they attend her,
Help her lie down.
                    And good Aeneas, longing

[20] A region in Asia Minor; Apollo had a great shrine there.

To ease her grief with comfort, to say something   420
To turn her pain and hurt away, sighs often,
His heart being moved by this great love, most deeply,
And still—the gods give orders, he obeys them;
He goes back to the fleet. And then the Trojans
Bend, really, to their work, launching the vessels
All down the shore. The tarred keel swims in the water,
The green wood comes from the forest, the poles are lopped
For oars, with leaves still on them. All are eager
For flight; all over the city you see them streaming,
Bustling about their business, a black line moving   430
The way ants do when they remember winter
And raid a hill of grain, to haul and store it
At home, across the plain, the column moving
In thin black line through grass, part of them shoving
Great seeds on little shoulders, and part bossing
The job, rebuking laggards, and all the pathway
Hot with the stream of work.
                              And Dido saw them
With who knows what emotion: there she stood
On the high citadel, and saw, below her,
The whole beach boiling, and the water littered   440
With one ship after another, and men yelling,
Excited over their work, and there was nothing
For her to do but sob or choke with anguish.
There is nothing to which the hearts of men and women
Cannot be driven by love. Break into tears,
Try prayers again, humble the pride, leave nothing
Untried, and die in vain:—"Anna, you see them
Coming from everywhere; they push and bustle
All up and down the shore: the sails are swelling,
The happy sailors garlanding the vessels.   450
If I could hope for grief like this, my sister,
I shall be able to bear it. But one service
Do for me first, dear Anna, out of pity.
You were the only one that traitor trusted,
Confided in; you know the way to reach him,
The proper time and place. Give him this message,
Our arrogant enemy: tell him I never
Swore with the Greeks at Aulis to abolish

The Trojan race, I never sent a fleet
460   To Pergamus,[21] I never desecrated
The ashes or the spirit of Anchises:
Why does he, then, refuse to listen to me?
What is the hurry? Let him give his lover
The one last favor: only wait a little,
Only a little while, for better weather
And easy flight. He has betrayed the marriage,
I do not ask for that again; I do not
Ask him to give up Latium and his kingdom.
Mere time is all I am asking, a breathing-space,
470   A brief reprieve, until my luck has taught me
To reconcile defeat and sorrow. This
Is all I ask for, sister; pity and help me:
If he grants me this, I will pay it ten times over
After my death." And Anna, most unhappy,
Over and over, told her tears, her pleading;
No tears, no pleading, move him; no man can yield
When a god stops his ears. As northern winds
Sweep over Alpine mountains, in their fury
Fighting each other to uproot an oak-tree
480   Whose ancient strength endures against their roaring
And the trunk shudders and the leaves come down
Strewing the ground, but the old tree clings to the mountain,
Its roots as deep toward hell as its crest toward heaven,
And still holds on—even so, Aeneas, shaken
By storm-blasts of appeal, by voices calling
From every side, is tossed and torn, and steady.
His will stays motionless, and tears are vain.

   Then Dido prays for death at last; the fates
Are terrible, her luck is out, she is tired
490   Of gazing at the everlasting heaven.
The more to goad her will to die, she sees—
Oh terrible!—the holy water blacken,
Libations turn to blood, on ground and altar,

---

[21] Before sailing to Troy, the Greeks assembled their forces at the port
of Aulis; it was there that the daughter of Agamemnon, Iphigenia, was
sacrificed so that the gods would grant favorable winds for the sailing.
Pergamus here means Troy, though strictly speaking it was the citadel
of Troy.

When she makes offerings. But she tells no one,
Not even her sister. From the marble shrine,
Memorial to her former lord, attended,
Always, by her, with honor, fleece and garland,
She hears his voice, his words, her husband calling
When darkness holds the world, and from the house-top
An owl sends out a long funereal wailing,   500
And she remembers warnings of old seers,
Fearful, foreboding. In her dreams Aeneas
Appears to hunt her down; or she is going
Alone in a lost country, wandering,
Trying to find her Tyrians, mad as Pentheus,
Or frenzied as Orestes, when his mother
Is after him with whips of snakes, or firebrands,
While the Avengers menace at the threshold.[22]
    She was beaten, harboring madness, and resolved
On dying; alone, she plotted time and method;   510
Keeping the knowledge from her sorrowing sister,
She spoke with calm composure:—"I have found
A way (wish me good luck) to bring him to me
Or set me free from loving him forever.
Near Ocean[23] and the west there is a country,
The Ethiopian land, far-off, where Atlas
Turns on his shoulders the star-studded world;
I know a priestess there; she guards the temple
Of the daughters of the Evening Star; she feeds
The dragon there, and guards the sacred branches,[24]   520
She sprinkles honey-dew, strews drowsy poppies,
And she knows charms to free the hearts of lovers
When she so wills it, or to trouble others;
She can reverse the wheeling of the planets,
Halt rivers in their flowing; she can summon
The ghosts of night-time; you will see earth shaking

[22] Pentheus was driven to insanity by Bacchus for opposing the worship of the god. Orestes was haunted by the Furies (Avengers) in revenge for his killing of his mother, Clytemnestra, who had murdered his father, Agamemnon.
[23] The waters believed to surround the world.
[24] The "daughters of the Evening Star" were the Hesperides, who, along with a dragon, watched over the golden apples in a garden at the western edge of the world.

Under her tread, and trees come down from mountains.
Dear sister mine, as heaven is my witness,
I hate to take these arts of magic on me!

530 Be secret, then; but in the inner courtyard,
Raise up a funeral-pyre, to hold the armor
Left hanging in the bower, by that hero,
That good devoted man, and all his raiment,
And add the bridal bed, my doom: the priestess
Said to do this, and it will be a pleasure
To see the end of all of it, every token
Of that unspeakable knave."

　　　　　　　　　And so, thought Anna,
Things are no worse than when Sychaeus perished.
She did not know the death these rites portended,

540 Had no suspicion, and carried out her orders.

　　The pyre is raised in the court; it towers high
With pine and holm-oak, it is hung with garlands
And funeral wreaths, and on the couch she places
Aeneas' sword, his garments, and his image,
Knowing the outcome. Round about are altars,
Where, with her hair unbound, the priestess calls
On thrice a hundred gods, Erebus, Chaos,
Hecate, queen of Hell, triple Diana.
Water is sprinkled, from Avernus fountain,[25]

550 Or said to be, and herbs are sought, by moonlight
Mown with bronze sickles, and the stem-ends running
With a black milk, and the caul[26] of a colt, new-born.
Dido, with holy meal and holy hands,
Stands at the altar, with one sandal loosened
And robes unfastened, calls the gods to witness,
Prays to the stars that know her doom, invoking,
Beyond them, any powers, if there are any,

[25] Erebus, Chaos, and Hecate (who was often represented as having three bodies and faces) were deities or powers associated with death and magic. Hecate was identified with Luna (the moon) in the sky, Diana on the earth, and Proserpina the queen of the Lower World. The entrance to the Lower World was near the lake of Avernus, in Italy.

[26] A membrane that sometimes envelops a newborn animal. Many commentators think, however, that Virgil is referring to the *hippomanes*, a growth on the head of newborn colts said to have power as a love-charm.

Who care for lovers in unequal bondage.
  Night: and tired creatures over all the world
Were seeking slumber; the woods and the wild waters   560
Were quiet, and the silent stars were wheeling
Their course half over; every field was still;
The beasts of the field, the brightly colored birds,
Dwellers in lake and pool, in thorn and thicket,
Slept through the tranquil night, their sorrows over,
Their troubles soothed. But no such blessèd darkness
Closes the eyes of Dido; no repose
Comes to her anxious heart. Her pangs redouble,
Her love swells up, surging, a great tide rising
Of wrath and doubt and passion. "What do I do?   570
What now? Go back to my Numidian suitors,
Be scorned by those I scorned? Pursue the Trojans?
Obey their orders? They were grateful to me,
Once, I remember. But who would let them take me?
Suppose I went. They hate me now; they were always
Deceivers: is Laomedon[27] forgotten,
Whose blood runs through their veins? What then? Attend
      them,
Alone, be their companion, the loud-mouthed sailors?
Or with my own armada follow after,
Wear out my sea-worn Tyrians once more   580
With vengeance and adventure? Better die.
Die; you deserve to; end the hurt with the sword.
It is your fault, Anna; you were sorry for me,
Won over by my tears; you put this load
Of evil on me. It was not permitted,
It seems, for me to live apart from wedlock,
A blameless life. An animal does better.
I vowed Sychaeus faith. I have been faithless."
So, through the night, she tossed in restless torment.
  Meanwhile Aeneas, on the lofty stern,   590
All things prepared, sure of his going, slumbers
As Mercury comes down once more to warn him,

[27] The notoriously dishonest former king of Troy. See III.3, III.248, and notes.

Familiar blond young god: "O son of Venus,
Is this a time for sleep? The wind blows fair,
And danger rises all around you. Dido,
Certain to die, however else uncertain,
Plots treachery, harbors evil. Seize the moment
While it can still be seized, and hurry, hurry!
The sea will swarm with ships, the fiery torches
600   Blaze, and the shore rankle with fire by morning.
Shove off, be gone! A shifty, fickle object
Is woman, always." He vanished into the night.
And, frightened by that sudden apparition,
Aeneas started from sleep, and urged his comrades:—
"Hurry, men, hurry; get to the sails and benches,
Get the ships under way. A god from heaven
Again has come to speed our flight, to sever
The mooring-ropes. O holy one, we follow,
Whoever you are, we are happy in obeying.
610   Be with us, be propitious; let the stars
Be right in heaven!" He drew his sword; the blade
Flashed, shining, at the hawser; and all the men
Were seized in the same restlessness and rushing.
They have left the shore, they have hidden the sea-water
With the hulls of the ships; the white foam flies, the oars
Dip down in dark-blue water.
                              And Aurora[28]
Came from Tithonus' saffron couch to freshen
The world with rising light, and from her watch-tower
The queen saw day grow whiter, and the fleet
620   Go moving over the sea, keep pace together
To the even spread of the sail; she knew the harbors
Were empty of sailors now; she struck her breast
Three times, four times; she tore her golden hair,
Crying, "God help me, will he go, this stranger,
Treating our kingdom as a joke? Bring arms,
Bring arms, and hurry! follow from all the city,
Haul the ships off the ways, some of you! Others,
Get fire as fast as you can, give out the weapons,
Pull oars! What am I saying? Or where am I?

[28] Goddess of the dawn; mate of Tithonus.

I must be going mad. Unhappy Dido, 630
Is it only now your wickedness strikes home?
The time it should have was when you gave him power.
Well, here it is, look at it now, the honor,
The faith of the hero who, they tell me, carries
With him his household gods, who bore on his shoulders
His aged father! Could I not have seized him,
Torn him to pieces, scattered him over the waves?
What was the matter? Could I not have murdered
His comrades, and Iulus, and served the son
For a dainty at the table of his father?[29] 640
But fight would have a doubtful fortune. It might have,
What then? I was going to die; whom did I fear?
I would have, should have, set his camp on fire,
Filled everything with flame, choked off the father,
The son, the accursèd race, and myself with them.
Great Sun, surveyor of all the works of earth,
Juno, to whom my sorrows are committed,
Hecate, whom the cross-roads of the cities
Wail to by night, avenging Furies, hear me,
Grant me divine protection, take my prayer.[30] 650
If he must come to harbor, then he must,
If Jove ordains it, however vile he is,
False, and unspeakable. If Jove ordains,
The goal is fixed. So be it. Take my prayer.
Let him be driven by arms and war, an exile,
Let him be taken from his son Iulus,
Let him beg for aid, let him see his people dying
Unworthy deaths, let him accept surrender
On unfair terms, let him never enjoy the kingdom,
The hoped-for light, let him fall and die, untimely, 660
Let him lie unburied on the sand. Oh, hear me,
Hear the last prayer, poured out with my last blood!
And you, O Tyrians, hate, and hate forever

---

[29] This atrocity is committed in a number of ancient Greek myths. It was, for example, an ancestral crime that formed part of a chain of evil leading to the murder of Agamemnon on his return from the Trojan war. The story is told in Aeschylus' great dramatic trilogy *The Oresteia*.

[30] Much of this curse is fulfilled in later parts of the poem (where, however, the death of Aeneas is not described).

The Trojan stock. Offer my dust this homage.
No love, no peace, between these nations, ever!
Rise from my bones, O great unknown avenger,[31]
Hunt them with fire and sword, the Dardan settlers,
Now, then, here, there, wherever strength is given.
Shore against shore, wave against wave, and war,
670   War after war, for all the generations."
      She spoke, and turned her purpose to accomplish
The quickest end to the life she hated. Briefly
She spoke to Barce, Sychaeus' nurse; her own
Was dust and ashes in her native country:—
"Dear nurse, bring me my sister, tell her to hurry,
Tell her to sprinkle her body with river water,
To bring the sacrificial beast and offerings,
And both of you cover your temples with holy fillets.
I have a vow to keep; I have made beginning
680   Of rites to Stygian[32] Jove, to end my sorrows,
To burn the litter of that Trojan leader."
Barce, with an old woman's fuss and bustle,
Went hurrying out of sight; but Dido, trembling,
Wild with her project, the blood-shot eyeballs rolling,
Pale at the death to come, and hectic[33] color
Burning the quivering cheeks, broke into the court,
Mounted the pyre in madness, drew the sword,
The Trojan gift, bestowed for no such purpose,
And she saw the Trojan garments, and the bed
690   She knew so well, and paused a little, weeping,
Weeping, and thinking, and flung herself down on it,
Uttering her last words:—
"Spoils that were sweet while gods and fate permitted,
Receive my spirit, set me free from suffering.
I have lived, I have run the course that fortune gave me,
And now my shade, a great one, will be going
Below the earth. I have built a noble city,

[31] Virgil is thinking of Hannibal (247–183 B.C.), the great Carthaginian general who led an invading army against Rome. Dido's curse anticipates the three Punic wars between Carthage and Rome in the third and second centuries B.C.

[32] Of the Styx, a river in the Lower World. Its ruler is Pluto or Hades (the "Stygian Jove").

[33] Feverish.

I have seen my walls, I have avenged a husband,
Punished a hostile brother. I have been
Happy, I might have been too happy, only   700
The Trojans made their landing." She broke off,
Pressed her face to the couch, cried:—"So, we shall die,
Die unavenged; but let us die. So, so,—
I am glad to meet the darkness. Let his eyes
Behold this fire across the sea, an omen
Of my death going with him."
                              As she spoke,
Her handmaids saw her, fallen on the sword,
The foam of blood on the blade, and blood on the hands.
A scream rings through the house; Rumor goes reeling,
Rioting, through the shaken town; the palace   710
Is loud with lamentation, women sobbing,
Wailing and howling, and the vaults of heaven
Echo the outcry, as if Tyre or Carthage
Had fallen to invaders, and the fury
Of fire came rolling over homes and temples.
Anna, half lifeless, heard in panic terror,
Came rushing through them all, beating her bosom,
Clawing her face:—"Was it for this, my sister?
To trick me so? The funeral pyre, the altars,
Prepared this for me? I have, indeed, a grievance,   720
Being forsaken; you would not let your sister
Companion you in death? You might have called me
To the same fate; we might have both been taken,
One sword, one hour. I was the one who built it,
This pyre, with my own hands; it was my voice
That called our fathers' gods, for what?—to fail you
When you were lying here. You have killed me, sister,
Not only yourself, you have killed us all, the people,
The town. Let me wash the wounds with water,
Let my lips catch what fluttering breath still lingers."   730
She climbed the lofty steps, and held her sister,
A dying woman, close; she used her robe
To try to stop the bleeding. And Dido tried
In vain to raise her heavy eyes, fell back,
And her wound made a gurgling hissing sound.
Three times she tried to lift herself; three times

Fell back; her rolling eyes went searching heaven
And the light hurt when she found it, and she moaned.
      At last all-powerful Juno, taking pity,
740   Sent Iris[34] from Olympus, in compassion
For the long racking agony, to free her
From the limbs' writhing and the struggle of spirit.
She had not earned this death, she had only sought it
Before her time, driven by sudden madness,
Therefore, the queen of Hades had not taken
The golden lock, consigning her to Orcus.
So Iris, dewy on saffron wings, descending,
Trailing a thousand colors through the brightness,
Comes down the sky, poises above her, saying,
750   "This lock I take as bidden, and from the body
Release the soul," and cuts the lock; and cold
Takes over, and the winds receive the spirit.[35]

[34] The rainbow-goddess; Juno's messenger.
[35] Orcus was another name for Pluto or Hades, king of the dead. His
queen, Proserpina, would normally take a lock of Dido's hair and thus
consecrate her to the powers of the Lower World, but Dido's suicide
prevents the goddess from doing so; Iris must perform the rite instead
of her.

BOOK VI

The
Lower World

OURNING for Palinurus, he drives the fleet
To Cumae's[1] coast-line; the prows are turned, the anchors
Let down, the beach is covered by the vessels.
Young in their eagerness for the land in the west,
They flash ashore; some seek the seeds of flame
Hidden in veins of flint, and others spoil
The woods of tinder, and show where water runs.
Aeneas, in devotion, seeks the heights
Where stands Apollo's temple, and the cave
Where the dread Sibyl dwells, Apollo's priestess,   10
With the great mind and heart, inspired revealer
Of things to come. They enter Diana's grove,
Pass underneath the roof of gold.[2]

                        The story
Has it that Daedalus fled from Minos' kingdom,
Trusting himself to wings he made, and travelled
A course unknown to man, to the cold north,

[1] A city, near the modern Naples, where Aeneas is to visit the Sibyl named Deiphobe, mythical prophet and priestess of Apollo, in preparation for his visit to the Lower World.

[2] The temple and its environs were sacred to both Apollo and Diana, his full sister. In her alter ego as Hecate, she was goddess of the Lower World and was sometimes associated with witchcraft.

Descending on this very summit; here,
Earth-bound again, he built a mighty temple,
Paying Apollo homage, the dedication
20   Of the oarage of his wings. On the temple doors
He carved, in bronze, Androgeos' death, and the payment
Enforced on Cecrops' children, seven sons
For sacrifice each year: there stands the urn,
The lots are drawn—facing this, over the sea,
Rises the land of Crete: the scene portrays
Pasiphae in cruel love, the bull
She took to her by cunning, and their offspring,
The mongrel Minotaur, half man, half monster,
The proof of lust unspeakable; and the toil
30   Of the house is shown, the labyrinthine maze
Which no one could have solved, but Daedalus
Pitied a princess' love, loosened the tangle,
Gave her a skein to guide her way. His boy,
Icarus, might have been here, in the picture,
And almost was—his father had made the effort
Once, and once more, and dropped his hands; he could
    not
Master his grief that much.[3] The story held them;
They would have studied it longer, but Achates[4]
Came from his mission; with him came the priestess,

---

[3] Minos was king of Crete. His wife Pasiphae, in a bovine disguise fabricated by the craftsman Daedalus, made love with a bull and then gave
birth to the Minotaur, half bull and half human. (Compare V.550–53.)
Minos then forced Daedalus to construct a labyrinth to contain the Minotaur. After the Athenians killed Androgeos, the son of Minos, the king
in revenge forced them (the "children" of Cecrops, an early king of Athens)
to sacrifice to the Minotaur, each year, the lives of seven young men and
seven young women, chosen by lots drawn from an urn. The Athenian
hero Theseus went to Crete and succeeded in killing the monster that
was devouring his compatriots. In this enterprise he was helped by Daedalus and the love-smitten Ariadne, Minos' daughter, who gave Theseus a
thread to guide him back out of the labyrinth. Imprisoned for his part
in this feat, Daedalus with his son Icarus escaped from Crete on wings
the father had constructed; Icarus, however, died when he flew too close
to the sun, which melted the wax fastenings of his wings. Daedalus, after
reaching Italy, built the temple and executed the carvings that Aeneas is
examining, though Virgil represents the artist as having been incapable,
in his grief, of representing his son's tragic story.
[4] Aeneas' most faithful friend.

Deiphobe, daughter of Glaucus,[5] who tends the temple   40
For Phoebus and Diana; she warned Aeneas:
"It is no such sights the time demands; far better
To offer sacrifice, seven chosen bullocks,
Seven chosen ewes, a herd without corruption."
They were prompt in their obedience, and the priestess
Summoned the Trojans to the lofty temple.
    The rock's vast side is hollowed into a cavern,
With a hundred mouths, a hundred open portals,
Whence voices rush, the answers of the Sibyl.
They had reached the threshold, and the virgin cried: 50
"It is time to seek the fates; the god is here,
The god is here, behold him." And as she spoke
Before the entrance, her countenance and color
Changed, and her hair tossed loose, and her heart was
        heaving,
Her bosom swollen with frenzy; she seemed taller,
Her voice not human at all, as the god's presence
Drew nearer, and took hold on her. "Aeneas,"
She cried, "Aeneas, are you praying?
Are you being swift in prayer? Until you are,
The house of the gods will not be moved, nor open   60
Its mighty portals." More than her speech, her silence
Made the Trojans cold with terror, and Aeneas
Prayed from the depth of his heart: "Phoebus Apollo,
Compassionate ever, slayer of Achilles
Through aim of Paris' arrow,[6] helper and guide
Over the seas, over the lands, the deserts,
The shoals and quicksands, now at last we have come
To Italy, we hold the lands which fled us:
Grant that thus far, no farther, a Trojan fortune
Attend our wandering. And spare us now,   70
All of you, gods and goddesses, who hated
Troy in the past, and Trojan glory. I beg you,
Most holy prophetess, in whose foreknowing
The future stands revealed, grant that the Trojans—

[5] Glaucus was a sea-god gifted with prophetic powers.
[6] Apollo, patron of archers, helped Paris to slay Achilles by shooting
him in the heel, the only part of his body not supernaturally protected.

I ask with fate's permission—rest in Latium
Their wandering storm-tossed gods. I will build a temple,
In honor of Apollo and Diana,
Out of eternal marble, and ordain
Festivals in their honor, and for the Sibyl
80   A great shrine in our kingdom, and I will place there
The lots and mystic oracles for my people
With chosen priests to tend them.[7] Only, priestess,
This once, I pray you, chant the sacred verses
With your own lips; do not trust them to the leaves,
The mockery of the rushing wind's disorder."[8]
    But the priestess, not yet subject to Apollo,
Went reeling through the cavern, wild, and storming
To throw the god, who presses, like a rider,
With bit and bridle and weight, tames her wild spirit,
90   Shapes her to his control. The doors fly open,
The hundred doors, of their own will, fly open,
And through the air the answer comes:—"O Trojans,
At last the dangers of the sea are over;
That course is run, but graver ones are waiting
On land. The sons of Dardanus will reach
The kingdom of Lavinia—be easy
On that account—the sons of Dardanus, also,
Will wish they had not come there. War, I see,
Terrible war, and the river Tiber foaming
100   With streams of blood. There will be another Xanthus,
Another Simois, and Greek encampment,
Even another Achilles, born in Latium,
Himself a goddess' son. And Juno further
Will always be there: you will beg for mercy,
Be poor, turn everywhere for help. A woman
Will be the cause once more of so much evil,
A foreign bride, receptive to the Trojans,
A foreign marriage.[9] Do not yield to evil,

[7] The Sibylline books, venerated in Virgil's day, were supposed to contain prophetic oracles important to the guidance of Rome.
[8] See Helenus' instructions to Aeneas in III.455–63,466–67.
[9] In short, it will be the Trojan war all over again. Xanthus and Simois were rivers at Troy. The second Achilles will be the Italian hero Turnus
(Continued)

Attack, attack, more boldly even than fortune
Seems to permit. An offering of safety,—   110
Incredible!—will come from a Greek city."[10]
   So, through the amplifiers of her cavern,
The hollow vaults, the Sibyl cast her warnings,
Riddles confused with truth; and Apollo rode her,
Reining her rage, and shaking her, and spurring
The fierceness of her heart. The frenzy dwindled,
A little, and her lips were still. Aeneas
Began:—"For me, no form of trouble, maiden,
Is new, or unexpected; all of this
I have known long since, lived in imagination.   120
One thing I ask: this is the gate of the kingdom,
So it is said, where Pluto reigns, the gloomy
Marsh where the water of Acheron[11] runs over.
Teach me the way from here, open the portals
That I may go to my belovèd father,
Stand in his presence, talk with him. I brought him,
Once, on these shoulders, through a thousand weapons
And following fire, and foemen. He shared with me
The road, the sea, the menaces of heaven,
Things that an old man should not bear; he bore them,   130
Tired as he was. And he it was who told me
To come to you in humbleness. I beg you
Pity the son, the father. You have power,
Great priestess, over all; it is not for nothing
Hecate gave you this dominion over
Avernus' groves. If Orpheus could summon
Eurydice from the shadows with his music,
If Pollux could save his brother, coming, going,
Along this path,—why should I mention Theseus,

(son of the nymph Venilia as Achilles had been the son of the nymph
Thetis), who will become Aeneas' rival for the princess Lavinia. Thus
woman will again be at the root of the troubles, as with Helen and (it
may be implied) Dido.
   [10] Pallanteum, a city on the site of the future Rome; it had been founded
by Evander, king of Arcadia (in Greece), who had emigrated to Italy. See
Book VIII.
   [11] One of the rivers of the Lower World.

140   Why mention Hercules?[12] I, too, descended
       · From the line of Jupiter." He clasped the altar,
       Making his prayer, and she made answer to him:
       "Son of Anchises, born of godly lineage,
       By night, by day, the portals of dark Dis
       Stand open: it is easy, the descending
       Down to Avernus.[13] But to climb again,
       To trace the footsteps back to the air above,
       There lies the task, the toil. A few, beloved
       By Jupiter, descended from the gods,
150   A few, in whom exalting virtue burned,
       Have been permitted. Around the central woods
       The black Cocytus glides, a sullen river;
       But if such love is in your heart, such longing
       For double crossing of the Stygian lake,[14]
       For double sight of Tartarus,[15] learn first
       What must be done. In a dark tree there hides
       A bough, all golden, leaf and pliant stem,
       Sacred to Proserpine. This all the grove
       Protects, and shadows cover it with darkness.
160   Until this bough, this bloom of light, is found,
       No one receives his passport to the darkness
       Whose queen requires this tribute. In succession,
       After the bough is plucked, another grows,

[12] The legendary musician Orpheus was allowed to lead his dead wife Eurydice out of the Lower World (though he lost her after all, being unable to obey the command not to look back as she followed him). Pollux, an immortal who was half-brother to the mortal Castor, wished to die with him but could not; Jupiter, however, agreed to let them exchange places daily, each living alternately in the heavens and in the world of the dead. Theseus and Pirithous had tried to abduct Proserpine, queen of the dead. (She is also called Proserpina and Persephone.) The most difficult of Hercules' famous "labors" was the theft of Cerberus, the three-headed dog guarding the Lower World. (See lines 415–21.)

[13] Dis, like Hades (Greek) and Orcus, is another name for the god Pluto, and also for his realm, the Lower World. Avernus in this passage also means the Lower World, named for a sulfurous volcanic lake near Cumae. See also line 136.

[14] The four rivers of the Lower World (besides Lethe, the river of forgetfulness) were Styx, Acheron, Cocytus, and Phlegethon.

[15] The place in the Lower World where evil was punished. Aeneas actually sees only the walls of Tartarus, but it is described, in lines 573–660. *Tartarus* can also mean the Lower World in general.

Gold-green with the same metal. Raise the eyes,
Look up, reach up the hand, and it will follow
With ease, if fate is calling; otherwise,
No power, no steel, can loose it. Furthermore,
(Alas, you do not know this!), one of your men
Lies on the shore, unburied, a pollution
To all the fleet, while you have come for counsel   170
Here to our threshold.[16] Bury him with honor;
Black cattle slain in expiation for him
Must fall before you see the Stygian kingdoms,
The groves denied to living men."
                                        Aeneas,
With sadness in his eyes, and downcast heart,
Turned from the cave, and at his side Achates
Accompanied his anxious meditations.
They talked together: who could be the comrade
Named by the priestess, lying there unburied?
And they found him on dry sand; it was Misenus,   180
Aeolus' son, none better with the trumpet
To make men burn for warfare. He had been
Great Hector's man-at-arms; he was good in battle
With spear as well as horn, and after Hector
Had fallen to Achilles, he had followed
Aeneas, entering no meaner service.
Some foolishness came over him; he made
The ocean echo to the blare of his trumpet
That day, and challenged the sea-gods to a contest
In martial music, and Triton, jealous, caught him,   190
However unbelievable the story,
And held him down between the rocks, and drowned
       him
Under the foaming waves.[17] His comrades mourned,
Aeneas most of all, and in their sorrow
They carry out, in haste, the Sibyl's orders,

[16] An unburied corpse was offensive for religious reasons. See the meeting with Palinurus later in Book VI.

[17] Triton was a sea-deity, son of Neptune, and was often portrayed as blowing a conch-shell trumpet. The classical gods did not like to be challenged at their own specialties. Appropriately, the father of the trumpeter Misenus (line 181) is the namesake of the god of the winds, Aeolus.

Construct the funeral altar, high as heaven,
They go to an old wood, and the pine-trees fall
Where wild beasts have their dens, and holm-oak rings
To the stroke of the axe, and oak and ash are riven
200   By the splitting wedge, and rowan-trees come rolling
Down the steep mountain-side. Aeneas helps them,
And cheers them on; studies the endless forest,
Takes thought, and prays: "If only we might see it,
That golden bough, here in the depth of the forest,
Bright on some tree. She told the truth, our priestess,
Too much, too bitter truth, about Misenus."
No sooner had he spoken than twin doves
Came flying down before him, and alighted
On the green ground. He knew his mother's birds,
210   And made his prayer, rejoicing,—"Oh, be leaders,
Wherever the way, and guide me to the grove
Where the rich bough makes rich the shaded ground.
Help me, O goddess-mother!" And he paused,
Watching what sign they gave, what course they set.
The birds flew on a little, just ahead
Of the pursuing vision; when they came
To the jaws of dank Avernus, evil-smelling,
They rose aloft, then swooped down the bright air,
Perched on the double tree, where the off-color
220   Of gold was gleaming golden through the branches.
As mistletoe, in the cold winter, blossoms
With its strange foliage on an alien tree,
The yellow berry gilding the smooth branches,[18]
Such was the vision of the gold in leaf
On the dark holm-oak, so the foil was rustling,
Rattling, almost, the bract[19] in the soft wind
Stirring like metal. Aeneas broke it off
With eager grasp, and bore it to the Sibyl.
        Meanwhile, along the shore, the Trojans mourned,
230   Paying Misenus' dust the final honors.
A mighty pyre was raised, of pine and oak,

[18] Mistletoe is a parasite with hardly visible roots, so that in winter it
contrasts in appearance with the tree it grows on and seems to live a
strange, self-sustaining life.
[19] A botanical term translating *brattea*, a thin metallic leaf.

The sides hung with dark leaves, and somber cypress
Along the front, and gleaming arms above.
Some made the water hot, and some made ready
Bronze caldrons, shimmering over fire, and others
Lave and anoint the body, and with weeping
Lay on the bier his limbs, and place above them
Familiar garments, crimson color; and some
Take up the heavy burden, a sad office,
And, as their fathers did, they kept their eyes   240
Averted, as they brought the torches nearer.
They burn gifts with him, bowls of oil, and viands,
And frankincense; and when the flame is quiet
And the ashes settle to earth, they wash the embers
With wine, and slake the thirsty dust. The bones
Are placed in a bronze urn by Corynaeus,
Who, with pure water, thrice around his comrades
Made lustral cleansing, shaking gentle dew
From the fruitful branch of olive; and they said
Hail and farewell! And over him Aeneas   250
Erects a mighty tomb, with the hero's arms,
His oar and trumpet, where the mountain rises
Memorial for ever, and named Misenus.[20]
    These rites performed, he hastened to the Sibyl.
There was a cavern, yawning wide and deep,
Jagged, below the darkness of the trees,
Beside the darkness of the lake. No bird
Could fly above it safely, with the vapor
Pouring from the black gulf (the Greeks have named it
Avernus, or A-Ornos, meaning *birdless*[21]),   260
And here the priestess for the slaughter set
Four bullocks, black ones, poured the holy wine
Between the horns, and plucked the topmost bristles
For the first offering to the sacred fire,
Calling on Hecate, a power in heaven,
A power in hell. Knives to the throat were driven,
The warm blood caught in bowls. Aeneas offered

[20] The promontory at the southwestern end of the Bay of Naples is
still called Cape Miseno.
[21] Most authoritative manuscripts of *The Aeneid* omit this parenthetical
statement.

A lamb, black-fleeced, to Night and her great sister,
A sterile heifer for the queen;[22] for Dis
270 An altar in the night, and on the flames
The weight of heavy bulls, the fat oil pouring
Over the burning entrails. And at dawn,
Under their feet, earth seemed to shake and rumble,
The ridges move, and bitches bay in darkness,
As the presence neared. The Sibyl cried a warning,
"Keep off, keep off, whatever is unholy,
Depart from here![23] Courage, Aeneas; enter
The path, unsheathe the sword. The time is ready
For the brave heart." She strode out boldly, leading
280 Into the open cavern, and he followed.
  Gods of the world of spirit, silent shadows,
Chaos and Phlegethon, areas of silence,
Wide realms of dark, may it be right and proper
To tell what I have heard, this revelation
Of matters buried deep in earth and darkness!
  Vague forms in lonely darkness, they were going
Through void and shadow, through the empty realm
Like people in a forest, when the moonlight
Shifts with a baleful glimmer, and shadow covers
290 The sky, and all the colors turn to blackness.
At the first threshold, on the jaws of Orcus,
Grief and avenging Cares have set their couches,
And pale Diseases dwell, and sad Old Age,
Fear, evil-counselling Hunger, wretched Need,
Forms terrible to see, and Death, and Toil,
And Death's own brother, Sleep, and evil Joys,
Fantasies of the mind, and deadly War,
The Furies' iron chambers,[24] Discord, raving,
Her snaky hair entwined in bloody bands.
300 An elm-tree loomed there, shadowy and huge,

[22] The sister of Night (Nox) was Earth (Tellus). The "queen" is Proserpine.
[23] At Roman religious ceremonies, the ritual dismissal of the uninitiated; here applied to Aeneas' companions, who must now leave him. The approaching "presence" (line 275) is that of the goddess Hecate, accompanied by her hounds.
[24] The Furies were primitive female agents of revenge and punishment for crime.

The aged boughs outspread, beneath whose leaves,
Men say, the false dreams cling, thousands on thousands.
And there are monsters in the dooryard, Centaurs,
Scyllas, of double shape, the beast of Lerna,
Hissing most horribly, Briareus,
The hundred-handed giant, a Chimaera
Whose armament is fire, Harpies, and Gorgons,
A triple-bodied giant.[25] In sudden panic
Aeneas drew his sword, the edge held forward,
Ready to rush and flail, however blindly,   310
Save that his wise companion warned him, saying
They had no substance, they were only phantoms
Flitting about, illusions without body.
    From here, the road turns off to Acheron,
River of Hell; here, thick with muddy whirling,
Cocytus boils with sand. Charon is here,
The guardian of these mingling waters, Charon,
Uncouth and filthy, on whose chin the hair
Is a tangled mat, whose eyes protrude, are burning,
Whose dirty cloak is knotted at the shoulder.   320
He poles a boat, tends to the sail, unaided,
Ferrying bodies in his rust-hued vessel.
Old, but a god's senility is awful
In its raw greenness. To the bank come thronging
Mothers and men, bodies of great-souled heroes,
Their life-time over, boys, unwedded maidens,
Young men whose fathers saw their pyres burning,
Thick as the forest leaves that fall in autumn
With early frost, thick as the birds to landfall
From over the seas, when the chill of the year compels them   330
To sunlight. There they stand, a host, imploring

---

[25] These lines are a catalogue of many of the most famous or fearsome
monsters of ancient fable. Centaurs were half man, half horse; Scylla was
a six-headed monster (described in III.432-44) who devoured sailors in
the straits of Messina; the beast of Lerna was the Hydra, a gigantic many-
headed serpent; Briareus, as the text states, was a giant with a hundred
hands; the fire-breathing Chimaera was a combination of lion, goat, and
serpent; the Harpies were foul bird-women (described in III.213-57); the
Gorgons (Medusa and her two sisters) were snake-haired female monsters
who literally petrified men who gazed on them; the triple-bodied giant
was named Geryon.

To be taken over first. Their hands, in longing,
Reach out for the farther shore. But the gloomy boatman
Makes choice among them, taking some, and keeping
Others far back from the stream's edge. Aeneas,
Wondering, asks the Sibyl, "Why the crowding?
What are the spirits seeking? What distinction
Brings some across the livid stream, while others
Stay on the farther bank?" She answers, briefly:
340   "Son of Anchises, this is the awful river,
The Styx, by which the gods take oath; the boatman,
Charon; those he takes with him are the buried,
Those he rejects, whose luck is out, the graveless.
It is not permitted him to take them over
The dreadful banks and hoarse-resounding waters
Till earth is cast upon their bones. They haunt
These shores a hundred restless years of waiting
Before they end postponement of the crossing."
Aeneas paused, in thoughtful mood, with pity
350   Over their lot's unevenness; and saw there,
Wanting the honor given the dead, and grieving,
Leucaspis, and Orontes, the Lycian captain,
Who had sailed from Troy across the stormy waters,
And drowned off Africa, with crew and vessel,[26]
And there was Palinurus, once his pilot,
Who, not so long ago, had been swept over,
Watching the stars on the journey north from Carthage.[27]
The murk was thick; Aeneas hardly knew him,
Sorrowful in that darkness, but made question:
360   "What god, O Palinurus, took you from us?
Who drowned you in the deep? Tell me. Apollo
Never before was false, and yet he told me
You would be safe across the seas, and come
Unharmed to Italy; what kind of promise
Was this, to fool me with?" But Palinurus
Gave him assurance:—"It was no god who drowned me,[28]

[26] For Orontes, see I.127–30. Leucaspis is not mentioned there, however.
[27] See V.796–838.
[28] Palinurus is ignorant of the role of the god of Sleep in casting him overboard. Apollo's promise is not mentioned elsewhere in the poem.

No falsehood on Apollo's part, my captain,
But as I clung to the tiller, holding fast
To keep the course, as I should do, I felt it
Wrenched from the ship, and I fell with it, headlong.   370
By those rough seas I swear, I had less fear
On my account than for the ship, with rudder
And helmsman overboard, to drift at the mercy
Of rising seas. Three nights I rode the waters,
Three nights of storm, and from the crest of a wave,
On the fourth morning, sighted Italy,
I was swimming to land, I had almost reached it, heavy
In soaking garments; my cramped fingers struggled
To grasp the top of the rock, when barbarous people,
Ignorant men, mistaking me for booty,[29]   380
Struck me with swords; waves hold me now, or winds
Roll me along the shore. By the light of heaven,
The lovely air, I beg you, by your father,
Your hope of young Iulus, bring me rescue
Out of these evils, my unconquered leader!
Cast over my body earth—you have the power—
Return to Velia's[30] harbor,—or there may be
Some other way—your mother is a goddess,
Else how would you be crossing this great river,
This Stygian swamp?—help a poor fellow, take me   390
Over the water with you, give a dead man
At least a place to rest in." But the Sibyl
Broke in upon him sternly:—"Palinurus,
Whence comes this mad desire? No man, unburied,
May see the Stygian waters, or Cocytus,
The Furies' dreadful river; no man may come
Unbidden to this bank. Give up the hope
That fate is changed by praying, but hear this,
A little comfort in your harsh misfortune:
Those neighboring people will make expiation,   400
Driven by signs from heaven, through their cities
And through their countryside; they will build a tomb,

---

[29] A man carrying valuable goods.
[30] A town near Cumae.

Thereto bring offerings yearly, and the place
Shall take its name from you, Cape Palinurus."[31]
So he was comforted a little, finding
Some happiness in the promise.

                      And they went on,
Nearing the river, and from the stream the boatman
Beheld them cross the silent forest, nearer,
Turning their footsteps toward the bank. He challenged:—
410   "Whoever you are, O man in armor, coming
In this direction, halt where you are, and tell me
The reason why you come. This is the region
Of shadows, and of Sleep and drowsy Night;
I am not allowed to carry living bodies
In the Stygian boat; and I must say I was sorry
I ever accepted Hercules and Theseus
And Pirithous, and rowed them over the lake,
Though they were sons of gods and great in courage.
One of them dared to drag the guard of Hell,
420   Enchained, from Pluto's throne, shaking in terror,
The others to snatch our queen from Pluto's chamber."[32]
The Sibyl answered briefly: "No such cunning
Is plotted here; our weapons bring no danger.
Be undisturbed: the hell-hound in his cavern
May bark forever, to keep the bloodless shadows
Frightened away from trespass; Proserpine,
Untouched, in pureness guard her uncle's threshold.[33]
Trojan Aeneas, a man renowned for goodness,
Renowned for nerve in battle, is descending
430   To the lowest shades; he comes to find his father.
If such devotion has no meaning to you,
Look on this branch at least, and recognize it!"
And with the word she drew from under her mantle
The golden bough; his swollen wrath subsided.
No more was said; he saw the bough, and marvelled
At the holy gift, so long unseen; came sculling

---

[31] As with Misenus and modern Cape Miseno (line 253), Palinurus' name
is still given today to a promontory on the Italian coast (Point Palinuro).
[32] See lines 139–41 and note.
[33] Proserpine's husband, Pluto, was also her uncle, since she was the
daughter of Jupiter, Pluto's brother.

The dark-blue boat to the shore, and drove the spirits,
Lining the thwarts, ashore, and cleared the gangway,
And took Aeneas aboard; as that big man
Stepped in, the leaky skiff groaned under the weight,   440
And the strained seams let in the muddy water,
But they made the crossing safely, seer and soldier,
To the far margin, colorless and shapeless,
Grey sedge and dark-brown ooze. They heard the baying
Of Cerberus, that great hound, in his cavern crouching,
Making the shore resound, as all three throats
Belled horribly; and serpents rose and bristled
Along the triple neck. The priestess threw him
A sop with honey and drugged meal; he opened
The ravenous throat, gulped, and subsided, filling   450
The den with his huge bulk. Aeneas, crossing,
Passed on beyond the bank of the dread river
Whence none return.
                        A wailing of thin voices
Came to their ears, the souls of infants crying,
Those whom the day of darkness took from the breast
Before their share of living. And there were many
Whom some false sentence brought to death. Here Minos
Judges them once again;[34] a silent jury
Reviews the evidence. And there are others,
Guilty of nothing, but who hated living,   460
The suicides. How gladly, now, they would suffer
Poverty, hardship, in the world of light!
But this is not permitted; they are bound
Nine times around by the black unlovely river;
Styx holds them fast.
                        They came to the Fields of Mourning,
So-called, where those whom cruel love had wasted
Hid in secluded pathways, under myrtle,
And even in death were anxious. Procris, Phaedra,
Eriphyle, displaying wounds her son
Had given her, Caeneus, Laodamia,   470
Caeneus, a young man once, and now again

[34] This Minos, who had given laws to and ruled Crete, seems to be
identical with the one mentioned in line 14 (see note to line 37), but
possibly his grandfather is intended.

A young man, after having been a woman.[35]
And here, new come from her own wound, was Dido,
Wandering in the wood. The Trojan hero,
Standing near by, saw her, or thought he saw her,
Dim in the shadows, like the slender crescent
Of moon when cloud drifts over. Weeping, he greets her:—
"Unhappy Dido, so they told me truly
That your own hand had brought you death. Was I—
480   Alas!—the cause? I swear by all the stars,
By the world above, by everything held sacred
Here under the earth, unwillingly, O queen,
I left your kingdom. But the gods' commands,
Driving me now through these forsaken places,
This utter night, compelled me on. I could not
Believe my loss would cause so great a sorrow.
Linger a moment, do not leave me; whither,
Whom, are you fleeing? I am permitted only
This last word with you."
                                    But the queen, unmoving
490   As flint or marble, turned away, her eyes
Fixed on the ground: the tears were vain, the words,
Meant to be soothing, foolish; she turned away,
His enemy forever, to the shadows
Where Sychaeus, her former husband, took her
With love for love, and sorrow for her sorrow.
And still Aeneas wept for her, being troubled
By the injustice of her doom; his pity
Followed her going.
                              They went on. They came
To the farthest fields, whose tenants are the warriors,
500   Illustrious throng. Here Tydeus came to meet him,

---

[35] Some of these figures (all women) were evil, some admirable. Procris'
jealousy of her husband led to his killing her by accident; Phaedra nursed
a guilty, unrequited love for her stepson; Eriphyle, having been bribed,
sent her husband to his death in war and was then, in return, killed by
her son; Laodamia, on the other hand, was the faithful wife of the first
man to die at Troy and gave up her life to be with him after his death.
The sex-changed Caeneus had been seduced, as a maiden named Caenis,
by Neptune. The translator omits two other women named here by Virgil:
Pasiphae (for her unnatural love, see line 26 and note) and Evadne, a
wife who immolated herself on her husband's funeral pyre.

Parthenopaeus came, and pale Adrastus,[36]
A fighter's ghost, and many, many others,
Mourned in the world above, and doomed in battle,
Leaders of Troy, in long array; Aeneas
Sighed as he saw them: Medon; Polyboetes,
The priest of Ceres; Glaucus; and Idaeus
Still keeping arms and chariot;[37] three brothers,
Antenor's sons; Thersilochus; a host
To right and left of him, and when they see him,
One sight is not enough; they crowd around him,   510
Linger, and ask the reasons for his coming.
But Agamemnon's men, the Greek battalions,
Seeing him there, and his arms in shadow gleaming,
Tremble in panic, turn to flee for refuge,
As once they used to, toward their ships, but where
Are the ships now? They try to shout, in terror;
But only a thin and piping treble issues
To mock their mouths, wide-open.
                                    One he knew
Was here, Deiphobus, a son of Priam,
With his whole body mangled, and his features   520
Cruelly slashed, and both hands cut, and ears
Torn from his temples, and his nostrils slit
By shameful wounds. Aeneas hardly knew him,
Shivering there, and doing his best to hide
His marks of punishment; unhailed, he hailed him:—
"Deiphobus, great warrior, son of Teucer,
Whose cruel punishment was this? Whose license
Abused you so? I heard, it seems, a story
Of that last night, how you had fallen, weary
With killing Greeks at last; I built a tomb,   530
Although no body lay there, in your honor,
Three times I cried, aloud, over your spirit,
Where now your name and arms keep guard. I could
     not,
Leaving my country, find my friend, to give him
Proper interment in the earth he came from."

---

[36] Three of the seven heroes who led a famous siege of the city of Thebes.
[37] Idaeus had been charioteer to Priam, king of Troy.

And Priam's son replied:—"Nothing, dear comrade,
Was left undone; the dead man's shade was given
All ceremony due. It was my own fortune
And a Spartan woman's[38] deadliness that sunk me
540   Under these evils; she it was who left me
These souvenirs. You know how falsely happy
We were on that last night; I need not tell you.
When that dread horse came leaping over our walls,
Pregnant with soldiery, she led the dancing,
A solemn rite, she called it, with Trojan women
Screaming their bacchanals;[39] she raised the torches
High on the citadel; she called the Greeks.
Then—I was worn with trouble, drugged in slumber,
Resting in our ill-omened bridal chamber,
550   With sleep as deep and sweet as death upon me—
Then she, that paragon of helpmates, deftly
Moved all the weapons from the house; my sword,
Even, she stole from underneath my pillow,
Opened the door, and called in Menelaus,
Hoping, no doubt, to please her loving husband,
To win forgetfulness of her old sinning.
It is quickly told: they broke into the chamber,
The two of them, and with them, as accomplice,
Ulysses came, the crime-contriving bastard.[40]
560   O gods, pay back the Greeks; grant the petition
If goodness asks for vengeance! But you, Aeneas,
A living man—what chance has brought you here?
Vagrant of ocean, god-inspired,—which are you?
What chance has worn you down, to come, in sadness,
To these confusing sunless dwelling-places?"

    While they were talking, Aurora's rosy car
Had halfway crossed the heaven;[41] all their time
Might have been spent in converse, but the Sibyl

---

[38] Helen, who had left her husband Menelaus and run off to Troy with
Paris; after his death she had become the wife of Deiphobus.

[39] Wild revels in honor of Bacchus, god of wine. Helen carried one of
the torches customary in such revels but used it treacherously, as a signal
to the Greeks.

[40] The insult is meant literally by Deiphobus, suggesting actual infidelity
by Ulysses' mother.

[41] Aurora was goddess of the dawn. It is now past noon on earth.

Hurried them forward:—"Night comes on, Aeneas;
We waste the hours with tears. We are at the cross-road,   570
Now; here we turn to the right, where the pathway leads
On to Elysium, under Pluto's ramparts.
Leftward is Tartarus, and retribution,
The terminal of the wicked, and their dungeon."
Deiphobus left them, saying, "O great priestess,
Do not be angry with me; I am going;
I shall not fail the roll-call of the shadows.
Pride of our race, go on; may better fortune
Attend you!" and, upon the word, he vanished.

As he looked back, Aeneas saw, to his left,   580
Wide walls beneath a cliff, a triple rampart,
A river running fire, Phlegethon's torrent,
Rocks roaring in its course, a gate, tremendous,
Pillars of adamant,[42] a tower of iron,
Too strong for men, too strong for even gods
To batter down in warfare, and behind them
A Fury, sentinel in bloody garments,
Always on watch, by day, by night. He heard
Sobbing and groaning there, the crack of the lash,
The clank of iron, the sound of dragging shackles.   590
The noise was terrible; Aeneas halted,
Asking, "What forms of crime are these, O maiden?
What harrying punishment, what horrible outcry?"
She answered:—"O great leader of the Trojans,
I have never crossed that threshold of the wicked;
No pure soul is permitted entrance thither,
But Hecate, by whose order I was given
Charge of Avernus' groves, my guide, my teacher,
Told me how gods exact the toll of vengeance.
The monarch here, merciless Rhadamanthus,[43]   600
Punishes guilt, and hears confession; he forces
Acknowledgment of crime; no man in the world,
No matter how cleverly he hides his evil,
No matter how much he smiles at his own slyness,
Can fend atonement off; the hour of death

[42] An extremely hard metal.
[43] Brother of Minos and, like him, a judge in the Lower World.

Begins his sentence. Tisiphone, the Fury,
Leaps at the guilty with her scourge; her serpents
Are whips of menace as she calls her sisters.
Imagine the gates, on jarring hinge, rasp open,
610 You would see her in the doorway, a shape, a sentry,
Savage, implacable. Beyond, still fiercer,
The monstrous Hydra dwells; her fifty throats
Are black, and open wide, and Tartarus
Is black, and open wide, and it goes down
To darkness, sheer deep down, and twice the distance
That earth is from Olympus.[44] At the bottom
The Titans crawl, Earth's oldest breed, hurled under
By thunderbolts; here lie the giant twins,
Aloeus' sons, who laid their hands on heaven
620 And tried to pull down Jove; Salmoneus here
Atones for high presumption,—it was he
Who aped Jove's noise and fire, wheeling his horses
Triumphant through his city in Elis, cheering
And shaking the torch, and claiming divine homage,
The arrogant fool, to think his brass was lightning,
His horny-footed horses beat out thunder!
Jove showed him what real thunder was, what lightning
Spoke from immortal cloud, what whirlwind fury
Came sweeping from the heaven to overtake him.
630 Here Tityos, Earth's giant son, lies sprawling
Over nine acres, with a monstrous vulture
Gnawing, with crooked beak, vitals and liver
That grow as they are eaten; eternal anguish,
Eternal feast.[45] Over another hangs
A rock, about to fall; and there are tables
Set for a banquet, gold with royal splendor,
But if a hand goes out to touch the viands,

[44] The dwelling-place of the gods.
[45] The Titans, giant offspring of Heaven and Earth, fought alongside
Saturn in his unsuccessful struggle against his son Jupiter. The sons of
Aloeus, Otus and Ephialtes, were giants who tried to assault the gods
by piling the mountains Ossa and Pelion on top of Olympus. Salmoneus
imitated Jove's thunder, in a city sacred to Jove, by driving a brass chariot
over a brass bridge. Tityos had sexually assaulted the goddess Latona,
who was avenged by her children Apollo and Diana.

The Fury drives it back with fire and yelling.
Why name them all, Pirithous, the Lapiths,
Ixion?[46] The roll of crime would take forever.   640
Whoever, in his lifetime, hated his brother,
Or struck his father down; whoever cheated
A client, or was miserly—how many
Of these there seem to be!—whoever went
To treasonable war, or broke a promise
Made to his lord, whoever perished, slain
Over adultery, all these, walled in,
Wait here their punishment. Seek not to know
Too much about their doom. The stone is rolled,
The wheel keeps turning; Theseus forever   650
Sits in dejection; Phlegyas, accursed,
Cries through the halls forever: *Being warned,*
Learn justice; reverence the gods![47] The man
Who sold his country is here in hell; the man
Who altered laws for money; and a father
Who knew his daughter's bed. All of them dared,
And more than dared, achieved, unspeakable
Ambitions. If I had a hundred tongues,
A hundred iron throats, I could not tell
The fullness of their crime and punishment."   660
And then she added:—"Come: resume the journey,
Fulfill the mission; let us hurry onward.
I see the walls the Cyclops[48] made, the portals
Under the archway, where, the orders tell us,
Our tribute must be set." They went together
Through the way's darkness, came to the doors, and halted,
And at the entrance Aeneas, having sprinkled
His body with fresh water, placed the bough
Golden before the threshold. The will of the goddess

---

[46] Ixion, king of the Lapiths, had attempted a sexual assault on Juno;
for Pirithous (son of Ixion), see lines 139–40 and note and lines 415–
21.

[47] Theseus is punished, presumably, for his attempt to abduct Proserpine
(see lines 415–21). Phlegyas (father of Ixion) had burned Apollo's temple
at Delphi.

[48] The Cyclops labored in the forge of Vulcan, the blacksmith god of
fire.

670   Had been performed, the proper task completed.
        They came to happy places, the joyful dwelling,
        The lovely greenery of the groves of the blessèd.
        Here ampler air invests the fields with light,
        Rose-colored, with familiar stars and sun.
        Some grapple on the grassy wrestling-ground
        In exercise and sport, and some are dancing,
        And others singing; in his trailing robe
        Orpheus strums the lyre; the seven clear notes
        Accompany the dance, the song.[49] And heroes
680   Are there, great-souled, born in the happier years,
        Ilus, Assaracus; the city's founder,
        Prince Dardanus.[50] Far off, Aeneas wonders,
        Seeing the phantom arms, the chariots,
        The spears fixed in the ground, the chargers browsing,
        Unharnessed, over the plain. Whatever, living,
        The men delighted in, whatever pleasure
        Was theirs in horse and chariot, still holds them
        Here under the world. To right and left, they banquet
        In the green meadows, and a joyful chorus
690   Rises through groves of laurel, whence the river
        Runs to the upper world.[51] The band of heroes
        Dwell here, all those whose mortal wounds were suffered
        In fighting for the fatherland; and poets,
        The good, the pure, the worthy of Apollo;
        Those who discovered truth and made life nobler;
        Those who served others—all, with snowy fillets
        Binding their temples, throng the lovely valley.
        And these the Sibyl questioned, most of all
        Musaeus,[52] for he towered above the center
700   Of that great throng:—"O happy souls, O poet,
        Where does Anchises dwell? For him we come here.
        For him we have traversed Erebus'[53] great rivers."

---

[49] For Orpheus, see lines 136–37 and note. He is playing on a seven-stringed lyre, or harp.
[50] Three illustrious ancestors of the Trojans.
[51] The river is Eridanus, believed in fable and folklore to be the underground source of the river Po.
[52] Legendary poet, taught by Orpheus.
[53] God of darkness; more generally, the Lower World itself.

And he replied:—"It is all our home, the shady
Groves, and the streaming meadows, and the softness
Along the river-banks. No fixed abode
Is ours at all; but if it is your pleasure,
Cross over the ridge with me; I will guide you there
By easy going." And so Musaeus led them
And from the summit showed them fields, all shining,
And they went on over and down.   710
    Deep in a valley of green, father Anchises
Was watching, with deep earnestness, the spirits
Whose destiny was light, and counting them over,
All of his race to come, his dear descendants,
Their fates and fortunes and their works and ways,
And as he saw Aeneas coming toward him
Over the meadow, his hands reached out with yearning,
He was moved to tears, and called:—"At last, my son,—
Have you really come, at last? and the long road nothing
To a son who loves his father? Do I, truly,   720
See you, and hear your voice? I was thinking so,
I was hoping so, I was counting off the days,
And I was right about it. O my son!
What a long journey, over land and water,
Yours must have been! What buffeting of danger!
I feared, so much, the Libyan realm would hurt you."
And his son answered:—"It was your spirit, father,
Your sorrowful shade, so often met, that led me
To find these portals. The ships ride safe at anchor,
Safe in the Tuscan sea. Embrace me, father;   730
Let hand join hand in love; do not forsake me."
And as he spoke, the tears streamed down. Three times
He reached out toward him, and three times the image
Fled like the breath of the wind or a dream on wings.
    He saw, in a far valley, a separate grove
Where the woods stir and rustle, and a river,
The Lethe, gliding past the peaceful places,
And tribes of people thronging, hovering over,
Innumerable as the bees in summer
Working the bright-hued flowers, and the shining   740
Of the white lilies, murmuring and humming.
Aeneas, filled with wonder, asks the reason

For what he does not know, who are the people
In such a host, and to what river coming?
Anchises answers:—"These are spirits, ready
Once more for life; they drink of Lethe's water
The soothing potion of forgetfulness.
I have longed, for long, to show them to you, name them,
Our children's children; Italy discovered,
750   So much the greater happiness, my son."
"But, O my father, is it thinkable
That souls would leave this blessedness, be willing
A second time to bear the sluggish body,
Trade Paradise for earth? Alas, poor wretches,
Why such a mad desire for light?" Anchises
Gives detailed answer: "First, my son, a spirit
Sustains all matter, heaven and earth and ocean,
The moon, the stars; mind quickens mass, and moves it.
Hence comes the race of man, of beast, of wingèd
760   Creatures of air, of the strange shapes which ocean
Bears down below his mottled marble surface.
All these are blessed with energy from heaven;
The seed of life is a spark of fire, but the body
A clod of earth, a clog, a mortal burden.
Hence humans fear, desire, grieve, and are joyful,
And even when life is over, all the evil
Ingrained so long, the adulterated mixture,
The plagues and pestilences of the body
Remain, persist. So there must be a cleansing,
770   By penalty, by punishment, by fire,
By sweep of wind, by water's absolution,
Before the guilt is gone. Each of us suffers
His own peculiar ghost.[54] But the day comes
When we are sent through wide Elysium,
The Fields of the Blessed, a few of us, to linger
Until the turn of time, the wheel of ages,
Wears off the taint, and leaves the core of spirit

---

[54] This notoriously elusive aphorism, typical of the formidable difficulties
in translating Virgil, probably means something like "Each endures his
own penance and lives with his own purgatorial consciousness" (though
other meanings have been suggested).

Pure sense, pure flame.[55] A thousand years pass over
And the god calls the countless host to Lethe
Where memory is annulled, and souls are willing   780
Once more to enter into mortal bodies."
    The discourse ended; the father drew his son
And his companion toward the hum, the center
Of the full host; they came to rising round
Where all the long array was visible,
Anchises watching, noting, every comer.
"Glory to come, my son, illustrious spirits
Of Dardan lineage, Italian offspring,
Heirs of our name, begetters of our future!
These I will name for you and tell our fortunes:[56]   790
First, leaning on a headless spear, and standing
Nearest the light, that youth, the first to rise
To the world above, is Silvius; his name
Is Alban; in his veins Italian blood
Will run with Trojan; he will be the son
Of your late age; Lavinia will bear him,
A king and sire of kings; from him our race
Will rule in Alba Longa. Near him, Procas,
A glory to the Trojan race; and Capys,
And Numitor, and Silvius Aeneas,   800
Resembling you in name, in arms, in goodness,
If ever he wins the Alban kingdom over.
What fine young men they are! What strength, what prowess!
The civic oak already shades their foreheads.
These will found cities, Gabii, Fidenae,
Nomentum; they will crown the hills with towers
Above Collatia, Inuus fortress, Bola,

[55] Certain rare and noble spirits remain in Elysian bliss rather than being reincarnated. Anchises is one of these.

[56] In lines 791–808, Anchises describes the Trojan lineage in Italy up to the time of Romulus, legendary founder (in 753 B.C., several centuries after Aeneas) of Rome proper. Alba Longa, forerunner of Rome, was the city founded by Ascanius (as we are told in I.278–83). Silvius was third in the line to rule after Aeneas and Ascanius/Iulus. The persons listed in lines 798–800 were subsequent Alban kings (one of whom, Silvius Aeneas, was denied the throne for a long time). The aboriginal towns mentioned in lines 805–08 were near Rome.

Cora, all names to be, thus far ungiven.
"And there will be a son of Mars; his mother
810   Is Ilia, and his name is Romulus,
Assaracus' descendant. On his helmet
See, even now, twin plumes; his father's honor
Confers distinction on him for the world.
Under his auspices Rome, that glorious city,
Will bound her power by earth, her pride by heaven,
Happy in hero sons, one wall surrounding
Her seven hills, even as Cybele, riding
Through Phrygian cities, wears her crown of towers,
Rejoicing in her offspring, and embracing
820   A hundred children of the gods, her children,
Celestials, all of them, at home in heaven.[57]
Turn the eyes now this way; behold the Romans,
Your very own. These are Iulus' children,[58]
The race to come. One promise you have heard
Over and over: here is its fulfillment,
The son of a god, Augustus Caesar, founder
Of a new age of gold, in lands where Saturn
Ruled long ago;[59] he will extend his empire
Beyond the Indies, beyond the normal measure
830   Of years and constellations, where high Atlas
Turns on his shoulders the star-studded world.[60]
Maeotia[61] and the Caspian seas are trembling
As heaven's oracles predict his coming,
And all the seven mouths of Nile are troubled.
Not even Hercules, in all his travels,
Covered so much of the world, from Erymanthus
To Lerna; nor did Bacchus, driving his tigers

[57] Cybele, a Phrygian (Trojan) deity considered the mother of the gods, was associated with the building and fortifying of cities.
[58] Iulus, Aeneas' son, was regarded as the progenitor of the Julian clan of Virgil's time, and thus of the line of Caesars.
[59] Augustus was "son of a god" because Julius Caesar, of whom Augustus was the adopted son, was deified at his death. Saturn, after being deposed by his son Jupiter, was supposed to have reigned in Italy during the mythical Age of Gold.
[60] The giant Atlas (sometimes identified with the north-African mountain) was imagined as supporting the heavens on his shoulders.
[61] Region north of the Black Sea.

From Nysa's summit.[62] How can hesitation
Keep us from deeds to make our prowess greater?
What fear can block us from Ausonian[63] land?   840
    "And who is that one yonder, wearing the olive,
Holding the sacrifice? I recognize him,
That white-haired king of Rome, who comes from Cures,
A poor land, to a mighty empire, giver
Of law to the young town. His name is Numa.
Near him is Tullus; he will rouse to arms
A race grown sluggish, little used to triumph.
Beyond him Ancus, even now too boastful,
Too fond of popular favor.[64] And then the Tarquins,
And the avenger Brutus, proud of spirit,   850
Restorer of the balance. He shall be
First holder of the consular power; his children
Will stir up wars again, and he, for freedom
And her sweet sake, will call down judgment on them,
Unhappy, however future men may praise him,
In love of country and intense ambition.[65]
    "There are the Decii, and there the Drusi,
A little farther off, and stern Torquatus,
The man with the axe, and Camillus, the regainer
Of standards lost. And see those two, resplendent   860
In equal arms, harmonious friendly spirits
Now, in the shadow of night, but if they ever
Come to the world of light, alas, what warfare,
What battle-lines, what slaughter they will fashion,
Each for the other, one from Alpine ramparts

---

[62] Erymanthus, a mountain range, and Lerna, a lake, were in Greece;
among the Twelve Labors of Hercules were victories over monsters inhabit-
ing these places. The mountain Nysa (located in India, according to one
tradition) was the boyhood home of Bacchus, the god of wine, whose
chariot was drawn by tigers.

[63] Italian.

[64] The religious and civic lawgiver Numa Pompilius, the warlike Tullus,
and Ancus (according to Virgil, a demagogue) were, respectively, the second, third, and fourth kings of Rome (Romulus having been the first).

[65] Brutus (not to be confused with the Brutus who assassinated Julius
Caesar centuries later) expelled the last (seventh) of the Roman kings,
Tarquinius Superbus, and founded the Roman republic in 509 B.C. He
had his sons executed for attempting to restore the old monarchical line.

Descending, and the other ranged against him
With armies from the east, father and son
Through marriage, Pompey and Caesar.[66] O my children,
Cast out the thoughts of war, and do not murder
870   The flower of our country. O my son,
Whose line descends from heaven, let the sword
Fall from the hand, be leader in forbearing!
      "Yonder is one who, victor over Corinth,
Will ride in triumph home, famous for carnage
Inflicted on the Greeks; near him another,
Destroyer of old Argos and Mycenae
Where Agamemnon ruled; he will strike down
A king descended from Achilles; Pydna
Shall be revenge for Pallas' ruined temple,
880   For Trojan ancestors. Who would pass over,
Without a word, Cossus, or noble Cato,
The Gracchi, or those thunderbolts of warfare,
The Scipios, Libya's ruin, or Fabricius
Mighty with little, or Serranus, ploughing
The humble furrow? My tale must hurry on:
I see the Fabii next, and their great Quintus
Who brought us back an empire by delaying.[67]
Others, no doubt, will better mould the bronze
To the semblance of soft breathing, draw, from marble,

[66] The Decii, Torquatus, and Camillus were military or civic heroes of
the fourth and third centuries B.C. The Drusi were ancestors of Livia,
wife of Caesar Augustus. The civil war (49–45 B.C.) between the forces
of Julius Caesar and those of his son-in-law Pompey, in Virgil's own lifetime, had been part of the chain of events culminating in the accession
of Augustus.

[67] The "victor over Corinth" (line 873) was Mummius; the "another"
of line 875 was probably Paullus (both second century B.C.). The latter,
by defeating a Greek opponent, descended from Achilles, at the battle
of Pydna, avenged Greek desecration of the Trojan temple of Pallas Athena
during the Trojan War; see I.48–50, II.430–32. These two heroes, along
with the other men named in lines 881–87, were among the greatest of
the Roman military and political figures from the fifth through the second
centuries B.C. The legacy of the episode with Dido is hinted at through
the mention of the two Scipios and Quintus Fabius Maximus ("Cunctator,"
or "Delayer," famous for his drawn-out avoidance tactics), all three of
whom won victories over Carthage in the Punic Wars (third and second
centuries B.C.).

The living countenance; and others plead   890
With greater eloquence, or learn to measure,
Better than we, the pathways of the heaven,
The risings of the stars: remember, Roman,
To rule the people under law, to establish
The way of peace, to battle down the haughty,
To spare the meek. Our fine arts, these, forever."[68]
    Anchises paused a moment, and they marvelled,
And he went on:—"See, how Marcellus[69] triumphs,
Glorious over all, with the great trophies
Won when he slew the captain of the Gauls,   900
Leader victorious over leading foeman.
When Rome is in great trouble and confusion
He will establish order, Gaul and Carthage
Go down before his sword, and triple trophies
Be given Romulus in dedication."
    There was a young man going with Marcellus,
Brilliant in shining armor, bright in beauty,
But sorrowful, with downcast eyes. Aeneas
Broke in, to ask his father: "Who is this youth[70]
Attendant on the hero? A son of his?   910
One of his children's children? How the crowd
Murmurs and hums around him! what distinction,
What presence, in his person! But dark night
Hovers around his head with mournful shadow.
Who is he, father?" And Anchises answered:—
"Great sorrow for our people! O my son,
Ask not to know it. This one fate will only
Show to the world; he will not be permitted
Any long sojourn. Rome would be too mighty,

---

[68] In these memorable lines, one of the most famous passages in all of literature, the "Others" (line 888), with whose accomplishments Anchises is comparing those of the Romans, are primarily the Greeks. In oratory the Greeks were in fact superior, but Anchises concedes even this area, so as to keep the distinction between the two peoples clean and emphatic.

[69] Roman general of the third century B.C.

[70] The Younger Marcellus—descendant of the Marcellus just described, nephew and son-in-law of Caesar Augustus, and presumed successor to him—died of malaria in 23 B.C. at the age of nineteen.

920   Too great in the gods' sight, were this gift hers.
       What lamentation will the field of Mars[71]
       Raise to the city! Tiber, gliding by
       The new-built tomb, the funeral state, bear witness!
       No youth from Trojan stock will ever raise
       His ancestors so high in hope, no Roman
       Be such a cause for pride. Alas for goodness,
       Alas for old-time honor, and the arm
       Invincible in war! Against him no one,
       Whether on foot or foaming horse, would come
930   In battle and depart unscathed. Poor boy,
       If you should break the cruel fates; if only—
       You are to be Marcellus. Let me scatter
       Lilies, or dark-red flowers, bringing honor
       To my descendant's shade; let the gift be offered,
       However vain the tribute."
           So through the whole wide realm they went together,
       Anchises and his son; from fields of air
       Learning and teaching of the fame and glory,
       The wars to come, the toils to face, or flee from,
940   Latinus' city and the Latin peoples,
       The love of what would be.
                                 There are two portals,
       Twin gates of Sleep, one made of horn, where easy
       Release is given true shades, the other gleaming
       White ivory, whereby the false dreams issue
       To the upper air. Aeneas and the Sibyl
       Part from Anchises at the second portal.[72]
       He goes to the ships, again, rejoins his comrades,
       Sails to Caieta's[73] harbor, and the vessels
       Rest on their mooring-lines.

[71] The Campus Martius, site of Marcellus' tomb.
[72] Why Aeneas should emerge through the gate of falsehood is one of the most mystifying problems in the entire poem. Virgil may mean no more than that Aeneas ends his visit to the Lower World early in the night, since dreams dreamt at that time were considered deceiving. (The reliable dreams were those dreamt just before waking.) But other interpreters scorn this notion, as too trivial to suit the apparently deliberate effect of high-solemn mystery.
[73] A town about 35 miles up the coast from Cumae and the modern Naples.

Ovid,
Metamorphoses,
Book 1

BOOK 1

In a short *Prologue* (1–4) Ovid announces his theme of meta-
morphosis: his stories of change will form one continuous poem,
ranging in time from the beginning of the universe to Ovid's
own lifetime.

The first great change is *The Creation* of the Universe (5–88)
out of Chaos, culminating in the appearance of Man. Ovid's
grand description draws on a variety of poetic and philosophical
sources, including the earlier Roman poet Lucretius (first century BC). We will naturally compare it with the biblical account
in Genesis, chapters 1 and 2. The process of change continues
through *The Four Ages* (89–150) of early human existence,
viewed as a degeneration from natural innocence and abund-
ance to a world governed by selfishness and aggression. At this
stage *The Giants* (151–62) attempt to oust the gods from their
home on Olympus but are struck down by Jupiter's lightning.
The Earth transforms their blood into new men whose brutality
is true to their origin.

Human depravity is exemplified by *Lycaön* (163–252), the
savage king of Arcadia. Jupiter calls an assembly to indicate his
intention to destroy mankind; but in response to objections
from the other gods, he promises to breed a new and better race.
Mankind's destruction follows in Ovid's description of *The
Flood* (253–312) and its transforming effects. (The story of a
world-wide flood recurs in the Greek and Near Eastern traditions, particularly in Genesis, chapters 6–9.) *Deucalion and
Pyrrha* (313–415) are the Greek Mr and Mrs Noah, two god-
fearing and mutually devoted survivors. After the flood's effects
are reversed, they miraculously produce a new race of hardy

men. The after-effects of the flood lead to the birth of strange
new creatures, including the terrifying *Python* (416–50), who
is killed by the god Apollo.

Apollo is the link with the first in a series of metamorphoses
involving the amours of gods. The next story concerns the
virginal nymph *Daphne* (451–567), who is relentlessly pursued
by Apollo but finally eludes capture by being transformed into
a laurel tree. The lighter tone and pace of this contrast vividly
with the earlier part of the book.

A noble description of the Vale of Tempe provides an ingeni-
ous transition to the parallel story of Jupiter's successful pursuit
of *Io* (568–686, 713–47), whom the god transforms to a cow
to protect her from Juno's jealousy. Here we can see an element
of comedy in the relationship between the gods, as well as of
touching pathos in Ovid's account of Io's unhappy predicament.
Here too we have the first inserted story, told by Mercury to
Io's hundred-eyed sentinel, Argus, of *Pan and Syrinx* (687–
712), another instance of a nymph pursued by a god and metamorphosed at the last minute.

The book concludes with an introduction to the story of
Phaëthon (748–79), which is to occupy a large part of Book 2.
When the young man's claim to be the child of the sun god is
questioned, he is determined to establish the truth and sets
out to find his father. The closing lines ring with excited
anticipation.

PROLOGUE*

Changes of shape, new forms, are the theme which my
    spirit impels me
now to recite. Inspire me, O gods (it is you who have even
transformed my art*), and spin me a thread from the
    world's beginning
down to my own lifetime, in one continuous poem.

THE CREATION

Before the earth and the sea and the all-encompassing
    heaven   5
came into being, the whole of nature displayed but a
    single
face, which men have called Chaos: a crude,
    unstructured mass,
nothing but weight without motion, a general
    conglomeration
of matter composed of disparate, incompatible elements.
No Titan the sun god was present to cast his rays on the
    universe,   10
nor Phoebe the moon to replenish her horns and grow to
    her fullness;
no earth suspended in equilibrium, wrapped in its folding
mantle of air; nor Amphitríte, the goddess of ocean,
to stretch her sinuous arms all round the earth's long
    coastline.
Although the land and the sea and the sky were involved
    in the great mass,   15
no one could stand on the land or swim in the waves of
    the sea,
and the sky had no light. None of the elements kept its
    shape,
and all were in conflict inside one body: the cold with the
    hot,

the wet with the dry, the soft with the hard, and weight
20   with the weightless.
    The god who is nature* was kinder and brought this
     dispute to a settlement.
He severed the earth from the sky and he parted the sea
     from the land;
he separated translucent space from the cloudier
     atmosphere.
He disentangled the elements,* so as to set them free
from the heap of darkness, then gave them their
25   separate places and tied them
down in a peaceful concordat: fire flashed out as a
     weightless
force in the vaulted heaven and found its rightful place
at the height of the firmament; air came next in position
     and lightness;
earth was denser than these, attracted the larger
     particles
and sank through the downward thrust of its weight; in
30   the nether region
came water, confining the solid disc in its liquid
     embrace.
    When the god, whichever one of the gods, had
     divided the substance
of Chaos and ordered it thus in its different constituent
     members,
first, in order that earth should hang suspended in
     perfect
symmetrical balance, he moulded it into the shape of a
35   great sphere.
Next he commanded the seas to scatter and swell as
     they fronted
the blast of the winds, surrounding the earth with its
     circle of shore.
To the ocean he added the springs, huge standing pools
     and the lakes,
and rivers to wind downstream as their sloping banks
     confined them.

These in their various places may be absorbed by the earth
    itself,   40
or travel as far as the sea, where they enter the broad
    expanse
of more open water and beat on the shore instead of their
    banks.
Then he commanded the plains to extend and the valleys to
    sink,
the woods to be decked in their leaves and the rock-faced
    mountains to soar.
And just as the sky is cut into zones, with two to
    northward,   45
two to the south and a fifth which burns with more heat
    than the others,
so with the earth which the sky encloses: the god in his
    wisdom
ordained five separate zones* or tracts to be traced on its
    surface.
The central zone is too hot for men to inhabit the region;
two are buried in snow; but two he placed in between,   50
and thus he blended the heat with the cold in a temperate
    climate.
    Hanging over the lands is the air, whose weight exceeds
that of fire by as much as the weight of earth exceeds that of
    water.
It was here that the god commanded the mists and the
    clouds to settle,
here that he posted the thunder to trouble the hearts of
    men,   55
with the winds which cause the lightning that burns and the
    lightning that flashes.*
Still the creator did not allow the winds dominion
over the whole wide range of air. As it is, they can scarcely
be stopped from tearing the world to pieces, though each of
    them governs
his blasts in a distant quarter; so angrily brothers can
    quarrel.   60

Eurus' retreat is the home of the dawn, from the realms of
            Arabia
and Persia through to the mountains* that gleam in the
            morning sunlight;
Zephyr is close to the evening and fans the shores that are
            warmed
by the setting sun. Bóreas, lord of the blizzard, sweeps
into Scýthia, land of the frozen north; while Auster,
65   opposite,
drenches the soil of the south with his clouds of
            incessant rain.
Above the turbulent lower air the creator imposed
the weightless translucent ether, untainted by earthly
            pollution.
    Nature had hardly been settled within its separate
            compartments
when stars, which had long been hidden inside the
70   welter of Chaos,
began to explode with light all over the vault of the
            heavens.
And lest any part of the world should be wanting its
            own living creatures,
the floor of heaven was richly inlaid with the stars and
            the planets,
the waves of the sea were assigned as the realm of the
            glinting fishes,
the earth was the home of the beasts, and the yielding
75   air of the birds.
    Yet a holier living creature, more able to think high
            thoughts,
which could hold dominion over the rest, was still to be
            found.
So Man came into the world. Maybe the great artificer
made him of seed divine in a plan for a better universe.
Maybe the earth that was freshly formed and newly
80   divorced
from the heavenly ether retained some seeds of its
            kindred element –

earth, which Prométheus, the son of Iápetus, sprinkled with
    raindrops
and moulded into the likeness of gods who govern the
    universe.
Where other animals walk on all fours and look to the
    ground,
man was given a towering head and commanded to stand   85
erect, with his face uplifted to gaze on the stars of heaven.
Thus clay, so lately no more than a crude and formless
    substance,
was metamorphosed to assume the strange new figure of
    Man.

THE FOUR AGES

First to be born was the Golden Age. Of its own free
    will,
without laws or enforcement, it did what was right and
    trust prevailed.   90
Punishment held no terrors; no threatening edicts were
    published
in tablets of bronze; secure with none to defend them, the
    crowd
never pleaded or cowered in fear in front of their
    stern-faced judges.
No pine tree had yet been felled from its home on the
    mountains and come down
into the flowing waves for journeys to lands afar;   95
mortals were careful and never forsook the shores of their
    homeland.
No cities were yet ringed round with deep, precipitous
    earthworks;
long straight trumpets and curved bronze horns never
    summoned to battle;
swords were not carried nor helmets worn; no need for
    armies,
but nations were free to practise the gentle arts of peace.   100

The earth was equally free and at rest, untouched by the
      hoe,
unscathed by the ploughshare, supplying all needs from
      its natural resources.
Content to enjoy the food that required no painful
      producing,
men simply gathered arbutus fruit and mountain
      strawberries,
cornel cherries and blackberries plucked from the prickly
105   bramble,
acorns too which they found at the foot of the
      spreading oak tree.
Spring was the only season. Flowers which had never
      been planted
were kissed into life by the warming breath of the
      gentle zephyrs;
and soon the earth, untilled by the plough, was
      yielding her fruits,
and without renewal the fields grew white with the
110   swelling corn blades.
Rivers of milk and rivers of nectar flowed in
      abundance,
and yellow honey, distilled like dew from the leaves of
      the ilex.
    When Saturn* was cast into murky Tártarus, Jupiter
      seized
the throne of the universe. Now there followed the age
      of silver,
meaner than gold but higher in value than tawny
115   bronze.
Gentle spring was no longer allowed to continue
      unbroken;
the king of the gods divided the year into four new
      seasons:
summer, changeable autumn, winter and only a short
      spring.
The sky for the first time burned and glowed with a dry
      white heat,

and the blasts of the wild winds froze the rain into hanging
    icicles.   120
People now took shelter in houses; their homes hitherto
had been caves, dense thickets or brushwood fastened
    together with bark.
For the first time also the corn was sown in long ploughed
    furrows,
and oxen groaned beneath the weight of the heavy yoke.
  A third age followed the Silver Age, the bronze
    generation,   125
crueller by nature, more ready to take up menacing
    weapons,
but still not vile to the core. The final age was of iron;
the floodgates opened and all the forces of evil invaded
a breed of inferior mettle. Loyalty, truth and conscience
went into exile, their throne usurped by guile and
    deception,   130
treacherous plots, brute force and a criminal lust for
    possession.
Sailors spread their sails to the winds they had tempted so
    rarely
before, and the keels of pine that had formerly stood stock
    still
on the mountain slopes presumptuously bobbed in the alien
    ocean.
The land which had been as common to all as the air or the
    sunlight   135
was now marked out with the boundary lines of the wary
    surveyor.
The affluent earth was not only pressed for the crops and
    the food
that it owed; men also found their way to its very bowels,
and the wealth which the god had hidden away in the home
    of the ghosts
by the Styx was mined and dug out, as a further incitement
    to wickedness.   140
Now dangerous iron, and gold – more dangerous even than
    iron –

had emerged. Grim War appeared, who uses both in his
        battles,
and brandished his clashing weapons in hands
        bespattered with slaughter.
Men throve on their thefts: no guest was safe from his
        host, no father
secure with his daughter's husband; love between
145   brothers was found
but seldom. Men and their wives would long for each
        other's demise;
wicked stepmothers brewed their potions of deadly
        wolfsbane;
sons would cast their fathers' horoscopes prematurely.
All duty to gods and to men lay vanquished; and
        Justice the Maiden*
was last of the heavenly throng to abandon the
150   blood-drenched earth.

THE GIANTS

The upper air was not to be left in greater peace
than the earth below. The story goes that the giants*
        aspired
to the throne of heaven and built a path to the stars on
        high,
by piling mountain on mountain. Then it was that
        almighty
Jupiter launched his lightning bolts to shatter Olympus,
and shook Mount Pélion down from its base on the
155   ridges of Ossa.
When, crushed by the mass they had raised, those
        fearsome bodies lay prostrate,
Mother Earth, as the story continues, now steeped and
        drenched
in the blood of her offspring, gave fresh life to the
        seething liquid.

Unwilling that all the fruits of her womb should be lost and
    forgotten,
she turned their blood into human form; but the new race
    also   160
looked on the gods with contempt. Their passionate lust for
    ferocious
violence and slaughter prevailed. You'd have known they
    were born of blood.

LYCAÖN

When Jupiter, son of Saturn, looked down from the heights
    of heaven,
he sighed, and remembered the gruesome banquet* served
    at Lycáön's
table, a recent event and not yet publicly rumoured.   165
Mightily angry, as only Jove can be angry, he called
a general assembly and all responded at once to his
    summons.
    In cloudless skies you can clearly see a path in the
    heavens;
men call it the Milky Way, well known for its brilliant
    whiteness.
This is the road which the gods must take to the mighty
    Thunderer's   170
royal palace. The well-thronged halls to the right and the
    left,
with their doors flung open, belong to the gods of the
    highest rank.
The common divinities live outside; right here the élite
and heavenly powers that be have established their hearths
    and homes.
And this is the place which, if I could muster the boldness to
    say it,   175
I'd not be afraid to describe as the Pálatine Hill* of the
    firmament.

After the gods had taken their seats in the marble
        chamber,
Jove, enthroned on a dais and clutching his ivory sceptre,
shook the awesome locks of his head three times and
        again,
so causing the earth and the sea and the constellations to
180   tremble,
then opened his lips to give vent to his wrath in the
        following manner:
'The fear that I feel today for the sovereign power of
        the universe
equals my fear when each of the snake-footed giants
        was striving
to lay his hundred hands on the sky and make it his
        own.
Fierce as that enemy was, its impetus sprang from a
185   single
body and source. But now I am forced to commit the
        whole race
of mankind to destruction wherever the ocean roars on
        the shore.
By the streams of the Stygian river below I swear I shall
        do it!
Let other cures be attempted first, but what is past
190   remedy
calls for the surgeon's knife, lest the parts that are
        sound be infected.
I have my demigods, all those powers of the
        countryside: nymphs,
and fauns and satyrs, my woodland spirits who dwell
        on the mountains.
These we have not yet chosen to welcome to heavenly
        honours,
but let us allow them at least to dwell on the earth we
195   have given them.
Or do your honours believe their safety is firmly
        assured,

when I, who am lord of the lightning and master of all you
      gods,
am the object of plots hatched up by that infamous savage,
      Lycaön?'
   The house was in uproar; passions blazed as they called
      for the blood
of the reckless traitor; as, when that band of disloyal
      malcontents   200
raged to extinguish the name of Rome by murdering
      Caesar,*
all mankind was suddenly struck by a terrible fear
of grievous disaster to come and the whole world shuddered
      in horror.
And just as your people's loyal devotion is welcome to you,
Augustus,* so was his subjects' to Jove. A word and a
      gesture   205
sufficed to control the murmuring hubbub and all were
      silent.
Then Jupiter broke the silence again to make his
      pronouncement:
'Lycaön has paid for his crimes, so far you may rest
      assured;
but let me describe his offence and the punishment meted
      out.   210
An evil report of the times had come to my ears. Desirous
of proving it false, I made my descent from the heights of
      Olympus
and wandered over the earth, a god disguised as a mortal.
It would take too long to recount the story of all the
      wickedness
I discovered. The truth was worse than rumour reported.   215
Crossing over the high Arcadian mountains (Maénalus,
home of wild beasts, Cylléne, and cold pine-covered
      Lycaéus),
I entered the palace of King Lycaön and ventured beneath
his inhospitable roof in the twilight hour of the nightfall.
I gave a sign that a god had come, and the common people 220

turned to their prayers. Lycaön began by mocking their
    piety;
then he said, "Is it a god or a mortal? I'll settle the matter
by using a simple test. There will be no doubt where the
    truth lies."
His plan was to make a sudden attack in the night on my
    sleeping
body and kill me. This was his chosen method of
225   proving
the truth. Not content with that, he applied his sword
    to the throat
of a hostage sent from Epírus and under my own
    protection;
and while the man's flesh still held some warmth, he
    roasted part of it
over the fire and poached the remainder in boiling
    water,
then set this repast on the table. My moment now had
230   arrived.
My lightning of vengeance struck, and the palace
    collapsed in ruins
on top of the household gods* who shared the guilt of
    the master.
Frightened out of his wits, Lycaön fled to the country
where all was quiet. He tried to speak, but his voice
    broke into
an echoing howl. His ravening soul infected his jaws;
his murderous longings were turned on the cattle; he
235   still was possessed
by bloodlust. His garments were changed to a shaggy
    coat and his arms
into legs. He was now transformed to a wolf. But he
    kept some signs
of his former self: the grizzled hair and the wild
    expression,
the blazing eyes and the bestial image remained
    unaltered.

One house has fallen, but more than one has deserved to
    perish.   240
The demon of madness is holding dominion the wide world
    over;
you'd think that the human race had joined in an evil
    conspiracy.
This is my sentence: let all of them speedily pay for their
    crimes!'
  Jove had spoken. Some fuelled his anger further by
    cheering
loudly, while others simply expressed their approval by
    clapping.   245
But still a murmur went round: 'The loss of the human race
will be widely deplored! And what will a world bereft of
    mortals
be like in the future? Who will bring to our altars the
    offerings
of incense? Is earth to be left to the mercies of ravaging wild
    beasts?'
Such were their questions; but Jupiter told them not to be
    anxious.   250
He would take care of the future, he said; and he promised
    to breed
a new race of miraculous birth, unlike the people before it.

THE FLOOD

The god was now on the point of launching his bolts on the
    whole wide
earth, but he feared that the conflagration might cause the
    holy
ether* to catch fire too in a blaze from pole to pole.   255
He also remembered the Fates' decree, that a time would
    arrive*
when the sea and the land and the royal palace of heaven
    would burst

into flames and the complex mass of the universe come
    to grief.
So he put the lightning, forged in the Cyclops' workshop,
    aside
and chose a different method of punishing mortals, by
260   massing
his storm-clouds over the sky and destroying the race
    in a great flood.
  All of the gales which scatter the gathering clouds,
    and among them
the north wind Áquilo, Jupiter promptly imprisoned
    inside
the caverns of Aéolus. Notus, the wind of the south, he
    released.
265 Notus flew out on his soaking wings, his terrible visage
covered in pitchy gloom; his beard was a bundle of
    rain-storms;
water streamed from his hoary locks; his forehead a
    cushion
for mists; his wings and the folds of his garments were
    sodden and dripping.
He squeezed the bank of menacing clouds like a
    sponge, and a thunderclap
followed. Instantly rain poured down from the sky in
    torrents.
Juno's messenger, decked in her mantle of many
270   colours,
Iris the rainbow, sucked up moisture to thicken the
    clouds.
The corn was flattened; the farmer wept for his wasted
    prayers;
and all the fruits of a long year's labour were gone to
    no purpose.
  Jupiter's anger did not stop short in the sky, his own
    kingdom;
Neptune the sea god deployed his waters to aid his
275   brother.

He summoned the rivers and, when they'd arrived at their
    master's palace,
he spoke to the meeting: 'No need for a lengthy harangue,'
    he said;
'Pour forth in the strength that is yours – it is needed! Open
    the floodgates,
down with the barriers, give full rein to the steeds of your
    streams!'   280
He had spoken. The rivers returned to relax the curbs on
    their sources,
and then rolled down to the ocean flats in unbridled
    career.
Neptune himself now struck the earth with his trident. It
    trembled
under the blow, and a raging torrent gushed from the
    chasm.
Bursting their confines, the rivers engulfed the plains and
    the valleys.   285
The orchards along with the crops, and the cattle along
    with the people,
houses and shrines with their sacred possessions were swept
    to oblivion.
Dwellings, which stood their ground and were able to face
    such an onslaught
untoppled, were still submerged from above by an
    overwhelming,
mountainous wave, which levelled their pinnacles deep in
    the floodtide.   290
  And now no more could the land and the sea be clearly
    distinguished.
The world was reduced to an ocean, an ocean without any
    coastline.
Look at the man on that hill, or sitting alone in his
    fishing-boat,
rowing across the fields where he recently guided his
    ploughshare.
Another is sailing above his cornfields or over the roof   295

of his vanished farmhouse, or casting his line in the top
    of an elm tree.
He might have dropped anchor to catch in the soil of a
    grassy meadow,
or else his dinghy is scraping the vineyard trellis below
    him.
There in the field where the slender goats were lately
    browsing
300 on tufts of grass, the seals are resting their clumsy bodies.
Under water the Néreïds gaze in utter amazement
at coppices, cities and buildings. The woods are
    invaded by dolphins,
blundering into the branches and bumping the trunks
    till they shake them.
Wolves are swimming among the sheep; tawny lions
and tigers are swept along in the flood; no use to the
305   boar
is his lightning strength, nor the speed of his legs to the
    floundering stag.
At the end of a tedious search for land and a resting
    place,
with wings exhausted the wandering bird flutters down
    to the waves.
Small hills are completely submerged by the sea in its
    limitless freedom,
and billows are strangely beating against the peaks of
310   the mountains.
All but a few have been drowned in the flood, and any
    survivors
for shortage of food are destroyed by long-drawn-out
    starvation.

DEUCALION AND PYRRHA

Phocis lies in the country between Boeótia and Thessaly,
fertile land, when still it was land. At the time of the flood
it was part of the sea and a plain of suddenly spreading
    water.   315
Here you can visit a twin-peaked mountain, called
    Parnássus,
towering up to the stars and hiding its head in the clouds.
This was the only feature the ocean had left uncovered;
and here Deucálion, sailing a tiny boat with his wife,
ran aground. On landing they paid the homage due to the
    nymphs   320
of the great Corýcian cave, to the mountain spirits and
    Themis,
goddess of prophecy, then in control of the Delphic oracle.
You'd never find a better or more right-minded man
than Deucalion, neither a more god-fearing woman than
    Pyrrha.
When Jupiter saw that the world was a pool of swirling
    water,
that only one was left of so many thousand men,   325
and only one was left of so many thousand women,
both of them guiltless of sin and both devout in their
    worship,
he scattered the mists; with the north wind's help he
    banished the storm-clouds,
Exposing the earth once more to the sky and the sky to the
    earth.
Neptune's anger subsided as well. Laying his trident   330
aside, he calmed the turbulent waters and called upon
    Triton,
the sea-green merman, who heaved his shoulders, encrusted
    by nature
with shells of the murex,* above the surface, with orders to
    blow

on his resonant conch and signal the rivers and waves to
    withdraw.
Triton lifted his hollow horn, which wreathes in a
335   spiral
up from its mouthpiece to broaden out to a bell, the
    horn
whose notes, when once he has filled it with breath in
    the midst of the deep,
rebound on the echoing shoreline from east to west. So
    then,
when the god had raised his instrument up to his lips,
    with the salt drops
streaming down from his beard, and the blast had
340   sounded the bidden
retreat, it was heard by all the water of land and ocean;
and all the waters by which it was heard were held in
    check.
The sea recovered its shores; the rivers, though full,
    were confined
to their channels; the flooding receded; the hills were
    seen to emerge.
The earth rose up; as the waves died down, dry land
345   expanded.
At the end of a long, long day the tops of the trees in
    the forest
began to appear, their leaves still thick with a coating
    of slime.

The world was restored; but when Deucalion saw it
    was empty
and felt the silence brooding over the desolate earth,
he burst into tears and said to Pyrrha, his dear
350   companion:
'My cousin, my wife, the only woman who still
    survives,
first we were tied by our kindred blood, and then by
    our marriage;

now our very danger unites us. Here is the world
with its glorious lands from east to west; and here are we,
an inglorious crowd of two. All else belongs to the sea.   355
As yet, indeed, we can hardly be certain the life that we
      have
is safely assured. These clouds still fill me with fear and
      foreboding.
How would you now be feeling, my poor dear love, if I
had been lost and you had been snatched from death? How
      could you have suffered
fear on your own, with no one there to comfort your
      sorrow?   360
Believe me, if you were lying beneath the waves, my
      beloved,
I should follow you there to be drowned in the waves beside
      you.
I wish I could use my father Prometheus' skill to create
mankind once again and breathe new life into moulded
      clay!
Today we two are all that is left of the human race.   365
That is the will of the gods. We survive as nothing but
      relicts.'
  He spoke and they wept. They then decided to pray to the
      heavenly
power of Themis and crave her help in a sacred oracle.
Speedily, side by side, they made their way to Cephísus;*
the river was still disturbed but cutting its usual channel.   370
Drawing some water, they sprinkled it over their heads and
      their garments,
and bent their footsteps towards the shrine of the holy
      goddess.
Its gable was pale with unsightly moss, and the fires on the
      altar
were dead. When they reached the temple steps, they both
      prostrated   375
themselves and fearfully pressed their lips on the cold, hard
      pavement,

saying aloud: 'If the prayers of the righteous can soften
    the hearts
of the gods and win them over, transforming their anger
    to kindness,
gentle Themis, declare to us how to repair the loss
of our wretched race, and come to the aid of our deluged
380   world.'
The heart of the goddess was moved and she gave her
    response to them, saying:
'Leave this sanctuary, cover your heads and ungirdle
    your garments,
then cast the bones of your mighty mother behind your
    backs.'
They were long dumbfounded. Pyrrha was first to
    break the silence
and voice her protest aloud. She refused to obey the
385   goddess'
commands. With trembling lips she begged for pardon,
    too frightened
to give such offence to her mother's ghost by casting
    her dead bones.
Meanwhile they silently pondered the words of the
    puzzling reply
which had come from the oracle's dark recess, and
    discussed them together.
Prometheus' son then gently suggested, to calm
390   Epimétheus'*
daughter: 'Unless my wits are awry and sorely
    deceiving me,
oracles must be holy and never command what is
    sinful.
Our mighty mother is Earth. I believe what is meant by
    her bones
are stones on her body, and these we are bidden to cast
    behind us.'
    Though Pyrrha was much impressed by her
395   husband's interpretation,

her hopes still wavered. They both distrusted the oracle's
    bidding,
but saw little harm in trying. Proceeding down from the
    temple,
they covered their heads, ungirdled their robes and,
    stepping out boldly,
scattered some stones behind their backs, as the oracle
    ordered.
Who would believe what ensued, if it wasn't confirmed by
    tradition?   400
The stones started to lose their essential hardness, slowly
to soften, and then to assume a new shape. They soon
    grew larger
and gathered a nature more gentle than stone. An outline
    of human
form could be seen, not perfectly clear, like a
    rough-hewn statue   405
partially carved from the marble and not yet properly
    finished.
But still, the part of the stones which consisted of earth
    and contained
some moisture was turned into flesh; the solid, inflexible
    matter
was changed into bones; and the veins of the rock into
    veins of blood.   410
In a moment of time, by the will of the gods, the stones
    that were thrown
from the hands of a man were transformed to take on the
    appearance of men,
and women were fashioned anew from those that were
    thrown by a woman.
And so our race is a hard one; we work by the sweat of
    our brow,
and bear the unmistakable marks of our stony origin.   415

PYTHON

Other creatures after their various kinds came forth
from the earth by spontaneous self-generation. The
      lingering moisture
was warmed by the rays of the sun, and the heat made
      the mud in the water-logged
marshes swell and expand. The seeds of animal life
were fed in the mother's womb of life-giving soil which
420   engendered them,
growing in course of time to the shapes of the different
      species.
Such we can see when the seven-mouthed Nile has
      withdrawn from the flood-drenched
fields and brought its waters back to their normal
      channels.
After the freshly deposited mud grows hot in the
      sunshine,
the farmers turning the clods with their ploughs
425   discover a horde
of new creatures. Some have arrived on the threshold
      of life and can even
be watched at the moment of birth, while others are
      still half-formed
and without their limbs; it will sometimes appear in a
      single body
that one of its parts is alive and the rest is composed of
      mere earth.
When heat and moisture are blended, we know that
430   they lead to conception;
everything owes its first beginning to these two
      elements.
Though fire is at war with water, their combination
      produces
the whole of nature – procreation from friendly
      enmity.*

So at the time straight after the flood, when the earth was
    muddy
and heated again from above by the rays of the sun, it
    produced   435
an infinite number of species. Some of the forms which
    emerged
were familiar before, but others were new and amazing
    creations.
  Amongst these forms was an unknown serpent, the
    monstrous Python,
also brought forth by Earth at the time, though she cannot
    have wished for it.
Sprawling over Parnassus, it horribly frightened the
    new-born   440
peoples, until it was killed by the deadly shafts of Apollo,
whose only targets before were the timid gazelles and the
    roe deer.
The snake was transfixed by a thousand arrows (the quiver
    was almost
emptied) and out of its wounds there spewed black gushes
    of venom.
In order that time should never destroy the fame of this
    exploit,   445
Apollo established the sacred games, attended by huge
    crowds,
the Pythian Games,* called after the serpent he vanquished,
    Python.
Here the athletes who won their events on track or on field,
or the chariot-race, would receive the glorious crown of an
    oak-wreath.
The laurel had not yet appeared, and Phoebus would
    garland the flowing
locks of his comely head with any available foliage.   450

DAPHNE

Apollo's first love was Daphne, the child of the river
    Penéüs.
Blind chance was not to be blamed but Cupid's spiteful
    resentment.
Phoebus, still in the flush of his victory over the
    serpent,
had noticed the love-god bending his bow and drawing
455   the string
to his shoulder, and asked him: 'What are you doing
    with grown-up weapons,
you mischievous boy? That bow would better be
    carried by me.
When I fire my shafts at my foes or beasts, they're
    unfailingly wounded.
My numberless arrows have just destroyed the
    venomous Python,
which filled whole acres of mountainside with its
460   belly's infections.
You be content with your torch and use it to kindle
    some passion
or other; but don't usurp any honours belonging to
    me!'
The son of Venus replied: 'Your arrows, Apollo, can
    shoot
whatever you choose, but I'll shoot you. As mortal
    creatures
must yield to a god, your glory will likewise prove to
465   be subject
to mine.' Then he beat his wings and cut a path
    through the atmosphere,
nimbly alighting upon the heights of shady Parnassus.
Once there he drew from his quiver two arrows of
    contrary purpose:
one is for rousing passion, the other is meant to repel it.

The former is made of gold, and its head has a sharp, bright
        point,   470
while the latter is blunt and weighted with lead one side of
        the reed shaft.
That was the arrow which Cupid implanted in Daphne's
        bosom;
the other was aimed at Apollo and smote to the core of his
        being.
Phoebus at once was filled with desire, but Daphne fled
from the very thought of a lover. She joyed in the forest
        lairs   475
and in spoils of captive beasts, like the virgin goddess
        Diana,
binding her carelessly flowing locks in a simple headband.
Courted by suitors in droves, Peneüs' daughter rejected
        them.
Stubbornly single, she'd roam through the woodland
        thickets, without
concern for the meaning of marriage or love or physical
        union.   480
Often her father remarked, 'You owe me a son, my
        daughter,'
or else he would say, 'Now when, my child, will you give
        me a grandson?'
Marriage torches to Daphne were nothing less than
        anathema.
Blushes of shame would spread all over her beautiful
        cheeks,
she would lovingly cling to her father's neck in a coaxing
        appeal   485
and say to him, 'Darling Father, I want to remain a virgin
for ever. Please let me. Diana's father allowed her that.'
Peneüs granted her wish; but Daphne's peculiar beauty
and personal charm were powerful bars to her prayer's
        fulfilment.
Phoebus caught sight of her, fell in love and longed to
        possess her.   490

Wishes were hopes, for even his powers of prophecy
    failed him.
Think of the flimsy stubble which burns in a harvested
    cornfield;
and think of a blazing hedgerow fired by a torch which a
    traveller
has carelessly brought too close or dropped behind him
    at daybreak.
So was the god as his heart caught fire and the flames
495   spread through
to the depths of his soul, and passion was fuelled with
    empty hope.
He eyes the hair hanging loosely over her neck, and
    murmurs,
'What if that hair were neatly arranged!' He looks at
    her bright eyes
burning and twinkling like stars; he studies her lips, so
    teasingly
tempting; he fondly admires her hands with their
500   delicate fingers;
he dotes on the shapely arms, so nearly bare to the
    shoulder;
what's hidden he thinks must be even better. But swift
    as the light breeze,
Daphne is gone, with never a pause as he calls out after
    her:
'Stop, dear Daphne, I beg you to stop! This isn't an
    enemy
chasing you. Stop! You would think I'm a wolf
505   pursuing a lamb,
a lion hunting a deer or an eagle pouncing on fluttering
doves in mid-air, but I'm not! It is love that impels me
    to follow you.
Have pity! How frightened I am that you'll fall and
    scratch those innocent
legs in the brambles. You mustn't be hurt on account
    of me!

The ground where you're rushing away is so rough. Slow
        down, my beloved,   510
I beg you. Don't run so fast and I promise to slow down
        too.
Now ask who it is that desires you. I'm not a wild
        mountain-dweller;
this isn't an uncouth shepherd, minding the flocks and the
        herds
round here. Impetuous girl, you have no idea who you're
        running from.
That's why you're running so fast. Listen! I am the master
        of Delphi,   515
Claros and Ténedos, Pátara's temple too. My father
is Jupiter. I can reveal the past, the present and future
to all who seek them. I am the lord of the lyre and song.
My arrows are deadly, but one is even more deadly than
        they are,
the shaft which has smitten a heart that has never been
        wounded before.   520
Healing is my invention, the world invokes me as Helper,
and I am the one who dispenses the herbs with the power to
        cure.
Alas! No herbs have the power to cure the disease of my
        love.
Those arts which comfort the whole of mankind cannot
        comfort their master!'
    Apollo wanted to say much more, but the terrified
        Daphne   525
ran all the faster; she left him behind with his speech
        unfinished.
Her beauty was visible still, as her limbs were exposed by
        the wind;
the breezes which blew in her face managed also to flutter
        her dress;
and the currents of air succeeded in blowing her tresses
        behind her.
Flight made her all the more lovely; but now the god in his
        youthful   530

ardour was ready no longer to squander his breath on
    wheedling
pleas. Spurred on by desire, he followed the trail with
    new vigour.
Imagine a greyhound, imagine a hare it has sighted in
    open
country: one running to capture his prey, the other for
    safety.
The hound is about to close in with his jaws; he believes
535   he is almost
there; he is grazing the back of her heels with the tip of
    his muzzle.
The hare isn't sure if her hunter has caught her, but
    leaps into freedom,
clear of the menacing jaws and the mouth which keeps
    brushing against her.
So with Apollo and Daphne, the one of them racing in
    hope
and the other in fear. But the god had the pinions of
540   love to encourage him.
Faster than she, he allowed her no rest; his hands were
    now close
to the fugitive's shoulders; his breath was ruffling the
    hair on her neck.
Her strength exhausted, the girl grew pale; then
    overcome
by the effort of running, she saw Peneüs' waters before
    her:
'Help me, Father!' she pleaded. 'If rivers have power
545   over nature,
mar the beauty which made me admired too well, by
    changing
my form!' She had hardly ended her prayer when a
    heavy numbness
came over her body; her soft white bosom was ringed
    in a layer
of bark, her hair was turned into foliage, her arms into
550   branches.

The feet that had run so nimbly were sunk into sluggish
    roots;
her head was confined in a treetop; and all that remained
    was her beauty.
  Tree though she was, Apollo still loved her. Caressing the
    trunk
with his hand, he could feel the heart still fluttering under
    the new bark.
Seizing the branches, as though they were limbs, in his arms'
    embrace,   555
he pressed his lips to the wood; but the wood still shrank
    from his kisses.
Phoebus then said to her: 'Since you cannot be mine in
    wedlock,
you must at least be Apollo's tree. It is you who will always
be twined in my hair, on my tuneful lyre and my quiver of
    arrows.
The generals of Rome shall be wreathed with you, when the
    jubilant paean   560
of triumph is raised and the long procession ascends the
    Capitol.
On either side of Augustus' gates your trees shall stand
    sentry,
faithfully guarding the crown of oak-leaves* hanging
    between them.
As I, with my hair that is never cut, am eternally youthful,
so you with your evergreen leaves are for glory and praise
    everlasting.'   565
Apollo the Healer had done. With a wave of her
    new-formed branches
the laurel agreed, and seemed to be nodding her head in the
    treetop.

IO (1)

Théssaly boasts a ravine called Tempe, enclosed on
    each side
by a rock face covered with trees; and down it the river
    Peneüs
pours and rolls on his foaming way from the foot of
570   Mount Pindus.
Powerfully tumbling, the cataract leaps into clouds of a
    wandering,
wispy vapour; the spray besprinkles the trees on the
    clifftops
like showers of rain; and a constant roar is returned
    from the distance.
This is the dwelling, the mansion, the innermost shrine
    of the mighty
575 river-god; here he dispenses justice, enthroned in a cave
carved out of the rock, to all of his waters and nymphs
    of the waters.
This was the gathering point of firstly the local rivers,
uncertain whether they ought to congratulate
    Daphne's father
or offer condolence: Spercheüs whose banks are
    bordered with poplars,
580 restless Enípeus, ancient Apídanus, gentle Amphrýsus
and Aéas. These were shortly followed by other
    streams,
who wander lazily down to the sea as their currents
    impel them.
Only Ínachus* failed to appear; he was buried away
in the depths of his cavern, adding tears to his waters,
    in pitiful
grief for the loss of his daughter Io. He didn't know
585   whether
she still was alive or had gone to the shades; but as she
    was nowhere

at all to be found, he feared the worst and believed she had
    vanished.
   What happened? As Io was one day coming away from
    her father's
river, Jupiter saw her and cried, 'You beautiful maiden,
worthy of Jove, how happy the husband who makes you his
    own!   590
You should rest in the depths of these shady woods,' and he
    pointed them out,
'while the sun is so high in the sky, at its zenith, and
    burning so fiercely.
If you are afraid to enter the wild beasts' lairs on your own,
you'll be safe with a god to guide you into the forest's
    secret
recesses – no ordinary god, but I who wield in my mighty   595
hand the sceptre of heaven and hurl the volatile lightning.'
She started to flee. 'Don't run from me now!' Already she'd
    left
the pastures of Lerna and woody Lyrcéan country behind
    her,
when Jupiter, throwing a mantle of darkness over the wide
    earth,
halted the flight of the runaway nymph and stealthily raped
    her.   600

Meanwhile Queen Juno directed her gaze on the middle of
    Argos.
The day had been bright and sunny, but now to her great
    surprise
the clouds had suddenly turned it to night. The mist didn't
    come
from the river, she saw; and it couldn't be due to the earth's
    own moisture.
Where was her husband? She looked all round. She was
    quite familiar   605
with Jupiter's amorous tricks, as she'd caught him straying
    so often.

As soon as she failed to find him in heaven, her instant
    reaction was,
'Either I'm wrong, or I'm wronged!' and, gliding down
    through the air,
she alighted on earth and commanded the mists to
    remove themselves.
610 The god, however, anticipating his consort's arrival,
had changed the daughter of Inachus into a
    snow-white heifer.
Even so she was perfectly lovely; Saturnian Juno,
much as it galled her, was forced to admire the
    beautiful creature.
'Whose is it? Whence does it come? What herd?' she
    enquired in pretended
ignorance. 'Born of the earth,' lied Jupiter, hoping to
615   silence
her searching questions. Juno then asked him, 'Please
    will you give her
to me as a present?' What was he to do? To surrender
    his love
would be cruelly painful, but not to give her would
    look suspicious.
Conscience would argue for her surrender; his love was
    against it.
Love indeed would have won the battle; but if he
    refused
the paltry gift of a cow to the wife who was also his
620   sister,
it could have appeared that the creature was not
    exactly a heifer.
    Juno's rival was now in her power, but her fears
    continued
to haunt her. She still suspected Jove and his
    treacherous wiles,
until she put Argus, the son of Aréstor, in charge of Io.
625 Argus' head had a hundred eyes, which rested in relays,
two at a time, while the others kept watch and
    remained on duty.

Whichever way he was standing, his eyes were always on Io;
even behind his back, she could never escape from his
    watchful
stare. She could graze in the daytime, but after sundown
    he'd pen her   630
inside an enclosure and tie her innocent neck with a halter.
Her food was tree leaves and bitter herbs; her bedding was
    earth,
not always too grassy; her water came from the muddy
    streams.
When Io wanted to supplicate Argus with outstretched
    arms,   635
no arms were there to outstretch. When she opened her
    mouth to complain,
her own voice startled her; all that emerged was a hideous
    lowing.
She came to the banks where so often she'd played, the
    banks of her father
Inachus. Here when she looked in the water and saw her
    reflected
head with its strange new horns, she recoiled from herself in
    a panic.   640
The naiads had no idea who she was, and even Inachus
failed to know her; but still she followed her father and
    sisters
quickly along, and allowed them to pat her back and
    admire her.
Inachus plucked some grass and tenderly held it out to her. 645
Licking and kissing her father's hands, she couldn't help
    weeping.
If only words could have followed her tears, she'd have
    begged him for help;
she'd have told him her name and described her plight. Two
    letters* were all
that could serve for words, two letters traced by a hoof in
    the dust,
which revealed her name and the sorry tale of her
    transformation.   650

'Woe and alas!' old Inachus cried, as he tenderly fondled
the horns and clung to the snowy neck of the moaning
  heifer.
'Woe and alas!' he repeated. 'Are you the daughter I
  searched for
over the whole wide world? My sorrow was not so heavy
when I was unable to find you. You're silent and cannot
655 reply
to my questions. You only respond with a deep, deep
  sigh from your heart.
When I speak to you, all you can offer me back is a
  melancholy low.
Blind to the future, I busied myself with plans for your
  wedding,
in hope to gain a new son and soon to become a
  grandfather.
Now your husband and children must come from a
660 herd of cattle.
If only death could allow me to end this terrible
  sorrow!
Sadly I have to remain a god and the gates of Hades
are barred to me. Grief must be my companion for ever
  and ever.'
So the father lamented, but star-eyed Argus discreetly
eased him aside and led the daughter away to more
665 distant
pastures. There he transferred himself to the heights of
  a mountain
summit, from where he could sit and keep watch in
  every direction.

The king of the gods could no longer endure his
  beloved Io's
pain and distress. He summoned his son, whom Maia
  the radiant
Pleiad had borne, and gave him his orders to murder
670 Argus.
Mercury only paused to don his winged sandals, cover

his head, and seize the sleep-giving wand which empowers
    his hand.
Thus attired, the offspring of Jupiter leapt from his father's
    citadel
down to the earth; once there he discarded his
    wide-brimmed hat,
took off his sandals and simply clung to his snake-twined
    staff,   675
which he used in herdsman's fashion to drive the goats he
    had rustled
along his way through the scrubland, playing the while on
    his reed pipe.
Juno's guard was entranced by the unfamiliar music.
'You there, whoever you are,' said Argus, 'do come over
and sit with me here on this rock. You'll find no richer
    abundance   680
of grass for your goats, and you see there's plenty of shade
    for a herdsman.'
Mercury then sat down and filled the lingering hours
with desultory chat. He attempted to conquer those
    watchful eyes
with the drone of his panpipes; but Argus fought to resist
    sleep's soft   685
seduction. While some of his hundred eyes were allowed to
    surrender,
others were kept awake. The pipe had been newly invented,
so Argus drowsily asked his companion about its invention.

INTERLUDE: PAN AND SYRINX

The god then told him a tale: 'In the cold Arcadian
    mountains,
among the Nonácrian wood-nymphs, there lived a
690   remarkable naiad
(Syrinx her sisters called her), whom all admired for her
    beauty.

More than once she'd eluded pursuit by lascivious
        satyrs
and all the various gods who dwell in the shadowy
        forests
and fertile fields. She modelled herself on the goddess
        Diana
in daily life and by staying chaste. When she dressed as a
695   huntress,
you might have been taken in and supposed she was
        Leto's daughter,
but for her bow, which was made of horn, where
        Diana's is gold.
Despite it, she passed for Diana. One day she was
        spotted returning
from Mount Lycaeus by Pan. Bedecked with a garland
        of sharp
pine needles, he spoke to her, saying –' but Mercury
700   broke off there,
and didn't describe how the nymph rejected the god's
        advances
and fled through the fields, until she arrived at the river
        Ladon
peacefully flowing between its sandy banks. Since the
        waters
were barring her way, she called on the nymphs of the
        stream to transform her.
So just at the moment when Pan believed that his
705   Syrinx was caught,
instead of a fair nymph's body, he found himself
        clutching some marsh reeds.
But while he was sighing in disappointment, the
        movement of air
in the rustling reeds awakened a thin, low, plaintive
        sound.
Enthralled by the strange new music and sweetness of
        tone, Pan exclaimed,
'This sylvan pipe will enable us always to talk
710   together!'

And so, when he'd bound some reeds of unequal length with
　　a coating
of wax, a syrinx – the name of his loved one – stayed in his
　　hands.

IO (2)

That was the story the god of Cyllene was going to tell,
when he saw that his enemy's drowsy eyes had all
　　succumbed
and were shrouded in sleep. At once he stopped talking and
　　stroked the sentry's   715
drooping lids with his magic wand to make sure he was out.
Then he rapidly struck with his sickle-shaped sword at his
　　nodding victim
just where the head comes close to the neck, and hurled him
　　bleeding
down from the rock to bespatter the cliff in a shower of
　　gore.
Argus was finished. The light that had glittered in all those
　　stars   720
was extinguished; a hundred eyes were eclipsed in a single
　　darkness.
　　Juno extracted those eyes and gave them a setting like
　　sparkling
jewels in the feathers displayed on the tail of the peacock,
　　her own bird.
Blazing with anger, she wasted no time in venting her
　　fury
by sending a horrible demon to frighten the eyes of Io   725
by day, and her mind at night. A goading terror was
　　planted
deep in her heart, which hounded her over the world in
　　flight.
At the end of the road was the Nile, where the tale of her
　　toils was concluded.

As soon as she reached it, she sank to her knees by the
    bank of the river,
looked up with her neck thrown back and, lacking the
730   arms to lift up
in prayer, uplifted her face to the stars. The groans that
    she uttered,
the tears that she shed and her piteous lowings, seemed
    to be challenging
Jupiter, pleading with him to grant her an end to her
    sufferings.
Jupiter then drew Juno gently into his arms
and asked her to punish Io no more: 'You may banish
735   your fears
for the future,' he said; 'she will never provide you
    with cause for vexation
again,' and he called on the Stygian marshes to witness
    his promise.
Once the goddess had been placated, Io recovered
her human face and her body, the horns shrank down,
740   the cow eyes narrowed,
the gaping mouth grew smaller, the shoulders and
    hands came back,
the hooves dissolved and faded away into five smooth
    toenails.
All that survived of the snow-white cow was its
    glowing beauty.
Happy once more to be standing on two feet only, the
    fair nymph
rose from the ground; but frightened to speak, in case
745   she still lowed
like a heifer, she nervously tried a few words in her
    long-lost language.
Attended by linen-clad priests, she is worshipped today
    as a goddess.*

PHAËTHON (1)

Finally, Io gave birth to a son, called Épaphus, thought
to be sprung from mighty Jupiter's seed; and throughout the
    cities
his temple is linked with his mother's. One of his peers and
    rivals   750
was Pháëthon, child of the sun god. On one occasion,
    Epaphus
took exception to Phaëthon's boastful talking, his failure
to show him respect and his arrogant pride in his father,
    Phoebus.
'Ridiculous booby,' he sneered, 'to believe every word that
    your mother
tells you. The picture you have of your father is false and
    inflated!'
Phaëthon's face grew red, but shame put a brake on his
    anger;   755
he went and reported Epaphus' gibes to his mother,
    Clýmene.
'To distress you further, dear mother,' he added, 'I,
    Phaëthon, known
as so open and savage-tempered, said nothing. I'm deeply
    ashamed
that these scandalous taunts should be thrown at our heads
    and I couldn't refute them.
Mother, if I am truly the son of a god, please give me   760
a sign of my glorious birth and establish my title in heaven!'
After he'd spoken, he threw his arms round his mother's
    neck,
imploring her, if she valued the life of himself and her
    husband
Mérops, and if she hoped that his sisters would happily
    marry,
to offer him positive proof that his father was really the sun
    god.

We cannot be sure whether Phaëthon's prayers or
765   Clymene's anger
at what was imputed against herself affected her more;
but she raised both arms to the sky and her eyes to the
       sun's bright beams,
to protest: 'By yonder resplendent orb with his
       glistening rays,
who hears and surveys us all, my child, I swear to you
       now
that the sun you gaze on in wonder, the sun which
770   governs the whole world,
is truly your father. If I speak false, may he ever refuse
       me
his light, and may this day be the last when my eyes
       shall behold him!
Small effort is needed to find your way to your father's
       hearth.
The domain from where he arises begins where our
       own land ends.
If your spirit impels you,* be off on your way and
775   question the sun god
himself!' As soon as his mother had finished speaking,
       Phaëthon
darted out in excitement. The sky was already his own!
Crossing his native Ethiopia and India, nearing
the land of the sun, he hastened east to discover his
       father.